MAKSIM GORKY
a reference guide

*A
Reference
Guide
to
Literature*

Barry Scherr
Editor

MAKSIM GORKY
a reference guide

EDITH W. CLOWES

G.K. HALL &CO.
70 LINCOLN STREET, BOSTON, MASS.

All rights reserved.
Copyright 1987 by Edith W. Clowes.

Library of Congress Cataloging-in-Publication Data

Clowes, Edith W.
  Maksim Gorky : a reference guide.

  (A Reference guide to literature)
  Includes indexes.
  1. Gorky, Maksim, 1868–1936—Bibliography.   I. Title.
II. Series.
Z8357.8.C55   1987   016.89178'309   87-20
[PG3465.Z8]
ISBN 0-8161-8722-3

This publication is printed on permanent/durable acid-free paper
MANUFACTURED IN THE UNITED STATES OF AMERICA

Contents

The Author vi

Preface vii

Introduction xi

Primary Bibliography xxix

Secondary Bibliography 1

Author Index 197

Subject Index 209

The Author

Edith Clowes is an assistant professor of Russian language and literature at Purdue University, West Lafayette, Indiana. Her research interests include early twentieth-century literature and German-Russian literary relations. Articles on the symbolist writers Dmitry Merezhkovsky and Konstantin Balmont have appeared in <u>Germano-Slavica</u> and <u>Slavic and East European Review</u>. She has published an article on Friedrich Nietzsche and Russian censorship in <u>Germano-Slavica</u>, and has contributed a chapter on the popular cult of Nietzsche to the book <u>Nietzsche in Russia</u> (Princeton: Princeton University Press). Work on Boris Pasternak is to appear in <u>Russian Language Journal</u> and on Maxim Gorky in the collection, <u>Fifty Years On: Gorky and His Time</u> (Nottingham: Astra Press).

Preface

Maksim Gorky and his works have been the subject of a large number of Soviet bibliographies. These publications are unfortunately biased and therefore only moderately useful: they register only Soviet sources and ignore Western and Russian émigré writing. In the English-speaking world, where Gorky has too often been reviled or simply ignored, he is starting to receive the attention he deserves. Scholars, however, still lack the research tools with which to engage in thorough studies of his life and art. As the first English-language research bibliography, the present work is intended to provide basic secondary sources. It could not and does not try to duplicate the massive Soviet bibliographies. Although it records Soviet memoir and archival materials and major critical approaches to Gorky, it omits the hundreds of Soviet reviews, scholarly articles, and books that merely repeat established patterns of interpretation. Here most attention is devoted to what the Soviets leave out: European (both East and West) and American sources as well as all available Russian émigré publications. The broad scope of Russian response in the prerevolutionary period and the ten years following 1917 is represented as fully as possible. My goal is to encourage recent efforts at a reassessment by presenting a large variety of approaches and evaluations and by raising as many questions about Gorky's life and art as possible. Particular attention is given to periods, issues, and themes about which scholars disagree.

The bibliography is organized in four parts. An introduction sketches the patterns in critical reading and biography writing and raises what seem to me to be the central issues in the study of Gorky. A primary bibliography provides the reader with publication data for Russian and English editions of Gorky's major works. This part is not exhaustive, however. It records only the famous stories and critical essays, as well as the major novels and plays that are mentioned in the secondary bibliography.

The secondary bibliography constitutes the bulk of this volume. Organized chronologically, the entries are accompanied by brief annotations that summarize the subject and works treated. Where it is relevant, I have given the author's line of argument and its place in the history of Gorky criticism. For collections of articles, such as

Preface

those in the serial <u>Gor'kovskie chteniia</u> [Readings in Gorky], I have provided a full table of contents in the main entry; articles of particular interest are given a separate entry. These items are fully cross-referenced. A translation of the volume title appears only in the entry for the book itself.

The fourth part, the author and subject indexes, determine the usefulness of the bibliography. My goal here is to give as full as possible representation to all aspects of Gorky study and to the major works, characters, biographical and critical issues, and historical figures. Titles of Gorky's works appear in their standard English translation.

Thanks are due to several people and institutions. The Kennan Institute supported my research for the bibliography. Ms. June Ferris at the University of Illinois helped me track down several hard-to-find sources. Dr. S.S. Zimina at the Gorky Institute of World Literature made it possible for me to work in the institute's Gorky Room. Ms. T.N. Markova kindly helped me during my weeks there. I am grateful to Ms. Ruth Rothenberg and Ms. Kathy Garner at Purdue's Interlibrary Loan Office for obtaining a large number of books and articles. I wish to thank Professor Barry Scherr for his interest in Gorky and his helpful suggestions for this bibliography. Ms. Borgna Brunner and Mr. Ara Salibian of G.K. Hall were very kind and helpful in matters of editing and deadlines. My deepest thanks are due to Ms. Carol Gog in the Department of Foreign Languages and Literatures for constant and careful work in typing and producing the manuscript on the word processor.

A variety of sources was used in the compilation of this bibliography. They included the <u>MLA Bibliography</u>, existing Russian bibliographies (see the subject index under "Bibliography"), as well as footnotes and bibliographies given in secondary sources. In addition, I consulted catalogs and holdings of the following libraries and institutes: the University of Illinois Library, the Library of Congress, the New York Public Library, the Regenstein Library at the University of Chicago, the Purdue University Library, La Bibliothèque Nationale in Paris, the University of Helsinki Library, the Lenin Library in Moscow, and the Gorky Room and the Gorky Archive at the Institute of World Literature in Moscow.

The system of transcription used is Thomas Shaw's System II. For the sake of ease in reading I have altered some last names as they appear in the annotations. For example, <u>-skii</u> becomes <u>-sky</u>, and diacritical marks have been dropped.

Since Soviet publishing houses often have cumbersome names, I have used the following system of abbreviation:

    ANSSSR--Akademiia nauk Soiuza Sovetskikh Sotsialisticheskikh Respublik
    Det. lit.--Detskaia literatura

Preface

Gor'k. obl. bibl. im. Vl. Lenina--Gor'kovskaia oblastnaia biblioteka imeni Vladimira Lenina
GIKhL--Gosudarstvennoe izdatel'stvo khudozhestvennoi literatury
Gosizdat--Gosudarstvennoe izdatel'stvo
Goslitizdat--Gosudarstvennoe literaturnoe izdatel'stvo
Izd. EGU--Izdatel'stvo Erevanskogo gosudarstvennogo universiteta
Izd. GGU--Izdatel'stvo Gor'kovskogo gosudarstvennogo universiteta
Izd. Kal. GU--Izdatel'stvo Kaliningradskogo gosudarstvennogo universiteta
Izd. Kaz. KGU--Izdatel'stvo Kazanskogo gosudarstvennogo universiteta
Izd. KGU--Izdatel'stvo Kievskogo gosudarstvennogo universiteta
Izd. knizh. sektora Gubono--Izdatel'stvo knizhnogo sektora Gubono
Izd. LGU--Izdatel'stvo Leningradskogo gosudarstvennogo universiteta
Izd. L'vov. GU--Izdatel'stvo L'vovskogo gosudarstvennogo universiteta
Izd. MGU--Izdatel'stvo Moskovskogo gosudarstvennogo universiteta
Izd. TGU--Izdatel'stvo Tbilisskogo gosudarstvennogo universiteta
Khud. lit.--Khudozhestvennaia literatura
Kuib. knizh. izd-vo.--Kuibishevskoe knizhnoe izdatel'stvo
Mosk. gos. ped. in-t.--Moskovskii gosudarstvennyi pedagogicheskii institut
Obshch. pol'za--Obshchestvennaia pol'za
Sov. pisatel'--Sovetskii pisatel'
Tash. gos. ped. in-t.--Tashkentskii gosudarstvennyi pedogogicheskii institut
Volgo-viat. knizh. izd-vo.--Volgo-viatskoe knizhnoe izdatel'stvo
Vses. gos. bibl. inostr. lit.--Vsesoiuznaia gosudarstvennaia biblioteka inostrannoi literatury
Vses. knizh. palata--Vsesoiuznaia knizhnaia palata

I have abbreviated the titles of a few frequently encountered journals as well:
SEEJ--<u>Slavic and East European Journal</u>
SEER--<u>Slavonic and East European Review</u>
<u>Vestnik MGU</u>--<u>Vestnik Moskovskogo gosudarstvennogo universiteta</u>

Introduction

The art and life of Maksim Gorky (born Aleksei Peshkov) is beset with an intriguing ambiguity that complicates the tasks of aesthetic evaluation and biographical accounts. In both areas fiction and fact become so intertwined that they are virtually impossible to separate. Despite their stylistic weakness, Gorky's fictional works are of tremendous historical importance. As the poet Aleksandr Blok put it in 1907, these stories, novels, and plays seemed to strike at the heart of some deeply Russian truth. In the years preceding the 1917 revolution, they changed the way Russian society saw itself. Whereas aesthetic considerations were secondary in Gorky's art, they were paramount in his life. The events of his life were the stuff that legends are made of, and he was enveloped in a legendary mystique. Indeed, several skeptical contemporaries accused Gorky of fabricating a rebellious, embittered persona (his pseudonym, "Gorky," means "bitter") to conceal Peshkov, the self-educated man from the lower middle class (1936.5, 9). What Yury Tynianov called "literary personality"--that fusion of the writer's character with the lives and characters of his heroes--would be effectively used to blur biographical fact.

Ambivalence pervades most aspects of Gorky's art and his life as activist: his literary style, his moral view, his social vision. Gorky's realist style combines the gift of hard, clear-sighted observation with a passion for scourging observed reality and transporting the reader with a utopian vision of life. Kornei Chukovsky noted a corresponding pattern of paired character types throughout Gorky's work (1909.1). Chukovsky found the archetypes for this pattern in "The Song of the Falcon" (1895). Here the sober pragmatism of a grass snake is subordinated to the wild, inspirational dream of a falcon. For over fifty years Soviet critics have seen this idiosyncratic combination of realism and romanticism as the essence of the literary method they call "socialist realism" (1939.1).

Many critics also find a fundamental ambiguity in Gorky's morality, both in his work and in his life. The enemy of false moral values, he crusaded in his early work against values that comfort and pacify. The play The Lower Depths is considered Gorky's most famous

Introduction

attack on the "comforting lie" (1978.3). Some memoirists, however, have suggested that the man who zealously exposed one kind of lie devoted himself to another: the "elevating lie" of Stalinist reconstruction (1939.5).

Gorky's attitude toward intellectuals and high culture reveals another aspect of his essential duality. He coveted the refinement and style of the educated, but he reviled their seeming passivity in the face of terrible social problems. Although many of his works "punished" intellectuals for their fecklessness, he remained fascinated by the intelligentsia and indeed wanted to belong to it. Thus, it seems inexplicable that although he was never accepted into the esoteric reaches of the high intelligentsia, Gorky after the Revolution became its champion and defender. In the 1920s he was seen by young Soviet writers as one of the intellectuals who had been on the "wrong" side of the Revolution (1927.2, 7).

In all aspects of his life and work, Gorky balanced what seemed to be mutually negating pairs of values: he denied his <u>meshchanstvo</u> (lower middle class) heritage and established himself as its enemy, but then wrote bourgeois family chronicles and devoted what some critics see as his best literary effort to the description of that heritage (1971.17; 1978.19). Failing to be accepted by "decadent" intellectuals, he established himself as their bitter opponent and engaged in vicious squabbles and discreditory polemics with them; but then he helped save those very people in their most difficult times. He railed about the moral destructiveness of philosophy and abstract thought, but, fascinated by the writers and thinkers he criticized so harshly, he continued his whole life to read philosophy and educate himself. It is these paradoxes that still puzzle and intrigue Gorky's readers.

The large majority of critics, no matter what their orientation, would probably agree with Anton Chekhov's observation that "there will be a time when Gorky's works will be forgotten, but it is highly unlikely that he himself will be forgotten even in a thousand years."[1] The historical figure seems to be more important than the texts he produced. Even in the Soviet Union where Gorky enjoys status as <u>the</u> twentieth-century classic, critics undermine his lofty station with repeated anxious assertions that Gorky is "relevant" for the present day (1977.17; 1978.3). By continually reaffirming Gorky's high place in Russian letters beside Pushkin and Tolstoy, by "studying" over and over again his broad national and international influence, they inadvertently cast doubt on his literary value. Indeed, such influential Gorky specialists as Boris Bialik and Aleksandr Ovcharenko convince this reader that Gorky is more valuable for his friendship with Lenin and his politically engaged fiction (read: fiction in praise of the Bolshevik cause) than for any independent aesthetic value. His status as literary classic is tied to his historical role as social activist. Most critics are interested in Gorky as an important actor in a crucial period in Russian history. The enormous amount of published memoirs and correspondence

Introduction

outweighs in mass and thematic interest the book-length studies on Gorky's literary work. This emphasis suggests that the historical figure imposes itself more strongly on readers' imaginations than his writings do.

In the light of this observation, it is surprising that no definitive biography of Gorky has yet been written. The obstacles in the way of such a book, however, are formidable. Intentional fictionalization, mystification, intrigue, lack of historical documentation have all played their part in thwarting biographies, and only recently have the first steps been taken toward a full understanding of the problem (1983.3).

In order to explain this unusual situation, it is important to understand Gorky's own attitude, as well as the attitude of radical prerevolutionary and Soviet critics, toward his life. Gorky himself was the first to commit the biographical fallacy on a grand scale. He mixed life with fiction and placed literary personality well above biographical fact. From his first years of literary life he disclaimed his family background of small-time, provincial business people. That he did so was understandable because the meshchanstvo was very hostile to anything but a strict, conservative Russian Orthodox outlook. As a group the meshchanstvo was widely despised by educated Russian society for its narrow outlook, its resistance to progress and enlightenment, its obsequiousness and dishonesty. To be a writer while conforming to meshchanstvo ways was impossible, and those with literary ambitions concealed their dreams and awaited the first chance to leave home.2 Gorky was quick to disassociate himself from this hated past and to develop a separate literary personality as outsider and social firebrand (1936.5). He gave himself a pseudonym designed at once to shock other people and to disguise his social heritage. The name "Maksim" he took from his father who came from a soldiering family. The epithet "Gorky" projected to readers of the day a compelling mood of alienation. The déclassé image was completed with the costume that soon became his trademark: the broad-brimmed hat, cape, peasant shirt, and high boots of a vagabond.

A two-volume collection of stories published in St. Petersburg in 1898 established Gorky as an instant best-seller at home and abroad. It has been shown that the young writer chose his stories for the collection with a careful eye to their image-making qualities (1983.3). Readers naturally wanted to know more about the mysterious upstart, but Gorky could be very unpleasant toward people who were too inquisitive about his past. As he wrote to his publishing partner, K.P. Piatnitsky, "My autobiography is my nuisance."3 He was enraged at the inquisitiveness of his first biographer, V.F. Botsianovsky (1903.1). He claimed that all information about his life "you can glean . . . from stories like 'My Traveling Companion' [Moi sputnik]." Ultimately, he argued, "what matters is not who I am, but what I want."5 Personality and his reputation as a self-made man mattered to Gorky, and his social background could be seen only as an obstacle to their fullest flowering. Seen in this light, it

Introduction

becomes more understandable that the young writer would extend fiction into life. Thus it was not by chance that he came to seem like a character from a novel (1902.1) come to life to shock his readers; in Gorky's view, life was the fundamental fiction to be shaped to his own ends.

During his mid-career, as more became known about his past, Gorky again tried to form a public persona, this time by writing an autobiography that is a superbly polished mixture of artifice and fact. The three-volume work--<u>Childhood</u>, <u>Apprenticeship</u>, and <u>My Universities</u>--clearly departs from historical fact (1952.6). Recent studies have shown how he deftly used literary device to shape reality (1979.17).

Throughout Gorky's career, radical critics played a role in creating a Gorky legend. At the turn of the century, populists and Marxists alike were looking eagerly for "writers from the people" who would justify their efforts at popular enlightenment and support their theories of social change from below. When Gorky appeared, he seemed to fit the image. Critics as different as the Populist Nikolai Mikhailovsky and the Marxists Vladimir Posse and Andreevich (Evgeny Solovev) labeled Gorky a proletarian (1900.1; 1901.7, 9). Bolsheviks like Georgy Plekhanov, Anatoly Lunacharsky, and Vladimir Lenin continued to develop the image after 1905, once they had claimed Gorky as their own.

The issue of Gorky's social heritage arose once again in the late 1920s. Now other writers who claimed a proletarian heritage for themselves were asking how a <u>meshchanin</u> could be a founder of proletarian literature and act as the stormy petrel of the workers' revolution (1926.2; 1927.2, 7). But old Bolsheviks, among them Petr Kogan and Anatoly Lunacharsky, revived Gorky's claim to belong to the working class and argued that he possessed proletarian consciousness if not a proletarian heritage. As Kogan saw it, although Gorky had been born to the family of a meshchanin, he had re-created himself as a proletarian (1928.12). Lunacharsky pointed out that some of the greatest revolutionaries came from a bourgeois background. Their greatness lay in their ability to recognize the role of the proletariat in the future development of society (1928.15).

A major topic that is shrouded in legend is the writer's relationship to the Bolshevik party and later the Soviet leadership. Vladimir Lenin was interested in using Gorky's popularity to broaden the base of his revolutionary effort. He praised Gorky as the spirit of Russia's future and a writer "who would do much for the proletarian cause" (1909.3). Gorky had the panache needed to arouse the popular imagination. Moreover, as Bertram Wolfe has shown, Gorky did not seriously hamper Lenin's organizational aims, although he was frequently critical in private (1967.18). It was easy enough to keep him out of the arena of political infighting. The few forays he did make into political life (1908 and 1917) were smoothed over and forgiven. In the Soviet Union, Gorky's relationship with Lenin stands at the center of political-artistic hagiography, and thus there is very

Introduction

little chance of it ever being fully described. Throughout Soviet biographies of Gorky resounds the fiction of Lenin as Gorky's political mentor, as a kindly if condescending older-brother figure who cajoled the "father of Soviet letters" into a politically correct point of view. Lenin, in the myth, is a staunch if somewhat stolid figure who could neither imagine nor allow any point of view other than his own. This legendary relationship between the two men has become the mythic archetype for party loyalty--that is, for the subordinate relationship of the arts to political goals in Soviet culture (1967.2). To change the legend would be to legitimize a different kind of relationship between cultural institutions and the government.

Some light was shed on the friendship with Lenin in Bertram Wolfe's study The Bridge and the Abyss (1967.18) and in Herman Ermolaev's collection of Gorky's dissenting articles from Novaia zhizn' (New life) from 1917 and 1918 (1971.1). The vehemence with which established Soviet critics such as Boris Bialik (1970.2) and East German colleagues (1970.8) responded, particularly to Wolfe's book, shows how important the myth still is to the supporters of the Soviet status quo. It is interesting to note that in recent years the perceived relationship between Lenin and Gorky and, by analogy, politics and the arts has changed slightly. For example, Volkov's book (1972.16) pictures the relationship between the two men less as teacher and student and more as two equals, each with his own point of view and each with justifiable disagreements. Nevertheless, the established icon of the "proletarian father of Soviet letters" and the hallowed friendship between Lenin and Gorky hinder a full factual assessment of Gorky's relations to the Bolsheviks and his view of politically engaged literature.

Yet another problem facing the biographer is the paucity of independent primary sources: few documents besides Gorky's own memoirs and Soviet accounts are available to illuminate certain key points in the author's life. His childhood and young manhood are veiled because of the lack of evidence other than his autobiography. There exist only a few memoirs by people who remembered Gorky in the 1870s and 1880s (for example, 1933.3). The meshchanstvo as a group refrained from writing anything, even in some cases business accounts. Diary or letter writing were not traditional cultural activities. Thus, there are no family accounts or sets of correspondence.

The late 1920s and 1930s are another period in which documentation is both limited and strongly controlled. This period saw a great deal of mythmaking. Gorky had lent his services to political organization one last time, for the consolidation of Stalinist power. But "demythifying" evidence seeps out through the cracks, for example, in the occasional footnote or side remark. Several biographical issues, however, remain unsolved, among them, why Gorky returned to the Soviet Union after a seven-year absence, what role he played in the founding of the Writers' Union, and under what conditions he

Introduction

died in 1936. Legend, as recorded by Gorky's major biographer Ilia Gruzdev (1946.2), says about the first subject that having recovered in some measure from his tuberculosis, he was homesick and anxious to participate in the "building of socialism" in his country. His role in the Writers' Union was that of founding father. His death has been explained in contradictory ways: as the work of Trotskyites and as the work of Stalin's chief of police. There has been a great deal of speculation about this point. The best work shows the inconsistency of Soviet sources (1970.7).

Despite all the problems, however, a great many biographical sources have become available. A large amount of absorbing correspondence and memoir material has appeared both in the Soviet Union and abroad in the last thirty years. Gorky was a pivotal figure in Russian literary life before and after the Bolshevik Revolution. He was a person toward whom no one remained neutral. Thus, memoirs are nearly always biased, inclined either to magnify him or to discredit him. The best, such as Khodasevich's (1939.5) or Berberova's (1967.1), are aware of and open about their biases. The least useful are those that smooth over historical complexities and make of Gorky's life an exercise in modern-day hagiography (1959.8). Oddly enough, the most hostile treatments, such as Gippius's (1923.1) or Mandelshtam's (1972.11), often raise fascinating issues and, despite their desire to sweep Gorky and the dilemmas he represents out of the way, ultimately admit his central importance, thus helping to define if not interpret his historical role.

The correspondence by and about Gorky is remarkable for its volume and richness. The Gorky archive holds about twenty-thousand letters, in the estimation of archive director S.S. Zimina.6 Despite an enormous effort--several volumes of letters, two volumes in the Literaturnoe nasledstvo series, and numerous smaller publications--only part of the archive has been published. These sources, too, are carefully edited and abridged. Their overall subject matter is designed to support the Soviet myth in its key points--to reinforce the concept of Gorky's student-mentor relationship with Lenin, his image as founder of socialist realism and enemy of modernism in art, and his enormous impact on prerevolutionary art, Soviet letters, and world literature (for example, 1958.42; 1960.10; 1963.8). Nonetheless, the documents themselves and the voluminous notes that accompany them often belie the myth and suggest a historical actuality that is much more complex, interesting, and worthy of a great literary figure. Everyone interested in Russian and European culture in the forty years around the Revolution can only look forward to the full publication of Gorky's correspondence.

In the Soviet Union, a great deal of effort has been expended in compiling bibliographies. Since the 1930s Soviet researchers have attempted to gather all published primary and secondary material on Gorky. Their bibliography, currently covering material to 1970, includes only Russian-language writings published in the Soviet Union. Foreign bibliographies (for example, 1968.91) focus on

Introduction

Gorky's reception in a given country and typically give greatest weight to leftist or radical publications.

Available Russian and foreign-language biographies are highly inadequate: most of them perpetrate biographical fallacy by claiming Gorky's autobiography as fact. Although Soviet specialists have been calling for a full critical biography of Gorky for several years (1981.12), Ilia Gruzdev's work (1960.12) is the only Russian-language biography that covers his whole life. It is more hagiography that biography, however. Other biographies tend to focus on one small portion of Gorky's life. The most useful material appears in the four-volume Chronicle of A.M. Gorky's Life and Work (1958.18), but this biography, too, has major problems: whether by chance or design, the volumes divide just at the periods of political crisis in Gorky's life, the times that give Soviet historians the greatest trouble. They are 1908-9, the Capri period and the disintegration of the Bolshevik party into factions; 1917-18, the Novaia zhizn' (New life) period when Gorky used that journal as a forum to criticize the Bolshevik party and its method of consolidating power; and 1928, the year of Gorky's return to Russia after seven years abroad.

The most complete English-language biography is still Alexander Kaun's (1931.2). It covers his life only to 1929, however, and thus does not treat Gorky's activities in Stalinist Russia. Other biographical studies, such as Filia Holtzman's (1948.2) and Dan Levin's (1965.8), romanticize Gorky's life. The best recent biographical treatment is given by Richard Hare (1962.3) who deals with discrepancies between fact and legend. The best literary biography is Irwin Weil's (1966.25).

Gorky's literary work is difficult to isolate from his life because of the function he assigned to art. Art was for him an extension of a whole personality and was meant largely to serve the social function of raising consciousness. The work judged by itself has often seemed to critics to be flawed. Indeed, Gorky himself was frequently displeased with his work (1982.25). It rarely received praise for aesthetic merit either at home or abroad. Even radical critics, such as Lunacharsky and Plekhanov, hesitated to discuss aesthetic, stylistic aspects of much of Gorky's work and limited themselves to discussion of its political spirit and its ideas (1906.4). What might spell failure for most writers, however, did not hurt Gorky. His work won acclaim and indeed succeeded in its efforts to rouse readers and make them debate the issues. Almost everyone agreed from the beginning that Gorky was more than the texts he produced: both in Russia and abroad he represented something deeply Russian (1907.1). He and his work got to the heart of Russian debates over culture, the way to social change, and the role of the intelligentsia in the future of Russian society.

Critics have been divided into two groups since before the writer's debut in 1898. They split roughly along the lines of those who believe that literary culture is a self-contained and self-referential system and those who want literature to serve a social and political function. In the 1890s the first group was represented by writers in the journal <u>Severnyi vestnik</u> (Northern herald). Gorky had approached these people and even published a small number of stories there. But an irreconcilable disagreement soon arose between him and the editors. Editorial board members--among them, Akim Volynsky (pseudonym of A. Flekser), Dmitry Merezhkovsky, Zinaida Gippius, and Nikolai Minsky--became Gorky's worst detractors. On the other hand, Gorky's most enthusiastic early supporters were socially oriented writers and publicists such as Vladimir Korolenko and Nikolai Mikhailovsky. These intellectuals and the large variety of Marxists who appeared in the early 1900s were ecstatic about Gorky. In their criticism they not only analyzed his work but helped shape the revolutionary romantic literary personality we now associate with him.

This dual approach to the writer became the major axis of opinion about Gorky in the prerevolutionary years. The one important exception was the response of younger symbolists Aleksandr Blok and Andrei Belyi, who tried to reconcile the two views of literature. They found more to admire in Gorky and his belles lettres than did their elders. The older view of the Gippius-Merezhkovsky group, however, lasted longer and formed the basis for opinion about Gorky among émigré writers after the Revolution. Like Gippius (1908.4), émigrés such as Nina Berberova (1967.1) or Vladimir Nabokov (1981.14) made clear they did not recognize Gorky as a writer, although they admitted that as a cultural phenomenon and a personality he was interesting, even pivotal for the age.

After the watershed of 1905, Gorky was increasingly claimed by Bolshevik critics and political activists. Plekhanov, Lunacharsky, and Lenin praised the propagandistic novels and plays of this period, particularly <u>Enemies</u> and <u>Mother</u>. The criticism of these three men prefigured the socialist realist aesthetic of the Stalin years (see, for example, 1975.16). Plekhanov liked the profile of will and courage that Gorky's play, <u>Enemies</u>, gave to masses of workers who otherwise seemed to be characterless (1907.6). Lunacharsky was the first to speak of Gorky's "positive hero" and claimed in several articles that Gorky was the fitting spokesman for a class that was taking history into its own hands (1903.5). He liked Gorky's insistence on the honor and the right to happiness and fulfillment of even the lowest members of society. It was Lenin who put forward the idea of <u>partiinost'</u> (party loyalty) in 1905 in his famous article, "Party Organization and Party Literature." Lenin called for a new literature founded on party guidance and collectivist principles, and Gorky was the first writer to fill the bill.

Gorky, however, had a significance for other than socialist readers and politicians. During the early years of his exile after 1905, Russian readers seemed to have forgotten him, but gradually they rediscovered and reclaimed him. In 1907, Dmitry Filosofov announced the "end of Gorky" as an artist (1907.2), but the lengthy

Introduction

and heated debate that ensued showed how alive the author was and how valued by his readers. Socialist critics insisted on Gorky's continued relevance. Modernists argued among themselves, and several felt compelled to affirm his significance as a writer. In 1907 Aleksandr Blok's had been a lone voice in favor of Gorky. Now Andrei Belyi (pseudonym of Boris Bugaev) joined him (1910.1; 1911.1), and even Gorky's enemies Zinaida Gippius and Dmitry Merezhkovsky bitterly admitted his larger significance for Russian society and culture (1908.4; 1916.3). In the post-1905 period a variety of histories of recent literature appeared (1907.3; 1912.2; 1915.4). Their authors universally placed Gorky above all intellectual and political movements including Bolshevism: he would outlast any one trend.

The revolutions of 1917, Gorky's quarrel with the new rulers in the Kremlin, and his subsequent long sojourn abroad led to yet another reassessment of his literary achievement and a number of speculative articles about his relationship to political power. Abroad, he came under renewed attack from Merezhkovsky, and his old admirers came to his defense (1922.1, 2). In the Soviet Union, he fell into disfavor with the futurists and proletarian writers, two groups who themselves were at loggerheads. Both groups saw him as a "fellow traveler," a writer out of step with the Revolution. The formalist critics Viktor Shklovsky and Boris Eikhenbaum and the futurist poet Vladimir Maiakovsky all suggested that Gorky's petit bourgeois heritage emerged in his consumer-oriented approach to letters and to culture in general (1926.4; 1929.1). Maiakovsky taunted the older poet of the Revolution with the reproach that anyone who experienced the Revolution from a distance in an armchair on a lovely Italian veranda was not really living with his time (1927.2). Members of the Russian Association of Proletarian Writers (RAPP) also questioned Gorky's proletarian heritage and his right to a place in Soviet letters (1979.7).

It is interesting and important to note that in a period when Gorky was least politically active, his literary work received perhaps its most positive aesthetic appraisals. Even those who questioned his relevance for Soviet life were interested in his latest writing. Viktor Shklovsky and others praised his memoiristic writings for their plotless structure and crisp prose (1924.6; 1926.4; 1927.3).

In the mid-1920s old Bolsheviks, including Lunacharsky and Petr Kogan, began to rally in Gorky's political defense. The image of Gorky, the stormy petrel of the Revolution, gradually regained its old glory and was further embellished. The year 1928 was a turning point in Gorky's Soviet reception. His sixtieth birthday was used as a reason to bring him back to the Soviet Union and to honor his revolutionary image. The resulting revival of the fighting spirit of 1905 and 1917 and Gorky's quasi-religious vision of the "new man" were both intended to support Stalin's effort to collectivize, industrialize, and root out remaining vestiges of the bourgeois spirit of personal enterprise and initiative. Gorky now became a mythic hero

in the most traditional sense: in him were fused the human and
superhuman. He joined the mighty few who had transfigured the
Russian land, saved it from the wastes of capitalism, and made it
into an earthly paradise. Now the "holy land" was "sanctified" with
his name. His hometown, Nizhny Novgorod, had formerly been a major
commercial center and the location of an enormous annual trade fair.
In 1928, it was renamed Gorky, thus blotting from the geographical
and spiritual map an age-old landmark of the Russian free market. In
addition, factories and new collective farms were named for him.
Gorky spent a great deal of time traveling to these places, giving
speeches and bestowing his blessing on the new man as he now saw him:
the selfless, collectivized Soviet worker.7

At times, Gorky seemed to play John the Baptist to Stalin's
Christ. In the 1930s there appeared a number of critical studies
that interpreted Stalin's consolidation of power as the realization
of Gorky's "humanitarian" dream of the transformation of human nature
(1936.6). Gorky was thus pictured as the prophet of an earthly
paradise brought to perfection by Stalin.

In the following years Gorky was magnified as a mythic father and
progenitor (rodonachal'nik) of socialist letters; critics demon-
strated his broad impact throughout Russia and the world by publishing impressively thick volumes of memoirs (1928.10; 1929.3) and
critical essays (1934.2), as well as extensive bibliographies of
primary and secondary material (1934.1; 1936.1). As in the period
after 1905, Lunacharsky now served as the critical mirror that
brightened and enlarged the profile of the writer (1931.3; 1933.1;
1938.9). Well-edited collections of his articles contained all the
elements of mythmaking. Lunacharsky wrote in an exultant, glorifying
tone, smoothing over the troublesome, discordant periods in the life
of the revolutionary genius and demonstrating Gorky's godlike perspective on history. He placed him beside the other great geniuses
of human history, particularly Goethe and Tolstoy. (Later and lesser
critics would compare him to the still loftier and more remote Dante
and Shakespeare [1939.1]). Above all, Lunacharsky emphasized Gorky's
support for socialist reconstruction and his Olympian relations with
political leaders, particularly Lenin. Others would assert his great
friendship with the "father of the people," Stalin (1936.6).

After Gorky's death, a concerted "scientific" effort at canoniza-
tion assured the writer a permanent position in the top rank of the
Stalinist iconostasis. The party assigned the job to older literary
critics and acquaintances of Gorky, as well as a few chosen doctoral
students (1968.77). These people formed the first and second generations of Gorky specialists devoted to what has become an institution
in Soviet literary criticism, gor'kovedenie (Gorky studies). They
set as their goals legitimate literary-critical tasks such as the
establishment of a Gorky archive and the publication and interpretation of his work. Their activities, however, frequently took them
beyond literary criticism, and their significance and influence went
much deeper. Gorky specialists soon became watchdogs and enforcers

Introduction

of party rules controlling both the production and critical study of belles lettres in the Soviet Union. They canonized the political-aesthetic code known as socialist realism, which compels all Soviet authors to write in a specific style, with a certain kind of hero, and with an actively supportive orientation toward the nation, the socialist government, the planned economic system, and above all the Communist party. Since the 1930s Gorkyists have asserted and reasserted the Gorky icon, the "progenitor of Soviet letters," the prophet of the "new man," and the mythic link between the old, corrupt world before the Revolution and the bright new paradise of Soviet life. More serious for ongoing cultural life, the Gorkyists have actively interpreted party guidelines and cultural policies to the public and to writers even in the post-Stalin period (for example, 1963.13; 1974.11; 1979.3). Some book-length studies--for example, I.S. Eventov's The Force of Sarcasm (1973.6)--have been explicitly intended to help contemporary writers find the right themes and the right point of view. Finally, Gorky specialists have stepped out of literary life altogether and invoked Gorky's name for all kinds of propagandistic purposes. Gorky "criticism" was used in the 1930s to enhance Stalin's image and legitimize forced collectivization and industrialization. Gorky has been invoked as a fighter against all the Soviet Union's "enemies." For example, he has been said to have died in 1936 with antifascist warnings on his lips. (Paradoxically, he also died a victim and martyr of "villainous Trotskyism"!) In later years, he has been quoted as the enemy variously of parliamentary democracy, Richard Nixon, and the Vietnam War (1979.3)! Gorkyists write this material, both legitimate and illegitimate, in a strange tone that mixes fierce militancy and saccharine sentimentality. One often finds here images of struggle and fighting intended to preserve in the reader vigilance and hatred for ideological enemies. On the other hand, Gorky is made to uphold an ill-defined notion of "socialist humanism"--some vague, sentimental combination of cruelty and kindness, toughness and tenderness.

In the 1930s Gorky studies helped significantly to codify aesthetic views that lay at the center of Soviet culture. They created the archetypal image of the artist and the proper cultural values. Gorkyist works trimmed and shaped their subject to fit the model of the ideal socialist activist and intellectual--a type in close step with the political leader enjoying the approximate status of naive, wayward, but ingenious younger brother. He may question from time to time but ultimately accepts the politician's moral and intellectual superiority. His art is warlike because art is meant to serve as a weapon in the struggle of the working class for liberation and of Bolshevik socialism for dominion.

The Soviet literary ideal defines itself best by what it is not, through its precedents whom it has surpassed and its enemies whose weaknesses it has long since revealed. Thus, Gorky as the founder of socialist realism has his literary roots in nineteenth-century critical realism and such giants of that school as Tolstoy and Chekhov. His art is seen as greater than theirs because, like theirs, it

Introduction

defines social dilemmas, but in addition anticipates the coming socialist paradise. Whereas critical realism points out the failings of present society, socialist realism in its ideal Gorkian form both criticizes the present and points the way to future greatness.

Gorky, it has been repeatedly shown (1965.12), delineated his own moral and aesthetic views through his discrediting of Russia's and Europe's two "sick geniuses," Dostoevsky and Nietzsche. The "sickness" of these two men has been "cured" in the Soviet age. The simple, extroverted, active, patriotic "positive hero" has conquered the complex, neurotic, megalomaniac, and ultimately corrosive superfluous man. In this view, Dostoevsky--the skeptic, the political reactionary, the religious thinker--dwells on the dark, sadomasochistic elements of human nature. His morality of compassion, Gorkyists point out, is weak: it is based on pessimism and is paralyzed by a morbid fascination with psychic sickness and deformity (1941.5). Nietzsche is disliked for his seemingly antisocial, misanthropic attitudes, his disdain for the broad masses of the people, and his encouragement of strong, self-willed individualism. Gorkyists are quick to identify Nietzsche as the philosopher of enemy number one, fascism. Both Dostoevsky and Nietzsche, and all the modernist poets and existentialist thinkers who followed them, are branded as supporters of political oppression and benighted irrationalism.

A traditional Gorkyist concern is the documentation of Gorky's "struggle" against the corrosive effects of <u>dostoevshchina</u> (Dostoevskyism) and <u>nitssheanstvo</u> (Nietzcheanism) in Russian culture. Before the Revolution, in their view, Gorky polemicized with neo-idealists, symbolists, and decadents (1978.8). He resisted Nietzsche in his effort to create a morality of constructive, active compassion. In the Soviet era, Gorky criticized the revival of interest in Dostoevsky. Gorkyists have pointed to their subject's relationship to Leonid Leonov as an example of his beneficial anti-Dostoevskian influence (1953.3).

The Soviet Gorkyists deserve more attention than they have received because of their impressive influence in the Soviet literary world. The mechanism of control and subordination of the arts to political needs and interests function partly through such people. They occupy positions of influence in literary and historical research institutes, universities, and archives, and on editorial boards. They enjoy the support of the Party; the Party gave them their mandate in 1937, and they have passed on this mandate from generation to generation. The fourth generation is on the horizon, but the second and third formed in Stalinist times are still in control.

The first Gorkyists were linked to the writer through personal acquaintance. V.A. Desnitsky, a political activist who knew Gorky in Nizhny Novgorod at the turn of the century, collected and edited an enormous amount of correspondence and unpublished manuscripts by the author and critical articles on him. He lived in Leningrad and was

Introduction

very active at the Herzen Institute, the Pushkin House, and Leningrad University. Ilia Gruzdev conducted a lengthy correspondence with Gorky during the 1920s and 1930s, was one of Gorky's chief boosters after the author's return in 1928 (1928.10; 1930.1), and became his primary Russian biographer-hagiographer (1946.2). The third major charter Gorkyist was S.D. Balukhatyi, a literary critic, who organized the effort to compile an ongoing Gorky bibliography. He also did his share of cultural enforcement (1938.2) and propaganda work (1938.3).

The second generation of Gorky specialists included people who in the 1930s were young graduate students and budding literary specialists. They included Boris Bialik, Ksenia Muratova, Boris Mikhailovsky, Evgeny Tager, and Sergei Kastorsky, among others. All of them occupied influential positions in major universities and institutes. Their work combined solid if tendentious literary criticism with some enforcing or controlling role in academic literary studies. Bialik and Muratova, for example, made their careers as theorists and historians of socialist realism.

Boris Bialik stands out as Gorky's greatest cheerleader in the post-Stalin period. He made his debut in the late 1930s when against Gorky's wishes he wrote a dissertation on the writer's aesthetic views. It was published as a book in 1939 (1939.1) and stands out to the present day as a classic on socialist realism. His other books deal with topics central to socialist realist doctrine, for example, party loyalty in literature (see his bombastic Rulers of Thoughts and Feelings: Lenin and Gorky [1970.2]) or literature as a vehicle for raising social-political awareness (M. Gorky the Playwright [1977.1]). Bialik, who is closely tied with the Institute of World Literature in Moscow, has edited many serial publications such as Gor'kovskie chteniia and has done an enormous amount of scholarly work. He exerts his greatest influence in his role as spokesman at home and abroad for official literary politics. He appears to be an important link between party and people on questions of Gorky, correct aesthetic judgment, and aesthetic-political education.

Ksenia Muratova has devoted her career to compiling bibliographies, studying Gorky's biography, and documenting his work as a literary organizer in the Soviet period. Muratova got her start as a close collaborator of Balukhatyi. She has been the director of the archive at the Pushkin House in Leningrad for many years and appears to be influential in Leningrad literary circles. Like Bialik, she edited many collections, some of them excellent (for example, 1968.78) and was active in guiding the course of Gorky studies in the 1950s and 1960s. If Bialik indicated to writers what they should write and the public what they should read, Muratova pointed out to Gorky specialists and other literary critics what subjects they should research (1968.77).

The third generation of Gorky specialists includes people such as Aleksandr Ovcharenko, I.I. Vainberg, and A.A. Volkov, who became prominent in the 1950s under the tutelage of their immediate elders. Ovcharenko is perhaps best known of all. He is director of the Gorky Archive, associate director of the Institute of World Literature in Moscow, professor at Moscow University, and spokesman for Soviet literature abroad. He has been active in the Writers Union and has worked for many years on the editorial board of the best known literary journal <u>Novyi mir</u>. To an American audience, it is interesting and important to point out that Ovcharenko has been very active in promoting American-Soviet cultural exchanges.8

This generation is more sophisticated and less belligerent than the previous one. Still, their readings of Gorky continue in the same tradition. They focus on much the same themes: Gorky as the progenitor of socialist realism, his influence on Soviet literature, his place as a classic among the nineteenth-century greats, his struggle against the moral sickness of modernism. Ovcharenko has tried to prove that socialist realism is one of the great twentieth-century aesthetic systems. The major contribution of this generation has been the rediscovery of Gorky's last work, <u>The Life of Klim Samgin</u>. Valuable work has been done on this book by Vainberg (1971.20) and Volkov (1968.122).

In the 1970s a crisis of generations arose among the Gorkyists. Bialik noted in print (1977.14) that Gorky did not appear to excite Soviet readers anymore. This comment is mild in the light of accounts by such émigrés as V. Maramzin who grew up in the Soviet Union and were forced against their will to read Gorky extensively (1976.26). The second generation is dying and the third aging, but a fourth generation of prominent Gorky specialists has not yet emerged. Younger scholars publish occasionally on Gorky, and one sees younger people studying him at the Institute of World Literature; but there are as yet no established figures who will take up the banner as the guardians of true socialist realism.

Other signs show the changing fortunes of Gorky studies. Major serial publications devoted to him have been relocated to the provincial city of Gorky. That they are no longer managed in Moscow and Leningrad suggests their lessening importance as tools of political control. Here we find grounds for hope: provincial publications occasionally produce interesting and unexpected interpretations, ones that depart significantly from accepted standards.

Other developments give grounds for optimism. Relatively fresh interpretations and new topics have appeared in the last fifteen years. For example, Volkov's book (1972.16) and Burian's article (1976.3) give a slightly different picture of the relationship between Lenin and Gorky, arguing that Gorky influenced Lenin at times and suggesting that each man had his own justifiable point of view on the issues. A great deal more work has been done on Gorky's relationship to modernist writers (1968.59; 1976.18; 1980.7) and even on modernist aspects of his work (1977.2).

Introduction

Gorky criticism has been used recently in some beneficial ways--for example, to rehabilitate a number of excellent early Soviet writers. Discussion of Gorky's relationship to the bohemian poet Sergei Esenin (1968.127) or the great but long silenced prosaist Andrei Platonov (1968.89) is but a pretext to broaden the circle of accepted writers. Particularly remarkable is the published discussion of a dystopian work by Platonov, Chevengur, that to this day has not been printed in the Soviet Union (1976.9).

Gorky's rather complex religious and philosophical tastes have received more attention in the last twenty years. Ermakova gives serious and thorough attention to Gorky's response to Dostoevsky (1973.5). Some recent articles deal with Gorky's controversial "God-building" period (1908-9) and related works such as Confession (1968.118-19). Gorky's use of religious imagery in his autobiography has been treated in a fresh and interesting way (1968.51). Belenky, Sukhikh, and Darialova have contributed important sustained work on Gorky's philosophical views--for example, his response to the Russian philosopher Nikolai Fedorov, as well as to the "decadent" philosophers Schopenhauer and Nietzsche (for example, 1961.3; 1978.21; 1980.2).

Some refinement of literary critical techniques have developed in some cases around the study of Gorky. Vainberg's work concerns the use of quotation and misquotation in The Life of Klim Samgin (1968.121); Mikhailov has written on the use of Old Russian sources in Gorky's prerevolutionary work (1982.15); and several articles have dealt with problems of influence in an innovative way (1968.122; 1969.39).

All these changes suggest that Gorky critics are at once paying attention to and giving a kind of official legitimacy to trends, writers, literary styles that already enjoy some popularity among readers and critics. The same basic structure and role of Gorky studies in Soviet letters remains intact, however. No real change of the archetypal relationship between art and government can be predicted.

Gorky's reception outside of Russia--in Eastern Europe, Western Europe, and English-speaking countries--often reflects the tone of general relations between those countries. In Eastern Europe, Gorky studies are used to create a cultural bond between the socialist countries and their Soviet senior partner and to spread the Soviet ideal of the writer. Writers in each country have produced at least a few articles on Gorky's reception in that country. The most zealous in their cooperation and support are the East Germans (for example, 1968.52). There is firm ground for legitimate study of Gorky's German reception; his work found a strong response in the art of such major German writers as Bertolt Brecht, Heinrich Mann, and Anna Seghers. Of particular note is Rolf Schroeder's serious work on Gorky and Thomas Mann (1971.17).

Introduction

The relative independence of art from political strictures in Eastern Europe can be seen in the occasional fresh approaches to Gorky. For example, the longest treatment in any language of Gorky's response to the thought of Friedrich Nietzsche was written by the Hungarian Bela Lengyel (1979.12). Lengyel's work starts with an interesting juxtaposition of sculptured busts of Gorky and Nietzsche: the two look remarkably alike. The text is larded with notes and quotations from Nietzsche and Gorky: although it is inaccessible to most readers (perhaps deliberately?), it seems a thorough and serious piece of literary criticism. Lengyel has also produced other important articles on Gorky and the modernist tradition (1975.15).

In France and West Germany, too, critical works on Gorky have appeared over the years. For example, Jean Pérus produced a thorough study of the most intense relationship of Gorky's later years--his friendship with Romain Rolland (1968.92). Hélène Imendörfer's book on narrative technique in The Life of Klim Samgin is one of the best studies of the novel in any language (1973.7).

Gorky's reception in English-speaking countries has never been particularly warm. His visit to New York in 1906 helped arouse a special feeling of antagonism in his American public (1908.9; 1949.5). At first he was welcomed enthusiastically, but when it was disclosed that he was not married to his traveling companion, M.F. Andreeva, he was ostracized, even by such a famous liberal and social activist as Mark Twain. It was now that Gorky created his embittered image of New York, "The City of the Yellow Devil," which has become part of the Soviet myth of the United States as the bastion of merciless, oppressive capitalism (1949.4; 1970.13; 1976.30).

As a writer of fiction Gorky is typically seen by English readers as second-rate. Critics frequently point out what they feel to be the inadequacy of his style: triteness, sentimentalism, hackneyed expression (1929.1; 1950.2; 1964.10). And they generally dislike the perceived moral inconsistency in his actions and views (1971.13). The one exception to the rule is Gorky's dramatic work. In particular, The Lower Depths is everywhere accepted as a classic of modern drama.

Given the generally low opinion of Gorky's achievements as a writer and of his overall worldview, literary critics have long since abandoned him to historians and political scientists. In these fields he is treated mostly in his relationship to political leaders (1964.7; 1967.18). In the mid-1960s, however, literary critics, particularly Irwin Weil, called for a reassessment of Gorky (1965.27). Although he has since then received more good-willed serious attention, he is still treated less as a writer than as an influential cultural figure and literary organizer (1962.3; 1966.24). Recently several dissertations and published articles by younger Slavists, including B.Y. Forman and M.L. Loe, have helped undermine the Gorkyist socialist-realist position and opened up Gorky as a far more interesting, complex writer than had long been thought (1977.9;

Introduction

1979.16; 1983.2). Most important, his prerevolutionary literary achievements are finally receiving the attention they deserve.

Much work remains to be done. Gorky is certainly one of the keys to understanding the complex shift of political, social, and cultural life that transformed the Western hemisphere in the first half of the twentieth century. It is time for a full reassessment of the man. In Europe and North America there are signs of renewed interest, but in the Soviet Union, Gorky and the religion of the "new man" have lost their hold on the popular imagination. The eventual publication of his complete essays and correspondence will no doubt undermine once and for all the simplistic Stalinist image of Gorky.

It is time, then, to produce a full critical biography of Gorky and to assign the complexities, the paradoxes, the failings and successes their place. None of the riddles of Gorky's life, literary development, and popular reception has been answered satisfactorily. It is still unclear who Peshkov the man was, what Gorky the writer wanted, and why the split between the two existed. No one has fully explained why Gorky had such a powerful grip on the Russian imagination at the turn of the century and why he was at the heart of so many intellectual disputes. Gorky's life as an émigré between 1921 and 1928, his return to Russia, and his role in literary politics in the 1930s--all these subjects need to be fully explored. A thorough intellectual-literary biography would illuminate both its subject and the period he helped form. Perhaps the main mission of the present bibliography is to restore Aleksandr Blok's idea: although Gorky has been marred "by a forced union with socialist thought," he remains important in a larger sense as a Russian writer.

<u>NOTES</u>

1. A.P. Chekhov, <u>Polnoe sobranie sochinenii: Pis'ma</u> (Moscow: Nauka, 1982), 11:164.
2. I.A. Belousov, <u>Literaturnaia Moskva: Pisateli iz naroda, pisateli-narodniki</u> (Moscow: Glavlit, 1926), 3-5; N. Teleshov, <u>Zapiski pisatelia: Vospominaniia i rasskazy o proshlom</u> (Moscow: Moskovskii rabochii, 1958), 134-35; 168-71; I.D. Sytin, <u>Zhizn' dlia knigi</u> (Moscow: G.I.P.L., 1962), 17-21.
3. A.M. Gor'kii, <u>Sobranie sochinenii v 30-i tomakh</u> (Moscow: G.I.Kh.L., 1954), 28:124.
4. Ibid., 129.
5. Ibid., 130.
6. Personal interview, IMLI, 14 March 1985.
7. Gor'kii, <u>Sobranie</u>, 24:292.
8. Telephone interview with Professor Irwin Weil, Purdue-Northwestern, 1 October 1985.

Primary Bibliography

I. COLLECTED WORKS

Sobranie sochinenii. 21 vols. Berlin: Kniga, 1923-28.

Sobranie sochinenii. 23 vols. Moscow-Leningrad: Gosizdat, 1928-30. Reprinted 1930-31.

Sobranie sochinenii v 30-i tomakh. Moscow: GIKhL, 1949-56.

Polnoe sobranie sochinenii. Moscow: Nauka, 1968-.
    1. Khudozhestvennye proizvedeniia v 25-i tomakh [Belles lettres in 25 volumes]. Moscow: Nauka, 1968-76.
    2. Varianty k khudozhestvennym proizvedeniiam [Variants to belles lettres]. 10 vols. Moscow: Nauka, 1974-82.

Collected Works in Ten Volumes. Moscow: Progress, 1979-82.

II. MAJOR INDIVIDUAL WORKS

1892

"Makar Chudra" [Makar Chudra]. Kavkaz (Tbilisi), no. 242 (12 September). For English translation, see Collected Works in Ten Volumes, vol. 1. See also A Sky-Blue Life and Selected Stories, trans. G. Reavey (New York: Signet, 1964).

1893

"O chizhe, kotoryi lgal, i o diatle-liubitele istiny" [The siskin and the woodpecker]. Volzhskii vestnik (Kazan), no. 226 (4 September).

Primary Bibliography

1894

"Ded Arkhip i Len'ka" [Grandfather Arkhip and Lenka]. Volgar' (Nizhnii Novgorod), nos. 35, 37, 39, 41, 43 (13-23 February). For English translation, see Collected Works in Ten Volumes, vol. 1.

"Ob odnom poete" [About a certain poet]. Volzhskii vestnik (Kazan), no. 163 (29 June).

"Moi sputnik" [My traveling companion]. Samarskaia gazeta, nos. 254, 257, 258, 264, 265, 267 (11-31 December). For English translation, see Collected Works in Ten Volumes, vol. 1.

1895

"Pesnia o Sokole" [Song of the falcon]. Samarskaia gazeta, no. 50 (5 March). For English translation, see Collected Works in Ten Volumes, vol. 1.

"Na plotakh" [On the rafts]. Samarskaia gazeta, no. 71 (2 April). For English translation, see A Sky-Blue Life and Selected Stories, trans. G. Reavey (New York: Signet, 1964).

"Starukha Izergil'" [Old woman Izergil]. Samarskaia gazeta, nos. 80, 86, 89 (16-27 April). For English translation, see Collected Works in Ten Volumes, vol. 1.

"Odnazhdi osen'iu" [One autumn]. Samarskaia gazeta, no. 154 (20 July); no. 156 (22 July). For English translation, see Collected Works in Ten Volumes, vol. 1. See also An Anthology of Russian Neo-Realism: The "Znanie" School of Maxim Gorky, ed. and trans. N. Luker (Ann Arbor: Ardis, 1982).

"Chelkash" [Chelkash]. Russkoe bogatstvo, no. 60. For English translation, see Collected Works in Ten Volumes, vol. 1. See also An Anthology of Russian Neo-Realism: The "Znanie" School of Maxim Gorky, ed. and trans. N. Luker (Ann Arbor: Ardis, 1982).

"Oshibka" [The mistake]. Russkaia mysl', no. 9.

1896

"Khan i ego syn" [The khan and his son]. Nizhegorodskii listok, no. 148 (31 May).

Primary Bibliography

1897

"Tovarishchi" [Comrades]. Nizhegorodskii listok, no. 5 (6 January); no. 7 (8 January).

"Konovalov" [Konovalov]. Novoe slovo, no. 6 (March). For English translation, see Collected Works in Ten Volumes, vol. 1.

"Byvshie liudi" [Creatures that were once men]. Novoe slovo, no. 1 (October); no. 2 (November). For English translation, see Best Short Stories of Maxim Gorki, ed. A. Yarmolinsky and M. Budberg (New York: Grayson, 1947).

"Suprugi Orlovy" [The Orlov couple]. Russkaia mysl', no. 10 (October). For English translation, see Collected Works in Ten Volumes, vol. 1.

"Mal'va" [Malva]. Severnyi vestnik', nos. 11-12 (November-December). For English translation, see Selected Short Stories. (New York: Frederick Ungar, 1966).

"Skuki radi" [For want of something better to do]. Samarskaia gazeta, no. 275 (25 December). For English translation, see Collected Works in Ten Volumes, vol. 1.

1898

"Varen'ka Olesova" [Varenka Olesova]. Severnyi vestnik, nos. 3-5 (March-May).

"Prokhodimets" [The rogue]. Zhizn', no. 15 (May).

"Chitatel'" [The reader]. Kosmopolis 12, no. 11 (December). For English translation, see Collected Works in Ten Volumes, vol. 1.

1899

"Kirilka" [Kirilka]. Zhizn', no. 1 (January).

Foma Gordeev [From Gordeev]. Zhizn', no. 4 (February); nos. 3-9 (March-September). For English translation, see Collected Works in Ten Volumes, vol. 2.

"Dvadtsat' shest' i odna" [Twenty-six and one]. Zhizn', no. 12 (December). For English translation, see Collected Works in Ten Volumes, vol. 1. See also An Anthology of Russian Neo-Realism: The "Znanie" School of Maxim Gorky, ed. and trans. N. Luker (Ann Arbor: Ardis, 1982).

Primary Bibliography

1901

"Pesnia o Burevestnike" [Song of the stormy petrel]. Zhizn', no. 4.
  For English translation, see Collected Works in Ten Volumes, vol.
  1. See also Selected Short Stories. (New York: Frederick
  Ungar, 1966).

Troe [The three of them]. In Rasskazy. Vol. 5. St. Petersburg:
  Znanie. For English translation, see The Three, trans.
  M. Wettlin (Moscow: Foreign Languages Publishing House, n.d.).

1902

Meshchane [The petit bourgeois]. St. Petersburg: Znanie. For
  English translation, see Collected Works in Ten Volumes, vol. 4.
  See also The Petty Bourgeois, trans. I. Kosin (N.p.: Washington
  State University Press, 1972).

1903

Na dne [The lower depths]. St. Petersburg: Znanie. For English
  translation, see Collected Works in Ten Volumes, vol. 4. See
  also Seven Plays of Maxim Gorky, trans. A. Bakshy and P. Nathan
  (New Haven: Yale University Press, 1978).

1904

"Chelovek" [Man]. Sbornik tovarishchestva "Znanie" za 1903 god.
  Vol. 1. St. Petersburg: Znanie. For English translation, see
  "The March of Man," Cosmopolitan, July 1905.

1905

"I eshche o cherte" [And still more on the devil]. Bor'ba, no. 1 (27
  November).

Dachniki [Summer folk]. Sbornik tovarishchestva "Znanie" za 1904
  god. Vol. 3. St. Petersburg: Znanie. For English translation,
  see Collected Works in Ten Volumes, vol. 4.

Deti solntsa [Children of the sun]. Sbornik tovarishchestva "Znanie"
  za 1905 god. Vol. 7. St. Petersburg: Znanie. For English
  translation, see The Children of the Sun, trans. M. Budberg
  (London: David-Poynter, 1973).

Primary Bibliography

"Anton Chekhov." Pt. 1: <u>Nizhegorodskii sbornik</u>. St. Petersburg: Znanie, 1905; Pt. 2: <u>Beseda</u>, no. 2 (August 1923). For English translation, see <u>Collected Works in Ten Volumes</u>, vol. 9.

1906

"Soldaty" [Soldiers]. <u>Krasnoe Znamia</u> (Paris), no. 3 (June).

<u>Mat'</u> [Mother]. First published in English: "Mother." <u>Appleton's</u> (December 1906; January-June 1907). As a book: New York: D. Appleton, 1907. In Russian: Berlin: I. Ladyzhnikov, 1907. First full appearance in Russia: <u>Sochineniia</u>. Vol. 15. For recent English translation, see <u>Collected Works in Ten Volumes</u>, vol. 3.

V <u>Amerike</u> [In America]. <u>Sbornik tovarishchestva "Znanie" za 1906 god</u>. Vols. 11, 12. St. Petersburg: Znanie.

<u>Vragi</u> [Enemies]. <u>Sbornik tovarishchestva "Znanie" za 1906 god</u>. Vol. 14. St. Petersburg: Znanie. For English translation, see <u>Collected Works in Ten Volumes</u>, vol. 4. See also <u>Seven Plays of Maxim Gorky</u>, trans. A. Bakshy and P. Nathan (New Haven: Yale University Press, 1978).

<u>Varvary</u> [Barbarians]. Stuttgart: Verlag von J.H.W. Dietz Nachfolger. For English translation, see <u>Seven Plays of Maxim Gorky</u>, trans. A. Bakshy and P. Nathan (New Haven: Yale University Press, 1945).

1908

<u>Zhizn' nenuzhnogo cheloveka</u> [The life of a superfluous man]. Berlin: I.P. Ladyzhnikov. For English translation, see <u>The Life of a Useless Man</u>, trans. M. Budberg (Harmondsworth: Penguin, 1975).

<u>Ispoved'</u> [The confession]. <u>Sbornik tovarishchestva "Znanie" za 1908 god</u>. Vol. 23. St. Petersburg: Znanie. For English translation, see <u>The Confession</u>, trans. R. Strunsky (New York: Frederick A. Stokes, 1916).

1909

<u>Leto</u> [Summer]. Berlin: I.P. Ladyzhnikov.

"Razrushenie lichnosti" [The disintegration of personality]. <u>Ocherki filosofii kollektivizma</u>. Vol. 1. St. Petersburg: Znanie. For English translation, see <u>Collected Works in Ten Volumes</u>, vol. 10.

Primary Bibliography

1910

Gorodok Okurov [The town of Okurov]. Sbornik tovarishchestva "Znanie" za 1909 god. Vols. 28-29. St. Petersburg: Znanie.

Chudaki [Eccentrics]. Sbornik tovarishchestva "Znanie" za 1910 god. Vol. 32. St. Petersburg: Znanie. For English translation, see Seven Plays of Maxim Gorky, trans. A. Bakshy and P. Nathan (New Haven: Yale University Press, 1945).

Vassa Zheleznova [Vassa Zheleznova]. Sbornik tovarishchestva "Znanie" za 1910 god. Vol. 33. St. Petersburg: Znanie. For English translation, see Collected Works in Ten Volumes, vol. 4. See also Seven Plays of Maxim Gorky, trans. A. Bakshy and P. Nathan (New Haven: Yale University Press, 1978).

1911

Zhizn' Matveia Kozhemiakina [The life of Matvei Kozhemiakin]. Sbornik tovarishchestva "Znanie" za 1910 god. Vols. 30-31, 35-37. St. Petersburg: Znanie. For English translation, see Collected Works in Ten Volumes, vol. 5.

1912

"Rozhdenie cheloveka" [A man is born]. Zavety, no. 1 (April). For English translation, see Collected Works in Ten Volumes, vol. 1. See also A Book of Short Stories, trans. A. Yarmolinsky and M. Budberg (New York: Cape, 1939).

1913

Detstvo [Childhood]. Russkoe slovo nos. 196, 208, 213, 219, 224, 230, 236, 260, 266, 271, 277, 283, 289, 295, 299; nos. 4, 12, 18, 24 (1914). For English translation, see Collected Works in Ten Volumes, vol. 6. See also My Childhood, trans. R. Wilks (Baltimore: Penguin, 1966).

1915

Skazki ob Italii [Tales of Italy]. All twenty-seven stories first collected in Sochineniia M. Gor'kogo [Works of M. Gor'kii]. Vol. 17. St. Petersburg: Zhizn' i znanie, 1915. For English translation, see Collected Works in Ten Volumes, vol. 6.

Po Rusi [Around Russia]. First eleven stories collected in Sochineniia M. Gor'kogo [Works of M. Gorky]. Vol. 19. St. Petersburg: Zhizn' i znanie, 1915. Last eighteen stories

Primary Bibliography

collected in <u>Eralash i drugie rasskazy</u> [Eralash and other stories]. Prague: Parus, 1918.

1916

<u>V liudiakh</u> [My apprenticeship]. <u>Letopis'</u>, nos. 1-12. For English translation, see <u>Collected Works in Ten Volumes</u>, vol. 7.

1917

<u>Nesvoevremennye mysli</u> [Untimely thoughts]. <u>Novaia zhizn'</u>, 1 May 1917-16 July 1918. For English translation of selected articles, see <u>Untimely Thoughts: Essays on Revolution, Culture, and Bolsheviks, 1917-1918</u>, trans. H. Ermolaev (New York: Paul S. Eriksson, 1968).

1919

"Lev Tolstoy." <u>Vospominaniia o L've Nikolaeviche Tolstom</u> [Memoirs of Lev Nikolaevich Tolstoy]. Petrograd: Z.I. Grzhebin. For English translation, see <u>Collected Works in Ten Volumes</u>, vol. 9.

1921

<u>Starik</u> [The old man]. Berlin: I.P. Ladyzhnikov. For English translation, see <u>Five Plays</u>, trans. M. Wettlin (London: Central Books, 1961).

1922

"Leonid Andreev." <u>Kniga o Leonide Andreeve: Vospominaniia</u> [A book about Leonid Andreev: Memoirs]. Petrograd: Z.I. Grzhebin. For English translation, see <u>Collected Works in Ten Volumes</u>, vol. 9.

1923

<u>Moi universitety</u> [My universities]. <u>Krasnaia nov'</u>, no. 2 (March-April); no. 3 (May); no. 4 (June-July). For English translation, see <u>Collected Works in Ten Volumes</u>, vol. 7. See also <u>My Universities</u>, trans. R. Wilks (Harmondsworth: Penguin, 1979).

"Rasskaz o bezotvetnoi liubvi" [A tale of unrequited love]. <u>Beseda</u>, no. 3 (September-October).

"O pervoi liubvi" [First love]. <u>Krasnaia nov'</u>, no. 6 (October-November). For English translation, see <u>Collected Works in Ten</u>

Primary Bibliography

Volumes, vol. 1. A Sky-Blue Life and Selected Stories, trans. G. Reavey (New York: Signet, 1964).

"Moi interv'iu" [My interviews]. Written 1906. First full publication of collection: Sobranie sochinenii. Vol. 13. Berlin: Kniga.

1924

"Rasskaz ob odnom romane" [The story of a certain romance]. Beseda, no. 4 (March).

"Rasskaz o geroe" [The story of a hero]. Beseda, no. 4 (March). For English translation, see Collected Works in Ten Volumes, vol. 1.

"V.I. Lenin." Izvestiia TsIK SSSR i VTsIK, no. 84 (11 April). See also Russkii sovremennik, no. 1 (May 1924); also in: Vospominaniia, Rasskazy, Zametki [Memoirs, stories, remarks]. Berlin: Kniga, 1927. For English translation, see Collected Works in Ten Volumes, vol. 9.

"Karamora." Beseda, no. 5 (June). For English translation, see Collected Works in Ten Volumes, vol. 1. See also A Book of Short Stories, trans. A. Yarmolinsky and M. Budberg (New York: Cape, 1939).

Zametki iz dnevnika: Vospominaniia [Fragments from my diary: Memoirs]. Berlin: Kniga. For English translation, see Fragments from My Diary, trans. M. Budberg (London: Penguin, 1972).

1925

Delo Artamonovykh [The Artamonov business]. Berlin: Kniga. For English translation, see Collected Works in Ten Volumes, vol. 8. See also The Artamonov Business, trans. A. Brown (London: Heron, 1969).

"Golubaia zhizn'" [A sky-blue life]. Published first in Italian as La vita azzurra. Translated by E. Lo Gatto. Rome: Stock. First Russian publication: Rasskazy 1922-1924 [Stories 1922-1924]. Berlin: Kniga, 1925. For English translation, see A Sky-Blue Life and Selected Stories, trans. G. Reavey (New York: Signet, 1964).

1927

Fal'shivaia moneta [Counterfeit money]. Written 1913. Berlin: Kniga.

Primary Bibliography

Zhizn' Klima Samgina [The life of Klim Samgin]. 4 vols. Vols. 1-2 in Sobranie sochinenii. Vols. 20-21. Berlin: Kniga, 1927-28. Vol. 3: Berlin: Kniga, 1931. Vol. 4: unfinished. For English translation, see Bystander [Klim Samgin, vol. 1], trans. B.G. Guerney (London: Cape, 1930); The Magnet [Klim Samgin, vol. 2], trans. A. Bakshy (London: Cape, 1931); Other Fires [Klim Samgin, vol. 3], trans. A. Bakshy (New York: Appleton, 1933); The Specter [Klim Samgin, vol. 4], trans. A. Bakshy (New York: Appleton, 1938).

1930

"Besedy o remesle" [Talks on craftsmanship]. Literaturnaia ucheba, no. 6 (June); no. 7 (July 1931); no. 9 (September 1931). For English translation, see Collected Works in Ten Volumes, vol. 10.

1932

Egor Bulychev i drugie [Egor Bulychev and others]. Berlin: Kniga. For English translation, see Collected Works in Ten Volumes, vol. 4. See also Seven Plays of Maxim Gorky, trans. A. Bakshy and P. Nathan (New Haven: Yale University Press, 1978).

1934

"Sovetskaia literatura" [Soviet literature]. Pravda, no. 228 (August 19). (Address delivered to the First All-Union Congress of Soviet Writers, 17 August 1934.) For English translation, see Collected Works in Ten Volumes, vol. 10.

Dostigaev i drugie [Dostigaev and others]. Almanakh: God semnadtsatyi (Almanac: The seventeenth year). Vol. 3. Moscow: N.p.

1941

Somov i drugie [Somov and others]. Arkhiv A. M. Gor'kogo. Vol. 2. Moscow: ANSSSR.

Secondary Bibliography

Undated

1   LEMOS, NESTOR. <u>Gorky como pedagogo de la literatura</u>.
    Mendoza, Argentina: N.p., 137 pp.
       Outlines Gorky's aesthetic theory.

1898

1   BATIUSHKOV, F.D. "V mire bosiakov" [In the world of tramps].
    <u>Kosmopolis</u> 12, no. 11:95-120.
       Gorky is a realist with many romantic impulses. Batiushkov notes the strong influence of Victor Hugo with whom Gorky shares a "romantic dreaminess." Gorky's freedom-loving tramps are refreshing after a long period of "naturalism" in literature.

2   B[OGDANOVICH], A. "<u>Ocherki i rasskazy</u> Maksima Gor'kogo. Dva toma" [M. Gorky's <u>Sketches and stories</u>. Two volumes]. <u>Mir bozhii</u>, no. 7:1-13.
       Gorky's characters can be divided into two types. The freedom-loving tramps and the "former people" who have failed in life. Gorky clearly sides with the freedom seekers.

3   FLEKSER, A. [Volynskii, A.L.]. "M. Gor'kii, <u>Ocherki i rasskazy</u>, St. Petersburg, 1898" [M. Gorky, <u>Sketches and stories</u>, St. Petersburg, 1898]. <u>Severnyi vestnik</u>, no. 10-12:206-12.
       Finds a certain artificiality in Gorky's tramps: they reflect recent European philosophy, especially Nietzsche. They often play the role of the "raisonneur," for which they are ill-equipped.

1899

1   VON ENGELHARDT, ALEXIS. "Echo der Zeitschriften." <u>Das literarische Echo</u> 8 (15 February).
       Gorky is a new, promising story writer.

1900

1   SOLOV'EV, EVGENII [Andreevich]. Kniga o Maksime Gor'kom i
    A.P. Chekhove [A book about Maksim Gorky and A.P. Chekhov].
    St. Petersburg: A.E. Kolpinskii, 259 pp.
       Gorky has brought about a literary revolution by creating a
    new hero, the bosiak [tramp]. The tramp-hero rebels against
    "petit bourgeois" self-interest and gives the reader a new perspective, a new love of freedom. Here Gorky satisfies the need
    felt by the intelligentsia for an uncompromising, vital, rebellious impulse. Andreevich finds Foma Gordeev Gorky's strongest
    work so far and a convincing expression of the tramp-proletarian
    spirit; notes a strong affinity with Friedrich Nietzsche.

1901

1   B[OGDANOVICH], A. "Mir bosiakov v izobrazhenii g. Gor'kogo"
    [Gorky's depiction of the world of tramps]. In Kriticheskie
    stat'i. Kiev: A.G. Aleksandrov, pp. 27-43.
       See 1901.3. Sees Gorky's "tramp brigade" as the "creation
    exclusively of the big cities," a product of industrialization.

2   BRANDES, GEORG. "Maksim Gor'kii." In Sobranie sochinenii.
    Translated by M.V. Luchitskaia. Vol. 19. St. Petersburg:
    N.p., pp. 285-99.
       Gorky as a novelist has no sense of idea or form. Like
    Tolstoy in War and Peace or Dostoevsky in all his novels, he
    "embraces too much." Gorky's women characters, such as Varenka
    Olesova, however, are wonderfully drawn.

3   GRINBERG, S., ed. Kriticheskie stat'i o proizvedeniiakh
    Maksima Gor'kogo [Critical articles on Maksim Gorky's works].
    Kiev: A.G. Aleksandrov, 254 pp.
       Contains the following articles:
       1. S.M., "Maksim Gor'kii (biograficheskii ocherk)" [Maksim Gorky
    (biographical sketch)]. See 1901.5.
       2. V. Posse, "Pevets protestuiushchei toski" [The singer
    of mutinous melancholy] (1898). See 1901.9.
       3. N. Minskii, "Filosofiia toski i zhazhda voli" [The
    philosophy of melancholy and the thirst for liberty] (1898).
    See 1901.8.
       4. A.B., "Mir bosiakov v izobrazhenii g. Gor'kogo" [Gorky's
    depiction of the world of tramps] (1898). See 1901.1.
       5. I. Ignatov, "Filosofiia bosiachestva" [The philosophy of
    the tramps] (1898).
       6. N. Mikhailovskii, "O g. Maksime Gor'kom i ego geroiakh"
    [About Mr. Maksim Gorky and his heroes] (1898). See 1901.7.
       7. A. Skabichevskii, "M. Gor'kii, ocherki i rasskazy" [M.
    Gorky, sketches and stories] (1898).
       8. A. Skabichevskii, "Novye cherty v talante g. M.
    Gor'kogo" [New qualities in Mr. M. Gorky's talent] (1898).
    See 1901.10.

9. A.B., "Krepnushchii talant" [A talent in the making] (1898).
10. Vl. Botsianovskii, "V pogone za smyslom zhizni" [In search of the meaning of life] (1900).
11. M. Men'shikov, "Krasivyi tsinizm" [Beautiful cynicism] (1900). See 1901.6.
12. N. Gekker, "'Dvadtsat' shest' i odna'" [Twenty-six and one] (1900).
13. N. Gekker, "O 'Muzhike' g. Gor'kogo" [About Mr. Gorky's "Peasant"].
14. L.E. Obolenskii, "'Dvadtsat' shest' i odna'" [Twenty-six and one] (1900).
15. L.E. Obolenskii, "Maksim Gor'kii i idei ego novykh geroev" [Maksim Gorky and the ideas of his new heroes] (1900).
16. L.E. Obolenskii, "Talant Maksima Gor'kogo" [The talent of Maksim Gorky] (1900).

4 HAPGOOD, ISABELLE. Introduction to Foma Gordeev. Translated by I.F. Hapgood. New York: Charles Scribner's, pp. v-x.
Gorky is the "most promising young writer in Russia." Compares and contrasts Gorky with Tolstoy.

5 M., S. "Maksim Gor'kii (biograficheskii ocherk)" [Maksim Gorky (biographical sketch)]. In Kriticheskie stat'i. Kiev: A.G. Aleksandrov, pp. vii-xvi.
See 1901.3. Tries to settle controversy over Gorky's biography and whether it has made a bigger impression on the public than his literary work. Gives a brief, clear, mostly accurate account of his life.

6 MEN'SHIKOV, M. "Krasivyi tsinizm" [Beautiful cynicism]. In Kriticheskie stat'i. Kiev: A.G. Aleksandrov, pp. 181-209.
See 1901.3. Gorky has become known partly on the merits of his talent and partly because of his unusual life. Author tries to separate what is worthwhile in Gorky's work from what is not.

7 MIKHAILOVSKII, N.K. "O g. Maksime Gor'kom i ego geroiakh" [On Mr. Maksim Gorky and his heroes]. In Kriticheskie stat'i. Kiev: A.G. Aleksandrov, pp. 53-105.
See 1901.3. Gorky is "fresh," an important change from positivist, progressivist writers. Finds his tramp hero a representative of a growing urban culture. Hostile to the peasant. Finds his characters amoral and cruel, less subtle than Dostoevsky's sadomasochists. Draws parallels to Nietzsche.

8 MINSKII, NIKOLAI. "Filosofiia toski i zhazhda voli" [The philosophy of melancholy and the thirst for liberty]. In Kriticheskie stat'i. Kiev: A.G. Aleksandrov, pp. 17-26.
See 1901.3. Gorky is a "fresh, unusual, . . . idiosyncratic" talent, but too sentimental and too tendentious. Compares Gorky with Nietzsche and Ibsen.

1901

9   POSSE, VLADIMIR. "Pevets protestuiushchei toski" [The singer of mutinous melancholy]. In Kriticheskie stat'i. Kiev: A.G. Aleksandrov, pp. 3-16.
    See 1901.3. Gorky is the "first talented artist-representative of the working proletariat." Uses mood of melancholy to create a sense of discontent in the reader.

10 SKABICHEVSKII, A. "Novye cherty v talante g. M. Gor'kogo" [New aspects of Mr. Gorky's talent]. In Kriticheskie stat'i. Kiev: A.G. Aleksandrov, pp. 125-45.
    See 1901.3. Gorky is moving away from the world of tramps and trying new themes in "Kirilka" and Foma Gordeev. Gorky's treatment of merchants shows his enthusiasm for Nietzsche's "man-god" [sic].

1902

1   BAIN, R. NISBET. "Biographical Sketch." Tales from Gorky. Translated by R.N. Bain. New York: Funk & Wagnalls, pp. 7-17.
    Gorky writing his own stories is like Oliver Twist becoming a writer.

2   DILLON, E.J. Maxim Gorky: His Life and Writings. London: Isbister, 383 pp.
    Deals with early biography, "new" heroes, the "over-tramp," reasons for Gorky's popularity, his "impressionist" style, his moral outlook.

3   HAPGOOD, ISABEL. A Survey of Russian Literature. New York: Chautauqua Press, pp. 268-72.
    Gorky is seen as the "successor" to Tolstoy. He is more than popular in Russia: he is "deeply loved." Has a genius for "painting absolutely living pictures." His main theme is the "uneasy man," who wants more than just to feed himself.

4   [Marxist.] "Maxim Ghorki, the Portrayer of Unrest." International Socialist Review (Chicago) (January):514-18.
    Review of Foma Gordeev. Likes Gorky's view that even the most degraded people are still humans. Compares and contrasts Gorky and Dostoevsky. Likes Gorky's lack of sentimentality. Argues with the opinion that Gorky is influenced by Nietzsche.

5   SOISSONS, C. de. "Maxime Gorky." Eclectic (Boston) 138 (March):316-24.
    Finds the "thirsty," "challenging" nature of Gorky's vagabonds fresh and original. Discusses "Chelkash" and "Malva." Compares Gorky's ideal to Nietzsche's superman.

6   STRANNIK, IVAN. "Preface: Maxime Gorky." In Twenty-Six and One. New York: J.F. Taylor, pp. 5-15.

Compares Gorky to Tolstoy and Maupassant. Notes the "trueness of Gorky's writing: everything is based on experience."

7 VOLKHOVSKY, F. "The Poet of the Awakening Personality." Free Russia, April, pp. 41-43.
   Likes Gorky's "vigorous self-assertion." Finds it healthy for the revolutionary movement. Denies Nietzsche's influence.

1903

1 BOTSIANOVSKII, V.F. Maksim Gor'kii: Kritiko-biograficheskii etiud [Maksim Gorky: A critical-biographical study]. St. Petersburg: A. Suvorin, 94 pp.
   First printed in 1901. Gorky's stories are all a truthful reflection of his own moods, his own desire for freedom. Records his biography and character in terms of his stories.

2 BURNS, JAMES. "Maxim Gorky: A Voice from the Depths." Westminster Review (London) 160, no. 2 (August):148-56.
   Gorky's biography is an example of the saying that "truth is stranger than fiction."

3 FILOSOFOV, DMITRII. "O 'lzhi' Gor'kogo" [About Gorky's "lie"]. Novyi put', no. 6:212-17.
   Continues a debate started in Novyi put', no. 5, about Gorky's moral view; discusses his treatment of the "great lie" in his character Luka. Affirms the need for the great lie, the need to revolt against God, in order to come to a real truth. Condemns Gorky's "watered-down" version of the problem in The Lower Depths [Na dne].

4 GEL'ROT, M. "Nitsshe i Gor'kii: Elementy nitssheanstva v tvorchestve Gor'kogo" [Nietzsche and Gorky: Elements of Nietzscheanism in Gorky's work]. Russkoe bogatstvo 5:25-68.
   Gelrot singles out "Nietzschean" themes in Gorky's work without trying to prove influence.

5 LUNACHARSKII, A.V. "Opyt literaturnoi kharakteristiki Gleba Uspenskogo" [An attempt at a literary sketch of Gleb Uspensky]. Obrazovanie, no. 8.
   See 1963.12.

1904

1 AMFITEATROV, ALEKSANDR. "Na dne" [The Lower Depths]. Literaturnyi al'bom. St. Petersburg: N.p., pp. 8-27.
   St. Petersburg's "bourgeoisie" has reacted very negatively to The Lower Depths [Na dne]. Amfiteatrov finds it morally honest and not cynical. He sees Satin as a Schillerian character.

He remarks that The Lower Depths grew in part from Tolstoy's The Power of Darkness [Vlast' t'my].

2   FILOSOFOV, DMITRII. "Zavtrashnee meshchanstvo" [Tomorrow's lower middle class]. Novyi put', no. 11:321-32.
    Review of Summer Folk [Dachniki]. This play exists "outside of literature." It is a "naive imitation of Chekhov . . . at his worst." Gorky plays up to the tastes and expectations of a "bourgeois" public. Laments that Gorky has changed from a "bright strong protester into the most mundane intellectual."

2A G., L. Inostrannaia kritika o Gor'kom [Foreign criticism on Gorky]. Moscow: Russkoe tovarishchestvo pechat. i izdat. dela, 324 pp.
    Includes reviews of Gorky's works from the English, German, French, Swedish, Danish, Italian, and Spanish press.

3   KINLOCH, A. "The Bossiak and Russia's Social Unrest." Fortnightly Review (London) 75 (January):60-68.
    Notes the difference between the "autocratic" government and the "democratic" literary culture of Russia.

4   KOROLENKO, V. [Zhurnalist]. "O sbornikakh tovarishchestva 'Znanie' za 1903 g." [On the "Znanie" almanacs for 1903]. Russkoe bogatstvo, no. 8:129-49.
    Gorky's old mentor criticizes "Man" ["Chelovek"] for its "tiredness" and its implied scorn for humanity.

5   STECH'KIN, N.IA. Maksim Gor'kii. St. Petersburg: Komarov, 259 pp.
    An attempt to discredit Gorky. Deals with his resounding reception among Russian readers, among whom he is popular because he answers their mood. Analyzes this mood.

1905

1   BRINTON, CHRISTIAN. "Career of Maxim Gorky." Everybody's Magazine 17, no. 4 (April):464-67.
    Gorky's life is "dismal" and "dazzling." His life is his art. Gorky's works are not great art but they do have social significance.

2   COOKE, GEORGE WILLIS. "Maxim Gorky: Tramp, Story-teller and Adventurer." New England (Boston) 32 (June):399-414.
    Discusses the social significance of Gorky's tales as warnings of revolution.

3   DIVIL'KOVSKII, A.A. "Maksim Gor'kii: Kriticheskii ocherk" [Maksim Gorky: A Critical Sketch]. Pravda 2:119-38; 3:83-97.

Dismisses Gorky's reputation as an "extreme individualist" as an image given him by his critics. His heroes are men of the people and his basic views are socially oriented.

4   L., R. "Maxim Gorky and the Russian Revolt." *Fortnightly Review* (London) 77 (April):608-21.
    Tells about the production of *Summer Folk* [*Dachniki*] in 1905.

5   LOURIE, OSSIP. "Maxime Gorki." *Open Court* (Chicago) 19, no. 592 (September):513-22.
    See 1905.7. An excerpt from the book *La psychologie des romanciers russes du XIXe siècle*. Gorky's tales are the natural outcome of nineteenth-century Russian social literature: Gogol's *Dead Souls*, Turgenev's *Hunter Sketches*, Dostoevsky's *Notes from the House of the Dead*.

6   LUNACHARSKII, A.V. "*Dachniki*" [*Summer Folk*]. *Pravda* (April).
    See 1964.20. Compares Gorky's and Nietzsche's "cruelty" and "honesty." Welcomes Gorky's attack on pity and moral falsity.

7   OSSIP-LOURIÉ, M. "Gorki." *La psychologie des romanciers russes du XIXe siècle*. Paris: Félix Alcan, pp. 381-417.
    Gorky is the logical end to the nineteenth-century Russian classical tradition. He is the voice of the people. His work shows how former serfs think and live.

8   TUMANOV, G.M. *Kharakteristiki i vospominaniia* [Character sketches and memoirs]. Tbilisi: Trud.
    Contains information on the "Sreda" literary gatherings and Gorky's participation.

1906

1   ANNENSKII, INNOKENTII. "Tri sotsial'nykh dramy: Drama na dne" [Three social dramas: Drama in the lower depths]. In *Kniga otrazhenii* [Book of reflections]. St. Petersburg: Izd. Brat'ev Bashmakovykh, pp. 127-46.
    Finds *The Lower Depths* [*Na dne*] an unusual play in that it fuses lyric-fantastic and dramatic-realistic impulses. Gorky is the "most sharply expressed Russian symbolist" after Dostoevsky. His characters are like masks that conceal the author. "The integrity of the new drama is based exclusively upon the idea of the author, the poetically disposed personality is the only mode of unifying colorful impressions of life."

2   CHESTERTON, G.K. Introduction to *Creatures that Once Were Men*. Translated by J.K.M. Shirazi. New York: Funk & Wagnalls, pp. v-xv.
    Culture "evolves" beyond the limits of national boundaries. Great "modern" literature has emerged from Russia without there

having been a "classical" literature. Uses Gorky as an example. Gorky is "Russian" in the sense that his temperament combines both "revolutionary" and "religious" aspects: he has an "attitude of primary and dogmatic assertion." Admires contrasting simplicity and rebelliousness. The story is the missing link between them.

3   GLINKA, A.S. [Volzhskii]. "O nekotorykh motivakh tvorchestva Maksima Gor'kogo" [On certain motifs in Maksim Gorky's work]. In Iz mira literaturnykh iskanii [From the world of literary explorations]. St. Petersburg: D.E. Zhukovskii, pp. 130-62.
    Gorky believes in the necessary lie. Discusses Luka in The Lower Depths [Na dne].

4   LUNACHARSKII, A.V. "Varvary" [Barbarians]. Vestnik zhizni, no. 2 (10 April).
    See 1964.20. Criticizes Gorky for the somber colors of his picture of Russian social reality. Finds here the clash of "wooden Russia" and "iron Russia."

5   MEREZHKOVSKII, D.S. Griadushchii kham: Chekhov i Gor'kii [The coming lout: Chekhov and Gorky]. St. Petersburg: M.V. Pirozhkov, 185 pp.
    Sees Chekhov's and Gorky's work as embodiments of the mediocrity and insignificance that threaten all Russian culture.

5A SPARGO, JOHN. "With Maxim Gorky in the Adirondacks." Craftsman 11, no. 2 (November):149-55.
    Page 148 contains a photograph of Gorky. Finds Gorky a man of the highest ideals, in search of freedom for Russia. Admires Maria Andreeva greatly. Useful background on Gorky's American hosts, the Martins. Emphasizes the language difference as a barrier to mutual understanding. Brings out other cultural differences--for example, that Gorky distrusts American measures of social progress: voter registration rather than "spiritual development."

6   "The Stormy Career of Maxim Gorky." Current Literature (New York) 40 (May):488-91.
    Gorky's philosophy is the "joy of life." Contains three photographs and reviews Gorky's life.

7   WELLS, H.G. "The Future in America. IX. Two Studies in Disappointment." Harper's Weekly (New York) 50 (8 September):1279-84.
    Uses Gorky's reception in the United States as an example of Americans' lack of social consciousness.

8   WILLCOX, LOUISE COLLIER. "Maxim Gorky." North American Review 183, no. 9 (7 December):1159-70.
    The Russian and American temperaments are "antipodal." Gorky is a great representative of Russia.

9   WILSHIRE, GAYLORD. "Gorky's Reception by New York and Mrs. Grundy." Wilshire Magazine 10, no. 5 (May):3, 10.
   On Gorky's reception in the United States. Attacks the newspaper World for perverting the facts about Gorky and Andreeva.

1907

1   BLOK, ALEKSANDR. "O realistakh" [About the realists]. Zolotoe runo [The golden fleece] 5:63-72.
   Agrees with recent opinions that Gorky's gift of "unconscious anarchism" has been ruined by a forced union with socialist thought. He feels the urge to say something good about him, however. "Gorky is more than he wants to be . . . because his 'intuition' is deeper than his consciousness. . . . by the fateful force of his talent, by blood, by the nobility of his striving, by the 'limitlessness of his ideal' . . . and by the extent of his spiritual torments, Gorky is a Russian writer."

2   FILOSOFOV, DMITRII. "Konets Gor'kogo" [The end of Gorky]. Russkaia mysl' 28, no. 4.
   Argues that Gorky's latest work--for example, Barbarians [Varvary] and Enemies [Vragi]--show the failure of his literary talent.

3   IVANOV-RAZUMNIK, R. Istoriia russkoi obshchestvennoi mysli [The history of Russian social thought]. Vol. 2. St. Petersburg: M.M. Stasiulevich, pp. 392-427.
   Compares and contrasts Gorky's and the Russian Marxist vision of humanity.

4   KRASIN, P. "Nravstvennye nachala (printsipy noveishei russkoi khudozhestvennoi literatury)" [Ethical origins (the principles of recent Russian fiction)]. Vera i razum, no. 5:622-40; no. 6:786-810; no. 7:81-96; no. 8:225-30.
   On Gorky's moral view. Finds that the romantic "influences" of Byron or Nietzsche served to "support" Gorky's own mood. Gorky's heroes arise out of a native Russian tradition of social protest and striving for a better life.

5   OSTWALD, HANS. Maxim Gorky. London: McClure, Phillips & Co., 78 pp.
   Provides an accurate but brief summary of Gorky's early life. Discusses early stories, Foma Gordeev, The Three of Them [Troe], The Petit Bourgeois [Meshchane], and The Lower Depths [Na dne]. Notes that Gorky's heroes depart from the typical Russian hero in that they are "virile" men of action. Gorky's narrative style is weakened by "hackneyed use of situations, materials, and ideas, suggestive of the hack writer."

6   PLEKHANOV, G.V. "K psikhologii rabochego dvizheniia: Maksim Gor'kii, Vragi" [On the psychology of the worker's movement: Maksim Gorky, Enemies]. Sovremennyi mir 5:1-16.
    See 1927.4.

1908

1   ALEKSANDROVICH, IURII. Posle Chekhova: Ocherk molodoi literatury poslednego desiatiletiia, 1898-1908. [After Chekhov: A sketch of recent literature of the last decade, 1898-1908]. Moscow: Obshch. pol'za, pp. 61-67.
    Gorky is at the center of a new buoyant trend in literature characterized by a mood of "yes, to life!" Gorky's heroes are "Nietzscheans." Discusses "Makar Chudra," "The Orlov Couple" ["Suprugi Orlovy"].

2   AMFITEATROV, ALEKSANDR. "Novyi Gor'kii" [The new Gorky]. Sovremenniki [Contemporaries]. Moscow: N.p., pp. 79-112.
    Although Gorky has written weak pieces in the period after The Lower Depths [Na dne], he remains Amfiteatrov's favorite writer and a major cultural figure. His strongest work is the short story "Soldiers" ["Soldaty"]. Gorky was "created for positive proselytizing, not for negative war." He has used his dramas to destroy a weak "bourgeois" intelligentsia that would not follow his lead. Now, with Mother [Mat'] he has created a didactic novel for a new reading public, the proletariat and has drawn the attention of the general public to the workers' movement.

3   BUGAEV, B. [A. Belyi]. "Na perevale" [At the pass]. Vesy, no. 9:59-62.
    Review of Confession [Ispoved']. Notes the fall in Gorky's popularity. Finds in Confession a reawakening of the best aspects of Gorky's gift. It shows real insight into the Russian soul.

4   GIPPIUS, ZINAIDA [Anton Krainii]. "Vybor meshka" [Taking sides]. In Literaturnyi dnevnik (1899-1907) [Literary diary (1899-1907)]. St. Petersburg: M.V. Pirozhkov, pp. 174-85.
    Although Gorky as a writer is forgotten, as a "social phenomenon" he is a touchstone for a whole series of issues.

4A GORNFEL'D, A.G. "Konchilsia li Gor'kii?" [Is Gorky finished?]. In Knigi i liudi [Books and people]. Vol. 1. St. Petersburg: Zhizn', pp. 102-11.
    Questions D. Filosofov's judgment that Gorky has failed as an artist (1907.2). Reviews early criticism of Gorky.

5   HUNEKER, JAMES. "Maxim Gorky's Nachtasyl." In Iconoclasts. 2d ed. New York: Charles Scribner, pp. 269-85.
    Focuses on The Lower Depths [Na dne] as the "last word in dramatic naturalism." Emile Zola should have gone to school to

learn the "alphabet" of naturalism from Gorky. Russian naturalism as founded by Gogol avoids the "melodrama" of Zola. Compares Gorky to Dickens. Although there is little "technical construction" in the play, Gorky brings about the necessary "collision of characters" through Luka.

6   K., I. "Bogostroitel'stvo M. Gor'kogo" [M. Gorky's God-building]. Moskovskii ezhenedel'nik 3, no. 35 (6 September): 3-16.
    Finds D. Filosofov's indictment of Gorky (1907.2) completely unfair. Although Gorky has "glued" a social-democratic "label" onto his work, he remains the same "passionately searching soul" as before. He has paused for only a short time in the "socialist kingdom of self-satisfied vulgarity." Reviews Confession [Ispoved']. Sees it as "God-seeking."

7   KOBYLINSKII, LEV. [Ellis]. "Eshche o sokolakh i uzhakh" [More on falcons and grass snakes]. Vesy, no. 7:53-58.
    Review of Barbarians [Varvary], Enemies [Vragi], The Last Ones [Poslednie]. Finds Gorky's transition from the form of the short story to the more complex form of the drama is not justified by any spiritual growth.

1909

1   CHUKOVSKII, KORNEI. "Maksim Gor'kii." In Ot Chekhova do nashikh dnei [From Chekhov to our days]. St. Petersburg: M.O. Vol'f, pp. 65-74.
    Makes fun of Gorky's moral view: Gorky's stories are like "little theorems" that all have the same opposition of "grass snakes" and "falcons" set forth in "The Song of the Falcon" ["Pesnia o sokole"]. Chukovsky: "To prove: the falcon is better than the grass snake."

2   LUNACHARSKII, A. "Dvadtsat' tretii sbornik 'Znaniia'" [The 23rd Znanie almanac]. In Literaturnyi raspad: Kriticheskii sbornik [Literary decline: A collection of critical essays]. Vol. 2. St. Petersburg: EOS, pp. 84-119.
    Devoted to Confession [Ispoved']. Finds in its "God-building pathos" the "spiritual center of the new world, of evolving collective, proletarian society," that is, the idea of "Man" ["Chelovek"]. It is a prototype for a "Marxist art." Revised: 1924.4.

2A PLEKHANOV, G.V. "O tak nazyvaemykh religioznykh iskaniiakh v Rossii" [On the so-called religious searching in Russia]. Sovremennyi mir, no. 10:188-200.
    Discusses Confession [Ispoved'] as an attempt to propagate the new religion of God-building. Argues that Gorky, like many great writers, is completely out of his depth when he deals in political theory or religious thought.

3   UL'IANOV, V.I. [V.I. Lenin]. "Basnia burzhuaznoi pechati ob iskliuchenii Gor'kogo" [The fable of the bourgeois press about Gorky's expulsion]. Proletarii, no. 50 (28 November).
    See 1958.42.

1910

1   BUGAEV, BORIS [A. Belyi]. "Simvolizm i sovremennoe russkoe iskusstvo" [Symbolism and contemporary Russian art]. In Lug zelenyi: Kniga statei [Green meadow: A book of articles]. Moscow: Al'tsiona, pp. 29-50.
    Discusses differences between symbolism and realism. Finds Gorky an enormous talent with a weak "credo." Likes Confession [Ispoved']. Puts Gorky at the center of Russian realism.

2   HARVEY, W.F. "The Genius of Gorky and Lagerlöf." Anglo-Russian Literary Society Proceedings (London), no. 58:5-23.
    Speech. Notes that Gorky has been widely read, but has received little critical attention. Finds Gorky a realist in the Russian tradition--that is, "realism leavened with romanticism," not naturalism. Ranks Gorky with Maupassant. Discusses Confession [Ispoved']. Urges that Russian writers be judged by their own standards.

1911

1   BUGAEV, BORIS [A. Belyi]. "Slovo pravdy" [A word of truth] (1908). In Arabeski [Arabesques]. Moscow: Musaget, pp. 295-98.
    The more fuss people make about Gorky the more his talent dries up. But one cannot forget his genuine works. Finds in Confession [Ispoved'] a resurgence of the best of Gorky.

2   PHELPS, W.L. "Gorki." In Essays on Russian Novelists. New York: Macmillan, pp. 215-33.
    Gorky's fame skyrocketed until 1906. His name became a "household word." Since then it has been waning. He is a worse artist than Leonid Andreev, but he is a "vital" person. Phelps gives background of Gorky's trip to the United States, especially his encounter with Mark Twain.

1912

1   GIPPIUS, ZINAIDA [Anton Krainii]. "Belletricheskie vody" [Belletristic waters]. Russkaia mysl', no. 8:25-28.
    Notes that Gorky is writing a great deal and in a much cleaner style than before. Is bewildered by the sense that all this work leads to a "big Nothing." His characters do not live

and are not memorable. Criticizes Gorky for not using his European exile to grow spiritually.

2   NAZAREVSKII, BORIS [Ben]. "Maksim Gor'kii." In <u>Sumerki russkoi literatury</u> [The twilight of Russian literature]. Moscow: Levenson, pp. 5-27.
    Quotes Filosofov (1907.2) that the "end of Gorky" is at hand. Argues that Gorky will still remain as an important writer in the history of Russian letters.

1913

1   "Gorky, the Bitter." <u>Lippincott's</u> (New York) 91 (January): 97-103.
    Introduction to "Comrades" ["Tovarishchi"], translated by J. Cournos. Notes that Gorky is an artist of "the unpleasant, the terrible, even the horrible." Questions the meaning of these qualities in his writing.

2   PERSKY, S.M. "Maxim Gorky." In <u>Contemporary Russian Novelists</u>. Translated by F. Eisemann. New York: Luce, pp. 142-98.
    Gorky is second only to Tolstoy in talent. He is popular because he has taken the familiar type of the tramp and has injected into it vigor, energy, restlessness.

1915

1   ANON. "Dva boga (<u>Detstvo</u> Maksima Gor'kogo)" [Two gods: Maksim Gorky's <u>Childhood</u>]. <u>Biulleten' literatury i zhizni</u>, no. 9 (January):582-86.
    Contrasts the two images of God, the grandmother's and the grandfather's, in <u>Childhood</u>.

2   BATOURENSKY, V. "Gorky, Dostoevsky, and Stendhal." <u>Twentieth Century Russia</u> (London) 1, no. 2 (December):136-45.
    Gorky belongs to a tradition of writers who seem to deny moral value but actually are interested in understanding the motives for action.

3   FOMIN, A.G. "Maksim Gor'kii (A.M. Peshkov)." In <u>Russkaia literatura XX veka</u>. Moscow: Mir, pp. 170-79.
    See 1915.6. Bibliography of works by and about Gorky.

4   L'VOV-ROGACHEVSKII, V.L. "Maksim Gor'kii." In <u>Russkaia literatura XX veka</u>. Moscow: Mir, pp. 201-34.
    See 1915.6. Gorky's work embraces all Russian society. It is the "eternal rebellion of a restless, mutinous soul" which has experienced and rejected all the major beliefs of the age:

Tolstoyanism, Nietzscheanism, Bolshevism, God-building, and his own brand of populism.

5   VENGEROV, S.A. "M. Gor'kii." In Russkaia literatura XX veka. Moscow: Mir, pp. 189-200.
    See 1915.6. Includes two autobiographical sketches from 1897 and 1899 and a description of Gorky's later literary reception both at home and abroad.

6   VENGEROV, S.A., ed. Russkaia literatura XX veka. [Russian literature of the twentieth century]. Moscow: Mir, pp. 170-79, 189-200, 201-34.
    Includes the following works on Gorky:
    1. S.A. Vengerov, "M. Gor'kii." See 1915.5.
    2. V.L. L'vov-Rogachevskii, "Maksim Gor'kii." See 1915.4.
    3. A.G. Fomin, "Maksim Gor'kii (A.M. Peshkov)." See 1915.3.
    Reprinted: 1972.16.

1916

1   ANDREEV, LEONID. "O 'Dvukh dushakh' M. Gor'kogo" [On M. Gorky's "Two Souls"]. Sovremennyi mir, no. 1 (January): 108-12.
    Criticizes Gorky's article "Two Souls" in Letopis' in which Russians' vices are blamed on their Asiatic heritage.

2   CHIRIKOV, E.N. "Nerazbirikha" [Confusion]. Sovremennyi mir, no. 1 (January):113-32.
    Deals with Gorky and the journal, Letopis'. Attacks Gorky's theory of the Russian soul as a combination of negative Eastern and positive Western elements.

2A KOROLITSKII, M. "Tvorchestvo Gor'kogo poslednikh let" [Gorky's recent work]. Vestnik evropy 51, no. 5:401-10.
    Discusses Gorky's work of the last five years: the Okurov cycle, Around Russia [Po Rusi], The Zykovs [Zykovy], Childhood [Detstvo]. Disagrees with D. Filosofov (1907.2) that Gorky has lost his literary talent. Finds Gorky's style clearer, harder, less melodramatic than in pre-1905 works.

3   MEREZHKOVSKII, D.S. "Ne sviataia Rus'" [Unholy Russia]. Russkoe slovo, no. 210 (11 September):2.
    Tolstoy is the last great "landmark" [vekha] of Russian thought, although Gorky would like to be seen as a landmark pointing to the future. Whereas great writers of the past represented "consciousness coming to the people," Gorky represents the "popular element [stikhiia] coming into consciousness" and "coming to power." Gorky the prophet of the "superhuman tramp" is dead, but a greater, stronger Gorky has come into being: he "is negating himself, overcoming [himself]" by sacrificing his

"personal" truth to the "truth of the many." Gorky's new consciousness is religious in essence. Discusses Childhood [Detstvo] and the grandmother's concept of God.

4   STRUNSKY, ROSE. "Gorky and the New Russia." Forum 55, no. 4 (April):441-53.
    A defense of Gorky's ideological use of literature: he saved Russia from its growing self-contempt.

5   _____. Introduction to The Confession. New York: Frederick A. Stokes, pp. v-xxii.
    Argues with the opinion that Gorky is only an ideological writer. Finds themes and attitudes that run through all his works: the same belief in the powers of the Russian people.

1917

1   "Bolee, chem original'no" [More than original]. Byloe, no. 1 (July):84-85.
    Primary material on the decision in 1902 not to admit Gorky to the Imperial Academy of Sciences.

1918

1   MASHIROV, M. [A.M.]. "Gor'kii i politika" [Gorky and politics]. Griadushchee, no. 4 (June):16.
    Criticizes Gorky's speech at a meeting of Culture and Freedom for putting culture above politics.

1920

1   HAMILTON, CLAYTON M. "Understanding the Russians: Maxim Gorki's Night Lodging." In Seen on the Stage. New York: Holt, pp. 138-43.
    Russians are different from Westerners: they "wallow" in misfortune. Night Lodging [The Lower Depths; Na dne] shows this side of the Russian character. Finds Luka the most interesting.

2   SAYLER, OLIVER M. "From Turgenieff to Gorky at the Art Theater." In The Russian Theater under the Revolution. Boston: Little, Brown, pp. 64-79.
    The Moscow Art Theater's production of The Lower Depths [Na dne] is the "peak of the modern realist stage" because of the close interaction of company, director, and dramatist.

3   SCHNITTKIND, HENRY T. Introduction to A Night's Lodging. Translated by E. Hopkins. Boston: Four Seas, pp. 5-8.
    Gorky's purpose is to show the "beauty that lurks within the heart of the submerged dregs of humanity." His plays are

"slices of life." Compared to Jerome K. Jerome's The Passing of the Third Floor Back and to Dickens.

1921

1   NIKOLAEVSKII, BORIS I. "'Pervoe prestuplenie' M. Gor'kogo" ["The first crime" of M. Gorky]. Byloe, no. 16:174-86.
    Uses police archives to reconstruct Gorky's political activity after his return to Nizhny Novgorod in 1889. Includes notes by Gorky.

2   RUSSELL, CHARLES EDWARD. Foreword to Mother. New York: D. Appleton, pp. v-xvi.
    Magnifies the Russian Revolution and its nameless heroes and heroines. Gorky is the "greatest delineator" of the Russian character and its extremes. Mother [Mat'] is his greatest book. He is the Russians' "prophet, exponent, interpreter, faultless painter."

1922

1   AMFITEATROV, ALEKSANDR. "Vozzvanie M. Gor'kogo" [Gorky's call]. In Gorestnye zamety: Ocherki krasnogo Petrograda [Sad comments: Sketches of red Petrograd]. Berlin: Grani, pp. 44-50.
    Attempts to defend Gorky from attacks of émigré intellectuals, for example, Merezhkovsky.

2   BUGAEV, BORIS [Andrei Belyi]. "K iubileiu Maksima Gor'kogo" [On Maksim Gorky's anniversary]. Novaia russkaia kniga (Berlin), no. 8:2-3.
    On the occasion of Gorky's thirtieth anniversary as a writer. Claims that Gorky is the great "symbol" of Russian life of the last thirty years: he is the "voice of the crisis of our age."

3   GOSSE, Sir E.W. "Unveiling of Tolstoi." In Books on the Table. New York: Scribner, pp. 75-82.
    Gorky's memoirs of Tolstoy "form the earliest work of pure literature which has appeared in Russian since the Lenin [sic] revolution." They are shocking and thrilling. Gosse compares Tolstoy to a "hippopotamus rolling about in a clouded pool."

4   LEWISOHN, LUDWIG. "Gorki and Arthur Hopkins." In Drama and the Stage. New York: Harcourt-Brace, pp. 72-77.
    Review of Night Lodging [The Lower Depths; Na dne]. Gorky's play is a new kind of tragedy: he throws out the conventions of character flaw, isolation, nobility of character.

1923

1. GIPPIUS, Z.N. [A. Krainii]. "Literaturnaia zapis': Polet v Evropu" [The Literary record: The flight to Europe]. Sovremennye zapiski (Paris) 18:123-38.

    A survey of Russian literature in exile; devotes pp. 134-36 to Gorky. Repeats her long-standing view that it is impossible to speak about Gorky the writer without taking into account Gorky the activist. Says Gorky's proselytizing has borne fruit in the Revolution. Has brought a catastrophe upon real Russian writers. Tries to explain why he is now living in Europe. Says he ruins, yet is in love with, "culture." Predicts that he will waver between Russia and Europe for the rest of his days and will produce nothing of value.

2. HARRIS, F. "Meetings with Maxim Gorki." In Contemporary Portraits. 4th ser. New York: Brentano's, pp. 174-89.

    Low opinion of Gorky's work. Compares him to O. Henry. Finds his autobiography a "good Dutch painting of poverty-stricken Russian home-life." Finds a "cruel strain" in the Russian psychology. Gorky says he hates cruelty, wants to understand it. Asks about the lack of curiosity about sex in Childhood. Gorky refuses to answer.

3. "Pis'ma V.V. Rozanova k M. Gor'komu" [V.V. Rozanov's letters to M. Gorky]. Beseda, no. 2:402-16.

    Six letters from Rozanov to Gorky.

1924

1. DEWEY, VERONICA, trans. Translator's note to Reminiscences of My Youth. London: Wm. Heinemann, pp. v-x.

    Although Gorky's work is flawed, he is a truly "Russian" writer: his works are "remarkable for their originality of thought, their vigor of description and honest analysis of character." Quotes Aleksandr Blok.

2. LENIN, V.I. Briefe an Maxim Gorki, 1908-1913. Vienna: Verlag für Literatur und Politik, 126 pp.

    Correspondence. Contains an introduction by L. Kamenev and thirty-four letters to Gorky written from 1908 to 1913.

3. LO GATTO, ETTORE. Massimo Gorkij. Rome: A.F. Formiggini, 58 pp.

    A popular introduction to Gorky the man and his early stories.

4. LUNACHARSKII, A.V. Kriticheskie etiudy [Critical essays]. Leningrad: Izd. knizh. sektora Gubono, pp. 108-21, 286-92, 293-320.

Contains the following:
1. "Literaturnyi raspad i kontsentratsiia intelligentsii" ["Literary Decline and the Concentration of the Intelligentsia"]. Revised from 1909.2.
2. "Varvary" ["Barbarians"]. See 1906.4.
3. "Dachniki" ["Summer Folk"]. See 1905.6.

This collection of articles from around 1905 is meant to document the development of a body of Marxist belles lettres and outline a Marxist method of literary criticism. Lunacharsky revokes his belief in "God-building" and claims that Gorky went too far with these ideas in Confession.

5   MILLER, NELLIE BURGET. The Living Drama: Historical Development and Modern Movements Visualized. New York: Century, pp. 215-18.

The Lower Depths [Na dne] is the "acme of naturalism." Here there is only a "fragile" plot. If there is a hero, it is Gorky himself.

6   SHKLOVSKII, VIKTOR. "Novyi Gor'kii" [The new Gorky]. Rossiia, no. 2:192-206.

Treats Gorky almost as an avant-garde writer. Discusses diary, reminiscences. Notes that Gorky writes better, more sharply than before. Likes Gorky's "plotless" works. Polemicizes against the continuation of the novel form.

7   WIENER, LEO. "Gorki as a Dramatist." In The Contemporary Drama of Russia. Boston: Little, Brown, pp. 125-31.

Focuses on The Lower Depths [Na dne]. Compares it to Hauptmann's The Weavers and Tolstoy's The Power of Darkness.

1925

1   BYKHOVSKII, N.IA. "Bulochnik Aleksei Maksimovich Peshkov i kazanskaia revoliutsionnaia molodezh' kontsa 80-kh godov" [The baker Aleksei Maksimovich Peshkov and the revolutionary youth of Kazan at the end of the 1880s]. Byloe, no. 32:202-21.

Biographical material on Gorky's education and political activity in Kazan in the late 1880s. Includes remarks and corrections by Gorky.

2   SVOBODOV, A.N. "M. Gor'kii kak literaturnyi kritik" [M. Gorky as a literary critic]. Krasnaia nov', no. 1 (January):302-10.

Claims that Gorky has attracted no attention in biographical literature as a literary critic. Finds his critical work important as a vehicle for creating expectations in the "new reader who has emerged from the working classes." Focuses especially on Gorky's view of Chekhov, Balmont, and Briusov.

1926

1. BELOZEROV, A.A. "Iz molodykh let Maksima Gor'kogo" [From Maksim Gorky's early years]. Novyi mir, no. 3 (March):115-27; no. 4 (April):123-36.
   Memoirs.

2. CHUZHAK, N. "Novyi roman M. Gor'kogo" [M. Gorky's new novel]. Zhizn' i iskusstvo, no. 34:8-9.
   Criticizes The Artamonov Business [Delo Artamonovykh].

3. MIRSKY, PRINCE DMITRY S. "Gorky." In Contemporary Russian Literature, 1881-1925. London: George Routledge; New York: Alfred A. Knopf, pp. 6-20, 106-20, 342-44.
   Gorky is the only Russian writer beside Tolstoy with a "really worldwide reputation," not one confined to the intellectual elite of various countries. Gives biographical background. Compares him to H.G. Wells. Finds Gorky a truly great short-story writer. Discusses the "Znanie" school and Gorky's influence. Gives bibliography of primary works. Claims that Gorky during 1918-21 was the "only independent public force outside the government in the whole of Soviet Russia." Politically, however, he has little power.

4. SHKLOVSKII, VIKTOR. Udachi i porazheniia Maksima Gor'kogo [Successes and failures of Maksim Gorky]. Tbilisi: Zakavkazskaia kniga, 66 pp.
   Analyzes Gorky's work in the context of the contemporary crisis in artistic prose--the disintegration of plot, the sharp divisions in form: formless "writer's notes," on the one hand, and simple Western-style adventure novels of the type of Jack London and Marietta Shaginian, on the other. Finds Gorky's Petrograd period his richest and his short prose his best work. His memoirs of Tolstoy are the best because they are made of "fragments."
   Finds Gorky a "preserver" of old culture: he has the attitude of a "consumer" rather than a "producer." "He loves things more than making, producing them." Gorky wants to write poetry and a "real novel." He left Russia to write "long things." Shklovsky sees The Artamonov Business [Delo Artamonovykh] as a rewarmed The Three of Them [Troe]. "The habits of raznochinets belles lettres . . . spoiled Gorky."

5. VORONSKII, A. "O Gor'kom" [On Gorky]. Pravda, no. 79 (7 April):2-3; no. 80 (8 April):3.
   Review of Gorky's collected works, vols. 16-19. Likes Gorky's autobiography and reminiscence of L.N. Tolstoy. The flesh-and-blood human being comes through. Gorky is important as an antidote to contemporary Soviet writers who "agitate, . . . observe, . . . give shreds of life" but don't write about people. Younger writers might learn something from him. He remains "our best writer."

1927

1. LUNACHARSKII, A.V. "Gor'kii na Capri" [Gorky on Capri]. Ogonek, no. 44 (30 October).
   Reprinted: 1964.20. Memoir. Praises Confession [Ispoved'] and Summer [Leto].

2. MAIAKOVSKII, VLADIMIR. "Pis'mo pisateliu A.M. Gor'komu" [A letter to the writer, A.M. Gorky]. Novyi lef, no. 1 (January):2-6.
   A poem by one literary figurehead of the Revolution to his older counterpart. Tries to displace and discredit Gorky by noting that he has gotten too comfortable in exile and is missing the "construction of our days." His day, according to Maiakovsky, is past. Calls himself and the coeditors of LEF the real builders of the future.

3. PERTSOV, V.V. "Kakaia byla pogoda v epokhu grazhdanskoi voiny?" [How was the weather during the civil war?]. Novyi lef, no. 7:36-45.
   Discusses My Universities. Sees Gorky as one of the best prose writers of the day. Likes Gorky's nonbelletristic, "chronicle" style.

4. PLEKHANOV, G.V. "K psikhologii rabochego dvizheniia: Maksim Gor'kii, Vragi" [On the psychology of the workers movement: Maksim Gorky, Enemies]. In Sochineniia [Works]. Vol. 24. Moscow: Gosizdat, pp. 257-76.
   See 1907.6. Review. Discusses Enemies [Vragi]. Affirms that "strong personalities" with a will to independence can arise among the proletariat. Gorky reflects proletarian consciousness in his play.

5. SVOBODOV, A.N. "Iz rannikh zametok M. Gor'kogo-publitsista" [From the early notes of M. Gorky the publicist]. Pechat' i revoliutsiia, no. 1:19-28.
   Analyzes Gorky's publicistic work in the Nizhny Novgorod newspaper, Nizhegorodskii listok, 1896-1902. Gives background of the paper itself. Describes Gorky's social work with homeless children in Nizhny Novgorod.

6. _____. "M. Gor'kii i studencheskoe dvizhenie 1901 goda" [M. Gorky and the student movement of 1901]. Katorga i ssylka, no. 35:68-77.
   Describes Gorky's literary activity at student meetings in Nizhny Novgorod in 1901. Mentions among others the story "About the Writer Who Put on Airs" ["O pisatele, kotoryi zaznalsia"].

7. VESHNEV, V.G. "Gor'koe lakomstvo" [Bitter delicacy]. Na literaturnom postu, no. 20:41-55.
   An attack by Proletkult. Criticizes Gorky's work in the postrevolutionary period for its lack of moral objectivity and

its choice of theme. Challenges Gorky to deal with Soviet subject matter.

1928

1 APOSTOLOV, N.N. "L.N. Tolstoi i M. Gor'kii [L.N. Tolstoy and M. Gorky]. In Lev Tolstoi i ego sputniki [Lev Tolstoy and his fellow travelers]. Moscow: Komissiia po oznamenovaniiu stoletiia so dnia rozhdeniia L.N. Tolstogo, pp. 184-99.
  Deals with Gorky's personal acquaintance with Tolstoy and Tolstoy's remarks on Gorky's work. Sees in Gorky's memoirs an apotheosis of Tolstoy and a diminishing of himself.

2 ASHUKIN, N. "Pis'ma Maksima Gor'kogo k V. Briusovu" [Maksim Gorky's letters to V. Briusov]. Pechat' i revoliutsiia, no. 5:54-66.
  Correspondence. Contains eleven letters from Gorky to Briusov from 1900 to 1917.

3 BESPALOV, I. "Logika obrazov rannego Gor'kogo" [The logic of the early Gorky's imagery]. Pechat' i revoliutsiia, no. 4: 7-27.
  Analyzes the "realist-artistic" strand of Gorky's early work. Focuses on the interworking of allegory, legend, and polemic. Finds that Gorky's early "restless" heroes are not "fabricated," but "correspond in their essence . . . to actual reality."

4 _____. "O tvorcheskom svoeobrazii Gor'kogo" [On Gorky's creative uniqueness]. Revoliutsiia i kul'tura, no. 5:26-30.
  See 1928.16. Gorky is great for his depictions of the dregs of petit bourgeois life, his vision of its bifurcation into the Artamonovs, on the one hand, and the working class, on the other.

5 BONCH-BRUEVICH, VLADIMIR. "Moi vstrechi s Gor'kim" [My meetings with Gorky]. Novyi mir, no. 5:187-94.
  These memoirs concern Bonch-Bruevich's first contact with Gorky in 1905 and his plans to publish and sell Gorky's collected works as a way to raise funds for the Bolsheviks.

6 CHUZHAK, N. "Opyt ucheby na klassikov" [An experiment in learning from the classics]. Novyi lef, no. 7:9-19.
  Writes in a mood of recalcitrance toward all "teachers." Gorky is typical example of a Russian classic that cannot teach real "revolutionary" writers anything new. Gorky is a "typical realist-comprehender" [realist-osoznavatel']. He is neither a builder nor an organizer, but a bookkeeper, a pedagogue." He is a conserver of the "gentry" novel, which was written slowly and painstakingly and which dealt with events that were sufficiently

far back in the past. Discusses The Artamonov Business [Delo Artamonovykh] and The Life of Klim Samgin [Zhizn' Klima Samgina].

7   DOROVATOVSKII, N.S. "Pis'ma Maksima Gor'kogo k S.P. Dorovatovskomu" [Maksim Gorky's letters to S.P. Dorovatovsky]. Pechat' i revoliutsiia, no. 2:68-88.
    Correspondence. Contains thirty letters from Gorky, written from 1897 to 1899. Introduction tells about Gorky's relations with the first publisher of his collected stories, S.P. Dorovatovsky. Gives a detailed account of the campaign to market the collection: broad advertising, requests for reviews, contracts for longer studies.

8   FRICHE, V.M. "Gor'kii kak obshchestvennik" [Gorky as a social activist]. Revoliutsiia i kul'tura, no. 5:6-10.
    See 1928.16. Gorky brought from his childhood and adolescence his rage against social injustice and oppression. Unable to move the "bourgeois" intelligentsia (that is, Teleshov, Briusov, Petersburg intellectuals), he grew ever closer to the Social Democrats and Lenin. Explains Lenin's victory in the Capri incident in terms of his superior political tactics. Openly discusses Gorky's disagreements with Lenin and the Social Democratic party, but claims that they are secondary to Gorky's attachment to the "Soviet country."

9   GORBOV, D. "Obshchestvennyi smysl tvorchestva Gor'kogo" [The social meaning of Gorky's art]. Revoliutsiia i kul'tura, no. 5:19-25.
    See 1928.16. Claims that Gorky is valuable for the proletarian reader; invokes Lenin's statement that Gorky is an "enormous plus . . . in the business of proletarian art." Gorky criticized and destroyed petit bourgeois "Okurovian Russia."

10 GRUZDEV, I., ed. Sbornik statei i vospominanii o M. Gor'kom [Collection of articles and memoirs about Gorky]. Moscow and Leningrad: Gosizdat, 480 pp.
    Memoirs and reminiscences of Gorky by V. Desnitskii, N. Semashko, S.Ia. Elpatevskii, S. Protopopov, I.A. Belousov, Aleksei Tolstoi, Vl. Nemirovich-Danchenko, K.S. Stanislavskii, V.V. Luzhskii, S. Marshak, Mikhail Prishvin, Ivan Novikov, A. Pinkevich, L. Frenkel, Viach. Shishkov, A. Demidov, R. Arskii, Efim Zozulia, Maks Bartel, Vs. Ivanov, K. Chukovskii, N. Nikitin, V. Shklovskii, D. Lutokhin, S. Sergeev-Tsenskii, P. Kerzhentsev, Vl. Lidin, P. Kogan, Olga Forsh, N. Aseev.

11 KAUN, ALEXANDER. "Maxim Gorky, 1898-1928." Dial 84, no. 5 (June):464-68.
    A tribute to Gorky's sixtieth birthday and an assessment of his work and his place in Russian culture.

12 KOGAN, PETR S. Gor'kii. Moscow and Leningrad: Gosizdat, 82 pp.

Secondary Bibliography 1928

Although Gorky on the surface of things is not a <u>Pravda</u> writer, says that nevertheless he is and analyzes why. Judging by his social background, his literary characters, his major themes, he is not a <u>Pravda</u>, but he made himself into one, and he appealed to <u>Pravda</u> readers.

13 KUSKOVA, E. "Mesiats soglashatel'stva" [A month of opportunism]. <u>Volia Rossii</u> (Prague), no. 3:150-679; no. 4:42-61; no. 5:58-78.

Discussion of the relationship of the intelligentsia to the Revolution. Describes the Committee for Aid to the Hungry and Gorky's part in it.

14 _____. "Obeskrylennyi sokol" [The falcon with clipped wings]. <u>Sovremennye zapiski</u>, no. 36:305-45.

Memoirs and literary criticism. Remembers with sadness Gorky's shift in 1918 from rage at the atrocities committed by the Bolsheviks to reconciliation. Discusses Gorky's "message" in the early works, his role in the Revolution.

15 LUNACHARSKII, A. "O khudozhestvennom tvorchestve i o Gor'kom" [On the artistic creation and on Gorky]. <u>Revoliutsiia i kul'tura</u>, no. 5:11-18.

See 1928.16. Distinguishes between the writer-poet and the writer as publicist and political activist. Argues that Belinsky's and Plekhanov's definition of literature as use of figurative language ("language of images") does not fully apply to the publicist type who writes in a "language of concepts" and who, Lunacharsky implies, oversimplifies the complexities of the actual world. Says the greatest writers cannot give themselves to one political platform and become simple propagandists. The great political leaders, Marx and Lenin, recognized and accepted this truth.

Gorky's greatness lies in the fact that he sensed the directions in which the Okurov petite bourgeoisie would develop: on one hand, into the "grande bourgeoisie," on the other, into the "proletariat."

Says that contemporary arguments about Gorky's nonproletarian family heritage miss the point: he, like Marx and others, came from the middling layers of society, but saw how society would evolve and understood the role the working class would play. Argues for acknowledging Gorky. Says the role of the Party is "to use Gorky's enormous gifts," to perfect his artistic work, "to subject it to additional criticism, to reworking for publicistic purposes." Invokes Lenin.

16 <u>Revoliutsiia i kul'tura</u>, no. 5.

Commemorates the thirty-fifth anniversary of Gorky's debut as a writer. Editors speak of Gorky as the defender of the Soviet Union and the proletariat against fascism. Contains the following articles:

1. V. Friche, "Gor'kii kak obshchestvennik" [Gorky as a social activist]. See 1928.8.
2. A. Lunacharskii, "O khudozhestvennom tvorchestve i o Gor'kom" [On the artistic creation and on Gorky]. See 1928.15.
3. D. Gorbov, "Obshchestvennyi smysl tvorchestva Gor'kogo" [The social meaning of Gorky's creative work]. See 1928.9.
4. I. Bespalov, "O tvorcheskom svoeobrazii Gor'kogo" [On Gorky's creative uniqueness]. See 1928.4.

17 RUDNEV, V.V. "Gor'kii revoliutsioner" [Gorky the revolutionary]. Novyi mir, no. 3 (March):190-218; no. 4 (April):165-86.
New materials on Gorky's literary-political activity.

1929

1 BESPALOV, I. "Gor'kii." In Literaturnaia entsiklopediia. Vol. 2. Moscow: Izd. Kommunisticheskoi Akademii, pp. 643-55.
Detailed, balanced biographical sketch. Early life taken from Gorky's autobiography. No information of the Novaia zhizn' (New Life) episode. Includes a good select bibliography.

1A EIKHENBAUM, BORIS. "Pisatel'skii oblik M. Gor'kogo" [M. Gorky's profile as a writer]. In Moi vremennik [My periodical]. Leningrad: Izd. pisatelei, pp. 115-20.
Finds the appearance of Gorky in the early 1890s an extremely important "literary fact" characteristic of the broadening of the literary profession in that period. The fact that the aesthetic quality of Gorky's work received less attention than his literary-social personality shows the "demand" of the mass reader for sensation, scandal, and literary "stars." He came to represent the lower layer of the artistic intelligentsia. Through the Revolution Gorky and his type became the "replacement of the Russian intelligentsia." Contrasts Gorky with Blok as representative of "high culture" and old intelligentsia.

2 KUNITZ, JOSHUA. Russian Literature and the Jew: A Sociological Inquiry into the Nature and Origin of Literary Patterns. New York: Columbia University Press, pp. 131-38.
Deals with Gorky's moral view. Finds that he sentimentalizes and idealizes Jewish characters out of a sense of guilt. Concentrates on "The Little Boy" and "Kain and Artem."

3 POSSE, VLADIMIR. Moi zhiznennyi put': Dorevoliutsionnyi period (1864-1917gg). [The course of my life: The prerevolutionary period (1864-1917)]. Moscow and Leningrad: Zemlia i fabrika.
These memoirs contain a great deal of information about Gorky's literary debut, political relationships, and early years.

4 VORONSKII, ALEKSANDER. "O Gor'kom" [About Gorky]. Literaturnye portrety v 2-kh tomakh [Literary portraits in two volumes]. Vol. 2. Moscow: Federatsiia, pp. 7-32.

A consideration of Gorky's work in the early 1920s from a Soviet point of view. It seems that Gorky is "drawing conclusions," is trying to record and define what from his point of view is "valuable, interesting and curious in Russian life and art." Discusses memoirs of Tolstoy, My Universities. Reprinted: 1982.25.

1930

1 GRUZDEV, IL'IA. Sovremennyi zapad o Gor'kom [The contemporary West on Gorky]. Leningrad: Priboi, 224 pp.
   Contains excerpts from Western reviews and articles on Gorky, writers' messages to him on his sixtieth birthday, reminiscences about him. Largely from German writers and the German press.

2 KAUN, ALEXANDER. "Maxim Gorky and the Bolsheviks." Slavonic Review 9, no. 26 (December):432-48.
   Deals with Gorky's political activities between 1906 and 1917.

3 _____. "Maxim Gorky and the Tsarist Police." Slavonic Review 8, no. 24 (March):636-61.
   Biographical material. Uses some tsarist police reports to help reconstruct Gorky's political development.

4 _____. "Maxim Gorky in the Revolution of 1905." Slavonic Review 9, no. 25 (June):133-48.
   On Gorky's political activism, his role in Bloody Sunday.

5 LEE, ROSE. "Maxim Gorky Emerges: The Russian Novelist Becomes a Member of the Soviet Inner Government." World Today (London) 56 (June):32-38.
   Reprinted from World's Work (New York) 58 (November 1928):86-89. Sees Gorky's election to the Central Executive Committee as a "gesture." Discusses Gorky's political views.

1931

1 CHANDLER, FRANK W. "Exponents of Russian Realism: Tolstoi and Gorky." In Modern Continental Playwrights. New York: Harper, pp. 64-78.
   Out of fourteen plays Gorky has written, only one is on the level of his work in fiction: The Lower Depths [Na dne]. This play is the "last word in dramatic naturalism." Finds The Children of the Sun [Deti solntsa] and The Smug Citizen [Petit Bourgeois; Meshchane] "less crude" and "more conventional" than the "chaotic yet striking" Lower Depths. Compares The Lower Depths with Jerome K. Jerome's Passing of the Third Floor Back.

2   KAUN, ALEXANDER. <u>Maxim Gorky and His Russia</u>. New York: Jonathan Cape and Harrison Smith, 620 pp.
    Biography. The most complete account of Gorky's life up to 1929, based partly on personal interviews. Includes a long appendix on Gorky's visit to the United States and a letter from Leon Trotsky on the <u>Novaia zhizn'</u> (<u>New Life</u>) affair in 1917 and 1918.

3   LUNACHARSKII, ANATOLII V. "V zerkale Gor'kogo" [In Gorky's mirror]. <u>Na literaturnom postu</u>, no. 12:6-12; no. 20-21:19-24.
    Sees Gorky's portrait writing as a "magic mirror" which makes its subject eternal. Reprinted: 1938.9.

1932

1   HOGARTH, C.J. Introduction to <u>Through Russia</u>. London: J.M. Dent; New York: E.P. Dutton, pp. vii-ix.
    Reprinted from 1921 edition (London: J.M. Dent). Gorky is a "naturalist" rather than a "realist." Compares him to Dostoevsky: both use the "hideous" not just for its own sake but to make a point. Gorky's work helps us understand the Russians.

2   "Maxim Gorky." <u>Soviet Union Review</u> (Washington, D.C.) 10, no. 11 (November):205-7.
    Reports the fortieth anniversary of Gorky's writing career.

2A PIKSANOV, N.K. "Gor'kii i fol'klor" [Gorky and folklore]. <u>Sovetskaia etnografiia</u>, no. 5-6:28-55.
    Devoted to Gorky's appropriation of oral culture.

3   PORTNOFF, G. <u>La literatura rusa en España</u>. New York: Instituto de las Españas en los Estados Unidos, pp. 80-86.
    Treats Gorky's reception in Spain. Contains a small annotated bibliography of works in Spanish on Gorky from 1901 to 1925.

4   RAIGUEL, G.E., and HUFF, N.K. <u>This Is Russia</u>. Philadelphia: Pennsylvania Publishing Co., pp. 416-19.
    Gorky as popular writer. He is a much greater artist than most "folk novelists" turn out to be.

1933

1   LUNACHARSKII, ANATOLII V. <u>Samgin</u>. Moscow: Zhurnal'no-gazetnoe ob"edinenie, 64 pp.
    Sees <u>The Life of Klim Samgin</u> [Zhizn' Klima Samgina] as a brilliant bildungsroman. Lunacharsky gives a sociohistorical account of capitalism in Russia from his own point of view.

2   OLGIN, M.J. Maxim Gorky: Writer and Revolutionist. New
    York: International Publishers, 64 pp.
        Popular biography. Gorky brought new life to the Russian
    intelligentsia, gave a real, unsentimental picture of poor people.

3   PERTSOV, P.P. Literaturnye vospominaniia [Literary memoirs].
    Moscow and Leningrad: Akademiia, pp. 30-31, 44.
        A rare memoir of Gorky in the late 1880s and early 1890s
    before his "noisy success."

1934

1   BALUKHATYI, S. Kritika o M. Gor'kom: Bibliografiia statei i
    knig 1893-1932g. [Critical work on M. Gorky: Bibliography of
    articles and books, 1893-1932]. Leningrad: GIKhL, 592 pp.
        Bibliography of Russian works published in Russia, 1893-
    1932. Organized by year.

2   DESNITSKII, V.A., ed. M. Gor'kii: Materialy i issledovaniia
    [M. Gorky: Materials and research]. Vol. 1. Leningrad:
    ANSSSR, 552 pp.
        Contains six sections:
        1. Forgotten or unpublished works of Gorky:
            a. Story: "Fedor Diadin" (1910).
            b. Sketches: "Pogrom" (1901); "Kak ia v pervyi raz
               uslyshal o Garibal'di" [How I heard about Garibaldi
               for the first time] (1907).
            c. Political satire: "O serom" [About gray things]
               (1905); "Pis'mo v redaktsiiu" [Letter to the
               editor] (1906).
            d. Publicistic articles: "Po povodu moskovskikh
               sobytii" [On events in Moscow] (1906); "'V shir'
               poshlo'" ["It is spreading"] (1911); "Pis'mo
               monarkhistu" [Letter to a monarchist] (1911); "O
               russkoi intelligentsii i natsional'nykh voprosakh"
               [On the Russian intelligentsia and national ques-
               tions] (1912); "Khronika zagranichnoi zhizni"
               [Chronicle of life abroad] (1912).
        2. Literary articles, reviews.
        3. Correspondence with L. Andreev, V. Briusov,
    K. Bal'mont, F. Sologub, A. Amfiteatrov, A. Kaliuzhnyi,
    G. Hauptmann, G.B. Shaw; poems dedicated to Gorky by Z. Gippius,
    K. Bal'mont.
        4. Correspondence with critics.
        5. Letters of young writers to Gorky: I.E. Vol'nov, M.P.
    Gerasimov, M.V. Zhuravleva, P.I. Karpov, I.E. Lavrent'ev, V.N.
    Lazarev, S.V. Malyshev, A.R. Palei, I.I. Sadof'ev, I.I.
    Tachalov, K.A. Trenev.
            6. Articles on textual history (shortened titles):
                a. N.Ia. Morachevskii, "'Vesennie melodii'" [Spring
                   melodies].

b. S.D. Balukhatyi, "'Deti solntsa'" [Children of the sun].
   c. B.P. Gorodetskii, "Obraz 'krasnogo peska'" [The image of "red sand"].
   d. Vasilii Gippius, "'Mordovka.'"

3 EASTMAN, MAX. *Artists in Uniform: A Study of Literature* and *Bureaucratism*. New York: Alfred A. Knopf, pp. 95-96, 218-20.
   Discusses Gorky and RAPP, and Gorky's view of Lenin.

4 MANNING, C.A. "Maxim Gorky." *South Atlantic Quarterly* (Durham) 33 (July):219-28.
   Compares Gorky to Rodin's *The Thinker*: his "thought is muscular rather than mental." Finds in Gorky's work the interwoven "threads" of "excellent narration" and "boring prophecy." Singles out the early stories and the autobiography as his best work.

1935

1 STRUVE, GLEB. "Gorky." In *Soviet Russian Literature*. London: George Routledge, pp. 5-8.
   Gorky is now the "doyen" of Soviet Russian literature: postrevolutionary writers have lately been trying to come nearer to his "Realism relieved by revolutionary Romanticism." Notes a change from the experimental mood of the 1920s. Recommends *The Artamonov Business* [*Delo Artamonovykh*].

1936

1 BALUKHATYI, S.D. *Literaturnaia rabota M. Gor'kogo* [Gorky's literary work]. Moscow and Leningrad: Academia, 521 pp.
   A bibliography of first editions and authorized publications from 1892 to 1934. Organized by year.

2 BALUKHATYI, S.D., ed. *Opisanie rukopisei M. Gor'kogo: Khudozhestvennye proizvedeniia* [Description of M. Gorky's manuscripts: Fiction]. Moscow and Leningrad: ANSSSR, 263 pp.
   Gives a description of authorized texts of Gorky's fictional works found in Soviet archives. Includes his corrections, censors' marks, and comments. Works are organized alphabetically.

3 BALUKHATYI, S.D., and DESNITSKII, V.A., eds. *M. Gor'kii: Materialy i issledovaniia* [M. Gorky: Materials and research]. Vol. 2. Moscow and Leningrad: ANSSSR, 484 pp.
   Contains two sections:
   1. Forgotten or unpublished works:
      a. Stories: "Sirota [Orphan] (1899); "Dobycha" [Booty] (1900); untitled (1901); "Rasskazy o zhizni

na okrainakh goroda" [Stories about life on the edge of town] (1901); "Skazka" [Tale] (1912); "Nesoglasnyi" [Not agreed] (1917).
b. Articles: "On Chekhov's 'In the ravine'" (1900); "V prostranstvo" [Into the distance] (1912).
2. Correspondence with A.P. Chekhov, F.D. Batiushkov, L.L. Tolstoy, A.F. Koni, D.Ia. Aizman; letters to Gorky: P. Iakubovich, I.A. Bunin.

4   BORDON, MANYA. "Gorky: Ancestor of Young Russia." Saturday Review of Literature (New York) 14 (1 August):3-4, 13.
Gorky belongs to the nineteenth-century tradition of socially engaged literature.

5   ERMILOV, VLADIMIR. Mechta Gor'kogo: Osnovnye idei tvorchestva [Gorky's dream: The basic ideas of artistic creation]. Moscow: Sovetskii pisatel', 194 pp.
In praise of Stalin. Gorky's creative dream of the "rebirth of humanity" from the depths of the "horror of Russian life of yesterday" was realized in Stalin's constitution, the "grandest document of the rebirth of humanity."

6   KUSKOVA, E. "Na rubezhe dvukh epokh: Pamiati A.M. Gor'kogo" [On the border of two epochs: To the memory of Gorky]. Poslednie novosti (Paris), 26 June, p. 2.
A member of the old activist intelligentsia, now in emigration, mourns Gorky's death. Reminisces about student political life in Nizhny Novgorod and about the events of 1905. Remarks that Gorky's political ideas were always incomprehensible. Calls him an "anarchist to the marrow of his bones." Quotes a letter from Gorky to the author, dated 22 January 1929, about his "rudeness" toward emigrants and about his moral views. Gives a dreamlike view of contemporary Soviet life.

7   LEGRAS, JULES. "Maxime Gorki." Le monde slave 13, no. 3 (September):396-406.
Considers in detail Gorky's meshchanstvo (lower-middle-class) background and sees it as the source of his "outlaw" social mentality. Reviews his literary output and finds his early stories and his autobiography best.

8   YOUZOVSKY, JOZEF. "Gorky and Bulychov." Theatre Arts Monthly (New York) 20 (September):718-25.
Gorky uses unconventional dramatic techniques. Does not build suspense; uses little action. Rather, is interested in portraying people through a series of "scenes." Egor Bulychev is built around that "property . . . deforms, corrupts, destroys humanity."

9   ZAMIATIN, EVGENY. "Maxime Gorki." La Revue de France (Paris) 16, no. 15 (August):509-26.

Reminiscence. Notes two beings in one person: Gorky and Peshkov. Peshkov the person is dead; Gorky the legend lives. Sees Gorky as an "American-Russian, self-made man" [in English]. Describes Gorky during the civil war and in the late 1920s and early 1930s when Gorky got Zamiatin an exit visa. Reprinted: 1967.19; 1970.22.

1937

1   IL'INSKII, ALEKSANDR. "Gor'kii i Briusov" [Gorky and Briusov]. In Literaturnoe nasledstvo. Vols. 27-28. Moscow: Zhurnal'no-gazetnoe ob"edinenie, pp. 639-60.

    Surveys Gorky's and Briusov's acquaintanceship from 1901 to 1921 when Gorky went abroad. Concentrates on years during World War I, the Revolution, and the civil war. Contrasts the two: Gorky as a writer with "life experience" envied by Briusov, and Briusov as the highly cultured poet and critic.

2   KAUN, ALEXANDER. "Obituary: Maxim Gorky, 1868-1936." Slavonic Review 15, no. 44 (January):440-42.

    Attempts an impartial appraisal of Gorky. Sees Gorky as a "courageous and effective dissenter" who helped to preserve cultural figures under the Soviet regime.

3   KHODASEVICH, V. "Gor'kii (vospominaniia)" [Gorky (memoirs)]. Sovremennye zapiski (Paris) 63:264-92.

    First part of Khodasevich's memoir. See 1939.5.

4   LAVRETSKY, A. "Gorky on Socialist Realism." International Literature, no. 4 (April):87-95.

    Gorky as one of the first theoreticians of socialist realism.

5   Literaturnyi kritik, no. 6.

    Devoted entirely to the first anniversary of Gorky's death:
    1. Iu. Iuzovskii, "Geroi i temy Maksima Gor'kogo" [Heroes and themes of Maksim Gorky].
    2. V. Aleksandrov, "Obraz materi" [Image of the mother].
    3. Andrei Platonov, "Pushkin i Gor'kii [Pushkin and Gorky]. See 1937.7.
    4. M. Gor'kii, "O romantizme, 'narodnosti,' Zhukovskom" [On romanticism, populism, Zhukovsky], an unpublished article.
    5. I. Vertsman, "M. Gor'kii o lozhnom realizme" [Maksim Gorky on false realism].
    6. A. Lavretskii, "Istoriko-literaturnye vzgliady Gor'kogo" [Historical-literary views of Gorky].
    7. I. Sergievskii, "Gor'kii v bor'be s dekadentskoi literaturoi" [Gorky in the struggle with decadent literature].
    8. M. Gor'kii, "Pol' Verlen i dekadenty" [Paul Verlaine and the decadents].

9. B. Emel'ianov, "P'esa Deti solntsa i ee kritiki" [The play Children of the Sun and its critics].
10. P. Maksimov, "O pometkakh Gor'kogo na rukopisiakh pisatelei" [Gorky's notes on writers' manuscripts].

6 LONDON, KURT. The Seven Soviet Arts. London: Faber & Faber, pp. 134-36.
Gorky is overestimated in the Soviet Union. His significance is in the area of ideology and cultural work rather than artistic creativity.

7 PLATONOV, ANDREI. "Pushkin i Gor'kii" [Pushkin and Gorky]. Literaturnyi kritik, no. 6:63-84.
See 1937.5. Sees Gorky as the beginning of the third great period of modern Russian literature, the first being Pushkin, the second the generation "after Pushkin." The "people 'intervened' sharply and gave birth to Maksim Gorky" and saved Russian literature from "declining into decadence."

1938

1 BALIKA, D.A. "Gor'kii nad stranitsami filosofskikh knig" [Gorky on the pages of philosophical books]. Novyi mir, no. 8:253-61.
Treats philosophical views. Discusses Gorky's marginalia in philosophical books collected in the period 1893-1900. Books treated here include E. Karo, Pessimism in the 19th Century [Pessimizm v XIX veke; Moscow, 1893]; Vl. Stein, Count Giacomo Leopardi and his theory infélicita [Graf Dzhiakomo Leopardi i ego teoriia infélicita; St. Petersburg, 1891].

2 BALUKHATYI, S.D. "Gor'kii i kul'tura" [Gorky and culture]. Vestnik AN SSSR, nos. 2-3:20-27.
Gorky's idea of culture is founded on the "usefulness of knowledge" and its "connection with social action."

3 BALUKHATYI, S., and MURATOVA, K. M. Gor'kii: Spravochnik. [M. Gorky: A handbook]. Leningrad: Khud. lit., 271 pp.
Popular bibliographical source meant to keep alive in the mind of the general reader "the light of Gorky's genius," so prematurely and unexpectedly snuffed out "by a band of murderers from the anti-Soviet right-Trotskyist block." Provides biographical material, fragments from correspondence, reminiscences, a survey of his literary works.

3A BEREZARK, I. "Gor'kii i khudozhestvennyi teatr" [Gorky and the Art Theater]. Literaturnyi sovremennik, no. 6:186-94.
See 1938.6A. Notes the similarities in Gorky's and Stanislavsky's visions of a national theater. Outlines the history of Gorky's work with the Moscow Art Theater.

3B   BIALIK, B. "Chelovek s bol'shoi bukvy" [Man with a capital M]. Literaturnyi sovremennik, no. 6:178-86.
      See 1938.6A. Discusses Foma Gordeev and Gorky's attempt to combine in his heroes the typical with the extraordinary. His approach to his heroes includes both realist and romantic elements.

4   BROWN, BENJAMIN W. Theatre at the Left. Providence, R.I.: Book Shop, pp. 72-73.
      Compares Gorky to Shaw. Discusses Egor Bulychev.

5   CLARK, BARRETT H. "Maxim Gorky." A Study of the Modern Drama. New York and London: Appleton-Century, pp. 51-56.
      Gorky's plays are interesting as the "by-products of a genius who must try all forms." He is not a fine stylist or technician. The Lower Depths [Na dne] is a series of pictures from life. Shows how the play departs from conventional drama.

5A   DAN'KO, E. "O dushevnoi shchedrosti" [About heartfelt generosity]. Literaturnyi sovremennik, no. 6:194-98.
      See 1938.6A. A factory worker reminisces about a meeting with Gorky in 1919.

5B   GRUZDEV, IL'IA. "Gor'kii v teatre (iz biograficheskikh materialov)" [Gorky in the theater (biographical materials)]. Literaturnyi sovremennik, no. 6:173-78.
      See 1938.6A. Includes a fragment written in 1915 which Gorky had at first wanted to put in the second volume of his autobiography, Apprenticeship [V liudiakh].

6   KOL'TSOV, MIKHAIL. Burevestnik: Zhizn' i smert' Maksima Gor'kogo [The stormy petrel: The life and death of Maksim Gorky]. Moscow: OGIZ, 96 pp.
      Gorky died too early, fighting the good fight. He was killed by "enemies of the people," fascists who want to establish capitalism in the Soviet Union. Trotskyite rightists murdered him because he was in their way.

6A   Literaturnyi sovremennik, no. 6.
      Memoirs of Gorky, includes:
      1. Iurii Tynianov, "Aleksei Maksimovich Gor'kii." See 1938.11A.
      2. Il'ia Gruzdev, "Gor'kii v teatre" [Gorky in the theater]. See 1938.5B.
      3. B. Bialik, "Chelovek s bol'shoi bukvy" [Man with a capital M]. See 1938.3B.
      4. I. Berezark, "Gor'kii i khudozhestvennyi teatr" [Gorky and the Art Theater]. See 1938.3A.
      5. E. Dan'ko, "O dushevnoi shchedrosti" [About heartfelt generosity]. See 1938.5A.

7 LUNACHARSKII, A.V. "Gor'kii na Kapri" [Gorky on Capri]. Stat'i o Gor'kom. Moscow: GIKhL, pp. 45-51.
See 1938.9. Reprinted from Ogonek, no. 44, 1927. Discusses the workers' school on Capri.

8 _____. "Pisatel' i politik" [The writer and the politician]. Stat'i o Gor'kom. Moscow: GIKhL, pp. 74-79.
See 1938.9. Reprinted from Izvestiia TsIK, no. 89 (31 March 1931). Discusses the political nature of all art, including seemingly apolitical art.

9 _____. Stat'i o Gor'kom [Articles on Gorky]. Moscow: GIKhL, 207 pp.
This collection includes mostly Lunacharsky's last articles on Gorky from 1927 to 1933. Contains the following reviews and articles:
    1. "Dachniki" [Summer folk] (1905). See 1905.6.
    2. "Varvary" [Barbarians] (1906). See 1906.4.
    3. "Gor'kii na Kapri" [Gorky on Capri] (1927).
    4. "M. Gor'kii" [M. Gorky] (1928).
    5. "Maksim Gor'kii [Maksim Gorky] (1928).
    6. "Pisatel' i politik" [The writer and the politician] (1928). See 1938.9.
    7. "V zerkale Gor'kogo" [In Gorky's mirror] (1931). See 1931.3.
    8. "Na zashchite sotsialisticheskoi stroiki" [In defense of the building of socialism] (1931).
    9. "Mirovoi pisatel'" [World-class writer] (1931).
    10. "M. Gor'kii-khudozhnik" [Gorky the artist] (1931).
    11. "Samgin" [Samgin] (1932). See 1933.1.
    12. "Maksim Gor'kii (predislovie k sochineniiam)" [Maksim Gorky (foreword to the works)] (1933).

10 MALAMUD, IRENE TITUS. "Psychological Approach to the Study of Social Crises." American Journal of Sociology (Chicago) 43, no. 4 (January):578-92.
Analyzes Gorky and Andreev as representatives of two sociopsychological types. Looks at their ways of coping with broad social crises.

10A PIKSANOV, N. Gor'kii i fol'klor [Gorky and folklore]. 2d ed. Leningrad: GIKhL, 192 pp.
Analyzes Gorky's links to oral culture and its use in literary works. Defines Gorky's narodnost' (national cultural identity).

11 SEMENOVSKII, D.M. A.M. Gor'kii: Pis'ma i vstrechi [A.M. Gorky: Letters and meetings]. Moscow: Sovetskii pisatel', 109 pp.
Memoirs. Shows Gorky as mentor of young "democratic" writers. Warns against modernism. Starts around 1912-13.

11A TYNIANOV, IURII. "Aleksei Maksimovich Gor'kii." Literaturnyi sovremennik, no. 6:171-73.
See 1938.6A. Writes about Gorky and his readers. Compares him to Pushkin and Tolstoy.

1939

1   BIALIK, BORIS. Esteticheskie vzgliady Gor'kogo [Gorky's aesthetic views]. Leningrad: Khud. lit., 230 pp.
The classical Soviet work on the development of Gorky's aesthetic views. Starts with his "battle" with decadence and arrives at his aesthetic of combining realism and romanticism. Conclusion is devoted to socialist realism. Compares Gorky with Dante--each opened a new era in human history.

2   GOR'KII, M. Istoriia russkoi literatury [History of Russian literature]. Edited by I.K. Luppol. Arkhiv A.M. Gor'kogo, vol. 1. Moscow: Khud. lit., 340 pp.
Notes for Gorky's lectures on Russian literature on Capri, 1908-9.

3   HUXLEY, ALDOUS. Foreword to A Book of Short Stories. Translated and edited by A. Yarmolinsky and Moura Budberg. New York: Cape, pp. vii-x.
Treats style and moral view. The effect and meaning of Gorky's work depends very much on verbal texture. His optimism-- the hope that there is an underlying "goodness" in people to be discovered--is implied, not stated.

4   KAUN, ALEXANDER S. "Maxim Gorky: In Search of a Synthesis." Slavonic Review (London) 17, no. 50 (January):429-44.
Analyzes Gorky's views of realism and romanticism.

5   KHODASEVICH, V. "Gor'kii." In Nekropol': Vospominaniia [Necropolis: Memoirs]. Brussels: Les éditions Petropolis, pp. 228-77.
See 1937.3; 1940.5. See 1976.16 for English translation. A candid, insightful view of Gorky's personality and moral view. Shows his ambiguous attitude toward truth.

1940

1   EL'SBERG, IA. "Trilogiia Gor'kogo i velikie avtobiografii proshlogo" [Gorky's trilogy and the great autobiographies of the past]. Krasnaia nov', no. 11-12:284-306.
Gorky's book fills the requirements of an "authentic" auto- biography. Its hero is from the people; he is a "new, progres- sive man of his own time." The author's convictions are in tune with "historical truth." Compares his work to Rousseau's, Goethe's, Herzen's.

2   GRINBERG, Z.G., and ZDOBNOV, N.V. Bibliografiia M. Gor'kogo: Proizvedeniia Gor'kogo i literatura o Gor'kom (1936-1937) [Bibliography of M. Gorky: Works by Gorky and critical literature on Gorky (1936-1937)]. Moscow and Leningrad: ANSSSR, 359 pp.

    Contains Soviet publications for the two years, 1936 and 1937. Organized by topic.

3   IUZOVSKII, IU. "Na dne" M. Gor'kogo: Materialy i issledovaniia [M. Gorky's The Lower Depths: Materials and research]. Moscow and Leningrad: Vserossiiskoe teatral'noe obshchestvo, 288 pp.

    This collection marks a renewal of interest in staging The Lower Depths. Five articles analyze important aspects of the play: Iu. Iuzovskii ("Idei i obrazy" [Ideas and images]) discusses Gorky's attempt to make a "general statement about [his] time." B. Neiman ("Iazyk p'esy" [The language of the play]) treats Gorky's use of speech and oral style as a major mode of characterization. S. Balukhatyi ("Kritika" [Criticism]) analyzes the play's reception. I. Berezark ("Stsenicheskaia istoriia" [Production history]) deals with the play's stage history in St. Petersburg, the provinces, and abroad, particularly in Germany. S. Balukhatyi ("Tsenzura" [The censors]) treats the reaction of the imperial censor to the play.

4   KASTORSKII, S.V. "Mat'" M. Gor'kogo: Tvorcheskaia istoriia povesti [Gorky's Mother: The creative history of the novel]. Leningrad: Khud. lit., 224 pp.

    Analyzes Gorky's work on Mother in the context of his publicistic activity around 1905. Discusses its reception among Russian workers, in various literary and political circles, and in the foreign press. Analyzes those aspects of style, structure, and imagery that make Mother the archetype of the socialist realist novel. Includes an analysis of the novel's sequel, Son [Syn].

5   KHODASEVICH, V.F. "Gor'kii." Sovremennye zapiski (Paris) 70:131-56.

    Second part of memoirs of Gorky. First part published in Sovremennye zapiski 63 (1937.3; see also 1939.5). Argues that Gorky left Russia in 1921 for reasons other than bad health. Discusses Gorky's and Andreeva's very poor relations with Kamenev and Zinovev. Recounts Gorky's failed efforts to save Sologub, Blok, Gumilev; the conditions surrounding the composition and publication of "V.I. Lenin"; and the political impact of E.P. Peshkova on Gorky's decision to make peace with Soviet power.

1941

1   BALUKHATYI, S.D. "'Pesnia o Sokole'" ["Song of the Falcon"]. In M. Gor'kii: Materialy i issledovaniia. Vol. 3. Moscow and Leningrad: ANSSSR, pp. 161-273.

See 1941.2. Analyzes the drafts of Gorky's "Song of the Falcon." Finds in this kind of analysis the basis for understanding Gorky's creative method. Treats ideological motifs and imaginative forms in this work. Focuses on Gorky's attitude to folklore and literary tradition. Discusses the political impact of the work.

2 BALUKHATYI, S.D., and DESNITSKII, V.A., eds. M. Gor'kii: Materialy i issledovaniia [M. Gorky: Materials and research]. Vol. 3. Moscow and Leningrad: ANSSSR, 464 pp.
Contains three sections:
1. Correspondence with V.S. Miroliubov (eighty-two letters, 1897-1928), S.A. Vengerov (twelve letters, 1907-16), D.N. Ovsianiko-Kulikovsky (twenty letters, 1911-13).
2. Articles:
    a. S.D. Balukhatyi, "'Pesnia o Sokole'" [Song of the falcon]. See 1941.1.
    b. V.Z. Golubev, "K voprosu o literaturnykh istochnikakh p'esy Deti solntsa" [On the question of the literary sources of the play Children of the Sun].
    c. S.V. Kastorskii, "Iz istorii sozdaniia povesti Mat'" [From the history of the creation of the novel Mother]. See 1941.7.
    d. V.A. Desnitskii. "Neosushchestvlennyi khudozhestvennyi zamysel M. Gor'kogo--roman o rossiiskom Zhan-Val'zhane, dobrodetel'nom katorzhnike" [An unrealized artistic plan of M. Gorky--a novel about the Russian Jean Valjean, the virtuous prisoner].
3. Materials and documents:
    a. Critical response in the American press of 1907 to Mother. See 1941.4.
    b. The tsarist censors on foreign editions of Gorky's work and foreign criticism on him. See 1941.9.

3 BALUKHATYI, S., and MURATOVA, K. Literaturnaia rabota M. Gor'kogo [The literary work of M. Gorky]. Moscow and Leningrad: ANSSSR, 195 pp.
Addition to primary bibliography of 1936.1. Brings it up to 1936. Organized by year.

4 BOBROVA, E.I., trans. "Kriticheskie otzyvy amerikanskoi pechati 1907g. o povesti Mat'" [Critical responses in the American press of 1907 to the novel Mother]. In M. Gor'kii: Materialy i issledovaniia. Moscow and Leningrad: ANSSSR, pp. 393-407.
See 1941.2. Gives ten American reviews of Mother, all of them basically positive. Notes impact of this novel on the American image of the Russian national character.

5   ERMILOV, VLADIMIR. O gumanizme Gor'kogo [On Gorky's humanism]. Moscow: GIKhL, 383 pp.
    Divided into three sections: "The Artist's Dream and Reality," "Gorky and Dostoevsky," "The Particularities of Gorky's Humanism." The first two deal with Gorky's response to Dostoevsky. The third deals with Gorky's own concept of the heroic and its realization in Stalinist Russia.

6   GOR'KII, M. P'esy i stsenarii [Plays and screenplays]. Edited by N.I. Belkina and V.N. Lanina. Arkhiv A.M. Gor'kogo, vol. 2. Moscow: Khud. lit., 343 pp.
    First publication of the following plays and sketches: Somov i drugie [Somov and others]; "Iakov Bogomolov," "Evgraf Bukeev," "Khristofor Bukeev," scenes for staging P. Sukhotin's My Apprenticeship [V liudiakh]; "Rabotiaga Slovotekov" [Workman Slovotekov], an opera libretto; "Propagandist" [The propagandist]; "Stepan Razin," "Zhizn' odnogo evreia" [Life of a Jew]; "Po puti na dno" [On the way to the bottom]; "Khod konia" [The knights' move]; "Prestupniki" [Criminals].

7   KASTORSKII, S.V. "Iz istorii sozdaniia povesti Mat'" [From the history of the creation of the novel Mother]. In M. Gor'kii: Materialy i issledovaniia. Moscow and Leningrad: ANSSSR, pp. 288-360.
    See 1941.2. Gorky's work on Mother is a model for Soviet writers to follow in their own work. Analyzes the six editions of the novel.

8   KUBLANOV, I. "M. Gor'kii i dekabr'skoe vosstanie" [Gorky and the December uprising]. Istorik marksist, no. 6:3-17.
    Discusses Gorky's part in the uprising of December 1905 in Moscow.

9   POLIANSKAIA, L.I., trans. "Materialy po tsarskoi tsenzure o zagranichnykh izdaniiakh sochinenii M. Gor'kogo i inostrannoi literature o nem" [Materials on the tsarist censorship of foreign editions of Gorky's works and of foreign criticism on him]. In M. Gor'kii: Materialy i issledovaniia. Moscow and Leningrad: ANSSSR, pp. 404-49.
    See 1941.2. Materials date from 1901-14. Discusses treatment of foreign Russian-language editions of Gorky's work.

10 SERGEEV-TSENSKII, S. "Moia perepiska i znakomstvo s Gor'kim" [My correspondence and acquaintance with Gorky]. In Izbrannoe [Selected works]. Moscow: Sovetskii pisatel', pp. 526-84.
    Includes letters from 1910 to the 1930s to Sergeev-Tsensky from Gorky. Information about Gorky's activities and literary life in this period.

11 SLONIMSKII, MIKHAIL. "Maksim Gor'kii: Vospominaniia" [Maksim Gorky: Memoirs]. Literaturnyi sovremennik, no. 6:97-113.

Remembers reading Gorky's stories and novels while on the battlefield in World War I. Recounts instances of Gorky's help for writers during the civil war. Discusses especially Fedor Sologub, Dmitry Merezhkovsky. Describes H.G. Wells's visit in 1920.

12   YARMOLINSKY, AVRAHM. "Maxim Gorki." *American Scholar* 11, no. 1 (Winter):89-98.
     Reprinted in part: 1969.43. Gorky's work marred by "sophomoric commentary" which intrudes on his story. Gives broad introduction. Verdict: Gorky is an "uneven writer"; to ignore his "serious faults" is to "fail to assess his virtues." He is a man who sacrificed his "free critical spirit" for what he thought were progressive sociopolitical forces. More time is needed for a real assessment.

1942

1   KAUN, ALEXANDER. "Gorky on Literature." *Books Abroad* 16, no. 4 (Fall):395-97.
    Review of *Nesobrannye literaturno-kriticheskie stat'i* [Uncollected literary critical articles], 1941. Sketches Gorky as a broadly read, deeply knowledgeable critic. Includes a lengthy quote from Gorky's sketch of Mark Twain.

2   VAN DOREN, MARK. "Where Nothing Happens." In *Private Reader*. New York: Holt, pp. 371-73.
    A review of Jean Renoir's 1928 film version of *The Lower Depths* [*Na dne*]. Film is made from a bad translation. Only occasionally does Renoir capture the atmosphere of the play.

1943

1   VAN GYSEGHEM, ANDRÉ. *Theatre in Soviet Russia*. London: Faber & Faber, pp. 51-53, 106-7.
    Gorky's plays are a protest against reality. Gorky gave the Moscow Art Theater a "social line," whereas Chekhov gave it an "artistic line."

1944

1   POOLE, ERNEST. "Maxim Gorky in New York." *SEER* 22, no. 58 (May):77-84.
    Memoirs by a man who knew Gorky at the time of his visit to the United States.

1945

1   THORGEVSKY, IVAN. De Gorki à nos jours: La nouvelle littérature russe. Paris: La Renaissance, pp. 13-32.
    Reviews life, stresses good relationship to political leaders, interest in high culture, dislike for peasants. Sees three stages in Gorky's literary development: romantic, militant Marxist, and memoirist and stock taker. Finds the first and third stages the best.

1946

1   FRIED, J. "Klim Samgin und die Menschheit." Sowjetliteratur, no. 1:73-83.
    An early effort to export Soviet socialist realism. Welcomes the publication of the fourth volume of The Life of Klim Samgin [Zhizn' Klima Samgina] in German translation. Gorky is great because he overcame the limitations of his own time and gained a view into the future. Gorky is the teacher of the spirit of "proletarian humanism" and a friend of Lenin and Stalin. Klim Samgin represents a dying society. He is "isolated" from his people and the world.

2   GRUZDEV, IL'IA. Gor'kii. Moscow and Leningrad: GIKhL, 127 pp.
    Biography. Outlines Gorky's growing alienation from his bourgeois background and his love for social struggle. Emphasizes Gorky's qualifications as a proletarian. Characterizes him as a passionate, romantic rebel against social oppression, a man close to the people. Gives strong emphasis to the relationship of Gorky to Lenin. Sidesteps difficult political and personal issues. Popularizes the Soviet legend of Gorky and canonizes "friends" and "enemies."

3   KALAUSHIN, M.M., ed. A.M. Gor'kii, zhizn' i tvorchestvo, 1868-1936. [A.M. Gorky, life and work, 1868-1936]. Moscow and Leningrad: ANSSSR, 99 pp. of pictures and 32 pp. introductory pamphlet.
    Loose-leaf collection of portraits of Gorky, caricatures, pictures, illustrations.

4   MIKHAILOVSKII, B.V. "A.M. Gor'kii i filosofiia kul'tury" [A.M. Gorky and the philosophy of culture]. In Uchenye zapiski: Trudy kafedry russkoi literatury (Moskovskii gosudarstvennyi universitet) no. 110:3-24.
    Gorky's theory of culture opposes Nietzsche's advocacy of a return to barbarism and amorality. Gorky sees the people as a whole as the creator of high culture.

5   ROSKIN, ALEXANDER. From the Banks of the Volga: The Life of Maxim Gorky. Translated by D.L. Fromberg. New York: Philosophical Library, 126 pp.

A popularized, romanticized biography. Stresses Gorky's early years; bypasses all problematic issues.

6 VAN DOREN, MARK. Introduction to Reminiscences. New York: Dover, pp. i-iii.
Gorky understands Tolstoy's mentality and religious views so well because he understands the whole man: his physical self, his habits, his speech.

1947

1 BIALIK, B. "Maxim Gorki und der Parteistandpunkt in der Literatur." Sowjetliteratur, no. 5:124-37.
Gorky showed in his 1934 speech at the First Congress of Soviet Writers that he understood the important guiding role that the Party must play in the creative life of each writer. The Party gives true "artistic freedom" in the sense that it makes the writer aware of the "strict teaching of history and its fundamental, organizing idea." That organizing idea is Leninism-Stalinism. Gorky fought hard against "pure art," "l'art pour l'art." Emphasizes the guiding, corrective effect Lenin had on Gorky, especially after 1905 and in 1917-18.

2 _____. O Gor'kom: Stat'i [On Gorky: Articles]. Moscow: Sovetskii pisatel', 331 pp.
Shows Lenin's and Stalin's impact on Gorky and through him on "progressive" art, particularly on the "best, most talented poet" of the Soviet era, V.V. Maiakovsky, and the "greatest reformers of Soviet theater," K. Stanislavsky and E. Vakhtangov. Also discusses the link between Gorky's work and folklore.

3 CLARK, BARRETT H., and FREEDLEY, GEORGE, eds. A History of Modern Drama. New York and London: D. Appleton-Century, pp. 419-31.
Surveys the stage history of all Gorky's dramas.

4 FAST, HOWARD. Introduction to Mother. New York: Citadel, pp. v-vii.
Models self as a self-made writer, influenced by Gorky. Sees Pelageia Vlasova as a great character because she embodies the "living process by which an ordinary person becomes, step by step, a fighter for justice." Speaks of the process as a "conversion" and of Gorky as a "great and saintly human being." Compares Gorky to Mark Twain.

5 GRIGOR'EV, M.A., ed. "Na dne": Materialy i issledovaniia [The Lower Depths: Materials and research]. Moscow: Vserossiiskoe teatral'noe obshchestvo, 151 pp.
Contains two lengthy articles on The Lower Depths. Iu. Iuzovskii in "Na dne: Idei i obrazy" [The Lower Depths: Ideas and images] contrasts the philosophies of the two characters,

Luka and Satin. Reprinted from 1940.3. In his article, "Stsenicheskii put' Na dne" [The stage history of The Lower Depths], M.B. Levin traces the lively polemic about Gorky's play in the Russian press both before the Revolution and after. He attempts to explain why Gorky himself criticized his play so harshly, twice claiming that it was hostile to his own worldview.

6   LAVRIN, J. "Maxim Gorky." In An Introduction to the Russian Novel. New York: McGraw-Hill, pp. 146-55.
    Gorky was the most outstanding example of a new kind of "self-made," "half intellectual" from the working class who perceived social and cultural needs differently from the traditional "high-brow" intellectuals. His creative urge came from a need to overcome a sense of social inferiority.

7   MOTYLJOVA, TAMARA. "Gorki und die internationale Bedeutung der Sowjetliteratur." Sowjetliteratur, no. 4:129-37.
    Praises nineteenth-century Russian literature as progressive in that it revealed to the world the injustice and oppression of tsarism. Gorky is greater than his nineteenth-century predecessors because he gave his contemporaries a "spiritual and aesthetic weapon for the active struggle for the liberation of humanity."

8   VENGROV, N. Človĕk Maxim Gorkij: Vzpominky současníků [Gorky the man: Memoirs of contemporaries]. Prague: Svoboda, 211 pp.
    In Czech. Edited translation of "M. Gor'kii v vospominaniiakh sovremennikov" [Gorky in the memoirs of contemporaries]. See 1955.3.

1948

1   BIALIK, B[ORIS]. "Gorki und Dostojewski." Sowjetliteratur, no. 10:149-57.
    Gorky held the same view of Dostoevsky all his life: although he was undoubtedly a genius, he was an "evil genius" who was fascinated with suffering and pain. Gorky warned of Dostoevsky's politically reactionary views and the harmfulness of his influence. Carried on a polemic with him in essays and fiction. Bialik discusses The Three of Them [Troe], The Old Man [Starik].

2   HOLTZMAN, FILIA. The Young Maxim Gorky, 1868-1902. Columbia University Press, 256 pp.
    Biography of the early Gorky.

3   NATHAN, G.J. "Long Way from Home." In Theatre Book of the Year, 1947-1948. New York: Knopf, pp. 255-57.

On The Lower Depths [Na dne]. Negative review of an adaptation of The Lower Depths in which Moscovite down-and-outers were changed into North Carolina blacks.

4   PIKSANOV, N.K. Gor'kii i nauka [Gorky and science]. Moscow and Leningrad: ANSSSR, 31 pp.
    This brochure is designed to acquaint the general reader with Gorky as a "profound scientist, an expert in the history of culture and science." Reviews Gorky's achievements in philosophy, history, art.

5   SERGIJEWSKIJ, A. "Gorkijs Kampf gegen die Dekadenz." Sowjetliteratur, no. 7:150-61.
    Gorky is greater than his nineteenth-century realist predecessors because he saw the way to social renewal in the rebellion of the working class against the old regime. He saw his role in "illuminating the difficult way forward of the millions." Gorky used his new vision to fight decadence in literature, especially Merezhkovsky, Balmont, Briusov, Poe, Verlaine.

1949

1   EGOLIN, A., MIKHAILOVSKII, B.V., and PETROV, S.M., eds. Gor'kovskie chteniia, 1947-1948 [Readings in Gorky, 1947-1948]. Moscow and Leningrad: ANSSSR, 524 pp.
    Contains the following articles:
    1. B.V. Mikhailovskii, "Tvorcheskie iskaniia molodogo Gor'kogo (osobennosti realizma rannego Gor'kogo)" [Creative explorations of the young Gorky (the peculiarities of the realism of the early Gorky)].
    2. N.P. Belkina, "Problema polozhitel'nogo geroia v avtobiograficheskoi trilogii Gor'kogo" [The problem of the positive hero in Gorky's autobiographical trilogy].
    3. V.A. Maksimova, "Iz tvorcheskoi istorii romana M. Gor'kogo Delo Artamonovykh" [From the creative history of M. Gorky's novel The Artamonov Business].
    4. V.N. Lanina, "Obraz Il'i Luneva (Glava iz monografii o romane M. Gor'kogo Troe)" [The image of Ilia Lunev (A chapter from a monograph on M. Gorky's novel The Three of Them)].
    5. B.V. Mikhailovskii and N.P. Belkina, "Bor'ba Gor'kogo s imperialisticheskoi reaktsiei i upadochnoi kul'turoi zapada" [Gorky's struggle with imperialist reaction and the decadent culture of the West].
    6. A.M. Egolin, "Gor'kii i russkaia literatura" [Gorky and Russian literature].
    7. D.D. Blagoi, "Pushkin v otsenke Gor'kogo" [Pushkin in Gorky's evaluation].
    8. B.V. Mikhailovskii, "Gor'kii i Gogol'" [Gorky and Gogol].
    9. N.L. Brodskii, "Gor'kii o Lermontove" [Gorky on Lermontov].

10. Ia.E. El'sberg, "Traditsiia Shchedrina v tvorchestve Gor'kogo" [The Shchedrin tradition in Gorky's work].
11. E.B. Tager, "Gor'kii i Chekhov" [Gorky and Chekhov].
12. M.N. Parkhomenko, "Gor'kii i ukrainskaia literatura" [Gorky and Ukrainian literature].
13. Mamed Arif, "Gor'kii v Azerbaidzhane" [Gorky in Azerbaijan].
14. Gurgen Ovnan, "Gor'kii i armianskaia literatura" [Gorky and Armenian literature].
15. K. Umbrasas, "Gor'kii i litovskaia literatura" [Gorky and Lithuanian literature].

2 HOLTZMAN, FILIA. "The Young Maxim Gorky, 1868-1902." Ph.D. diss., Columbia University, 256 pp.
Biography and criticism. Published as a book: 1948.2.

3 PIMENOV, VS., ed. Rabota rezhissera nad p'esoi M. Gor'kogo "Meshchane" [The director's work on Gorky's play The Petit Bourgeois]. Moscow and Leningrad: Iskusstvo, 155 pp.
Contains the full play, staging materials edited by A.D. Popov and A.A. Kharlamov, sketches of costumes by Fedotov, and drawings of sets by Petrachenko.

4 SURKOW, E. "Maxim Gorkis Pamphlete über Amerika." Sowjetliteratur, no. 7:142-49.
Gorky's works on the United States are more relevant than ever as criticism of capitalism. Nothing has changed in the intervening years. He is a harsh critic of bankers, business people, and corrupt politicians, but distinguishes the American people from their "exploiters."

5 WERNER, M.R. "That Was New York: L'Affaire Gorky." New Yorker (30 April):62-71.
A full description of Gorky's reception in the United States in 1906.

6 WILCZKOWSKI, CYRILLE. "Gorki." Ecrivains soviétiques. Paris: Editions de la revue des jeunes, pp. 184-210.
Gorky's biggest service to the Revolution was to preserve and incorporate Russian classic literature in the new Soviet society.

1950

1 ALEXINSKY, GRÉGOIRE. La vie amère de Maxime Gorki. Grenoble: B. Arthaud, 284 pp.
This biography is advertised as more than the usual romanticized version of Gorky's life. The author uses his own acquaintance with Gorky as well as available biographical materials. Stresses Gorky's political development. Contains appendixes on the trial of the Trotskyites in 1938, which deals with Gorky's death.

1950

2   BOWEN, ELIZABETH. "Gorki Stories." In <u>Collected Impressions</u>.
    New York: Longmans, Green, & Co., pp. 153-56.
        Review from the <u>New Statesman</u> and the <u>Nation</u> of <u>A Book of
    Short Stories</u>, which was translated by Yarmolinsky and M.
    Budberg. Gorky's stories show "virtuosity on a scale with his
    seriousness." The reviewer distinguishes between "austerity,"
    which Gorky possesses, and "toughness," which has a "maudlin
    streak." Gorky sometimes overuses certain narrative techniques;
    for example, his endings are often the same.

2A BUNIN, IVAN. "Gor'kii." In <u>Vospominaniia</u> [Memoirs]. Paris:
    Vozrozhdenie, pp. 118-29.
        Against legend making. Finds Gorky a vexing character who
    was always playing a role and never seemed genuine. He feels
    that Gorky's fame was "unequaled" but "undeserved," and rests in
    part on Gorky's effort to create legends about himself.
    Reprinted: 1981.2.

3   IVANOV, VSEVOLOD. <u>Vstrechi s M. Gor'kim</u> [Encounters with M.
    Gorky]. Moscow: Pravda, 64 pp.
        Memoir containing several letters from Gorky to Ivanov from
    the 1910s and 1920s.

4   JERMILOV, W. "Gorki und die Verteidigung des Friedens."
    <u>Sowjetliteratur</u>, no. 11:5-9.
        Gorky stood for an active, humanistic view. He "fought"
    against exploitation for human happiness. His hero, the working
    person, the person who creates values, has become the positive
    hero of Soviet literature. The "struggle for peace in the whole
    world" is the "heart and soul" of this trend in literature.

5   PROSHOGIN, W. "Das Thema der Arbeit in Gorkis Werken."
    <u>Sowjetliteratur</u>, no. 6:165-73.
        The theme of work dominates Gorky's creative work. He
    differs from earlier writers such as Dickens who saw the worker
    as an object of pity. For Gorky, the theme of work was related
    to the theme of revolutionary struggle. He hated all cooperation
    between classes, all reform movements.

1951

1   ANON. "Imia, kotoroe chtut narody" [The name the peoples
    honor]. <u>Literaturnaia gazeta</u>, no. 71 (16 June):1.
        See 1951.9. Discusses the hundreds of Soviet cities,
    towns, farms, businesses, parks named after Gorky. For example,
    nearly one thousand collective farms, two hundred schools, one
    hundred libraries carry his name.

2   BURSOV, B.I. <u>Roman M. Gor'kogo "Mat'" i voprosy
    sotsialisticheskogo realizma</u> [M. Gorky's novel <u>Mother</u> and

Secondary Bibliography 1951

questions of socialist realism]. Moscow and Leningrad: GIKhL, 167 pp.

Mother contains the kernel of socialist realism. It emerged as a response to the critical realism of Tolstoy and Chekhov.

3   CLARK, BARRETT H. "Maxim Gorky: The Happy Exile." In Intimate Portraits; Being Recollections of M. Gorky . . . and Others. New York: Dramatists Play Service, pp. 1-26.

Memoir of Clark's encounter with Gorky near Berlin in 1923. Gives Gorky's impressions of American writers. Gorky calls O'Neill "too Russian." Gives Gorky's views on his own writing and on Tolstoy.

4   DESNITSKII, V.A., and MURATOVA, K.D., eds. M. Gor'kii: Materialy i issledovaniia [M. Gorky: Materials and research]. Vol. 4. Moscow and Leningrad: ANSSSR, 402 pp.

Contains the following articles:
1. V.A. Desnitskii, "K voprosu ob avtobiograficheskikh povestiakh M. Gor'kogo Detstvo i V liudiakh" [On the question of Gorky's autobiographical novels Childhood and My Apprenticeship].
2. S.V. Kastorskii, "Povest' Leto" [The novel Summer].
3. K.D. Muratova, "Skazki ob Italii" [Tales of Italy].
4. I.S. Eventov, "M. Gor'kii v otsenke dooktiabr'skoi bol'shevistskoi kritiki" [M. Gorky in the evaluation of pre-revolutionary Bolshevik criticism].
5. K.N. Grigor'ian, "M. Gor'kii i Ter'ian" [M. Gorky and Teryan].
6. F.F. Kanaev, "Zhizn' Klima Samgina kak istoricheskii roman-khronika" [The Life of Klim Samgin as a historical novel-chronicle].
7. A.S. Bushmin, "M. Gor'kii i A. Fadeev" [M. Gorky and A. Fadeev].

Bibliography: first-time publications of poems, letters, articles from 1888 to 1936.

5   EGOLIN, A.M., MIKHAILOVSKII, B.V., and PETROV, S.M., eds. Gor'kovskie chteniia, 1949-1950 [Readings in Gorky, 1949-1950]. Moscow: ANSSSR, 483 pp.

Contains the following materials from the Gorky Archive:
1. Sketches, variants, fragments of various drafts of the first part of The Life of Klim Samgin.
2. Gorky's comments on The Life of Klim Samgin.
3. The plan of the novel, The Life of Mr. Platon Il'ich Penkin.

Contains the following articles:
1. N.P. Belkina, "Zhizn' Klima Samgina (glavnye obrazy romana)" [The Life of Klim Samgin (the main images in the novel)].

2. A.A. Saburov, "Rabota Gor'kogo nad pervoi chast'iu romana Zhizn' Klima Samgina [Gorky's work on the first part of the novel The Life of Klim Samgin].
3. Z.M. Karasik, "'Zapiski doktora Riakhina' (iz tvorcheskoi istorii obraza Klima Samgina)" ["The notes of Doctor Riakhin" (from the creative history of the image of Klim Samgin)].
4. A.M. Egolin, "M. Gor'kii--borets za mir i demokratiiu" [M. Gorky--fighter for peace and democracy].
5. A.A. Volkov, "Gor'kii i dooktiabr'skaia proletarskaia pressa" [Gorky and the pre-October proletarian press].
6. V.A. Maksimova, "Ocherki Gor'kogo Po soiuzu sovetov" [Gorky's sketches, Around the Union of Soviets].
7. B.V. Mikhailovskii, "Tema intelligentsii v rannei dramaturgii Gor'kogo" [The theme of the intelligentsia in Gorky's early drama].
8. A.I. Ovcharenko, "Obraz Pavla Gracheva" [The image of Pavel Grachev].
9. B.A. Bialik, "Bor'ba Gor'kogo--khudozhnika protiv reaktsionnykh idei Dostoevskogo" [The struggle of Gorky the artist against the reactionary ideas of Dostoevsky].
10. N.T. Fedorenko, "Nasledie M. Gor'kogo i sovetskaia literatura v Kitae" [The heritage of M. Gorky and Soviet literature in China].

6 FEDIN, KONSTANTIN. "Glashatai novoi zhizni" [The herald of the new life]. Literaturnaia gazeta, no. 71 (16 June):1.
    See 1951.9. Legend making. Recounts Gorky's return to the Soviet Union in 1928. Gorky felt that he was "going from miracle to miracle," that his life dream was coming true: "the new man had arrived, [and] with his hands, mind, [and] soul was building a life worthy of a free people." Calls for a thorough investigation of all Gorky's activities in the last eight years of his life "as one of the organizers of Soviet society, one of the leaders (vozhd') of the cultural revolution."

7 GOR'KII, A.M. M. Gor'kii i A. Chekhov: Sbornik materialov [M. Gorky and A. Chekhov: A collection of materials]. Moscow: GIKhL, 287 pp.
    Contains fifty-four letters of Gorky to Chekhov, thirty-nine letters from Chekhov to Gorky, an introductory article, Gorky's comments on Chekhov's story "In the Ravine," reminiscences of Chekhov, and remarks of each writer about the other. See 1951.7.

8 _____. Povesti, vospominaniia, publitsistika, stat'i o literature [Stories, reminiscences, polemics, articles on literature]. Edited by V.N. Guseva, V.N. Lanina, A.Ia. Tararaev, and M.M. Iunovich. Arkhiv A.M. Gor'kogo, vol. 3. Moscow: Khud. lit., 298 pp.

Contains:
1. Fragments from stories and novels: "Izlozhenie faktov i dum" [A presentation of facts and thoughts]; "Biograf[iia]" [Biography]; "Mudraia red'ka" [The wise radish]; "O komarakh" [On mosquitoes]; "'Pervyi raz ia uvidel etu zhenshchinu'" [The first time I saw this woman]; "Na stantsii" [At the station]; "'Diadia Vitia'" [Uncle Vitya]; "Ob I.E. Repine i kn. I.R. Tarkhanove" [On I.E. Repin and Prince I.R. Tarkhanov]; "'Ia vam ne pomeshaiu?'" [I won't bother you?]; from the Okurov cycle; "Bol'shaia liubov'" [A great love]; "Sluchai s Luzginym" [The case of Luzgin]; "Sny" [Dreams]; "Pravdivoe izlozhenie . . ." [A truthful presentation . . .]; "Ovrag" [Ravine].
2. Reminiscences of N.K. Mikhailovsky, A.N. Aleksin, Pavel Rozanov; notes from Gorky's diary.
3. Publicistic articles: fragment from "O protivorechiiakh" [On contradictions]; "SSSR na stroike" [The USSR at the construction sites]; "Poema v proze" [A poem in prose]; "O burzhuaznoi presse" [On the bourgeois press]; preface to 60 reisov [60 Flights]; "O nauke" [On science]; sketch for the book K chemu vse eto? [What Is All This For?]; "Beseda" [Conversation]; "Po povodu chuda" [A propos of a miracle]; on the program for the book Gor'kovskii krai [Gorky region]; "Zapiska o vuzakh" [A note about institutes of higher education].
4. Literary history and criticism: a fragment from Razrushenie lichnosti [The Destruction of Personality]; on the theater of the heroic; foreword to Tales of Italy; foreword to the English-language edition of Pushkin's works; "Molodaia literatura i ee zadachi" [Young literature and its tasks]; "O rabote redaktsii zhurnalov i litgazet" [On the work of editorial boards of journals and literary newspapers]; foreword to the French edition of Mother; "O rabote literaturnykh izdatel'stv" [On the work of literary presses]; "O fol'klore" [On folklore]; On "Proekt programmy dlia litkruzhkov" [Project for literary circles]; foreword to a history of literature for soldiers and sailors; "Nechto ob epose i prochem" [On the epic and other things].

9 Literaturnaia gazeta, no. 71 (16 June).
Devoted to the unveiling of the statue of Gorky on Belorusskaia Square. Contains the following articles:
1. K. Fedin, "Glashatai novoi zhizni" [The herald of the new life]. See 1951.6.
2. G. Fish, "Dlia schast'ia chelovechestva! M. Gor'kii i preobrazovanie prirody" [For the happiness of humanity! M. Gorky and the transformation of nature].
3. Anon., "Imia, kotoroe chtut narody" [The name the peoples honor]. See 1951.1.
4. Vl. Bakhmet'ev, "Na rodnoi zemle" [In one's native land].

5. S. Sergeev-Tsenskii, "Luchshii pamiatnik" [The best monument].
   6. Vera Inber, "Trud i masterstvo" [Labor and mastery].
   7. N. Pogodin, "Perechityvaia Gor'kogo" [Rereading Gorky].

10 MIKHAILOVSKII, B.V. Dramaturgiia M. Gor'kogo epokhi pervoi russkoi revoliutsii [M. Gorky's drama from the period of the first Russian revolution]. Moscow: ANSSSR, 200 pp.
    Analyzes Gorky's earliest plays, 1901-6. Establishes historical verisimilitude in these plays. Discusses the importance of Bolshevik [sic] ideas for Gorky's early work. Concentrates especially on The Petit Bourgeois [Meshchane], The Lower Depths [Na dne], Enemies [Vragi].

11 MUCHNIC, HELEN. "Circe's Swine: Plays by Gorky and O'Neill." Comparative Literature, 3:119-28.
    Compares the vision of humanity in The Lower Depths [Na dne] and The Iceman Cometh. Sees both as "parables of life." Reprinted: 1961.19.

12 SERGIEVSKII, I.V. "Gor'kii i Chekhov" [Gorky and Chekhov]. Introduction to M. Gor'kii i A. Chekhov. Moscow: GIKhL, pp. 6-20.
    See 1951.7. Discusses Chekhov's recognition of the young Gorky and Gorky's defense of Chekhov against claims of spiritual and moral emptiness. Both writers shared a distaste for everything "petit bourgeois" [meshchanskii].

1952

1   BURSOW, B. "Der sozialistische Realismus in Gorkis Roman Die Mutter." Sowjetliteratur, no. 8:169-74.
    Understanding the origin of socialist realism is crucial for "progressive literature" in all countries. Analyzes Mother as a work the goal of which was to urge workers of all countries to fight for liberation.

2   LUKÁCS, GEORG. "Maxim Gorki." In Der russische Realismus in der Weltliteratur. 3d ed. Berlin: Aufbau, pp. 261-309.
    Two chapters: "Der Befreier" (1936) and "Die menschliche Komödie des vorrevolutionären Rußland" (1936). Calls Gorky the "greatest writer of the present time." Gorky was more than a "master" to young socialist writers; he was a "liberator." Created not just great art but a whole social-cultural consciousness. In the second essay Lúkács defines Gorky as a "realist" in the sense that he grappled in his art with the greatest social reality of his time: the crisis of revolution. Compares him to Balzac: both are "historians of society" and "prophetic creators of forms" that were later realized. For English translation, see 1964.19.

3 PROOST, KAREL F. <u>Maxim Gorki: Zijn leven en werken</u> [Maxim Gorky: His life and works]. Arnheim: Van Loghum Slaterus, 193 pp.
   In Dutch. A biographical treatment.

4 SPECTOR, IVAR. "Maxim Gorky: 1868-1936." In <u>Golden Age of Russian Literature</u>. 4th ed. Caldwell, Idaho: Caxton, pp. 271-94.
   Reviews Gorky's life; gives plot summaries of <u>The Lower Depths</u> [<u>Na dne</u>] and <u>Mother</u> [<u>Mat'</u>].

5 STANISLAVSKI, CONSTANTIN. <u>My Life in Art</u>. Translated by J.J. Robbins. New York: Theater Arts Books, pp. 390-98, 439-40.
   Describes the political atmosphere around the staging of <u>The Petit Bourgeois</u> [<u>Meshchane</u>], <u>The Lower Depths</u> [<u>Na dne</u>], <u>Summer Folk</u>, [<u>Dachniki</u>].

6 ZABURDAEV, N.A. "Muratovy, Kashiriny, Peshkovy po dokumentam" [The Muratovs, Kashirins, Peshkovs in the documents]. <u>Volzhskii al'manakh</u>, no. 9:245-95.
   Uses the Gorky regional archives to trace the background of Gorky's family. Finds that his autobiography <u>Childhood</u> [<u>Detstvo</u>] differs from the documents at times.

1953

1 CHOLODOW, JEFIM. "Gorki-Aufführungen." <u>Sowjetliteratur</u>, no. 7:116-27.
   Discusses productions of Gorky's last plays, <u>Egor Bulychev</u>, <u>Dostigaev and Others</u>, and the second version of <u>Vassa Zheleznova</u> written in the 1930s. All show qualities typical of people in the "dying capitalist world."

2 DESNITSKII, V.A., and BUSHMIN, A.S., eds. <u>Voprosy sovetskoi literatury</u> [Questions of Soviet literature]. Vol. 1. Moscow and Leningrad: ANSSSR, 412 pp.
   Contains the following articles on Gorky:
   1. K.D. Muratova, "Publitsistika Gor'kogo" [Gorky's publicistic writing]. See 1953.5.
   2. V.V. Timofeeva, "Gor'kii i Maiakovskii" [Gorky and Maiakovsky]. See 1953.8.
   3. V.A. Kovalev, "Gor'kii i Leonov (20-e gody)" [Gorky and Leonov (the 1920s)]. See 1953.3.
   4. I.P. Dmitrakov, "Gor'kii i narodnoe tvorchestvo" [Gorky and folklore].
   5. V.N. Zlobin, "Gor'kii v Krymu" [Gorky in the Crimea].
   6. F.P. Vasil'ev, "Gor'kii v Leningrade (khronika, 1928-1931)" [Gorky in Leningrad (a chronicle, 1928-1931)].
   7. K.D. Muratova, "Vyskazyvaniia sovetskikh pisatelei o Gor'kom" [Remarks of Soviet writers about Gorky].

3   KOVALEV, V.A. "Gor'kii i Leonov (20-e gody)" [Gorky and Leonov (the 1920s)]. In Voprosy sovetskoi literatury. Vol. 1. Moscow and Leningrad: ANSSSR, pp. 200-244.
    See 1953.2. Analyzes Gorky's impact upon Leonov as a case study of his influence in creating a "new kind of writer." Discusses Gorky's response to Badgers. Stresses Gorky's stance against the influence of Dostoevsky and his desire that writers portray the "high qualities of the progressive Soviet person" and the failure of bourgeois individualism.

4   LAMM, MARTIN. "Maxim Gorky." In Modern Drama. Translated by Karin Elliot. New York: Philosophical Library, pp. 216-21.
    Discusses The Lower Depths [Na dne]. Influenced by Tolstoy's The Power of Darkness and Hauptmann's The Weavers.

5   MURATOVA, K.D. "Publitsistika Gor'kogo" [Gorky's publicistic writing]. In Voprosy sovetskoi literatury. Vol. 1. Moscow and Leningrad: ANSSSR, pp. 83-141.
    See 1953.2. Gorky's essays written after a six-year sojourn abroad cast in a new light the momentous changes going on in Russian society, economy, and in the Soviet moral character.

6   ORLOV, ALEXANDER. "The Medical Assassinations: The Death of Maxim Gorky." In The Secret History of Stalin's Crimes. New York: Random House, pp. 261-76.
    Shows how Stalin used Gorky's death to support his claim that old Bolshevik terrorist groups were undermining Soviet power.

7   PAWLENKO, PJOTR. "Maxim Gorky." Sowjetliteratur, no. 3: 167-77.
    Memoirs about Gorky's post-1905 years and how inspiring Mother [Mat'] was. Compares Gorky to Lomonosov. Stresses Gorky's role as a mentor to other writers.

8   TIMOFEEVA, V.V. "Gor'kii i Maiakovskii" [Gorky and Maiakovsky]. In Voprosy sovetskoi literatury. Vol. 1. Moscow and Leningrad: ANSSSR, pp. 142-99.
    See 1953.2. Analyzes Gorky's and Maiakovsky's relations after 1917. Shows "how close Maiakovsky's views on the essence and the purposes of art . . . were to Gorky's esthetic program."

9   WILSON, EDMUND. To the Finland Station. Garden City, N.Y.: Doubleday, pp. 380, 383, 384, 397-99, 448-49.
    Uses Gorky's sketch of Lenin as a historical source. Draws a parallel between Lenin's affectionate relationship to his younger brother Dmitry and his "half-protective attitude" to Gorky.

10 YAKOBSON, SERGIUS. "Introduction to 'The Letters of Maksim Gor'kij to V.F. Xodasevič, 1922-1925.'" Translated and edited by H. McLean. Harvard Slavic Studies 1:279-334.

These letters help penetrate the hagiographical image of Gorky created in the Soviet Union. They show a lesser known part of Gorky's life--his years in Europe after the 1917 Revolution. Contain a great deal of information on the journal Beseda [Conversation]. Notes to the letters are by Khodasevich.

1954

1. APLETIN, M.IA., ed. Proizvedeniia sovetskikh pisatelei v perevodakh na inostrannye iazyki, 1945-53 [Works by Soviet writers in foreign-language translation, 1945-53]. Moscow: Soiuz pisatelei, Vses. gos. bibl. inostr. lit-y., pp. 52-74.
   Bibliography. Lists primary literature in foreign languages.

2. BEERBOHM, SIR MAX. "Lower Depths." In Around Theatres. New York: Simon & Schuster, pp. 302-5.
   A review from 5 December 1903. Objects to the lack of artistic unity in The Lower Depths [Na dne].

3. GASSNER, J. "Maxim Gorky and the Soviet Drama." In Masters of the Drama. 2d ed. New York: Dover, pp. 526-41.
   Gorky was central in turning the Moscow Art Theater from a "middle-class" institution to a "proletarian" one. Traces Gorky's development and the growth of Soviet theater.

4. GOR'KII, A.M. Pis'ma k K.P. Piatnitskomu [Letters to K.P. Piatnitsky]. Edited by I.N. Uspenskii. Arkhiv A.M. Gor'kogo, vol. 4. Moscow: Khud. lit., 448 pp.
   Contains 455 letters and telegrams to the director of Znanie press. Most published for the first time.

5. KUSKOVA, E.K. "Tragediia Maksima Gor'kogo" [The tragedy of Maksim Gorky]. Novyi zhurnal 38:224-45.
   Maksim Gorky's "coarse" "romanticism of revolution" became the spirit that inspired the intelligentsia to revolution. His bold, challenging mood and his pathos set the tone for the official popular history of the Revolution. Now he is barely remembered in the driest, most formal way. Explains on the basis of her acquaintance with him why he did not accept the Revolution.

6. LAVRIN, J. "Maxim Gorky." In Russian Writers: Their Lives and Literature. New York: Van Nostrand, pp. 231-53.
   Gorky stands out as Russia's first proletarian writer. The artist and social reformer converge and strengthen each other in Gorky's work. His goal is to transform human existence through his art.

7. "Maksim Gor'kii." In Istoriia russkoi literatury [History of Russian literature]. Edited by M.P. Alekseev et al. Moscow and Leningrad: ANSSSR, pp. 207-402.

Contains five chapters dealing with Gorky's literary development in the years before the Revolution. He is seen primarily as the "founder of socialist realism." This account is an attempt to rectify a perceived overemphasis on the part of literary historians of "bourgeois-gentry" literary developments, for example, symbolism, acmeism, and underemphasis of developments in "socialist realism."

8   MAKSIMOVA, V. Kak Gor'kii redaktiroval rukopisi [How Gorky edited manuscripts]. Moscow: Iskusstvo, 72 pp.
    Uses analysis of Gorky's editing techniques as way of showing his concrete influence on Soviet literature.

9   MIKHAILOVSKII, B.V., PETROV, S.M., and FETISOV, M.I., eds. Gor'kovskie chteniia [Readings on Gorky]. Moscow: ANSSSR, 447 pp.
    Contains the following materials:
    1. Correspondence of Gorky with F.I. Shaliapin.
    2. A letter from Gorky to N.E. Burenin.
    3. Shaliapin's reminiscence of Gorky.
    4. Gorky's and Shaliapin's inscriptions on photographs.
    5. Gorky's remarks on D.A. Shmarinov's illustrations for The Life of Matvei Kozhemiakin [Zhizn' Matveia Kozhemiakina].
    Contains the following articles:
    1. I.N. Uspenskii, "Krest'ianstvo v tvorchestve M. Gor'kogo" [The peasantry in Gorky's work].
    2. B.A. Bialik, "P'esa Na dne i russkaia deistvitel'nost' nachala 900-kh godov" [The play The Lower Depths and Russian reality in the early 1900s].
    3. A.I. Ovcharenko, "Poema M. Gor'kogo 'Chelovek'" [M. Gorky's poem "Man"].
    4. V.N. Lanina, "O p'ese Varvary" [On the play Barbarians].
    5. E.B. Tager, "Avtobiograficheskie rasskazy Gor'kogo 20-kh godov" [Gorky's autobiographical stories of the 1920s].
    6. A.I. Ovcharenko, "O nekotorykh osobennostiakh publitsistiki M. Gor'kogo" [On certain peculiarities of M. Gorky's publicistic works].
    7. A.Ia. Tararaev, "O rabote M. Gor'kogo nad iazykom romana Zhizn' Klima Samgina" [On Gorky's work on the language of the novel The Life of Klim Samgin].
    8. "E.G. Bushkanets, "A.M. Gor'kii i Volzhskii Vestnik" [A.M. Gorky and Volzhskii Vestnik].

1955

1   ARAGON, LOUIS. "La lumière de Gorki." La nouvelle critique 7, no. 67 (July-August):162-83.
    Aragon's memoirs. Notes Gorky's tremendous popularity. See 1955.2.

Secondary Bibliography 1955

2 _____. "La lumière de Gorki." In <u>Littératures soviétiques</u>. Paris: Editions Denoël, pp. 245-70.
   Memoir on Gorky. Gorky seemed like forbidden fruit around 1907. Remarks on Gorky's tremendous personal influence on him, gave him a grand vision of the future. Loves in him all that is "great and beautiful in socialism," the "perpetual renewal" of humanity.

3 BRODSKII, N.L., et al., eds. <u>M. Gor'kii v vospominaniiakh sovremennikov</u> [M. Gorky in the reminiscences of his contemporaries]. Moscow: GIKhL.
   Contains memoirs of Bolshevik activists and contemporary intellectuals who became prominent in the Soviet state--for example, N. Krupskaia, A.N. Tolstoy, Vl. Nemirovich-Danchenko.

4 EVENTOV, I. "Gor'kii v 1905 godu" [Gorky in 1905]. <u>Zvezda</u> 32, no. 3:128-39.
   Discusses Gorky's political activity in the years leading up to and including 1905.

5 GOR'KII, A.M. <u>Pis'ma k E.P. Peshkovoi, 1895-1906</u> [Letters to E.P. Peshkova, 1895-1906]. Edited by E.P. Peshkova. Arkhiv A.M. Gor'kogo, vol. 5. Moscow: Khud. lit., 310 pp.
   First volume of Gorky's letters to his first wife. Includes 225 letters from June 1895 to October 1906. Some letters are abridged.

6 KAZIN, ALFRED. "Maxim Gorky and the Master Friends." In <u>Inmost Leaf: A Selection of Essays</u>. New York: Harcourt, pp. 28-35.
   Reviews Gorky's reminiscences of Russian writers--Tolstoy, Chekhov, Andreev, Blok. The memoir of Tolstoy is the best. The others are affected by Gorky's attention to "those elements . . . which were overtly against the regime." For example, he makes a "fellow-insurgent" out of Chekhov.

7 LONDON, JACK. "<u>Foma Gordeev</u>." In <u>Sochineniia v 8-i tomakh</u>. [Works in 8 volumes]. Vol. 5. Moscow: Khud. lit., pp. 633-38.
   Taken from the collection <u>Revolution</u> (New York, 1910); first published in the serial <u>Impressions</u> (San Francisco) (November 1901). Gorky's style is coarse and crude, but he tells the truth about bourgeois society.

8 PANKOV, VIKTOR. <u>Sovetskaia deistvitel'nost' v izobrazhenii M. Gor'kogo</u> [Soviet reality in Gorky's depiction]. Moscow: Sovetskii pisatel', 254 pp.
   See 1968.87. An attempt to discuss systematically Gorky's works on the Soviet state. Deals in particular with Gorky's activities during the civil war; his relationship to Lenin; his collections of stories, <u>Around the Soviet Union</u> [<u>Po soiuzu</u>

sovetov], Stories of Heroes [Rasskazy o geroiakh]; his play, Somov and Others [Somov i drugie].

8A VOLKOV, A.A. Ocherki russkoi literatury kontsa XIX i nachala XX veka [Sketches of Russian literature of the late 19th and early 20th centuries]. 2d ed. Moscow: GIKhL, pp. 53-232.
Contains four chapters on the early Gorky, Gorky and 1905, Gorky in the interregnum, and Gorky's political activities.

1956

1 AGAPOW, BORIS. "Gorki und die Dokumentarprosa." Sowjetliteratur, no. 6:203-11.
Gorky's publicistic writing and sketches are as colorfully written as his fiction. He is no "slave to facts." He can be compared with Swift and Voltaire in the way he wields rhetoric. The author focuses on "The City of the Yellow Devil." This number also includes reminiscences by Konstantin Fedin, Mikhail Isakovskii, Nikolai Mikhailov, all of which portray Gorky as the great teacher.

2 AMSTERDAM, A. "V shkole velikogo mastera (o rabote Gor'kogo s nachinaiushchimi pisateliami)" [In the school of the great master (on Gorky's work with beginning writers)]. In Gor'kii i voprosy sovetskoi literatury. Leningrad: Sovetskii pisatel', pp. 439-83.
See 1956.14. Discusses Gorky's ideas on the "education" (vospitanie) of writers.

3 BOURNE, R.S. "In the World of Maxim Gorky: A Book Review." In History of a Literary Radical and Other Papers. New York: S.A. Russell, pp. 135-39.
In his autobiography Gorky turns a horrible and vile experience into a "thing of significance and growth."

4 EVENTOV, I. "Poeziia revoliutsionnogo dela" [Poetry of the revolutionary cause]. In Gor'kii i voprosy sovetskoi literatury. Leningrad: Sovetskii pisatel', pp. 161-206.
See 1956.14. Reviews Gorky's remarks on prerevolutionary modernist poetry. Discusses his relations with Vl. Maiakovsky and S. Esenin.

5 GROMOV, P. "Gor'kii i sovetskaia proza tridtsatykh godov o liudiakh sotsialisticheskogo truda" [Gorky and Soviet prose of the 1930s on socialist laborers]. In Gor'kii i voprosy sovetskoi literatury. Leningrad: Sovetskii pisatel', pp. 104-60.
See 1956.14. Discusses Gorky's role in promoting the theme of the heroic worker in the 1930s. Discusses Gorky's evaluation of belles lettres devoted to the theme of labor.

6   KASTORSKII, S. "Gor'kii i Bunin" [Gorky and Bunin]. Zvezda, no. 3:144-53.
    Explores Gorky and Bunin's literary-political relationship: they worked together successfully on Gorky's journals, Znanie and Letopis', despite Bunin's strong resistance to Gorky's sociopolitical orientation. Sees Gorky's "influence" on Bunin in the slight change in Bunin's views on "writers from the people."

7   _____. "Gor'kovskie traditsii v sovetskom ocherke" [Gorkian traditions in the Soviet sketch]. In Gor'kii i voprosy sovetskoi literatury. Leningrad: Sovetskii pisatel', pp. 207-261.
    See 1956.14. Discusses Gorky's energetic support for sketch writing as a form of service in the name of "building socialism."

8   KOSTELIANETS, B. "Gor'kii i problema tvorcheskoi individual'nosti pisatelia" [Gorky and the problem of the writer's creative personality]. In Gor'kii i voprosy sovetskoi literatury. Leningrad: Sovetskii pisatel', pp. 3-54.
    See 1956.14. Discusses the development of Gorky's aesthetic views and individual personality. Set in the context of debate raised at the Second Writers' Congress concerning the schematic, stereotypic quality of Soviet belles lettres.

9   MURATOVA, K.D. Seminarii po Gor'komu [Seminar on Gorky]. Leningrad: Izd. ministerstva prosveshcheniia, 275 pp.
    Selected bibliography. Five sections: (1) books on Gorky's life and work; gives a survey of the history of Soviet Gorky studies; (2) survey of important dates in Gorky's life; (3) selected bibliography divided into topics such as Gorky as political writer, his relations with contemporary Soviet writers, his individual works, his aesthetic views, Gorky as editor and organizer, his importance for world literature, Gorky and art, Gorky and culture; (4) the main editions of Gorky's collected works; (5) main bibliographies devoted to Gorky.

10 NIKULINA, N.I. "O nekotorykh khudozhestvennykh osobennostiakh avtobiograficheskoi trilogii M. Gor'kogo" [On some artistic peculiarities of Gorky's autobiographical trilogy]. Vestnik Leningradskogo universiteta 11, no. 2:71-94.
    Gorky's autobiography is significant for its combination of a "passionate, truthful story" of a person's life and its "relentless exposure of the 'leaden vileness' of petit bourgeois existence."

11 OVCHARENKO, A. O polozhitel'nom geroe v tvorchestve M. Gor'kogo, 1892-1907 [On the positive hero in M. Gorky's work, 1892-1907]. Moscow: Sovetskii pisatel', 585 pp.
    Concentrates on the image of the worker in Gorky's early work. Starts with the stories, analyzes The Petit Bourgeois [Meshchane], "Man" ["Chelovek"], and Mother [Mat']. Sees Gorky's

image of the worker struggling to build a new world as the basis for the Soviet socialist realist concept of the positive hero. This character type serves as a model for Soviet writers to use in fulfilling the 1954 Party directive to create monumental works showing the "heroism of the Russian proletariat and the Leninist party" in 1905 and 1917. Sees Gorky also as a model for writers from Third-World countries.

12 PLOTKIN, L. "Gor'kii i problema romana-epopei" [Gorky and the problem of the epic novel]. In Gor'kii i voprosy sovetskoi literatury. Leningrad: Sovetskii pisatel', pp. 55-103.
    See 1956.14. Rectifies a perceived gap in Soviet literary criticism by defining Gorky's role in the development of the Soviet epic. Deals with The Artamonov Business [Delo Artamonovykh] and The Life of Klim Samgin [Zhizn' Klima Samgina]. Analyzes epic works of A. Tolstoy, M. Sholokhov, and I. Erenburg.

12A PUKHOV, IU.S. "M. Gor'kii i F. Gladkov (20-e gody)" [M. Gorky and F. Gladkov (the 1920s)]. Voprosy sovetskoi literatury 3:381-417.
    Analyzes Gorky's impact on Gladkov and early Soviet literature.

13 SHNEERSON, M.A. "Fol'klor v povesti M. Gor'kogo Foma Gordeev" [Folklore in Gorky's novel Foma Gordeev]. Voprosy sovetskoi literatury, no. 4:33-60.
    Songs, tales, poetry from the people create a reality that contrasts with the "rotten world of predators and parasites."

14 TSIMBAL, S.L., ed. Gor'kii i voprosy sovetskoi literatury: Sbornik statei [Gorky and questions of Soviet literature: A collection of articles]. Leningrad: Sovetskii pisatel', 484 pp.
    Contains the following articles:
    1. B. Kostelianets, "Gor'kii i problema tvorcheskoi individual'nosti pisatelia" [Gorky and the problem of the writer's creative personality]. See 1956.8.
    2. L. Plotkin, "Gor'kii i problema romana-epopei" [Gorky and the problem of the epic novel]. See 1956.12.
    3. P. Gromov, "Gor'kii i sovetskaia proza tridtsatykh godov o liudiakh sotsialisticheskogo truda" [Gorky and Soviet prose of the 1930s on socialist laborers]. See 1956.5.
    4. I. Eventov, "Poeziia revoliutsionnogo dela" [Poetry of the revolutionary cause]. See 1956.4.
    5. S. Kastorskii, "Gor'kovskie traditsii v sovetskom ocherke" [Gorkian traditions in the Soviet sketch]. See 1956.7.
    6. A. Ninov, "Master rasskazov (zametki o stile rannego Gor'kogo)" [A master of tales (notes on the style of the early Gorky)].
    7. I. Berezark, "V bor'be za pravdu dramaturgicheskogo obraza" [In the struggle for the truth of the dramatic image].

8. D. Zolotnitskii, "Satiricheskie motivy gor'kovskoi dramy" [Satiric motifs of the Gorkian drama].
9. A. Fedorov, "Gor'kii i voprosy khudozhestvennogo perevoda" [Gorky and questions of artistic translation].
10. A. Amsterdam, "V shkole velikogo mastera (o rabote Gor'kogo s nachinaiushchimi pisateliami)" [In the school of the great master (on Gorky's work with beginning writers)].

15 ZAKHAROVA, V.A. "Fol'klor v povestiakh M. Gor'kogo Detstvo i V liudiakh" [Folklore in M. Gorky's novels Childhood and Apprenticeship]. Voprosy sovetskoi literatury 4:61-75.
Shows how Gorky used folkloric themes and oral forms to convey the beauty and moral force of the Russian people.

1957

1 ELIZAROV, S. "Bor'ba M. Gor'kogo protiv reaktsionnykh tendentsii v literature (1892-1904)" [Gorky's struggle against reactionary trends in literature (1892-1904)]. In Stat'i o Gor'kom. Moscow: GIKhL, pp. 269-347.
See 1957.12. A relatively detailed account of Gorky's "struggle" with Minsky, Volynsky, Sologub, Filosofov, Briusov, and Balmont. Discusses the close relationship between naturalism and decadence.

2 ELIZAROV, S.S., et al., eds. M. Gor'kii v epokhu revoliutsii 1905-1907 godov: Materialy, vospominaniia, issledovaniia [Gorky in the epoch of the 1905-1907 revolution: Materials, memoirs, studies]. Moscow: ANSSSR, 410 pp.
Contains letters to A.A. Divilkovsky, Z.F. Stürmer, V.V. Rozanov, Charles Wright, N.E. Burenin, V.G. Sorin; memoirs from this period; the following articles:
   1. V.Ia. Orlova, "M. Gor'kii--uchastnik pervoi russkoi revoliutsii" [Gorky as participant in the first Russian revolution].
   2. A.Ia. Tararaev, "Tema Deviatogo ianvaria v tvorchestve M. Gor'kogo" [The theme of 9 January in Gorky's work].
   3. S.S. Elizarov, "1905 god v romane Zhizn' Klima Samgina" [1905 in the novel The Life of Klim Samgin].
   4. B.V. Mikhailovskii, "P'esa Poslednie" ["The play The Last Ones"].
   5. A.I. Ovcharenko, "Publitsistika M. Gor'kogo (1905-1907)" [Gorky's publicistic works (1905-1907)].
   6. V.A. Maksimova and Iu.I. Makarova, "Ob uchastii Gor'kogo v izdanii bol'shevistskoi gazety Vpered" [On Gorky's part in publishing the Bolshevik newspaper Forward].
   7. Z.M. Karasik, "M. Gor'kii i satiricheskie zhurnaly Zhupel i Adskaia pochta" [Gorky and the satirical journals, Bogey and Hell's Mail].
   8. S.Ia. Brodskaia, "O deiatel'nosti M. Gor'kogo v Amerike v 1906 godu (po materialam amerikanskoi pechati)" [On Gorky's

activities in America in 1906 (according to materials from the American press)].

3   GORCHAKOV, NIKOLAI A. The Theater in Soviet Russia. Translated by E. Lehrman. New York: Columbia University Press, pp. 39-40, 49-50, 312-14.
    Treats Soviet productions of Gorky's plays: The Lower Depths [Na dne], The Petit Bourgeois [Meshchane], Children of the Sun [Deti solntsa], Dostigaev and Others, Egor Bulychev and Others, Enemies [Vragi], among others.

4   GOR'KII, A.M. A.M. Gor'kii i V.G. Korolenko: Perepiska, stat'i, vyskazyvaniia [Gorky and Korolenko: Correspondence, articles, statements]. Moscow: GIKhL, 287 pp.
    Contains fifty-four pieces of correspondence between Gorky and Korolenko, nine between Gorky and Korolenko's relatives, fragments by Gorky on Korolenko (1919), "Vremia Korolenko" ["Korolenko's Time"] (1922), "V.G. Korolenko" (1922).

5   _____. Khudozhestvennye proizvedeniia, plany, nabroski, zametki o literature i iazyke [Artistic works, plans, sketches, notes on literature and language]. Edited by A. Ia. Tararaev. Arkhiv A.M. Gor'kogo, vol. 6. Moscow: Khud. lit., 263 pp.
    Includes two finished works, "Spectators" ["Zriteli"] and "Father Gapon" ["Pop Gapon"], thirty-two unfinished prose works, seven dramatic sketches, twenty-one poems, sixty-one small sketches, twenty-one plans for fictional works, and twenty-three notes on literature and language, which include remarks on Goncharov, Andrei Belyi, Viach. Ivanov, M.M. Prishvin, Anton Chekhov, G. Vico, O. Henry, Jack London, Leonid Andreev.

6   IAKOVLEV, N.V. "Satira v tvorchestve Gor'kogo i nasledie Saltykova-Shchedrina" [Satire in Gorky's work and the heritage of Saltykov-Shchedrin]. Voprosy sovetskoi literatury, no. 5:64-105.
    Reviews Gorky's reception of Saltykov-Shchedrin. Notes that both writers use a passionate, acidic satiric style. Focuses on Gorky's polemical essays.

7   KASTORSKII, S.V. "K istorii 'Okurovskogo tsikla' Gor'kogo" [On the history of Gorky's Okurov cycle]. Voprosy sovetskoi literatury, no. 6:7-51.
    Discusses Gorky's plans for his cycle on the provincial town of Okurov.

8   LEVIN, J.D. Muzei A.M. Gor'kogo: Kratkii putevoditel' [The Gorky Museum: A concise guide]. Moscow: Sovetskaia Rossiia, 55 pp.
    A description of books, letters, and other exhibits in the Gorky Museum on ul. Vorovskogo 25-a, Moscow.

8A LIVANOVA, T. Muzyka v proizvedeniiakh M. Gor'kogo [Music in M. Gorky's works]. Moscow: Akademiia nauk, 339 pp.
    Analyzes Gorky's use of music from a musicological point of view.

9   MURATOVA, KSENIIA D. "Gor'kii i sovetskaia satira (1919-1936)" [Gorky and Soviet satire (1919-1936)]. Voprosy sovetskoi literatury, no. 5:106-47.
    Satire is a powerful weapon in the "struggle with negative elements in life." It should not just expose but inspire with the will to overcome the object of satire. Discusses Gorky's view of satire and uses it to analyze satirists of the 1920s and 1930s, especially M. Zoshchenko, and the journal Krokodil.

10 PIRADOV, B. U istokov tvorchestva Maksima Gor'kogo [At the sources of Maksim Gorky's creative work]. Tbilisi: Zaria Vostoka, 109 pp.
    Deals with Gorky's sojourn in Tbilisi, 1891-92, especially his political acquaintances.

11 POZNER, VLADIMIR. Souvenirs sur Gorki. Paris: Les éditeurs français réunis, 145 pp.
    Memoirs. Contains nine photographs, six-page summary of Gorky's biography. Deals with Gorky's life between 1914 and 1922 in Russia, and 1932 in Sorrento. On page 137, calls Gorky "Prométhée aux pommettes saillantes, le nez en trompette et les cheveux en bataille, il venait de voir, du haut de son rocher, la nuit des hommes s'éclairer d'une multitude de feux."

12 SOLOV'EV, G., ed. Stat'i o Gor'kom: Sbornik [Articles on Gorky: A collection]. Moscow: GIKhL, 421 pp.
    Contains the following articles:
    1. B. Piradov, "K istorii rannikh revoliutsionnykh sviazei A.M. Gor'kogo (Gruziia, 1891-1892)" [Toward the history of Gorky's early revolutionary contacts (Georgia, 1891-1892)].
    2. V. Borshchukov, "U istochnikov sotsialisticheskogo realizma" [At the sources of socialist realism].
    3. A. Lektorskii, "Obrazy rabochikh revoliutsionerov v tvorchestve M. Gor'kogo nakanune i v gody pervoi russkoi revoliutsii" [Images of worker-revolutionaries in Gorky's work on the eve and during the years of the first Russian revolution].
    4. S. Elizarov, "Bor'ba M. Gor'kogo protiv reaktsionnykh tendentsii v literature (1892-1904)" [Gorky's struggle against reactionary trends in literature (1892-1904)]. See 1957.1.
    5. V. Vdovichenko, "Slovo, kotoroe voodushevliaet milliony" [The word which animates millions].

1958

1   BIALIK, B.A., et al., eds. Letopis' zhizni i tvorchestva A.M. Gor'kogo [A chronicle of A.M. Gorky's life and work]. Vol. 2. Moscow: ANSSSR, 623 pp.
    See 1958.18. Biographical chronology. Covers Gorky's life from 1908 to 1916.

2   BIALIK, B.A. "Razvitie traditsii klassicheskoi literatury v tvorchestve M. Gor'kogo" [The development of the classical tradition in Gorky's work]. In Tvorchestvo M. Gor'kogo i voprosy sotsialisticheskogo realizma. Moscow: ANSSSR, pp. 5-99.
    See 1958.19. Looks at Gorky's appropriation of nineteenth-century classical Russian literary traditions, especially of radical writers, for example, Herzen, Turgenev, Dobroliubov, Korolenko.

3   BOGUSLAVSKII, A.O. "Gor'kovskie traditsii v russkoi sovetskoi dramaturgii" [Gorkian traditions in Russian Soviet drama]. In Tvorchestvo M. Gor'kogo i voprosy sotsialisticheskogo realizma. Moscow: ANSSSR, pp. 254-305.
    See 1958.19. Defines the "Gorkian tradition" in Soviet drama.

4   GANELIN, R. "M. Gor'kii i amerikanskoe obshchestvo v 1906 godu" [M. Gorky and American society in 1906]. Russkaia literatura 1, no. 1:200-222.
    Treats Gorky's reception in the United States. The persecution of Gorky in the United States was politically motivated and showed how much the upper levels of American society feared and hated the Russian Revolution. Contains:
    1. An article from the magazine Weekly People (4 August 1906).
    2. Gorky's article "The City of Mamon," from Appleton's Magazine 8 (1906):177-82.

5   GRECHNEV, V. I.A."Literaturnyi portret M. Gor'kogo 'L.N. Tolstoi'" [Gorky's literary portrait "L.N. Tolstoy"]. Voprosy sovetskoi literatury, no. 7:413-36.
    Analyzes Gorky's technique of portraiture, especially how he unfolds Tolstoy's moral and intellectual being.

6   INBER, VERA. "O Gor'kom" [On Gorky]. In Sobranie sochinenii [Collected works]. Vol. 3. Moscow: Khud. lit., pp. 490-95.
    Looks at the exactness of Gorky's descriptions in "January 9," "Strasti-mordasti," My Universities [Moi universitety], among others.

7   IUR'EVA, L.M. "M. Gor'kii i peredovaia zarubezhnaia literatura" [M. Gorky and progressive foreign literature]. In

Tvorchestvo M. Gor'kogo i voprosy sotsialisticheskogo realizma. Moscow: ANSSSR, pp. 371-451.
    See 1958.19. Following the experience of Soviet literature, helps progressive foreign writers to fight antirealist art and the reactionary ideology that goes with it. Discusses special cases of Henri Barbusse, Romain Rolland, Louis Aragon, Ralph Fox, Theodore Dreiser, Heinrich Mann, Bertold Brecht, among others.

8   JACKSON, ROBERT LOUIS. "Maksim Gorky and Notes from the Underground." In Dostoevsky's Underground Man in Russian Literature. The Hague: Mouton, pp. 127-46.
    Examines Gorky's polemic with Dostoevsky and with "underground" psychology. Gorky sees the effects of this psychology upon Russian political behavior in the Revolution. Sees "The Story of a Hero" ["Rasskaz o geroe," 1924] and "Karamora" (1924) as exposés of the underground mentality. Gorky's struggle with Dostoevsky's work is a "focal point in his struggle for the regeneration of Russia."

9   KARASIK, Z., ed. "A.M. Gor'kii v perepiske sovremennikov" [A.M. Gorky in the correspondence of contemporaries]. Voprosy literatury, no. 3:67-99.
    See 1958.44. Materials on Gorky. Includes letters from N.D. Teleshov, I.A. Bunin, L.V. Sredin, K.S. Stanislavskii, V.E. Meierhold, V.Ia. Briusov, E.P. Peshkova, A.L. Volynsky, Vl.I. Nemirovich-Danchenko, among others.

10 KASTORSKII, S.V. "M. Gor'kii i poety 'znan'evtsy'" [M. Gorky and the Znanie poets]. In M. Gor'kii i poety 'Znaniia'. Leningrad: Sovetskii pisatel', pp. 5-58.
    See 1958.11. Discusses Gorky's own efforts at poetry writing and his use of poetic forms to parody decadents. Gives considerable background on the Znanie almanacs and the poets and prose writers who contributed to it.

11 _____. M. Gor'kii i poety 'Znaniia' [M. Gorky and the Znanie poets]. Leningrad: Sovetskii pisatel', 421 pp.
    Collection of poetry by Gorky as well as that by contributors to the Znanie almanacs, particularly Skitalets, A.A. Luk'ianov, E.M. Tarasov, I.K. Voronov, A.S. Cheremnov, I.A. Bunin. Contains a lengthy introduction. See 1958.10.

12 _____. "Nekotorye itogi i zadachi izucheniia povesti Mat' M. Gor'kogo" [Some conclusions and issues in the study of Gorky's novel Mother]. Voprosy sovetskoi literatury, no. 7:305-58.
    Affirms the popularity and importance of Mother. Discusses the question of its genre--whether it is a novel or novella. Reviews the history of its reception in the USSR.

13 MARCHESE, RICCARDO. "Appunti su Gor'kij." Ponte, no. 14: 208-20.
    A reconsideration of Gorky's main themes.

14 MATHEWSON, R.W. "Lenin and Gorky: The Turning Point." In The Positive Hero in Russian Literature. New York: Columbia University Press, pp. 200-226.
See 1975.16.

15 MEILAKH, BORIS. "Gor'kii i poeticheskoe tvorchestvo" [Gorky and poetry]. In Voprosy literatury i estetiki [Questions literary and aesthetic]. Leningrad: Sovetskii pisatel', pp. 499-530.
Reprinted from 1947 edition. Gorky wrote poems almost daily, yet destroyed many of them and published very few of them. Analyzes role of poetry writing in Gorky's creative process.

16 ———. "Iz temy: Lenin i Gor'kii" [From the topic of Lenin and Gorky]. In Voprosy literatury i estetiki [Questions literary and aesthetic]. Leningrad: Sovetskii pisatel', pp. 106-25.
Deals with Gorky's participation in the Capri school organized by A. Bogdanov in 1909.

17 MIASNIKOV, A.S. "Literaturnyi portret Lenina v tvorchestve Gor'kogo" [The literary portrait of Lenin in Gorky's creative work]. In Idei i obrazy khudozhestvennoi literatury [Ideas and images in literature]. Uchenye zapiski, no. 35. Edited by A.S. Miasnikov et al. Moscow: Akademiia obshchestvennykh nauk, pp. 3-52.
Contrasts the three versions of Gorky's portrait of Lenin. Discusses the development of his vision of Lenin the private person.

18 MIKHAILOVSKII, B.V., et al., eds. Letopis' zhizni i tvorchestva A.M. Gor'kogo [A chronicle of A.M. Gorky's life and work]. Vol. 1. Moscow: ANSSSR, 702 pp.
Covers Gorky's life from 1868 to 1907. Ordered by year. Information on Gorky's family, his biography, and his literary activity is taken from parish records, letters, memoirs, contemporary articles, and other written documents, as well as Gorky's own autobiographical works and Soviet publications. The four volumes of the chronicle are broken into the following segments: 1868-1907, 1908-16, 1917-29, 1930-36. See also 1958.1; 1959.4; 1960.1.

19 ———. Tvorchestvo M. Gor'kogo i voprosy sotsialisticheskogo realizma [M. Gorky's creative work and questions of socialist realism]. Moscow: ANSSSR, 502 pp.
Devoted to questions of tradition and innovation. Contains the following articles:
1. B.A. Bialik, "Razvitie traditsii klassicheskoi literatury v tvorchestve M. Gor'kogo" [The development of the classical tradition in Gorky's work]. See 1958.2.
2. E. Tager, "Problema eposa v tvorchestve M. Gor'kogo" [The problem of the epic in Gorky's work]. See 1958.38.

3. A.D. Siniavskii, "O khudozhestvennoi strukture romana Zhizn' Klima Samgina" [On the artistic structure of the novel, The Life of Klim Samgin].

4. A.M. Shumskii, "Tema sotsialisticheskogo stroitel'stva v publitsistike M. Gor'kogo" [The theme of building socialism in Gorky's publicistic work]. See 1958.34.

5. L.I. Timofeev, "K voprosu o gor'kovskikh traditsiiakh v russkoi sovetskoi literature" [On the question of Gorkian traditions in Russian Soviet literature]. See 1958.40.

6. A.O. Boguslavskii, "Gor'kovskie traditsii v russkoi sovetskoi dramaturgii" [Gorkian traditions in Russian Soviet drama]. See 1958.3.

7. K.L. Zelinskii, "M. Gor'kii i razvitie sotsialisticheskogo realizma v literaturakh narodov SSSR" [Gorky and the development of socialist realism in national literatures of the USSR].

8. L.M. Iur'eva, "M. Gor'kii i peredovaia zarubezhnaia literatura" [M. Gorky and progressive foreign literature]. See 1958.7.

9. V. Shcherbina, "Problemy izucheniia tvorchestva M. Gor'kogo" [Problems in the study of Gorky's work]. See 1958.31.

20 MOTYLEVA, T.L., ed. Proizvedeniia A.M. Gor'kogo v perevodakh na inostrannye iazyki [A.M. Gorky's works in translation]. Moscow: Vsesoiuz. knizh. palata, 610 pp.

Bibliography. Contains collected works and separate editions in foreign languages for the years 1900 to 1955. Organized alphabetically according to Russian titles.

21 MURATOVA, K.D. M. Gor'kii v bor'be za razvitie sovetskoi literatury [M. Gorky in the struggle for the development of Soviet literature]. Moscow and Leningrad: ANSSSR, 484 pp.

A classic treatment of Gorky as the founder of socialist realism. Treats his activity as an organizer of literary life after the Revolution. Recounts his early political "mistakes," his sojourn abroad, his late "struggle" to develop Soviet writers and a worthy Soviet literature. Characterizes the nature of Gorky's influence upon Soviet literary culture.

22 _____. "Novye knigi o M. Gor'kom (1955-1957)" [New books on M. Gorky (1955-1957)]. Russkaia literatura 1, no. 1:250-59.

Review of Soviet Gorky criticism. During a meeting in Moscow in 1954, postwar works on Gorky were generally criticized for their schematic, simplistic quality, primitive approach to sociological questions, lack of concern for the literary process and Gorky's place in it. Gorky criticism of the late 1950s has suffered from some of the same problems. Criticizes Ovcharenko's book On the Positive Hero in Gorky's Work (1956.11) for its simplistic discussion of the positive hero in Gorky's work and its lack of insight into the impact of this hero on Soviet literature.

23 NAUMOV, E. M. Gor'kii v bor'be za ideinost' i masterstvo sovetskikh pisatelei [M. Gorky in the struggle for ideational correctness and literary mastery of Soviet writers]. Moscow: Goslitizdat, 407 pp.
    Analyzes Gorky's role in the creation of a "Soviet literature," from his "mistaken" activities of 1917-18 to the first congress of the Writers' Union in 1934. Describes Gorky's role in establishment of socialist realism. Gorky is pictured as the "true son of his people, friend of Lenin, leading fighter for the realization of the ideas of the Communist Party."

24 NEDELJKOVIC, DRAGAN. "Réponse caractéristique de Romain Rolland à une autocritique de Maxime Gorki." Bulletin de la Faculté des lettres de Strasbourg, 36, no. 7:365-75.
    About one stage of the Gorky-Rolland friendship which illuminates Gorky's intellectual character. Discussion of Flaubert.

25 NILSSON, NILS ÅKE. "Strindberg, Gorky, and Blok." Scando-Slavica 4:23-42.
    Analyzes the impression made by Strindberg's personality on Gorky and Blok. Gorky liked Strindberg as a rebel and as a "kindred being."

26 PERIUS, ZH. (J. Pérus). "M. Gor'kii i R. Rolland ob Anatole Franse" [M. Gorky and R. Rolland on Anatole France]. Russkaia literatura 1, no. 3:173-81.
    Gorky's article "On Anatole France" (1922) helped revive France's faded popularity.

27 PÉRUS, JEAN. "Maxime Gorkij dans la littérature française." Revue des études slaves 34:109-11.
    Gorky's influence on French literature is still an unstudied question.

28 PLEKHANOV, G.V. "Tri pis'ma G.B. Plekhanova k A.M. Gor'komu" [Three letters of Plekhanov to Gorky]. In Literatura i estetika [Literature and aesthetics]. Vol. 2. Moscow: GIKhL, pp. 516-18.
    Correspondence from 1911 to 1913. Comments on The Life of Matvei Kozhemiakin.

29 PUSHKAREV, V.A. "Illiustratsii B.A. Dekhtereva k proizvedeniiam A.M. Gor'kogo" [B.A. Dekhterev's illustrations of Gorky's works]. In Idei i obrazy khudozhestvennoi literatury [Ideas and images in literature]. Uchenye zapiski, no. 35. Edited by A.S. Miasnikov et al. Moscow: Akademiia obshchestvennykh nauk, pp. 242-71.
    Illustrating Gorky's works has been a kind of training in realism for many Soviet artists, for example, Kukryniksov, D. Shmarinov, B. Dekhterev, and others.

30 SCOTT-JAMES, R.A. "A Great Hater." New Republic 138 (26 May):18-20.
   Review of The Letters of Gorky and Andreev. Compares Gorky with other "greater haters," Swift and Nietzsche. Finds that Gorky after 1905 "admired" nothing and thus was the "perfect" hater. Gorky later "ceased to be human because he gave himself up to that sort of hatred and cult of cruelty which has been one of the marks of Russian communism."

31 SHCHERBINA, V. "Problemy izucheniia tvorchestva M. Gor'kogo" [Problems in the study of Gorky's work]. In Tvorchestvo M. Gor'kogo i voprosy sotsialisticheskogo realizma. Moscow: ANSSSR, pp. 452-501.
   See 1958.19. An overview of Gorky studies.

32 SHEGALOW, NIKOLAI. "Maxim Gorkis Briefwechsel mit ausländischen Schriftstellern." Sowjetliteratur, no. 3: 98-111.
   Discusses Gorky's correspondence with Romain Rolland, Henri Barbusse, Stefan Zweig, George Bernard Shaw, H.G. Wells. Shows Gorky as a literary leader of world-class proportions.

33 SHUB, D.K. "Maksim Gor'kii i kommunisticheskaia diktatura" [Gorky and the Communist dictatorship]. Mosty (Munich) 1: 239-52.
   Argues that Gorky stood up for creative freedom of each person against any concept of "party loyalty" [partiinost'] and against the "dictatorship of party bureaucrat over literature." Discusses Stalin's attempts to get Gorky to write a sketch in praise of him. Discusses how his works have been abridged and "edited" for The Collected Works.

34 SHUMSKII, A.M. "Tema sotsialisticheskogo stroitel'stva v publitsistike M. Gor'kogo" [The theme of building socialism in Gorky's publicistic work]. In Tvorchestvo M. Gor'kogo i voprosy sotsialisticheskogo realizma. Moscow: ANSSSR, pp. 175-215.
   See 1958.19. Argues that Gorky in the Soviet period upheld the principle of art as propaganda: the major purpose of art is to propagandize the "historic advances of the USSR." Uses material from late 1920s and early 1930s.

35 SINIAVSKII, A.D. "O khudozhestvennoi strukture romana Zhizn' Klima Samgina" [On the artistic structure of the novel, The Life of Klim Samgin]. In Tvorchestvo M. Gor'kogo i voprosy sotsialisticheskogo realizma. Moscow: ANSSSR, pp. 132-74.
   See 1958.19. Finds coherence in the composition, plot, and imagery of Gorky's last novel-epic. The logic of the novel's structure is based on socialist-realist principles of the author: historicism of thought, depiction of life in its gradual movement toward socialism, the affirmation of the people as the creator of

history, Communist Party loyalty. The grouping of characters is built around a mirror principle, with Klim Samgin at the center.

36 SLONIM, M.L. "Gorky and Russian Prose before 1917." In Outline of Russian Literature. Oxford: Oxford University Press, pp. 192-204.

Reinforces the legend of Gorky as impoverished "proletarian." Gives an inaccurate biographical survey. Finds Gorky's appointed place in Russian literature unmerited.

37 TAGER, E.B. "Tvorchestvo M. Gor'kogo sovetskoi epokhi" [Gorky's creative work in the Soviet era]. In Russkaia sovetskaia literatura [Russian Soviet literature]. Edited by L.I. Timofeev and A.G. Dement'ev. Moscow: Gos. uch.-ped. izd-vo., pp. 78-138.

Repeats the clichés about Gorky: he is the founder of socialist realism; he is the mentor of Soviet writers. Discusses Luka in The Lower Depths [Na dne] as Gorky's "enemy"; Nil in The Petit Bourgeois [Meshchane] as Gorky's new hero; Mother [Mat'] as the "poem" about the "birth of a revolutionary party." Devotes sections to his memoirs, The Artamonov Business [Delo Artamonovykh], The Life of Klim Samgin, and his dramas.

38 _____. "Problema eposa v tvorchestve M. Gor'kogo" [The problem of the epic in Gorky's work]. In Tvorchestvo M. Gor'kogo i voprosy sotsialisticheskogo realizma. Moscow: ANSSSR, pp. 100-131.

See 1958.19. Studies Gorky's concept of epic literature and his attempts to create an epic hero: in Mother [Mat'] Gorky recreates the people in the image of epic hero.

39 TELESHOV, N. Zapiski pisatelia: Vospominaniia i rasskazy o proshlom [Notes of a writer: Reminiscences and stories of the past]. Moscow: Moskovskii rabochii, pp. 89-111.

These memoirs treat Gorky's participation in Teleshov's Moscow literary circle Sreda. Information on Znanie almanacs. Description of earliest readings and première of The Lower Depths [Na dne].

40 TIMOFEEV, L.I. "K voprosu o gor'kovskikh traditsiiakh v russkoi sovetskoi literature" [On the question of Gorkian traditions in Russian Soviet literature]. In Tvorchestvo M. Gor'kogo i voprosy sotsialisticheskogo realizma. Moscow: ANSSSR, pp. 216-53.

See 1958.19. Sees Gorky's influence in the creation of new socioaesthetic values.

41 VERRET, GUY. "Maxime Gorkij et Alexis Tolstoj à la crisée des chemins." Revue des études slaves 34:144-50.

Sees in Gorky's and A. Tolstoy's unexpected friendship a prism for studying Russian literary culture in the early 1920s.

42 V.I. Lenin i A.M. Gor'kii: Pis'ma, vospominaniia, dokumenty [V.I. Lenin and A.M. Gorky: Letters, reminiscences, documents]. Edited by B.A. Bialik, S.S. Zimina, and N.I. Krutikova. Moscow: ANSSSR, 431 pp.

Contains correspondence between Lenin and Gorky. Also includes material in which one man writes about the other. Includes memoirs of N.K. Krupskaia, M. Ul'ianova, M. Andreeva, E.P. Peshkova, among others. See 1909.3.

43 VOGT, HELGER. "Die zeitgenössische deutsche Literaturkritik zum Frühwerk Maxim Gorkis." Zeitschrift für Slawistik 3, no. 2-4:590-619.

Discusses Gorky's early reception in Germany.

44 Voprosy literatury, no. 3.

Devoted to Gorky's ninetieth anniversary. Contains the following articles and materials:
  1. N. Zhegalov, "Samginshchina i dekadans" [Samginism and decadence]. See 1958.49.
  2. B. Mikhailovskii, "Gor'kii i Ibsen" [Gorky and Ibsen].
  3. I. Ziuzenkov et al., "Maksim Gor'kii--komissar tipografii 'Kopeika'" [Maksim Gorky as the commissar of the typography "Kopeck"].
  4. Z. Karasik, ed., "A.M. Gor'kii v perepiske sovremennikov (1895-1916)" [A.M. Gorky in the correspondence of contemporaries (1895-1916)]. See 1958.9.

45 YERSHOV, PETER, ed. Introduction to Letters of Gorky and Andreev, 1899-1912. New York: Columbia University Press, 1957; London: Routledge & Kegan Paul, pp. 3-13.

These letters reflect the development of two streams of literary, social, political taste in the period before the Revolution.

46 _____. Letters of Gorky and Andreev, 1899-1912. New York: Columbia University Press, 1957; London: Routledge & Kegan Paul, 200 pp.

English translation of the correspondence.

47 ZAVALISHIN, V. "Gorki and the Realists: Maxim Gorki." Early Soviet Writers. New York: Praeger, pp. 61-63.

Enumerates Gorky's postrevolutionary works.

48 ZELINSKII, K.L. "M. Gor'kii i razvitie sotsialisticheskogo realizma v literaturakh narodov SSSR" [Gorky and the development of socialist realism in national literatures of the USSR]. In Tvorchestvo M. Gor'kogo i voprosy sotsialisticheskogo realizma. Moscow: ANSSSR, pp. 306-70.

See 1958.19. Gorky as educator. He was one of the earliest Russian writers to take an interest in and encourage literary talent among other nationalities.

49   ZHEGALOV, N. "Samginshchina i dekadans" [Samginism and decadence]. <u>Voprosy literatury</u>, no. 3:3-30.
   See 1958.44. Finds Samgin a representative of the "middling intelligentsia," raised with populist values and later faced with the spiritual crisis of decadence.

1959

1   APLETIN, M. IA., ed. <u>Proizvedeniia sovetskikh pisatelei v perevodakh na inostrannye iazyki, 1954-1957</u>. Moscow: Soiuz pisatelei SSSR, Vses. gos. bibl. inostr. lit., pp. 49-68.
   Bibliography. Continuation of 1954.1.

2   BAKSHY, ALEXANDER. "The Theater of Maxim Gorky." In <u>The Lower Depths and Other Plays</u>. New Haven: Yale University Press, pp. vi-xx.
   Sketches Gorky's career as a dramatist. Gives plots of some of the plays.

3   BIALIK, B.A., ed. <u>Gor'kovskie chteniia, 1953-1957</u> [Readings in Gorky, 1953-1957]. Moscow: ANSSSR, 783 pp.
   Contains seven sections:
   Section 1 contains sixty-nine letters to A.N. Tikhonov.
   Section 2 contains Gorky's story "Music" ["Muzyka"] (1910) published in Russian for the first time.
   Section 3 contains the following articles:
     1. V.A. Keldysh, "Ideino-khudozhestvennaia problematika sbornika 'Po Rusi'" [The ideational-artistic problems of the cycle "Around Russia"].
     2. V.S. Barakhov, "Ocherk 'Lev Tolstoi'" [The sketch "Lev Tolstoy"].
     3. N. Vengrov, "A. Blok i M. Gor'kii" [A. Blok and M. Gorky]. See 1959.18.
     4. I.P. Kochetova, "Rabota M. Gor'kogo nad tekstom p'esy <u>Dachniki</u>" [M. Gorky's work on the text of the play <u>Summer Folk</u>].
     5. Z.M. Karasik, "O nezakonchennoi povesti 'Bol'shaia liubov'" [On an unfinished novella, "A Great Love"].
     6. "Il'ia Gruzdev, "M. Gor'kii v Samare" [M. Gorky in Samara].
     7. "A.I. Ovcharenko, "Publitsistika M. Gor'kogo samarskogo perioda" [M. Gorky's publicist work of the Samara period].
   Section 4 contains the following articles on Gorky's reception abroad:
     1. Iu.A. Kozhevnikov, "M. Gor'kii v Rumynii" [M. Gorky in Rumania].
     2. O.K. Rossiianov, "M. Gor'kii i vengerskaia literatura" [M. Gorky and Hungarian literature].
     3. R.N. Krendel', "M. Gor'kii v Bolgarii" [M. Gorky in Bulgaria].

4. Sh.Sh. Bogatyrev, "Pervye postanovki Meshchan na cheshskoi stsene" [First productions of The Petit Bourgeois on the Czech stage].
5. A.Ia. Tararaev, "Sviazi A.M. Gor'kogo s ital'ianskimi pisateliami" [A.M. Gorky's connections with Italian writers].
6. S.Ia. Brodskaia, "Tvorchestvo M. Gor'kogo za rubezhom (Obzor)" [M. Gorky's work abroad (a survey)].

Section 5 reports on meetings devoted to Gorky around the Soviet Union. Lists Gorky museums.

Section 6 contains the following articles:
1. I.M. Kasatkina, "O pometakh A.M. Gor'kogo na knigakh ego lichnoi biblioteki v Gorkakh" [On A.M. Gorky's marginalia in books from his personal library in Gorki].
2. N.A. Zaburdaev, "Avtografy M. Gor'kogo" [M. Gorky's autographs].

Section 7 contains two bibliographies--one of texts published in the Soviet Union, 1951-56 (I.I. Sokolova) and one of texts published abroad (S.Ia. Brodskaia). See 1959.7. Also includes a short summary of Gorky's works and secondary literature published in Ukrainian.

4 BIALIK, B.A., et al., eds. Letopis' zhizni i tvorchestva A.M. Gor'kogo [A chronicle of A.M. Gorky's life and work]. Vol. 3. Moscow: ANSSSR, 767 pp.

Biographical material. Covers the years 1917 to 1929. See 1958.1, 1958.18, 1960.1.

5 BIALIK, B.A. "Dusha, ob"iavshaia soboiu vsiu Rus' [M. Gor'kii o L've Tolstom)" [A soul that embraced all Russia in itself (M. Gorky on Lev Tolstoy)]. Voprosy literatury, no. 11: 117-43.

Sees in the relationship between Tolstoy and Gorky the key to understanding the relationship between realism and socialist realism.

6 BILL, VALENTINE T. The Forgotten Class: The Russian Bourgeoisie from the Earliest Beginnings to 1900. New York: Praeger, pp. 187-201.

Discusses the image of the merchant in The Life of Matvei Kozhemiakin, The Artamonov Business [Delo Artamonovykh], and The Life of Klim Samgin.

7 BRODSKAIA, S.IA. "Publikatsii tekstov M. Gor'kogo za rubezhom" [Foreign publication of M. Gorky's texts]. In Gor'kovskie chteniia. Moscow: ANSSSR, pp. 761-74.

See 1959.3. Contains a list of letters, open letters, inscriptions published outside Russia from 1905 to 1933.

8 DESNITSKII, V. A.M. Gor'kii: Ocherki zhizni i tvorchestva [Gorky: Sketches of his life and work]. Moscow: GIKhL.

Contains memoirs from acquaintances in Nizhny Novgorod, the revolution of 1905, and on Capri. Also has literary-critical articles on Gorky and Leonid Andreev, Mother [Mat'], the autobiography. Gorky is pictured here as a "proletarian writer" who is hostile to parliamentary democracy.

9   GIUSTI, W. "Massimo Gor'kij e l'Italia." Annali, Sezione slava, Istituto universitario orientale (Naples) 2:71-120.
    Recounts Gorky's impressions of Italy before the Revolution of 1917. Includes background on the image of Italy in nineteenth-century Russian literature.

10 GOR'KII, A.M. Pis'ma k pisateliam i I.P. Ladyzhnikovu [Letters to writers and I.P. Ladyzhnikov]. Edited by V.P. Matreenko. Arkhiv A.M. Gor'kogo, vol. 7. Moscow: Khud. lit., 382 pp.
    Correspondence. Includes 160 letters to writers and editors, among others, V.A. Posse, V.V. Veresaev, N.D. Teleshov, I.D. Belousov, Sholom Aleikhem, A.S. Serafimovich, S.A. Naidenov, L.A. Nikiforova, S.G. Skitalets, A.I. Kuprin. Has 190 letters to the publisher, I.P. Ladyzhnikov.

11 IUZOVSKII, IU. Maksim Gor'kii i ego dramaturgiia [Maksim Gorky and his dramatic work]. Moscow: Iskusstvo, 779 pp.
    Studies aesthetic and stylistic structures in Gorky's plays. Three parts: the first is a discussion of the "key idea" of the liberation of labor in Gorky's plays; the second gives a historical overview comparing Gorky's drama with Chekhov's, the "Znanie" writers, the modernists, especially Blok, Sologub, Western dramatists, Ibsen and Hauptmann; the third part analyzes Gorky's place in the history of Russian drama.

12 KASTORSKII, S.V., ed. Iz istorii russkikh literaturnykh otnoshenii XVIII-XX vekov [From the history of Russian literary relations from the 18th to the 20th century]. Moscow and Leningrad: ANSSSR.
    Dedicated to V.A. Desnitsky on his death. Contains the following articles:
    1. K.D. Muratova, "M. Gor'kii i sovetskii teatr (1918-1921 gody)" [Gorky and Soviet theater (1918-1921)].
    2. S.S. Danilova, "Gor'kii na natsional'noi stsene" [Gorky on the national stage].
    3. I.A. Gruzdev, "Zametki o Gor'kom" [Remarks on Gorky].
    4. I.A. Alekseev, "Literaturnyi fond i Gor'kii" [The literary fund and Gorky].

13 NORĒS, DOMINIQUES. "Le Petits bourgeois de Gorki." Les lettres nouvelles (Paris), no. 26 (21 October):19-21.
    Gorky's play, The Petit Bourgeois [Meshchane], is being restaged only because of a popular "samovar mystique."

14 REMPEL, MARGARETA. "L. Tolstoi, G. Hauptmann and M. Gorky, a Comparative Study." Ph.D. diss., State University of Iowa, 186 pp.

Compares Tolstoy's, Gorky's, and Hauptmann's views on social, sexual, and religious issues. Argues that all three helped shape the modern perception of these issues.

15   RÜHLE, I. "Maxim Gorkis letztes Wort." Monat 11, no. 125:70-78.
     The Life of Klim Samgin [Zhizn' Klima Samgina] is "one of the great works of our century," a key to understanding modern Russia. Not meant to be a traditional "well-structured" novel but a chronicle of events of the forty years before the Revolution.

16   SALGALLER, EMANUEL. "Gorky's Letters to Piatnitsky--A Sidelight on His Attitude toward Leonid Andreev." American Slavic and East European Review 18, no. 4:579-89.
     Analyzes the political and aesthetic reasons for Gorky and Andreev's estrangement.

17   SMIRNOV, S.V. M. Gor'kii i zhurnalistika kontsa XIX-nachala XX vv [M. Gorky and journalism of the late 19th-early 20th centuries]. Leningrad: Izd. LGU, 185 pp.
     Covers Gorky's publicistic work and his work on various journals and newspapers from 1895 to 1907. Uses Gorky's activities as an approach to discussing larger ideological debates of the period. Deals with Gorky's participation on Volga papers (Volzhskii vestnik, Samarskaia gazeta), the "liberal" press, Gorky's relation to Severnyi vestnik, the Social Democratic press, satiric journals from 1905 to 1906, and Krasnoe znamia. Draws particular attention to Gorky's "struggle" with the reactionary press.

18   VENGROV, N. "A. Blok i M. Gor'kii" [A. Blok and M. Gorky]. Gor'kovskie chteniia, 1953-1957 [Readings in Gorky, 1953-1957]. Moscow: ANSSSR, pp. 200-261.
     See 1959.3. Claims that Blok's view of Gorky as a truly "great writer of his people" had an impact on his own reassessment of the goals of art in the years after 1905. Blok's attitude to the people and the native language and his view of the artist were both affected by his reading of Gorky. Notes Gorky's strong interest in Blok.

19   ZWEIG, STEFAN. "Maxim Gorky." Introduction to Selected Short Stories. New York: Frederick Ungar, pp. 1-8.
     Reprinted from the Virginia Quarterly Review, 1929. Gorky as Russian writer. Nineteenth-century Russian writers worshiped "the people," but Gorky actually spoke for them. In him the masses found their first voice.

1960

1   BIALIK, B.A., et al., eds. Letopis' zhizni i tvorchestva A.M. Gor'kogo [A chronicle of A.M. Gorky's life and work]. Vol. 4. Moscow: ANSSSR, 723 pp.
     See 1958.1, 18; 1959.4. Includes an index for all volumes.

2   BIALIK, BORIS. "On ne tue pas une âme ressuscitée." Europe 38:31-39.
    See 1960.7. Discusses Mother [Mat'] as a treatment of the "evolution of human conscience."

3   BLOCH, JEAN-RICHARD. "Gorki et la responsabilité de l'écrivain." Europe 38:199-204.
    See 1960.7. A speech given at the Congress of the Writers' Union, 29 June 1946. Gorky as model of politically engaged writer. Talks about the social-political responsibilities of a writer to "fight" for "democracy" and "peace."

4   ____. "Image de Gorki." Europe 38:7-13.
    See 1960.7. Memoir from a meeting with Gorky in Moscow, 1934.

5   BOCHAROV, S.G. "Psikhologicheskoe raskrytie kharaktera v russkoi klassicheskoi literature i tvorchestvo Gor'kogo" [The psychological development of character in Russian classical literature and Gorky's work]. In Sotsialisticheskii realizm i klassicheskoe nasledie [Socialist realism and the classical heritage]. Edited by N.K. Gei and Ia.E. El'sberg. Moscow: GIKhL, pp. 89-210.
    Analyzes modes of characterization in two different periods of the realist tradition. Concentrates on Tolstoy and Gorky as major representatives of their respective epochs and analyzes what Gorky inherited from Tolstoy.

6   DUN, A. "M. Gor'kii i Skitalets" [Gorky and Skitalets]. Russkaia literatura 3:166-69.
    Gorky as influence. The poet Skitalets (S.G. Petrov) was encouraged through his friendship with Gorky around 1900 to emphasize a "revolutionary mood" in his poetry.

7   Europe: Revue mensuelle 38, no. 370-371 (February-March).
    This issue is devoted to Gorky:
    1. Pierre Abraham, "Conjonction."
    2. Jean-Richard Bloch, "Image de Gorki." See 1960.4.
    3. Romain Rolland, "Un séjour chez Gorki." See 1960.25.
    4. Boris Bialik, "On ne tue pas une âme ressuscitée." See 1960.2.
    5. Franz Hellens, "Maxim Gorki à Sorrente." See 1960.13.
    6. Maxime Gorki, "Le groupe des 'Frères Sérapion.'"
    7. Vladimir Pozner, "Sur une lettre inédite de Gorki." See 1960.22.
    8. Lucien Psichari, "Fraternité France-Gorki." See 1960.23.
    9. Pierre Paraf, "Avec Paul Vlassov." See 1960.19.
    10. Pierre Gamarra, "Jeunesse de Gorki." See 1960.9.
    11. Jean-Richard Bloch, "Gorki et la responsabilité de l'écrivain." See 1960.3.
    12. Vladimir Pozner, "Biographie de Gorki." See 1960.21.

8   FARBER, L.M., and KUZ'MICHEV, I.K., eds. M. Gor'kii v nizhegorodskoi gor'kovskoi pechati, 1893-1958 [M. Gorky in the Nizhny Novgorod-Gorky press, 1893-1958]. Gorky: Gor'k. obl. bibl. im. Vl. Lenina, 415 pp.
    Bibliography. Two sections:
    1. Primary texts published in Nizhny Novgorod (Gorky).
    2. Secondary works: letters, materials, reviews, studies published in that region.
    Entries contain brief annotations.

9   GAMARRA, PIERRE. "Jeunesse de Gorki." Europe 38:67-74.
    See 1960.7. Gorky bridged two epochs. One cannot understand the new art of socialist realism without understanding Gorky.

10 GOR'KII, M. Perepiska A.M. Gor'kogo s zarubezhnymi literatorami [A.M. Gorky's correspondence with foreign writers]. Arkhiv A.M. Gor'kogo, vol. 8. Moscow: ANSSSR, 445 pp.
    Contains correspondence with writers largely from Europe but also from Argentina, Brazil, India, China, United States, Japan. Includes correspondence with Stefan Zweig, G.B. Shaw, Herbert Wells, G. Hauptmann, J. Becher, Thomas Mann, A. Seghers, Knut Hamsun, Upton Sinclair, Alexander Kaun (Gorky's first American biographer), R. Rolland, H. Barbusse.

11 GOURFINKEL, NINA. Gorky. London: Evergreen, 191 pp.
    A popular romanticized biography. With photographs.

12 GRUZDEV, IL'IA. Gor'kii. 2d ed. Zhizn' zamechatel'nykh liudei. Moscow: Molodaia gvardiia, 366 pp.
    Biography. First published in 1958. Expanded softened version of 1946 sketch. Gives greatest emphasis to Gorky as a politically engaged writer.

13 HELLENS, FRANZ. "Maxime Gorki à Sorrente." Europe 38:40-44.
    See 1960.7. Memoir. Describes his visit to Gorky in the early 1920s.

13A KASTORSKII, S. Povesti M. Gor'kogo [M. Gorky's novels]. Leningrad: Sovetskii pisatel', 379 pp.
    Treats the novels of the Okurov cycle, The Town of Okurov [Gorodok Okurov] and The Life of Matvei Kozhemiakin [Zhizn' Matveia Kozhemiakina]. Sees them as a new stage in Gorky's development of a realist style.

14 KELDYSH, V.A. "Tip rasskazchika v novellakh i ocherkakh Gor'kogo (k probleme polozhitel'nogo geroia v tvorchestve pisatelia)" [The type of the narrator in Gorky's novellas and sketches (on the problem of the positive hero in the writer's work)]. In O khudozhestvennom masterstve M. Gor'kogo. Moscow: ANSSSR, pp. 72-130.

See 1960.18. Analyzes the nature of the autobiographical hero and the development of Gorky's first-person narrator.

15   LANINA, V.N. "Gruppovye obrazy v romanakh Gor'kogo" [Images of groups in Gorky's novels]. In O khudozhestvennom masterstve M. Gor'kogo. Moscow: ANSSSR, pp. 230-68.
See 1960.18. Analyzes the use of portraits of social groups in Gorky's work and how they influence the development of the idea of masses-as-hero.

16   MARSHAK, SAMUIL. "My Meeting with Gorky." Translated by B. Koten. Atlantic 205 (June):41-44.
Contains one section from the memoirs published in Novyi mir. Recounts Marshak's first acquaintance with Gorky in 1904.

17   MIKHAILOVSKII, B.V. "Iz etiudov o romantizme rannego Gor'kogo" [From studies on the romanticism of the early Gorky]. In O khudozhestvennom masterstve M. Gor'kogo. Moscow: ANSSSR, pp. 5-71.
See 1960.18. Theme of Don Quixote in Gorky's work. Gorky's early heroes often acquire a Quixotic kind of humor because of the perceived incongruity between an ideal world and the actual world. These heroes are unable to realize their dreams because they have no support from the "collective" and are vague and impractical. Discusses "The Siskin and the Woodpecker" ["O chizhe, kotoryi lgal"], "Cursory Notes" ["Beglye zametki"], and "The Mistake" ["Oshibka"].

18   MIKHAILOVSKII, B.V., and TAGER, E.B., eds. O khudozhestvennom masterstve M. Gor'kogo [On the artistic mastery of M. Gorky]. Moscow: ANSSSR, 418 pp.
Contains the following articles:
1. B.V. Mikhailovskii, "Iz etiudov o romantizme rannego Gor'kogo" [From studies on the romanticism of the early Gorky]. See 1960.17.
2. V.A. Keldysh, "Tip rasskazchika v novellakh i ocherkakh Gor'kogo [The type of the narrator in Gorky's novellas and sketches]. See 1960.14.
3. A.D. Siniavskii, "Gor'kii-satirik" [Gorky as satirist]. See 1960.26.
4. B.V. Neiman, "Rech' personazhei v p'esakh Gor'kogo" [The speech of characters in Gorky's plays].
5. V.N. Lanina, "Gruppovye obrazy v romanakh Gor'kogo" [Images of groups in Gorky's novels]. See 1960.15.
6. M.G. Petrova, "Priemy obraznoi kharakteristiki v romane Zhizn' Klima Samgina" [Use of images in characterization in the novel The Life of Klim Samgin].
7. I.A. Reviakina, "O prirode dramaticheskogo konflikta p'esy Dostigaev i drugie" [On the nature of dramatic conflict in the play Dostigaev and Others].
8. A.A. Tarasova, "Rabota Gor'kogo nad tekstami rannikh rasskazov (podgotovka sobraniia sochinenii v izdatel'stve

Kniga 1923-1927 gody)" [Gorky's work on the texts of the early stories (the preparation of the collected works at Kniga publishers, 1923-1927]. See 1960.27.

9. E.B. Tager, "Zhanr literaturnogo portreta v tvorchestve Gor'kogo" [The genre of the literary portrait in Gorky's work].

19 PARAF, PIERRE. "Avec Paul Vlassov." Europe 38:62-67.
    See 1960.7. Remembers what Mother meant to students before World War I.

20 PASCAL, ROY. Design and Truth in Autobiography. Cambridge, Mass.: Harvard University Press, pp. 9-11.
    Argues that Gorky is My Childhood [Detstvo] is describing social realities and the people around him rather than his own inner world.

21 POZNER, VLADIMIR. "Biographie de Gorki." Europe 38:204-8.
    See 1960.7. Brief biography. Gives a chronicle of Gorky's life.

22 _____. "Sur une lettre inédite de Gorki." Europe 38:48-52.
    See 1960.7. Hopes for a full collection of Gorky's correspondence, which in itself is remarkable and extremely interesting. Publishes a letter to an aspiring writer A.N. Novitsky from 1933.

23 PSICHARI, LUCIEN. "Fraternité France--Gorki." Europe 38: 52-62.
    See 1960.7. Anatole France and Gorky shared a belief in universal communal will. Analyzes France and Gorky's relationship.

24 REZNIKOV, L. "Zhizn' Klima Samgina (tekstologichskie zametki)" [The Life of Klim Samgin: Textual notes]. Russkaia literatura 3:186-91.
    A review of the text of The Life of Klim Samgin as it was published in The Collected Works in 30 Volumes.

25 ROLLAND, ROMAIN. "Un séjour chez Gorki." Europe 38:13-30.
    See 1960.7. Excerpts from his diary from 1935.

26 SINIAVSKII, A.D. "Gor'kii-satirik" [Gorky as satirist]. In O khudozhestvennom masterstve M. Gor'kogo. Moscow: ANSSSR, pp. 131-73.
    See 1960.18. Gorky uses satire as a "whip" to awaken and chastise people and to reveal the evils of an "inhuman bourgeois reality." His work provides the first example in world literature of socialist realist satire. Analyzes "About a Certain Poet" ["Ob odnom poete"]; satire from 1905-6, especially "And Still More on the Devil" ["I esche o cherte"], satire from the postrevolutionary period.

1960

27   TARASOVA, A.A. "Rabota Gor'kogo nad tekstami rannikh rasskazov (podgotovka sobraniia sochinenii v izdatel'stve Kniga, 1923-1927 gody)" [Gorky's work on the texts of the early stories (preparing the collected works at Kniga publishers, 1923-1927)]. In O khudozhestvennom masterstve M. Gor'kogo. Moscow: ANSSSR, pp. 332-74.
   See 1960.18. Gorky's work as editor of his early stories shows the essential shift in his belletristic style.

28   WEIL, IRWIN A. "Four Novels by Maksim Gor'kij." Ph.D. diss., Harvard University.
   Published as a book, 1966.24.

29   _____. "Gor'kij's Relations with the Bolsheviks and Symbolists." Slavic and East European Journal 4:201-19.
   Shows the complexity of Gorky's literary and political consciousness. Asks why Soviet leaders were so tolerant of a writer who was so frequently critical of them.

30   ZELINSKII, KORNELII. "Gor'kii i 'Vsemirnaia literatura'" [Gorky and "World Literature"]. In Na rubezhe dvukh epokh: Literaturnye vstrechi 1917-1920 godov [On the border of two epochs: Literary encounters, 1917-1920]. Moscow: GIKhL, pp. 256-67.
   Deals with Gorky and Lenin's relationship from 1917 to 1920.

1961

1   AKIMOV, IU.L. "M. Gor'kii v vospominaniiakh sovremennikov" [Gorky in the memoirs of contemporaries]. In Stat'i o russkikh pisateliakh [Articles on Russian writers]. Moscow: Goslitizdat, pp. 80-131.
   Reviews Russian memoir literature about Gorky. Involuntarily shows the process of creating the Gorky "legend," and himself contributes to this process by sanctifying everything Gorky did: "Everything that Gorky created in the realm of art is a great contribution to the treasurehouse of culture of the coming communist society. [His work] will always be the pride and glory of a nation which produced such an artist."

2   ARNAUTOVÁ, MAITA. "Předrevoluční dramatická tvorba M. Gorkého a tradice čechovovského dramatu" [M. Gorky's prerevolutionary dramas and the Chekovian tradition]. Československá rusistika 6, no. 3:129-39.
   In Czech. A comparison of Gorky and Chekhov and their treatment of themes of social self, alienation, spiritual bankruptcy.

3   BELIN'KII, E.I. "Zametki ob aforizmakh M. Gor'kogo" [Remarks about M. Gorky's aphorisms]. Uchenye zapiski omskogo pedagogicheskogo instituta (Omsk) 15:76 pp.
    Analyzes Gorky's use of aphorisms in his belles lettres and their influence upon such writers as L. Leonov and V. Gusev. The author notes their close relationship to folk aphorisms and the influence of Schopenhauer's and Nietzsche's aphoristic styles upon Gorky. He analyzes their use in characterization.

4   BERBEROVA, NINA. "Tri goda zhizni M. Gor'kogo, 1922-1925" [Three years of Gorky's life, 1922-1925]. Mosty, no. 8: 262-77.
    Biographical material. Notes with interest the publication of the Chronicle of Gorky's Life (Letopis'; see 1958.1, 18; 1959.4; 1960.1). Criticizes lack of detail at important points: for example, February and October 1917, Gorky's return in 1928, and the years in between. Recommends Khodasevich's memoir in Nekropol' (see 1939.5). Gives all entries concerning Gorky in Khodasevich's notes from 1922 to 1925.

5   BURMISTRENKO, O.I. Iazyk i stil' romana M. Gor'kogo "Mat'" [Language and style of M. Gorky novel Mother]. Kiev: Izd. KGU, 117 pp.
    Analyzes use of folk language, publicistic style, and organizing metaphors in Mother, and how they contribute to the novel's purpose of mass political awakening.

6   EOFF, SHERMAN H. "The Persuasion to Passivity." In The Modern Spanish Novel. New York: New York University Press, pp. 148-85.
    On Foma Gordeev as a novel about metaphysical meaninglessness and paralysis of will. Compares the modern Spanish writer Pio Baroja with Gorky.

7   FARBER, L. "Novye dokumenty o revoliutsionnoi deiatel'nosti M. Gor'kogo" [New documents on Gorky's revolutionary activities]. Russkaia literatura 4, no. 3:164-67.
    Gorky's political activity. Mentions Gorky's efforts at organizing a demonstration in May 1901, in which young radicals and older liberals met.

8   FOMINA, M.I. "Sredstva sozdaniia ironii i satiry v rannikh publitsisticheskikh proizvedeniiakh A.M. Gor'kogo" [Ironic and satiric devices in A.M. Gorky's early publicistic works]. Russkii iazyk v shkole 22:36-42.
    See 1961.23. Gorky creates irony by juxtaposing words and idioms of different stylistic levels.

9   GOR'KII, A.M. V.I. Lenin i A.M. Gor'kii: Pis'ma, vospominaniia, dokumenty [V.I. Lenin and A.M. Gorky: Letters, memoirs, documents]. 2d ed. Edited by N.I. Krutikova et al. Moscow: ANSSSR, 476 pp.

Second edition is expanded. This collection is intended to show "what an enormous role V.I. Lenin played in the creative activity of the progenitor (rodonachal'nik) of proletarian literature." Letters document Lenin's interest in Gorky's ideological growth, how he corrected Gorky's "serious philosophical and political mistakes." This relationship presents a "remarkable example of the power and fruitfulness of party direction which helps a writer to generalize and objectivize reality."

10 GRUZDEV, IL'IA. "Moi vstrechi i perepiska s M. Gor'kim" [My meetings and correspondence with M. Gorky]. Zvezda 38, no. 1:141-84.
    Memoirs of Gorky's most famous Soviet biographer.

11 ILIE, PAUL. "Unamuno, Gorky, and the Cain Myth: Toward a Theory of Personality." Hispanic Review 29, no. 4:310-23.
    Looks at the impact of Gorky's story, "Kain and Artem" on Unamuno's fictional use of the Cain myth, especially on the two works "Abel Sanchez" (1917) and "Artemio, Heautontimoreumenos" (1918). Ilie identifies through the juxtaposition of these works Unamuno's conception of "personality."

12 IUNOVICH, M. A.M. Gor'kii: Propagandist nauki [A.M. Gorky: A propagandist for science]. 2d ed. Moscow: Sovetskii pisatel', 175 pp.
    Gorky the critic and historian worked for "science" in the broad sense of "learning." He made important observations about oral folk culture and folk movements. Discusses Gorky's relationship with the biologist K.A. Timiriazev, his play Children of the Sun [Deti solntsa], and his efforts to use technical and scientific advances as material for literary appropriation.

13 KASTORSKII, S.V. "L. Tolstoi i M. Gor'kii" [L. Tolstoy and M. Gorky]. Russkaia literatura, no. 2:108-20.
    Contrasts Tolstoy and Gorky, in particular with regard to their concepts of the "people." Sees in their relationship a shift in the moral and aesthetic values of all Russian literary culture.

14 _____. "Povest' M. Gor'kogo Delo Artamonovykh" [Gorky's novel The Artamonov Business]. Voprosy sovetskoi literatury, no. 9:7-81.
    Sees the focus of The Artamonov Business on capitalist business and how it affects people's lives, not on the members of the family. Compares it with other Russian and European family chronicles.

15 LESNÁKOVA, SOŇA. Maxim Gorkij v slovenskej kultúre [Maxim Gorky in Slovenian culture]. Bratislava: Vydavatel'stvo Slovenskej Akadémie Vied, 171 pp.
    In Slovenian. Reviews Gorky's reception in Eastern European countries, particularly Poland, Bulgaria, Yugoslavia,

Czechoslovakia. Discusses productions of Gorky's plays in Slovenia. Contains a bibliography of his work translated into Slovenian.

16   MIKHAILOVSKII, B.V. "M. Gor'kii i zapadnoevropeiskaia dramaturgiia kontsa XIX-nachala XX v." [M. Gorky and West European drama of late 19th and early 20th centuries]. In Gor'kii i zarubezhnaia literatura. Moscow: ANSSSR, pp. 5-81.
     See 1961.24. Compares Gorky's drama with works of Ibsen, Shaw, Björnson, Hauptmann, Rolland, Galsworthy in order to illuminate his contribution to world drama.

17   _____. "Roman M. Gor'kogo Troe i literatura XIX-nachala XX v." [Gorky's novel The Three of Them and literature of the 19th and early 20th centuries]. In Gor'kii i zarubezhnaia literatura. Moscow: ANSSSR, pp. 108-76.
     See 1961.24. Looks at Gorky's second novel, The Three of Them [Troe], in the light of nineteenth-century Continental bourgeois literature and in the context of social realities in prerevolutionary Russia.

18   MIKHAILOVSKII, B.V., and TAGER, E.B., eds. Gor'kovskie chteniia, 1958-1959 [Readings in Gorky, 1958-1959]. Moscow: ANSSSR, 451 pp.
     Contains 125 pieces of correspondence between Gorky and Ivan Bunin from 1899 to 1917. Contains the following articles:
     1. B.V. Mikhailovskii, "Roman Foma Gordeev" [The novel Foma Gordeev].
     2. V.N. Lanina, "O postroenii obrazov v pervykh romanakh Gor'kogo" [On the structure of images in Gorky's first novels].
     3. M.G. Petrova, "Sistema obrazov v romane Zhizn' Klima Samgina" [System of images in The Life of Klim Samgin].
     4. N.N. Zhegalov, "Gor'kii v bor'be s filosofskimi i esteticheskimi ideiami dekadansa (roman Zhizn' Klima Samgina)" [Gorky in the fight with the philosophical and aesthetic ideas of decadence (the novel The Life of Klim Samgin)].
     5. I.I. Vainberg, "Literaturnye motivy v romane Zhizn' Klima Samgina" [Literary motifs in the novel The Life of Klim Samgin].
     6. A.Ia. Tararaev, "Rabota Gor'kogo nad tsiklom rasskazov 'Publika'" [Gorky's work on the story cycle, "The Public"].
     7. M.L. Surpin, "Gor'kii i Pavlenko" [Gorky and Pavlenko].
     8. V.B. Levitina, "P'esy Gor'kogo na stsene Malogo teatra" [Gorky's plays on the stage of the Maly Theater].

19   MUCHNIC, HELEN. "The Irrelevancy of Belief: The Iceman and The Lower Depths." In O'Neill and His Plays. Edited by O. Cargill, N.B. Fagin, and W.J. Fisher. New York: New York University Press, pp. 431-42.
     See 1951.11.

20 _____. "Maxim Gorky." In From Gorky to Pasternak. New York: Random House, pp. 29-103.

Reviews Gorky's biography at length. Remarks on his double aesthetic "truth": to transform life and to record his own abundant impressions of the life around him.

21 PÉRUS, JEAN. "A propos de la correspondance étrangère de Gorki." Cahiers du monde russe et soviétique 2:256-61.

Notes a lack of studies devoted to Gorky's place in world literature. Praises K.D. Muratova's work, M. Gor'kii v bor'be za razvitie sovetskoi literatury and efforts of the Gorky Archive to publish his correspondence.

22 PIKSANOV, N.K. "Tolstoi i Gor'kii: Lichnye, ideinye i tvorcheskie vstrechi" [Tolstoy and Gorky: Personal, ideational, and creative meetings]. L.N. Tolstoi: Uchenye zapiski Gor'k. un-ta, no. 56:5-36.

Analyzes Tolstoy and Gorky's relationship in terms of the larger umbrella of Tolstoy's social and philosophical influence in the late nineteenth century. Gives a detailed picture of their personal meetings.

23 Russkii iazyk v shkole 22, no. 3.

This number dedicated to the twenty-fifth anniversary of Gorky's death. Contains:

1. E.M. Galkina-Fedorchuk, "O iazyke i stile A.M. Gor'kogo" [On A.M. Gorky's language and style].
2. Vl.A. Kovalev, "O stile ocherka A.M. Gor'kogo 'V.I. Lenin'" [On the style of A.M. Gorky's sketch "V.I. Lenin"].
3. E.A. Maimin and E.V. Popova, "Iazyk i stil' povesti A.M. Gor'kogo Detstvo" [The language and style of A.M. Gorky's novel Childhood].
4. V.I. Mitrokhina, "K izucheniiu skazki A.M. Gor'kogo 'Simplonskii tunnel'' v VIII klasse" [On studying A.M. Gorky's fable "Simplonsky Tunnel" in the 8th class].
5. M.I. Fomina, "Sredstva sozdaniia ironii i satiry v rannikh publitsisticheskikh proizvedeniiakh A.M. Gor'kogo" [Ironic and satiric devices in A.M. Gorky's early publicistic works]. See 1961.8.
6. V.V. Litvinov, "Nabliudeniia nad iazykom rannei romanticheskoi prozy A.M. Gor'kogo" [Observations on the language of A.M. Gorky's early romantic prose].

24 SAMARIN, R.M., ed. Gor'kii i zarubezhnaia literatura [Gorky and foreign literature]. Moscow: ANSSSR, 276 pp.

Includes the following articles:

1. B.V. Mikhailovskii, "M. Gor'kii i zapadnoevropeiskaia dramaturgiia kontsa XIX-nachala XX v." [M. Gorky and West European drama of late 19th-early 20th centuries]. See 1961.16.
2. G.V. Shatkov, "M. Gor'kii i skandinavskie pisateli" [Gorky and Scandinavian writers]. See 1961.26.

3. B.V. Mikhailovskii, "Roman M. Gor'kogo Troe i literatura XIX-nachala XX v." [Gorky's novel, The Three of Them, and literature of the 19th and early 20th centuries]. See 1961.17.
4. M. Botura, "M. Gor'kii i cheshskaia literatura" [Gorky and Czech literature].
5. A.P. Sarukhanian, "Iz istorii vospriiatiia M. Gor'kogo v Anglii (900-e gody)" [From the history of Gorky's reception in England (1900s)]. See 1961.25.
6. R.I. Khlodovskii, "M. Gor'kii v sovremennoi ital'ianskoi pechati (materialy pressy 1944-1958 gg.)" [Gorky in the contemporary Italian press (materials from 1944 to 1958)].

25 SARUKHANIAN, A.P. "Iz istorii vospriiatiia M. Gor'kogo v Anglii (900-e gody)" [From the history of Gorky's reception in England (1900s)]. In Gor'kii i zarubezhnaia literatura. Moscow: ANSSSR, pp. 218-41.
See 1961.24. Reviews English criticism on Gorky.

26 SHATKOV, G.V. "M. Gor'kii i skandinavskie pisateli" [M. Gorky and Scandinavian writers]. In Gor'kii i zarubezhnaia literatura. Moscow: ANSSSR, pp. 82-107.
See 1961.24. Surveys Gorky's attitudes to Scandinavian folklore and modern Scandinavian literature, and response of young Scandinavian writers to Gorky.

27 SLONIM, MARC. Russian Theater from the Empire to the Soviets. London: Methuen, pp. 136-47, 323-24.
Discusses Gorky as an important representative of sociopolitical, critical realist drama. Minimizes Gorky's importance for the development of the Moscow Art Theater. Considers The Lower Depths and Egor Bulychev to be his best plays.

28 SNOW, C.P. Introduction to Childhood. Translated by M. Wettlin. Revised by J. Coulson. London: Oxford University Press, pp. vii-xii.
Summarizes the Soviet legend of Gorky. Unjustly neglected in the West, he was not as great a writer as Chekhov or Sholokhov, but he was more than just a writer: he was the "epic poet of the Russian poor, just at the point when that poor was going to take history by the scruff of the neck."

29 SOKRUTENKO, JE.JU. "Hor'kyj i Korolenko" [Gorky and Korolenko]. Radjans'ke literaturoznavstvo, no. 3:66-75.
Analyzes how Korolenko and Gorky deal differently with their tramp characters and the theme of the dregs of humanity.

1962

1 BRODSKAIA, S.IA. "Zarubezhnaia kritika o Gor'kom (50-e gody): Obzor" [Foreign Gorky criticism of the 1950s: A survey]. In <u>Gor'kovskie chteniia, 1959-1960</u>. Moscow: ANSSSR, pp. 300-316.
    See 1962.6. Gorky's foreign reception. Claims that Gorky criticism in "people's democracies" is devoted to elucidation of his influence on literary and social views, whereas Gorky criticism in "bourgeois-reactionary" countries aims at distortion and discreditation of the writer.

2 CHUKOVSKII, KORNEI. "Gor'kii." In <u>Sovremenniki: Portrety i etiudy</u> [Contemporaries: Portraits and studies]. Moscow: Molodaia gvardiia, pp. 323-76.
    Reminiscences of Gorky during the civil war.

3 HARE, RICHARD. <u>Maxim Gorky: Romantic Realist and Conservative Revolutionary</u>. London: Oxford University Press, 156 pp.
    Argues with the view of Gorky as the first proletarian writer. Points out the paradoxes and contradictions in his personality and his literary-political activity.

4 HOLTZMAN, FILIA. "A Mission That Failed: Gor'kii in America." <u>SEEJ</u> 6, no. 3:227-35.
    Recounts Gorky's trip to the United States and the scandal over his relationship to Maria Andreeva that made his political mission a failure.

5 JUIN, H. "Le réalisme russe et Maxime Gorki." <u>Critique</u> (Paris) 18, no. 181 (June):509-32.
    Defines Russian nineteenth-century realism and contrasts it with Gorky's "active" realism, which is meant to "transform the world."

6 KELDYSH, V.A., and MIKHAILOVSKII, B.V., eds. <u>Gor'kovskie chteniia, 1959-1960</u> [Readings in Gorky, 1959-1960]. Moscow: ANSSSR, 383 pp.
    Contains the following materials:
    1. Letters of Gorky to Morkis Hillquit.
    2. Manuscript variants of <u>Barbarians</u> [<u>Varvary</u>].
    3. Variants of <u>Barbarians</u>.
    4. Letters of foreign writers on Gorky. See 1962.7.
    5. A rare picture of August Strindberg.
    Contains the following articles:
    1. B.V. Mikhailovskii, "Izobrazhenie proletariata v literature vtoroi poloviny XIX-nachala XX v. (k voprosu o novatorstve Gor'kogo v romane <u>Mat'</u>)" [The depiction of the proletariat in belles lettres from the second half of the 19th century and the beginning of the 20th century (on Gorky's innovations in the novel <u>Mother</u>)]. See 1962.12.

2. E.B. Tager, "O zhanre i stile romana Mat'" [On the genre and style of the novel Mother]. See 1962.19.
3. I.A. Bocharova, "Dve Vassy" [Two Vassas].
4. L.N. Ul'rikh, "Samarkandskie legendy Gor'kogo (legendy o Tamerlane, legenda o Mokaime)" [Gorky's Samarkand legends (legends of Tamerlane, the legend of Mokaim)].
5. A.A. Volkov, "Plodotvornoe vzaimodeistvie (opyt sovetskoi literatury i ego znachenie dlia Gor'kogo)" [Fruitful interaction (the experience of Soviet literature and its meaning for Gorky)].
6. V.A. Maksimova, "Gor'kii o zadachakh sovetskikh dramaturgov (beseda s pisateliami 4 aprelia 1935)" [Gorky on the tasks of Soviet dramatists (his conversation with writers on 4 April 1935)]. See 1962.11.
7. A.A. Tarasova, "Rabota M. Gor'kogo nad tekstom romana Foma Gordeev (Podgotovka sobraniia sochinenii v izdatel'stve Kniga, Berlin, 1923-1927 gg.)" [M. Gorky's work on the text of the novel Foma Gordeev (preparation of the collected works in Kniga press, Berlin, 1923-1927)]. See 1962.20.
8. N.M. Lobikova, "Pomety Gor'kogo na poliakh sochinenii Pushkina" [Gorky's marginalia on works of Pushkin]. See 1962.10.
9. S.Ia. Brodskaia, "Zarubezhnaia kritika o Gor'kom (50-e gody): Obzor" [Foreign Gorky criticism of the 1950s: A survey]. See 1962.1.
10. S.Ia. Brodskaia, "Publikatsiia tekstov A.M. Gor'kogo v SSSR (1957-1958)" [The publication of Gorky's texts in the USSR (1957-1958)].

7 KORITSKAIA, N.F. "Sovremennye zarubezhnye pisateli o Gor'kom" [Contemporary foreign writers on Gorky]. Gor'kovskie chteniia, 1959-1960. Moscow: ANSSSR, pp. 91-119.
See 1962.6. Gorky's reception in developing countries. A collection of correspondence mostly by literary figures from Third World countries.

8 LARIN, B.A., ed. Slovoupotreblenie i stil' M. Gor'kogo [M. Gorky's word usage and style]. Leningrad: Izd. LGU, 148 pp.
Devoted to questions of Gorky's vocabulary and the semantic fields of specific words. Contains the following articles:
1. B.A. Larin, "Osnovnye printsipy Slovaria avtobiograficheskoi trilogii M. Gor'kogo" [The basic principles of the Dictionary of Gorky's autobiographical trilogy].
2. L.S. Kovtun, "O spetsifike slovaria pisatelia" [On the specific character of the writer's vocabulary].
3. Iu.S. Iazikova, "Osnovnye priemy obraznogo slovoupotrebleniia M. Gor'kogo (na materiale povesti V liudiakh)" [The basic devices of Gorky's figurative use of words (on material from the novel My Apprenticeship)].
4. M.B. Borisova, "Stilisticheskoe ispol'zovanie mnogoznachnosti slova v dramaturgii M. Gor'kogo (na materiale

p'es Egor Bulychev i drugie, Dostigaev i drugie, Somov i drugie)" [The stylistic usage of multiple meanings in Gorky's dramatic work (On material from Egor Bulychev, Dostigaev, and Somov and Others)].
    5. I.L. Gorodetskaia, "Ob individual'nom upotreblenii frazeologizmov v avtobiograficheskoi trilogii M. Gor'kogo" [On the individual usage of phraseologisms in Gorky's autobiographical trilogy].
    6. O.I. Rak, "Opyt tekstual'nogo izucheniia sinonimov v iazyke pisatelia (na materiale avtobiograficheskoi trilogii M. Gor'kogo)" [An attempt at textual study of synonyms in the writer's language (on the material of Gorky's autobiographical trilogy)].
    7. A.I. Germanovich, "Mezhdometiia i zvukopodrazhatel'nye slova v stile M. Gor'kogo" [Interjections and onomatopoetic words in Gorky's style].
    8. G.A. Lilich, "O slove seryi v tvorchestve M. Gor'kogo" [On the word gray in Gorky's work].
    9. S.V. Trifonova, "O priamom i obraznom upotreblenii slova goluboi u M. Gor'kogo" [On the direct and figurative use of the word blue in Gorky's work].

9   LEWIS, A. "The Theatre of Socialist Realism: Maxim Gorky." In The Contemporary Theatre. New York: Crown, pp. 111-27.
        On Egor Bulychev. This trilogy of plays (Egor Bulychev and Others, Dostigaev and Others, Somov and Others) is the product of Gorky's maturity and a classic of realist drama. The first of the three about the merchant Bulychev is the best. Shows a self-made man who possesses a social conscience. Lewis provides a definition and discussion of socialist realism.

10 LOBIKOVA, N.M. "Pomety Gor'kogo na poliakh sochinenii Pushkina" [Gorky's marginalia in the works of Pushkin]. In Gor'kovskie chteniia, 1959-1960. Moscow: ANSSSR, pp. 287-299.
        See 1962.6. Discussion of Gorky's efforts to popularize Pushkin.

11 MAKSIMOVA, V.A. "Gor'kii o zadachakh sovetskikh dramaturgov (beseda s pisateliami 4 aprelia 1935g.)" [Gorky on the tasks of Soviet dramatists (his conversation with writers on 4 April 1935)]. In Gor'kovskie chteniia, 1959-1960. Moscow: ANSSSR, pp. 237-54.
        See 1962.6. Gives summary of Gorky's views on theater and his activities in organizing politically active theater in the Soviet Union.

12 MIKHAILOVSKII, B.V. "Izobrazhenie proletariata v literature vtoroi poloviny XIX-nachala XX v. (k voprosu o novatorstve Gor'kogo v romane Mat')" [The depiction of the proletariat in belles lettres from the second half of the 19th century and the beginning of the 20th century (on Gorky's innovations in

the novel Mother)]. In Gor'kovskie chteniia, 1959-1960. Moscow: ANSSSR, pp. 125-56.
See 1962.6. Places the treatment of the proletariat in Mother in the context of earlier treatments of this topic in European and Russian literature. Selects for analysis works by Charles Dickens, George Sand, Emile Zola, Romain Rolland, Upton Sinclair, Serafimovich, Mamin-Sibiriak.

13 MIROWA, E. "Perepiska A.M. Gor'kogo s zarubezhnymi literatorami" [Review of Gorky's correspondence with foreign writers]. Zeitschrift für Slawistik 7, no. 2:309-11.
Review. Emphasizes Gorky's impact on "progressive" German writers.

14 REEVE, F.D. Introduction to Foma Gordeev. Translated by M. Wettlin. New York: Dell, pp. 1-11.
Gorky gave himself a cause by "celebrating himself," his own experience of rising from the dregs of society to the status of writer. He embodied the purpose that the men of the 1860s and 1870s had served: the goal of opportunity and social equality. Discusses Gorky's relations with Tolstoy and Chekhov. Compares him to Galsworthy.

15 SALGALLER, EMANUEL. "Strange Encounter: Rilke and Gorky on Capri." Monatshefte 54, no. 1:11-21.
Rilke's meeting with Gorky brings out his views on socialism, Russia, and two contrasting positions on politics and art.

16 SHUMSKII, A. M. Gor'kii i sovetskii ocherk [M. Gorky and the Soviet sketch]. Moscow: Sovetskii pisatel', 404 pp.
Looks at Gorky's Soviet sketches as a literary-ideological genre in the tradition of Radishchev and others.

17 STRAUKAITE, D. "M. Gor'kii o N.S. Leskove" [M. Gorky on N.S. Leskov]. Literatūra (Vilnius) 4:7-96.
Gorky sees Leskov as one of his precursors. Leskov, in his view, was an excellent narrator.

18 STROKOV, P. Epopeia M. Gor'kogo Zhizn' Klima Samgina [M. Gorky's epic The Life of Klim Samgin]. Moscow: Sovetskii pisatel', 415 pp.
The first full treatment of Gorky's longest work. Deals with the composition of the plot, the principles of characterization, the ideological aspects of the novel such as the exposure of "Samginism" and the image of the people. Sees Gorky's novel as a picture of the "bourgeois-capitalist" epoch, which paved the way for socialism in Russia.

19 TAGER, E.B. "O zhanre i stile romana Mat'" [On the genre and style of the novel Mother]. Gor'kovskie chteniia, 1959-1960. Moscow: ANSSSR, pp. 157-72.

See 1962.6. Analyzes structure of Mother through comparison with Emile Zola's Germinal.

20 TARASOVA, A.A. "Rabota M. Gor'kogo nad tekstom romana Foma Gordeev (Podgotovka sobraniia sochinenii v izdatel'stve Kniga, Berlin, 1923-1927 gg.)" [M. Gorky's work on the text of the novel Foma Gordeev (preparation of the collected works in Kniga press, Berlin, 1923-1927)]. Gor'kovskie chteniia, 1959-1960. Moscow: ANSSSR, pp. 255-86.
See 1962.6. Enumerates changes that Gorky made in his fourth reworking of Foma Gordeev in 1923.

1963

1 ALEKSEEV, K.S. [K. Stanislavskii]. "Production Play for The Lower Depths, a Scene from Act II." In Directors on Directing. Edited by T. Cole and H.K. Chinoy. Indianapolis: Bobbs-Merrill, pp. 281-95.
Contains an excerpt from My Life in Art on preparation for producing The Lower Depths, and a small part of Stanislavsky's prompt book.

2 ALEXANDROVA, VERA. A History of Soviet Literature. Translated by M. Ginsburg. Garden City, N.Y.: Doubleday, pp. 1-8, 125-28.
Argues with the Soviet view of Gorky. Points out where fact departs from the official Soviet story: Untimely Thoughts, relations with proletcult, the question of Gorky's literary influence. Discusses Gorky's attitude to the merchant class.

3 BOWEN, ELIZABETH. "Bowen on Gorki." In Storytellers and Their Art. Edited by G.S. Trask and C. Burkhart. Garden City, N.Y.: Doubleday, pp. 339-42.
Reprint of 1950.2.

4 BRODSKAIA, S. "Maksim Gor'kii v zarubezhnoi kritike (1959-1962)" [Gorky in foreign criticism (1959-1962)]. Voprosy literatury 7, no. 3 (March):187-94.
Foreign research on Gorky, the continuing publication of related memoirs, the production of his plays abroad all show that Gorky is of international importance. Discusses recent publications on Gorky--mostly in Eastern Europe and some in France and Italy. Finds Ilie's article on Gorky and Unamuno (1961.10) "formalist," Richard Hare's book (1962.3) "hostile to Gorky and to Soviet literature." Hare's book is "tendentious," "distortive," "one-sided." Finds Salgaller's article on Gorky and Rilke interesting (1962.15).

5 DUBNOVA-ERLIKH, SOFIIA S. Obshchestvennyi oblik zhurnala Letopis' [The social character of the journal Chronicle]. New

York: Interuniversity project on the history of the Menshevik movement, paper no. 14, 61 pp.
Memoir about Dubnova-Erlikh's work with Gorky's journal Chronicle (1915-17). Finds Chronicle an important voice for major social and political issues of the World War I years. Emphasizes Gorky's efforts to preserve monuments of old culture and to inject a sober mood of reflectiveness and reason into the emotional wartime atmosphere.

6 ERIKSON, E. "The Legend of Maxim Gorky's Youth." In Childhood and Society. New York: W.W. Norton, pp. 359-402.
Analyzes the movie of Gorky's Childhood. Compares the patterns of Gorky's and Hitler's childhood experiences, especially their relations with tyrannical father figures. Sees Gorky as an illustration of a "protestant" frame of mind belatedly emerging in the East.

7 FREY, DANIEL. "La mère: De Gorki à Bertolt Brecht à travers trente ans d'histoire." Etudes de lettres (Lausanne) 4: 125-51.
Gives textual history. Shows Brecht's increasing departure from Gorky's text. Contrasts styles and themes.

8 GOR'KII, A.M. Literaturnoe nasledstvo: Gor'kii i sovetskie pisateli [Literary inheritance: Gorky and Soviet writers]. Vol. 70. Moscow: Nauka, 734 pp.
Contains unpublished correspondence with Soviet writers, among others, Babel, Gladkov, Zoshchenko, Kaverin, Leonov, Pasternak, Pilniak, Platonov, Tynianov, Fedin, Forsh, Sholokhov. Also contains Gorky's response to a variety of stories, novels, and speeches by Soviet writers.

9 KALEPS, BORISS A. Bibliographie Maksim Gorkii, 1868-1936. Heidelberg and Kirchheim: Alfred Wörner, 107 pp.
Bibliography of works by and about Gorky in English, French, German, Italian, Spanish, and Latvian. Organized according to language and critical genre. Contains newspaper references to Gorky's visit to the United States in 1906.

10 KASTORSKII, S.V. Gor'kii-khudozhnik [Gorky the artist]. Moscow and Leningrad: GIKhL, 348 pp.
Deals with The Artamonov Business, My Universities, and the portrait of Tolstoy, as well as with Gorky's ideological development in his early plays and poetry. Shows Gorky's concept of party loyalty (partiinost').

11 _____. Dramaturgiia M. Gor'kogo [M. Gorky's dramatic works]. Moscow and Leningrad: ANSSSR, 171 pp.
Devoted to aesthetic questions about Gorky's dramatic works. Analyzes structures of sociopolitical conflict in plays; contrasts with Chekhov's style.

12 LUNACHARSKII, A.V. "Opyt literaturnoi kharakteristiki Gleba Uspenskogo" [An attempt at a literary sketch of Gleb Uspensky]. In Sobranie sochinenii v 8-i tomakh [Works in 8 volumes]. Vol. 1. Moscow: Khud. lit., pp. 286-89.

Reprinted from 1903.5. Sees Gorky as the representative of a new stage in socially oriented belles lettres. Uspensky focused on the suffering of the masses. Gorky focuses on their spirit of protest, their pride, their sense of honor.

13 OVCHARENKO, A.I. "Gumanizm Gor'kogo i sovremennaia literatura" [Gorky's humanism and contemporary literature]. In Gumanizm i sovremennaia literatura [Humanism and contemporary literature]. Edited by I.I. Anisimov et al. Moscow: ANSSSR, pp. 384-96.

Puts Gorky in the context of the fight between communist humanism (the goal of which is the "flowering of human selfhood [lichnost']") and capitalism (which means survival in the fight of all against all). Gorky stands for "class humanism."

14 SHCHERBINA, V. "Khudozhnik, realizm, vremia (M. Gor'kii i nekotorye problemy sovremennoi literatury)" [Artist, realism, time (Gorky and some problems of contemporary literature)]. Voprosy literatury 7, no. 9 (September):3-22.

Demands for the philosophical and human enrichment of art became apparent at the June 1963 plenary meeting of the Central Committee with the artistic intelligentsia. Gorky is a model who guides our search; in the direct bond of the artist with life in his "struggle for national ideals" for progressive ideas lies the path to innovation and enrichment. Negative lessons that Gorky teaches: "modernism" and "realism" are irreconcilable; subjective individual perception, which distorts an apolitical attitude, is bourgeois and "hostile to man."

15 SHOPTERIANU, V. "Iz istorii vospriiatiia tvorchestva M. Gor'kogo v Rumynii" [From the history of Gorky's reception in Rumania]. Romanoslavica (Bucharest) 9:361-86.

Traces Gorky's literary reception in Rumania from the early twentieth century.

16 VAINBERG, I. "Put' k romanu (zametki o romane Zhizn' Klima Samgina)" [The road to the novel (notes on the novel The Life of Klim Samgin)]. Znamia 38, no. 3:222-41.

Discusses the role of historical "fact" in this "ideological" novel. Discusses Gorky's use of cultural facts, for example, Shaliapin's concerts, poetry readings of Z. Gippius, publication of Artsybashev's novel Sanin, the rise of philosophical idealism.

17 ZHELIABUZHSKAIA, MARIIA [M.F. Andreeva]. Perepiska-vospominaniia-stat'i-dokumenty-vospominaniia o M.F. Andreevoi [Correspondence-memoirs-articles-documents-memoirs of M.F. Andreeva]. Moscow: Iskusstvo.

Contains a great deal of information about all aspects of Gorky's middle and late career.

1964

1   BECHER, JOHANNES R. "Wir müssen von Gorki lernen." Zeitschrift für Slawistik 9, no. 1:14-17.
    Discusses Gorky's significance for "revolutionary writers" in Germany.

2   BIALIK, B., KELDYSH, V.A., and SAMARIN, R.M., eds. Gor'kovskie chteniia, 1961-1963: Dramaturgiia i teatr [Readings in Gorky, 1961-1963: Drama and theater]. Moscow: Nauka, 315 pp.
    Contains Gorky's article "O teatre" and manuscript variants of The Petit Bourgeois [Meshchane]. This volume contains the following articles:
    1. Shio Chitadze, "Iz tsikla statei 'Maksim Gor'kii i ego tvorchestvo'" [From the cycle "Maksim Gorky and His Work"]. See 1964.4.
    2. B.A. Piradov, "M. Gor'kii i Shio Chitadze" [M. Gorky and Shio Chitadze].
    3. L.N. Iokar, "Iz tvorcheskoi istorii p'esy Vragi" [From the creative history of the play Enemies].
    4. R.G. Beislekhem, "Materialy k stsenicheskoi istorii p'esy Vragi" [Materials for a stage history of Enemies].
    5. B.A. Bialik, "Materialy k stsenicheskoi istorii p'esy Somov i drugie" [Materials for a stage history of Somov and Others].
    Several articles are devoted to Gorky and provincial theater:
    1. B.A. Piradov, "M. Gor'kii i gruzinskii teatr (1900-1917)" [M. Gorky and Georgian theater (1900-1917)].
    2. S.V. Pisareva, "P'esy Gor'kogo na stsene Kazanskogo dramaticheskogo teatra (1900-1917)" [Gorky's plays on the stage of the Kazan dramatic theater (1900-1917)].
    3. M.S. Konstantinova, "Pechat' Turkestana o dramaturgii M. Gor'kogo (1901-1907)" [The Turkestani press on M. Gorky's plays (1901-1907)].
    Four articles focus on Gorky's reception in other countries:
    1. Lila Gerrero, "Dramaturgiia Gor'kogo v Argentine" [Gorky's plays in Argentina]. See 1964.9.
    2. N.F. Koritskaia, "O Lile Gerrero" [On Lily Gerrero].
    3. Natal'ia Frederiksen, "Gor'kii v Norvegii" [Gorky in Norway]. See 1964.8.
    4. L. Kim, "Na dne M. Gor'kogo i iaponskii teatr" [M. Gorky's The Lower Depths and Japanese theater]. See 1964.17.
    One article recounts the history of drama in the Znanie group:
    1. B.S. Bugrov, "Dramaturgiia 'Znaniia'" [Znanie plays]. See 1964.3.

Eight articles give new biographical materials:
1. S.A. Golovina, "Portrety A.M. Gor'kogo raboty T.A. Steinlena" [T.A. Steinlen's portraits of Gorky].
2. A.M. Gak, "Iz istorii uchastiia A.M. Gor'kogo v ekspertnoi komissii Narkomvneshtorga v 1919-1921 gg." [From the history of A.M. Gorky's participation in the expert commission of Narkomvneshtorg from 1919 to 1921].
3. L.Z. Korabel'nikova, "Pesnia o burevestnike: Kantata Ia. Veinberga" [The Song of the Stormy Petrel: A cantata by Ia. Veinberg].
4. Iosif Utkin, "O Gor'kom" [On Gorky].
5. N.S. Tuikov, "A.M. Gor'kii v Forose" [A.M. Gorky in Foros].
6. E.G. Balatova, "Materialy k letopisi gor'kovskikh spektaklei (1957-1962)" [Materials for a chronicle of Gorky's plays (1957-1962)].
7. L.M. Farber, "Novye materialy ob A.M. Gor'kom (1896-1903)" [New materials on A.M. Gorky (1896-1903)].
8. A.V. Sigorskii, "Obshchestvennaia deiatel'nost' A.M. Gor'kogo v Nizhnem Novgorode (biobibliograficheskii obzor)" [A.M. Gorky's public activities in Nizhny Novgorod (a biobibliographical survey)].

3   BUGROV, B.S. "Dramaturgiia 'Znaniia'" [Drama of the Znanie group]. In Gor'kovskie chteniia. Moscow: Nauka, pp. 154-88.
    See 1964.2. Traces development of drama in the Znanie group, particularly S. Naidenov's Vaniushin's Children [Deti Vaniushina], Money [Den'gi], Avdotia's Life [Avdot'ina zhizn']; E.M. Chirikov's In the Yard in the Outbuilding [Na dvore vo fligele], Friends of Publicity [Druz'ia glasnosti], After Fame [Za slavoi], Ivan Mironych; L.N. Andreev's To the Stars [K zvezdam]; S. Iushkevich's King Hunger [Korol' Golod]; D. Aizman's The Thornbush [Ternovyi kust].

4   CHITADZE, SHIO. "Iz tsikla statei 'Maksim Gor'kii i ego tvorchestvo'" [From the cycle of articles "Maksim Gorky and his creative work"]. In Gor'kovskie chteniia. Moscow: Nauka, pp. 51-60.
    See 1962.2. First published in the Georgian progressive newspaper Znobis Purtseli [News Sheet] in 1906. Discusses Summer Folk [Dachniki] and Children of the Sun [Deti solntsa]. Hails Gorky's call to rebel against social injustice.

5   CHRISTIAN, R.F. "An Unpublished Letter by Maksim Gorky." SEER 42, no. 98:189-91.
    Contains a letter from Gorky to Galsworthy from 1923.

6   DEMENT'EV, A. "Gor'kii i kniga" [Gorky and the book]. Novyi mir 40, no. 5 (May):218-26.
    Discusses Gorky's contributions to Soviet culture in the area of book publishing.

7   FRANK, VICTOR S. "Maxim Gorky's Correspondence." Survey, no. 53 (October):165-70.
    Review of Literaturnoe nasledstvo, no. 70. Notes lack of mention of Gorky's visit to Solovka labor camp and his role in the volume dedicated to the White Sea-Baltic Canal. Discusses possible reasons for Gorky's political change of heart in the 1930s. Notes a "Nietzschean contempt for man in his present state."

8   FREDERIKSEN, NATAL'IA. "Gor'kii v Norvegii" [Gorky in Norway]. In Gor'kovskie chteniia. Moscow: Nauka, pp. 196-202.
    See 1964.2. Outlines Gorky's reception in the Norwegian press from 1899, production of plays, translation and publication of his works.

9   GERRERO, LILA. "Dramaturgiia Gor'kogo v Argentine: Iz materialov Arkhiva A.M. Gor'kogo" [Gorky's plays in Argentina: From materials in the archive of A.M. Gorky]. In Gor'kovskie chteniia. Moscow: Nauka, pp. 189-94.
    See 1964.2. Summarizes the history of Gorky's reception in Argentina from 1908 onward, focusing particularly on production of his plays in the 1950s. Calls Gorky's work the "banner of all progressive literature in the world."

10 GIFFORD, HENRY. "Gorky and Proletarian Writing." In The Novel in Russia: From Pushkin to Pasternak. New York: Harper & Row, pp. 133-45.
    Analyzes the use of the "elevating lie" in Gorky's work. Discusses "The Siskin and the Woodpecker" ["O chizhe, kotoryi lgal"], early tramp stories, Mother [Mat'], Childhood [Detstvo]. As a writer he is overestimated.

11 GOR'KII, A.M. Gor'kii i nauka: Stat'i, rechi, pis'ma, vospominaniia [Gorky and science: Articles, speeches, letters, memoirs]. Moscow: Nauka, 282 pp.
    Contains articles from the Soviet period. Correspondence includes letters to and from Lenin, K.A. Timiriazev, H.G. Wells.

12 _____. M. Gor'kii i sovetskaia pechat' [M. Gorky and the Soviet Press]. Edited by R.P. Pantaleeva et al. Book 1. Arkhiv A.M. Gor'kogo, vol. 10. Moscow: Nauka, 415 pp.
    Book 1 contains the following correspondence and appendixes:
    1. V.V. Vorovsky with agreements of 1918 and 1919 to establish the press World Literature [Vsemirnaia literatura]; one report of 1923 on the achievements of World Literature.
    2. The printing press Time [Vremia].
    3. V.I. Narbut.
    4. I.I. Ionov and the establishment of Academia.
    5. A.B. Khalatov and the publication of Russian classics in cheap editions; plans for the journal Building Place [Stroika].

6. N.N. Nakorianov.
7. Leningrad writers' press.
8. L.Z. Mekhlis and the book, Two Five-year Plans [Dve piatiletki].
9. A.S. Shcherbakov and children's literature.

13 _____. "Uchit'sia nadobno u masterov (Pis'ma v redaktsiiu Literaturnoi ucheby)" [One must study with the masters (letters to the editor of Literary study)]. Edited by T. Dmitrieva. Voprosy literatury 8, no. 12 (December):88-111.
    Correspondence. Contains twelve letters with advice on organizing and editing a journal for young literary talent in the factories.

14 GRECHNEV, VIACHESLAV IA. Zhanr literaturnogo portreta v tvorchestve M. Gor'kogo [The genre of the literary portrait in M. Gorky's work]. Moscow and Leningrad: Nauka, 132 pp.
    Studies the generic character of Gorky's literary portraits and how they work as a cycle of portraits.

15 IDZIKOWSKI, I. "Zur Aufnahme von Maksim Gorkijs Werk und Persönlichkeit in der Westdeutschen Presse von 1945 bis 1960." Zeitschrift für Slawistik 9, no. 1:23-36.
    Affirms the commitment made by East German writers and publishers to popularize Gorky. Criticizes West German publishers for not producing his works "in proportion to [his] meaning for world literature."

16 KELDYSH, V.A. Problemy dooktiabr'skoi proletarskoi literatury: Gor'kii i russkaia revoliutsionnaia poeziia [Problems of pre-October proletarian literature: Gorky and Russian revolutionary poetry]. Moscow: Nauka, 238 pp.
    Analyzes workers' and artisans' circles in the 1900s and Gorky's ideological development in this period.

17 KIM, L. "Na dne M. Gor'kogo i iaponskii teatr" [M. Gorky's The Lower Depths and Japanese theater]. In Gor'kovskie chteniia. Moscow: Nauka, pp. 203-17.
    See 1964.2. Sees Gorky's play as a touchstone for political taste in Japan. Analyzes its impact upon developments in Japanese theater.

18 LAZAREV, L. "Ozhivshaia istoriia" [History come alive]. Voprosy literatury 8, no. 4 (April):11-31.
    Praises the seventieth volume of Literaturnoe nasledstvo on Gorky and Soviet writers as one of a very few publications that deals in depth with Gorky and the establishment of Soviet literature. Calls for more work on this subject.

19 LUKÁCS, GEORG. "The Human Comedy of Pre-revolutionary Russia." In Studies in European Realism. New York: Grosset & Dunlap, pp. 206-41.

English translation of 1952.2. Written in 1938. Gorky is the "great social historian of pre-revolutionary Russia" who grasped the evolutionary tendencies of his own time. He shows the development of class differentiation and class consciousness.

20 LUNACHARSKII, A.V. Sobranie sochinenii v 8-i tomakh [Works in 8 volumes]. Vol. 2. Moscow: Khud. lit., pp. 7-202.
   Contains sixteen articles on Gorky. Prerevolutionary articles are republished from Soviet editions.
   1. "Dachniki" [Summer Folk].
   2. "Varvary" [Barbarians].
   3. "Gor'kii na Kapri" [Gorky on Capri].
   4. "O khudozhestvennom tvorchestve i o Gor'kom" [On artistic creation and on Gorky].
   5. "V eti dni" [In these days].
   6. "O Gor'kom" [On Gorky].
   7. "Maksim Gor'kii [Maksim Gorky]. A speech at Mossovet, 31 May 1928.
   8. "Maksim Gor'kii: Literaturnoobshchestvennaia kharakteristika" [Maksim Gorky: A literary-social character sketch].
   9. "Pisatel' i politik" [The writer and the politician].
   10. "V zerkale Gor'kogo" [In Gorky's mirror].
   11. "Na zashchite sotsialisticheskoi stroiki" [At the defense of socialist construction].
   12. "Mirovoi pisatel'" [A world-class writer].
   13. "M. Gor'kii--khudozhnik" [M. Gorky--the artist].
   14. "Maksim Gor'kii" [Maksim Gorky]. Preface to the collected works, 1928.
   15. "Gor'kii"--On his fortieth anniversary as a writer.
   16. "Samgin."

21 MATSAI, A. "Vozmozhnyi istochnik pervogo znakomstva Gor'kogo s Shevchenko" [A possible source of Gorky's first acquaintance with Shevchenko]. Russkaia literatura 7, no. 4:189-92.
   Discussion relates to Gorky's literary biography in the early 1880s.

22 MIKHAILOVSKII, B.V. "Gor'kii." In Kratkaia literaturnaia entsiklopediia [Concise literary encyclopedia]. Vol. 2. Moscow: Sovetskaia entsiklopediia, pp. 285-96.
   A concise presentation of the orthodox view of Gorky's biography, literary development, and use in Soviet literary politics.

23 NINOV, A. "Na rubezhe veka (Gor'kii i Bunin, 1899-1902 gody)" [At the turn of the century (Gorky and Bunin, 1899-1902)]. Voprosy literatury 8, no. 12 (December):130-47.
   The relationship between Gorky and Bunin left a mark on the work of both writers. Each had his own point of view on the issues, but their common interest in social and aesthetic issues

was the basis for a bond of friendship. Discusses their work in the Marxist journal Zhizn' and the literary circle, Sreda.

24   PERTSOV, V.O. "Maiakovskii i Gor'kii" [Maiakovsky and Gorky]. Izvestiia ANSSSR 23, no. 3:291-304.
    Discusses the hostility between Vladimir Maiakovsky and Gorky.

25   PRITCHETT, V.S. "The Young Gorky." In The Living Novel and Later Appreciations. 2d ed. New York: Random House, pp. 426-33.
    In Gorky's best books, his autobiography and his portraits of Tolstoy and Andreev, he writes in a clean, unsentimental, unmoralistic realist style. Gorky has the energy, tenacity, and incorruptibility of a puritan. Notes the visual quality of Russian literary art and Gorky's, in particular. Gorky was a "life rather than a novelist."

26   REZNIKOV, L.IA. Povest' M. Gor'kogo "Zhizn' Klima Samgina": Problemy zhanra i stilia [M. Gorky's novel The Life of Klim Samgin: Problems of genre and style]. Petrozavodsk: Karel'skoe knizhnoe izd-vo., 532 pp.
    Analyzes the meaning given the word povest' by Gorky and Gorky's generic innovations in The Life of Klim Samgin. Studies the novel in the light of traditions of bildungsroman and historical epic.

27   SOUVARINE, BORIS. "Gorki censuré." Preuves 161:60-61.
    Gorky and Soviet censorship. There are many cases in the thirty-volume collected works (1948-56) in which Gorky's original text has been heavily censored. For example, descriptions of a pogrom and of peasant cruelty have been deleted from "On the Russian Peasant."

28   STAUCHE, I. "Zur Geschichte der Berliner 'Nachtasyl'--Aufführungen." Zeitschrift für Slawistik 9, no. 1:118-21.
    Outlines impact of The Lower Depths [Na dne] on German theater history and social consciousness.

29   TAGER, E.B. Tvorchestvo Gor'kogo sovetskoi epokhi [Gorky's works of the Soviet period]. Moscow: Nauka, 379 pp.
    Sees Gorky as the one writer in whose work the old and new eras were joined. Studies Gorky's later work, from My Universities on.

29A WEIL, IRWIN. "Gorky and Others: Impressions of a Visiting Professor." Survey, no. 51 (April):3-9.
    A spirited and humorous sketch of the atmosphere in Soviet university circles of the early 1960s. Particular emphasis on the gor'kovedy (Gorky specialists).

30   WINKEL, HANS-JÜRGEN, ed. "Unbekannte Briefe von Gogol', Turgenev, Gor'kij und Sienkiewicz." Zeitschrift für slavische Philologie 31, no. 2:261-64.
     Letter to Z.I. Gzhebin from March 1924.

31   ZAMOSHKIN, N.I. "Gor'kii-sozdatel' i redaktor zhurnala Kolkhoznik" [Gorky as founder and editor of the journal the Collective Farmer]. In Sputniki nashei zhizni: Sbornik statei i retsenzii [Fellow travelers of our life: A collection of articles and reviews]. Moscow: Sovetskii pisatel', pp. 171-90.
     Written in 1937. Tells about Gorky's effort to create a journal that would bring to rural areas "real belles lettres" and "truthful" reportage on culture.

32   ZASURSKII, IA.N. "U istokov sotsialisticheskogo realizma v SShA." [At the sources of socialist realism in the U.S.A.]. In Problemy istorii literatury SShA [Problems of literary history of the U.S.A.]. Moscow: Nauka, pp. 347-72.
     Mentions Gorky's impact upon Sherwood Anderson and the critic Randolph Bourne.

1965

1   ANISIMOV, I.I., ed. Iz tvorcheskogo naslediia sovetskikh pisatelei [From the creative legacy of Soviet writers]. In Literaturnoe nasledstvo. Vol. 74. Moscow: Nauka, pp. 53-188.
     Includes the following materials:
     1. The first edition of Counterfeit Money [Fal'shivaia moneta] and a version of "Amateur Show" [Liubitel'skii spektakl'].
     2. Excerpts from early drafts of The Life of Klim Samgin [Zhizn' Klima Samgina].
     3. Gorky's reworking of Vassa Zheleznova.

2   CHEMERISKII, I.A. "Iz istorii klassovoi bor'by v 1921 g. (Vserossiiskii Komitet Pomoshchi Golodaiushchim)" [From the history of class struggle in 1921 (the All-Russian Committee on Aid for the Hungry)]. Istoricheskie zapiski, no. 77: 190-208.
     Gorky's social activity. Discusses his role in the Committee on Aid for the Hungry.

3   CZIKOWSKY, ERWIN. "Zur Reise Maksim Gor'kijs nach Westeuropa und den Vereinigten Staaten von Amerika im Jahre 1906." Wissenschaftliche Zeitschrift der Universität Berlin 14, no. 2:245-51.
     Uses police records to show plans to hinder Gorky's efforts to raise funds for the Bolshevik party.

4   GIROD, MARIANNE. "Maksim Gor'kijs Verhältnis zur
    Weltliteratur, am Beispiel des 'Molodoi chelovek XIX
    stoletiia' in Verbindung mit Zhizn' Klima Samgina."
    Wissenschaftliche Zeitschrift der Universität Berlin 14,
    no. 2:237-43.
        Surveys works that had an impact on The Life of Klim
    Samgin.

5   GOR'KII, A.M. M. Gor'kii i sovetskaia pechat' [M. Gorky and
    the Soviet press]. Edited by A.G. Dement'ev et al. Book 2.
    Arkhiv A.M. Gor'kogo, vol. 10. Moscow: Nauka, 502 pp.
        Book 2 contains materials and correspondence associated
    with the following journals:
        1. Krasnaia nov' [Red Virgin Soil]: A.K. Voronsky, F.F.
    Raskolnikov.
        2. Novyi mir [New World]: V.P. Polonsky.
        3. Ogonek [Little Flame]: E.D. Zozulia.
        4. Nashi dostizheniia [Our Achievements]: the editorial
    board, K.A. Maltsev, N.K. Koltsov, S.B. Uritsky, I.S.
    Shkapa, I.M. Razin, V.T. Bobryshev. With materials on the
    journal.
        5. Za rubezhom [Abroad]: T. Kostrov, A.S. Gurovich, M.E.
    Koltsov, with materials on the journal.
        6. Literaturnaia ucheba [Literary Studies]: A.D.
    Kamegulov, P.I. Chagin, E.S. Dobin, K.Ia. Gorbunov with addi-
    tional materials.
        7. Kolkhoznik [The Collective Farm Worker]: the editorial
    board, V.Ia. Zazubrin, with additional materials, V.M.
    Proskuriakov.

6   ILEK, BOHUSLAV. "Gorkij a Klim Samgin" [Gorky and Klim
    Samgin]. Ceskoslovenská Rusistika 10, no. 3:141-44.
        In Czech. Analyzes how Gorky achieves an "objective" nar-
    rative point of view in The Life of Klim Samgin.

7   IUR'EVA, LIDIIA M. "Maxim Gor'kij und die fortschrittlichen
    deutschen Schriftsteller des XX. Jahrhunderts."
    Wissenschaftliche Zeitschrift der Universität Berlin 14,
    no. 2:217-23.
        Gorky's reception in Germany. Outlines Gorky's impact upon
    "critical realists" J.R. Becher, Gerhart Hauptmann, Thomas Mann,
    Stefan Zweig, Berthold Brecht, Anna Seghers, Heinrich Mann.

8   LEVIN, DAN. Stormy Petrel: The Life and Work of Maxim Gorky.
    New York: Appleton-Century, 332 pp.
        Biography. Presents Gorky's life in its political, social,
    cultural context. Devotes most literary analysis to works less
    frequently discussed in existing criticism, for example, The
    Confession [Ispoved'].

9   _____. "'Stormy Petrel': A Study of Maxim Gorki." Ph.D.
    diss., University of Chicago.
        See 1965.8.

10 Literaturnoe nasledstvo: Gor'kii i Leonid Andreev [Literary inheritance: Gorky and Leonid Andreev]. Vol. 72. Moscow: Nauka, 630 pp.
    Contains:
    1. K.D. Muratova, "Maksim Gor'kii i Leonid Andreev" [Maksim Gorky and Leonid Andreev]. See 1965.14.
    2. Unpublished correspondence of Gorky and Andreev.
    3. Gorky's reminiscence of Andreev.
    4. Gorky's forward to Andreev's novel Sashka Zhegulev.
    5. Material on the two writers from articles by them.
    6. Interviews with Andreev.
    7. Memoirs of other figures.

11 LUKIRSKAIA, K.P., and MORSHCHIKHINA, A.S. Literatura o M. Gor'kom: Bibliografiia, 1955-1960 [Literature on Gorky: Bibliography, 1955-1960]. Edited by K.D. Muratova. Moscow and Leningrad: Nauka, 406 pp.
    Bibliography of Soviet Russian-language works about Gorky and his image in belletristic prose published between 1955 and 1960.

12 MIKHAILOVSKII, B.V. Tvorchestvo M. Gor'kogo i mirovaia literatura [The creative work of M. Gorky and world literature]. Moscow: Nauka, 646 pp.
    Corrects overemphasis by different schools of critics on romantic and realist trends in Gorky's work. Mikhailovsky sees a complex of styles in his works. Cites Hugo, Sand, Shelley as sources of Gorky's romanticism, notes a similarity to Ibsen, argues against influence of Nietzsche. The realist period starts with Foma Gordeev, which treats the emergence of the Russian bourgeoisie.

13 MIKOLAITIS, J. "Gor'kii i Lunacharskii i spory nachala 30-kh godov o putiakh razvitiia sovetskoi dramaturgii" [Gorky and Lunacharsky and the debates at the beginning of the 1930s about the further development of Soviet theater]. Literatūra (Vilnius) 8:60-78.
    Gorky and Lunacharsky were in agreement about the course of future development of socialist theater. Here their views are set out and contrasted with the two other sets of opinion that made up the debate.

14 MURATOVA, KSENIIA D. "Maksim Gor'kii i Leonid Andreev" [Maksim Gorky and Leonid Andreev]. In Literaturnoe nasledstvo. Vol. 72. Moscow: Nauka, pp. 9-60.
    See 1965.10. Speaks of the men's "love-hate" relationship, which revealed a great deal about issues, moods, trends in the period before the Bolshevik Revolution. Discusses in detail the stages of their friendship.

15 "Neopublikovannoe pis'mo M. Gor'kogo" [An unpublished letter of M. Gorky]. Novyi zhurnal 79:285-87.

A letter from the archive of the American journalist I.D. Levin. To a woman, dated 10 June 1922, Berlin. Herbert Hoover's efforts to help with famine in Russia have restored to Russian people a sense of their own humanity. Brings attention to the plight of the intelligentsia.

16   NINOV, A. "Kapriiskie vstrechi (Lenin i Gor'kii v 1908-1910 godakh)" [Capri encounters (Lenin and Gorky from 1908 to 1910)]. <u>Voprosy literatury</u> 9, no. 7:3-26.
   The Capri incident marks an important stage in the development of socialist realism. Discusses the deep impression Lunacharsky's book <u>Religion and Socialism</u> made on Gorky.

17   NOVICH, IOANN SAVEL'EVICH. <u>Khudozhestvennoe zaveshchanie Gor'kogo: "Zhizn' Klima Samgina"</u> [Gorky's artistic testament: <u>The Life of Klim Samgin</u>]. Moscow: Sovetskii pisatel', 538 pp.
   Analyzes major philosophical and intellectual-historical themes treated in Gorky's epic, particularly the intellectual's role in revolution, the relationship of the individual to government and society. Much attention is given to the relationship of historical "reality" of the prerevolutionary period and the image of it in <u>The Life of Klim Samgin</u>.

18   NOVIKOV, V.V. "Rabota Gor'kogo-dramaturga nad slovom" [The work of Gorky the dramatist on the word]. <u>Russkaia literatura</u> 8, no. 2:187-94.
   Analyzes how Gorky uses speech as a device of characterization and typologization.

19   _____. <u>Tvorcheskaia laboratoriia M. Gor'kogo-dramaturga</u> [The creative laboratory of M. Gorky the playwright]. Moscow: Sovetskii pisatel', 528 pp.
   Concentrates on <u>Summer Folk</u> [<u>Dachniki</u>], <u>The Barbarians</u> [<u>Varvary</u>], and <u>Dostigaev and Others</u> [<u>Dostigaev i drugie</u>].

20   OJETTI, FERNANDA. "Gorky a Firenze nel 1907." <u>Osservatore politico letterario</u> 11, no. 12:65-75.
   Biographical material. Ojetti's diary from November 1907.

21   OVCHARENKO, A. <u>Publitsistika M. Gor'kogo</u> [Publicistic writings of M. Gorky]. Moscow: Sovetskii pisatel', 626 pp.
   Covers Gorky's entire career as journalist and publicist. Stresses the positive influence of Lenin and the Communist press. Distorts and simplifies the polemic between <u>Novaia zhizn'</u> and <u>Pravda</u> of 1917 and 1918.

22   _____. <u>Roman-epopeia M. Gor'kogo "Zhizn' Klima Samgina"</u> [M. Gorky's novel-epic <u>The Life of Klim Samgin</u>]. Moscow: Khud. lit., 165 pp.

A popularized interpretation of Gorky's last novel. Compares The Life of Klim Samgin with Dante's Divine Comedy and Goethe's Faust.

23 PACHMUSS, TEMIRA. "Zinaida Gippius as a Literary Critic, with Particular Reference to Maksim Gorky." Canadian Slavonic Papers 7:127-42.
Gorky stands out as the opposite of Gippius in outlook, cultural values, style. Her discussion of him gives a clearer picture of her own metaphysical view.

24 PÉRUS, JEAN. "Gorki et Rolland devant la mort d'A. France." Europe 43, nos. 439-440:242-61.
Deals with Gorky's and Romain Rolland's views of Anatole France shortly before France's death. Shows the view of each person on the issue of philosophical skepticism.

25 SOUVARINE, BORIS. "Gorky, Censorship, and the Jews." Dissent 12, no. 1:83-85.
Notes instances of Soviet censorship of passages comparing Jews favorably with Russians. Sees this censorship as official anti-Semitism.

26 ULAM, ADAM B. The Bolsheviks. New York: Macmillan; London: Collier-Macmillan, pp. 272-73, 449-51, 492-93, 525-28.
Focuses on Gorky's relationship with Lenin.

27 VALENTINOV, N., and VOL'SKII, N.V. "Vstrechi s M. Gor'kim" [Meetings with M. Gorky]. Novyi zhurnal, no. 78:120-39.
Reminiscences about Gorky around the years of the Revolution, his attitude to politics, and his relationships with Lenin and Stalin in the early 1930s. Addresses Gorky's views on Russia and Europe.

28 WEIL, IRWIN. "A Prophet and a Prisoner." Saturday Review 48 (24 July):44-45.
Review of Levin (1965.8). Calls for a reassessment of Gorky: he was not a "mere lackey of the Stalinist régime."

29 ZHEGALOV, NIKOLAI. Roman M. Gor'kogo "Zhizn' Klima Samgina": Osnovnye problemy i obrazy [M. Gor'kii's novel, The Life of Klim Samgin: Basic problems and images]. Moscow: Prosveshchenie, 311 pp.
Devoted to analysis of characterization and psychological development of the novel's hero and heroine. Gives abundance of information about the "history of the bourgeois intelligentsia" of the prerevolutionary period.

30 ZHELTOVA, NINEL' I. M. Gor'kii i izobrazitel'noe iskusstvo [M. Gorky and representational art]. Moscow and Leningrad: Nauka, 121 pp.

Uses portraits and materials from the museum and archives of the Pushkin House in Leningrad. Includes a list of portraits of Gorky as well as black and white reproductions of fourteen sculptures and portraits.

31 _____. "V.V. Stasov o Gor'kom" [V.V. Stasov on Gorky]. Russkaia literatura 8, no. 3:226-34.
Discusses the critic Stasov's acquaintance with Gorky in the early 1900s.

1966

1 AKHUNDOVA, B. "Sputniki 'Materi' (tema proletariata v russkoi proze nachala XX veka)" [Fellow travelers of Mother (the theme of the proletariat in Russian prose of the early 20th century)]. In Gor'kovskie chteniia. Moscow: Nauka, pp. 302-17.
See 1966.23. Discusses image of the worker in several novels and stories by minor authors from the early twentieth century--for example, I. Grivsky, "Zapiski rabochego" ["Notes of a Worker"], F. Postupaev, "Posrednik" ["Mediator"], A. Mashitsky, "V ogne" ["In the Fire"].

2 ASTAF'EV, A. "Zabytyi pisatel' (A.A. Zolotarev)" [A forgotten writer (A.A. Zolotarev)]. In Gor'kovskie chteniia. Moscow: Nauka, pp. 318-44.
See 1966.23. Gives a biographical sketch of Zolotarev and discusses his work in the Znanie almanacs.

3 BABEL', ISAAK. Izbrannoe [Selected writings]. Moscow: Khud. lit., pp. 315-18, 427-28, 431-35.
Contains the following memoirs and letters:
1. "Nachalo" [The beginning] (1937).
2. "M. Gor'kii" (1937).
3. Seven letters to Gorky, 1925-33.

4 GIROD, MARIANNE. "Das Menschenbild Maxim Gorkis." Homo homini homo: Festschrift für Joseph E. Drexel zum 70. Geburtstag. Munich: C.H. Beck, pp. 99-111.
Points out that Gorky's early heroes are not utopian models: rather they are capable of feeling, protest, action. Discusses Satin in The Lower Depths. Contrasts Gorky and Nietzsche.

5 GOR'KII, A.M. Perepiska A.M. Gor'kogo s I.A. Gruzdevym [A.M. Gorky's correspondence with I.A. Gruzdev]. Edited by B.A. Bialik. Arkhiv A.M. Gor'kogo, vol. 11. Moscow: Nauka, 384 pp.
Contains 206 letters plus 3 letters in an appendix. Gruzdev's letters are published here for the first time.

6   GOR'KII, A.M. Pis'ma k E.P. Peshkovoi, 1906-1932 [Letters to E.P. Peshkova, 1906-1932]. Arkhiv A.M. Gor'kogo, vol. 9. Moscow: Khud. lit., 479 pp.
    Correspondence. Includes 415 letters from October 1906 to February 1932. Continuation of volume 5. See 1955.5.

7   IOKAR, L. "Garin-Mikhailovskii i Gor'kii" [Garin-Mikhailovskii and Gorky]. In Gor'kovskie chteniia. Moscow: Nauka, pp. 226-57.
    See 1966.23. Illuminates creative relations between Gorky and Garin. Draws attention to Gorky's literary portrait of Garin.

8   JÜNGER, HARRI. "Maxim Gorkis Klim Samgin: Ein aktuelles Meisterwerk der Weltliteratur." Wissenschaftliche Zeitschrift der Friedrich-Schiller Universität Jena. 15:143-50.
    The Life of Klim Samgin is a "modern" novel; has an innovative structure that permits a broad view of history, deeper insight into the human psyche.

9   KORETSKAIA, I. "Gor'kii i Kuprin" [Gorky and Kuprin]. In Gor'kovskie chteniia. Moscow: Nauka, pp. 119-61.
    See 1966.23. Compares themes of industrialization and capitalism in early works of both authors, particularly Foma Gordeev, "Chelkash" of Gorky and Moloch of Kuprin. Discusses Kuprin's work in the Znanie almanacs, focusing on Gorky's encouragement of Kuprin.

10 LEVIN, F. "Stranitsy proshlogo" [Pages of the past]. Neva, no. 4:182-89.
    Tells about meetings with Gorky and Rolland in 1934.

11 MIERAU, FRITZ. Maxim Gorki. Leipzig: VEB Bibliographisches Institut, 94 pp.
    Popular biography with photographs.

12 MIKHAILOV, O. "'Derevnia' Bunina i M. Gor'kii" [Bunin's "The Country" and M. Gorky]. In Gor'kovskie chteniia. Moscow: Nauka, pp. 34-61.
    See 1966.23. Contrasts Gorky and Bunin socially, politically, and aesthetically. Remarks upon Gorky's high valuation of Bunin's poetry. Concentrates on Bunin's story "The Country," and its relation to works of L.N. Tolstoy and A.P. Chekhov. Compares it to Gorky's treatment of rural themes.

13 MURATOVA, K.D. Vozniknovenie sotsialisticheskogo realizma v russkoi literature [The rise of socialist realism in Russian literature]. Moscow and Leningrad: Nauka, 279 pp.
    Shows Gorky as the founder of the socialist realist school in the years before 1917. Focuses on five stages:

1. Gorky's innovative approach to the literary crisis of the 1890s.
2. The Znanie group.
3. Mother [Mat'] and Enemies [Vragi] as typical exemplars of the new method.
4. Symbolists against Gorky's school.
5. Neorealists and proletarian writers.

14 NAUMOV, E. "Ispytannoe vremenem" [Tested by time]. Neva, no. 7:169-73.

Despite his "mistaken" positions on certain political issues--for example, his argument with Lenin in 1918--Gorky's sense of "aesthetic truth" is right. Against "enslavement to facts."

15 NINOV, A. "M. Gor'kii i I. Bunin na Kapri" [M. Gorky and I. Bunin on Capri]. In Gor'kovskie chteniia. Moscow: Nauka, pp. 62-118.

See 1966.23. Contains rich biographical information about Gorky's life in Italy, 1906-1913.

16 _____. "M. Gor'kii i Letopis'" [Gorky and Chronicle]. Neva, no. 1:176-81.

Discusses Gorky's activity as editor of the journal Letopis' in 1916. Sees his work in the Nekrasovian tradition of "democratic," antitsarist, antiwar journalism. Mentions Gorky's work with Bunin, Babel, and the biologist Kliment Timiriazev.

17 "Pasternak-Gor'kii: Z korrespondence." Plamen (Prague) 8, no. 6:52-58.

Contains correspondence between Boris Pasternak and Gorky.

18 PETROVA, M. "V shkole Gor'kogo (o tvorchestve Skital'tsa)" [In Gorky's school (on the creative work of Skitalets)]. In Gor'kovskie chteniia. Moscow: Nauka, pp. 162-225.

See 1966.23. Defines Gorky's literary influence on Skitalets.

19 ROMANOVA, E.S., ed. Proizvedeniia sovetskikh pisatelei v perevodakh na inostrannye iazyki, 1958-1964 [Works by Soviet writers in foreign-language translation, 1958-1964]. Moscow: Kniga, pp. 58-73.

Bibliography. Continuation of 1954.1; 1959.1.

20 SEREBROV, ALEKSANDR [A.N. Tikhonov]. "Rozhdenie 'Cheloveka'" [Birth of "Man"]. In Vremia i liudi: Vospominaniia, 1898-1905 [Time and people: Memoirs, 1898-1905]. Moscow: Moskovskii rabochii, pp. 142-61.

Recounts Gorky's first reading of "Man" ["Chelovek"] and his account of how he came to this "Promethean" myth.

21 SHKAPA, IL'IA. <u>Sem' let s Gor'kim: Vospominaniia</u> [Seven years with Gorky: Memoirs]. Moscow: Sovetskii pisatel', 387 pp.
    Memoirs devoted to Gorky at the end of his life, from 1928 on.

22 SURPIN, M. "O realisticheskoi proze 10-kh godov (M. Gor'kii i S.N. Sergeev-Tsenskii)" [On realist prose of the 1910s (M. Gorky and S.N. Sergeev-Tsensky)]. In <u>Gor'kovskie chteniia</u>. Moscow: Nauka, pp. 258-301.
    See 1966.23. Analyzes relationship of Gorky and Sergeev-Tsensky in 1910s.

23 TAGER, E.B., ed. <u>Gor'kovskie chteniia, 1964-1965: Gor'kii i russkaia literatura nachala XX veka</u> [Readings in Gorky, 1964-1965: Gorky and Russian literature of the early 20th century]. Moscow: Nauka, 399 pp.
    Contains the following materials:
    1. Drafts of the novel <u>The Artamonov Business</u>.
    2. The end of <u>The Artamonov Business</u> in the second redaction.
    Contains the following articles on Gorky's relations with writers from the Sreda group:
    1. O. Mikhailov, "'Derevnia' Bunina i M. Gor'kii" [Bunin's "Country" and M. Gorky]. See 1966.12.
    2. A. Ninov, "M. Gor'kii i I. Bunin na Kapri" [M. Gorky and I. Bunin on Capri]. See 1966.15.
    3. I. Koretskaia, "Gor'kii i Kuprin" [Gorky and Kuprin]. See 1966.9.
    4. M. Petrova, "V shkole Gor'kogo (o tvorchestve Skital'tsa)" [In Gorky's school (on Skitalets's work)]. See 1966.18.
    5. L. Iokar, "Garin-Mikhailovskii i Gor'kii" [Garin-Mikhailovsky and Gorky]. See 1966.7.
    6. M. Surpin, "O realisticheskoi proze 10-kh godov (M. Gor'kii i S.N. Sergeev-Tsenskii)" [On realist prose of the 1910s (M. Gorky and S.N. Sergeev-Tsensky)]. See 1966.22.
    7. B. Akhundova, "Sputniki 'Materi' (tema proletariata v russkoi proze nachala XX veka)" [<u>Mother</u>'s fellow travelers (the theme of the proletariat in Russian prose of the early 20th century)]. See 1966.1.
    8. A. Astaf'ev, "Zabytyi pisatel' (A.A. Zolotarev)" [A forgotten writer (A.A. Zolotarev)]. See 1966.2.
    There are two articles on literary decadence:
    9. V. Chuvakov, "A.S. Serafimovich protiv 'literaturnogo raspada'" [A.S. Serafimovich against "literary decadence"].
    10. I. Vainberg, "Russkoe dekadentstvo i literatura reaktsii na stranitsakh <u>Zhizni Klima Samgina</u>" [Russian decadence and the literature of reaction on the pages of <u>The Life of Klim Samgin</u>]. See 1966.24.
    There are two articles on Gorky's early biography:

11. N. Nemudrov, "Iz Nizhnego v Tiflis" [From Nizhny to Tbilisi].
12. R. Vul', "O date priezda A.M. Gor'kogo v Samaru v 1895 g." [On the date of A.M. Gorky's arrival in Samara in 1895].

24 VAINBERG, I. "Russkoe dekadentstvo i literatura reaktsii na stranitsakh Zhizni Klima Samgina" [Russian decadence and the literature of reaction on the pages of The Life of Klim Samgin. In Gor'kovskie chteniia. Moscow: Nauka, pp. 356-74.
    See 1966.23. Reconstructs a "true" historical picture of Russian literary "decadence" from Gorky's novel. Calls the novel an "artistically conceived sociology of literary tastes."

25 WEIL, IRWIN. Gorky: His Literary Development and Influence on Soviet Intellectual Life. New York: Random House, 238 pp.
    Literary biography. Studies Gorky's art and literary activity in relationship to the social and political environment in which it arose and which it was designed to influence. Adds to the attempt to understand Gorky's precise role in the history of Russian literary life. At the end, compares Gorky with two younger writers, Iury Kazakov and Aleksandr Solzhenitsyn.

26 WILKS, RONALD. Introduction to My Childhood. Harmondsworth: Penguin, pp. 5-12.
    Surveys Gorky's biography, oversimplifies some difficult points, is inaccurate at times. Gorky is compassionate to people even "at their lowest." Compares Gorky's autobiography to Tolstoy's.

1967

1 BERBEROVA, NINA. "Kursiv moi" [The italics are mine]. Novyi zhurnal 87:30-53.
   Memoirs. See 1961.4; 1969.4; 1972.1. Deals with Gorky's life in Europe between 1922, when he lived near Berlin, and 1925, in Italy. Gorky is separated from his "legends," and his personal taste, behavior, manner comes through. Impressions of Gorky's literary taste, his relationships with Bunin, Rolland. Tries to explain why Gorky finally returned to Russia.

2 BIALIK, BORIS. "V.I. Lenin i M. Gor'kii [V.I. Lenin and M. Gorky]. Znamia 37, no. 4 (April):212-31.
   This relationship is important for people who want to understand the principle of "party loyalty" [partiinost'] in literature and what true artistic freedom means. Discusses the variants of Gorky's portrait of Lenin, the question of "God-building," Gorky's God-building work, Confession [Ispoved'], the Novaia zhizn' debacle. Lenin shown as a mentor, a guiding hand.

3 BORRAS, F.M. Maxim Gorky the Writer: An Interpretation. Oxford: Clarendon, 190 pp.

Shows from two standpoints how Gorky's works might appeal to a Soviet reader and to a Western reader. Discusses works by genre.

4   BRODSKAIA, SOFIIA. Publikatsiia tekstov A.M. Gor'kogo v SSSR (1959-1963) [The publication of A.M. Gorky's texts in the USSR (1959-1963)]. Moscow: Nauka, 253 pp.
    Bibliography of correspondence and other documents published from 1959 to 1963. Organized by the year the letter was written.

5   DUKES, A. "Russia: Tolstoi, Gorky and Tchekhov." In Modern Dramatists. New York: Books for Libraries, pp. 181-210.
    Reprinted from 1912 edition. Russian dramatists are unique in questioning "life as an existing fact." The Lower Depths [Na dne] is composed of each person telling his own story and "ignoring the others in a dream-monologue of egoism." The gloom of this play never becomes "monotonous."

6   HINGLEY, RONALD. Russian Writers and Society, 1825-1905. New York and Toronto: McGraw-Hill, pp. 21-22, 175-76, 245-46.
    Mentions Gorky's work as important description of urban sectors of society. His most important pieces are his autobiography and his reminiscences.

7   IDZIKOWSKII, ILSE. "Das Vorbild Gor'kii: Zur Rezeption des Dichters in der Deutschen Demokratischen Republik." In Slawistische Beiträge aus der Deutschen Demokratischen Republik. Edited by H.H. Bielfeldt. Vol. 48. Berlin: Akademie, pp. 121-38.
    Discusses Gorky's "new reception" in Germany since World War II.

8   KESICH, LYDIA W. "Gorky and the Znanie Volumes, 1904-1913." Ph.D. diss., Columbia University, 277 pp.
    DAI 28: 1820A-21A. Argues that Gorky used his Znanie almanacs to challenge populist literary canons and to redefine literature's fresh social function.

9   KOVALEV, V.A. "Leonov i Gor'kii (aspekty sopostavitel'nogo izucheniia)" [Leonov and Gorky (aspects of a comparative analysis)]. Russkaia literatura 10, no. 2:3-24.
    Approaches influence as a mutual interaction. Continuation of earlier work from 1953.

10 KROPOTKIN, PETER. "Maxim Gorky." In Russian Literature. New York: Benjamin Blom, pp. 240-60.
    Reprint from 1905. Gorky's rapid rise to popularity is justified in his "fine analysis of complicated and struggling human feelings." He is a realist who idealizes his characters and believes "we must idealize." Gorky is great at writing short

stories, but bad at novels. Analyzes "The Reader" ["Chitatel'"] as Gorky's confession of faith.

11   MANUKHIN, I.I. "S. Botkin, I. Mechnikov, M. Gor'kii." Novyi zhurnal 86:139-58.
    Memoir. Treats acquaintance with Gorky on Capri, 1913, and in Petrograd, 1920.

12   OLIVA, L. JAY. "Maxim Gorky Discovers America." New York Historical Society Quarterly 51, no. 1:45-60.
    Biographical material. A detailed account of Gorky's visit to America. Discusses how Gorky's sketches have affected the Soviet image of America. Illustrated.

13   PEISAKHOVICH, M. "Velikii roman veka" [The great novel of the century]. Voprosy literatury 11, no. 3 (March):204-13.
    This lengthy review remarks on the rediscovery of Gorky's "novel-epic" The Life of Klim Samgin as the novel of the century. Reviews Novich (1965.17), Zhegalov (1965.29), and mentions several others. Notes that none of these researchers has discussed the impact of Gorky's epic on Soviet and foreign writers. Their analyses not connected enough with the theory of socialist realism.

14   PETROV, S.M. "Literatura romantizma i sotsialisticheskii ideal" [Romantic literature and the socialist ideal]. Vestnik Moskovskogo universiteta 22, no. 2:3-20.
    Traces romantic themes in socialist literature. Devotes pages 15-16 to Gorky.

15   RADÓ, GYÖRGY. Gorkij élete [Gorky's life]. Budapest: Móra.
    A popular biography.

16   SCHRÖDER, RALF. "Maxim Gorki, Thomas Mann und die Überwindung der spätbürgerlichen Romankrise." Weimarer Beiträge, no. 2:246-314; no. 2 (1968):277-342.
    Contrasts the "last bourgeois" Thomas Mann with Gorky. Mann saw Gorky's treatment of the Russian Revolution as a model of renewal. Finds Gorky's and Mann's careers parallel at many points: both started at the same time, both dealt with the bourgeois world in crisis. There is no attempt here to differentiate German and Russian middle classes. The second part deals with the theme of Faust in works of Tolstoy, Dostoevsky, Goethe, and Mann.

17   SEMENOVA, G.P. "G.V. Plekhanov i M. Gor'kii" [G.V. Plekhanov and M. Gorky]. Russkaia literatura 10, no. 3:51-71.
    Discusses Gorky and Plekhanov's relationship after 1906. Focuses on the drama of this period, Mother [Mat'] and Confession [Ispoved'].

18 WOLFE, BERTRAM D. The Bridge and the Abyss: The Troubled Friendship of Maxim Gorky and V.I. Lenin. New York: Praeger, 180 pp.

   An extremely controversial and influential study. Analyzes Gorky's relationship to Lenin. Sees Gorky's relationship to political power as morally ambivalent: he was concerned with the search for justice but wanted to believe in the "salutary lie."

19 ZAMIATIN, EVGENII. "M. Gor'kii" [M. Gorky]. In Litsa [Faces]. N.p.: Mezhdunarodnoe lit. sodruzhestvo, pp. 81-98.
   Memoir. Reprint of 1936.9. Translated: 1970.22.

1968

1 "A.M. Gor'kii i A.K. Vinogradov: Perepiska" [Gorky and A.K. Vinogradov: A correspondence]. Znamia 38, no. 3:174-207.
   Complete correspondence between Gorky and the literary historian Anatoly Vinogradov (1928-1933).

2 ADLING, WILFRIED. "Gorkis Weg zu dramatischer Meisterschaft und das sozialistisch-humanistische Menschenbild." In Theater hier und heute. Edited by Rolf Rohmer et al. Berlin: Henschel, pp. 109-60.
   Gorky's social and aesthetic heritage and his development in conscious interaction with the working movement make him a master of socialist-realist drama. Analyzes Nil [The Petit Bourgeois] and later "proletarian" characters as embodiments of Gorky's "humanism."

3 ALEKSANDROVA, L.P. "M. Gor'kii i voprosy istorizma v literature sotsialisticheskogo realizma" [M. Gorky and questions of historicism in socialist realism]. In Velikii rodonachal'nik sotsialisticheskoi literatury. Kiev: Izd. KGU, pp. 35-43.
   See 1968.125. Differentiates the "critical realist" historical novel with its consideration of past and present from the "socialist realist" historical novel with its emphasis on the future. Considers Mother [Mat'] and The Life of Klim Samgin [Zhizn' Klima Samgina].

4 ALEKSINSKAIA, TAT'IANA. "Iz zapisok russkoi sotsial-demokratki: Na Kapri u Gor'kogo" [From the notes of a Russian Social Democrat: At Gorky's on Capri]. Mosty (Munich), nos. 13-14:352-63.
   Memoir from 1909. Deals with the organization of the school for workers on Capri.

5 Anon. "Maxim Gorky in Indian Languages." Indian Literature 11, no. 1:68-73.
   A selected bibliography of Gorky in translation.

6   "Auswahlbibliographie der monographischen Werke von und über Gorki in deutscher Sprache." Kunst und Literatur 16, no. 3:317-32.
    A selected bibliography of primary and secondary works in German.

7   BALIKA, D.A. "Filosofskie interesy molodogo M. Gor'kogo" [The philosophical interests of the young M. Gorky]. In Gor'kovskii sbornik. Gorky: Volgoviat. knizh. izd-vo, pp. 70-84.
    See 1968.32. Traces the patterns of Gorky's interest in philosophy, particularly his critique of pessimist worldviews and the evolution of his thought toward dialectical materialism.

8   BECHER, JOHANNES R. Die realistisch-zeitgenössische Vervollkommnung des klassischen Ideals." In Mit der Menschheit auf du und du. Edited by R. Schröder. Berlin: Kultur und Fortschritt, pp. 57-63.
    See 1968.102. Written in 1938. Gorky is the model of a national poet. He represents a return to "classical" standards of art, in that he creates works of national character but has raised himself to the level of a "universal," "harmonic" personality.

9   _____. "Die Unteilbarkeit von Leben und Dichtung." In Mit der Menschheit auf du und du. Edited by R. Schröder. Berlin: Kultur und Fortschritt, pp. 63-68.
    See 1968.102. Written in 1936. Memoir of Becher's meetings with Gorky.

10 BIALIK, BORIS. "A Great Epopee." Soviet Literature, no. 3:147-52.
    On The Life of Klim Samgin. Traces its prehistory to the turn of the century. Affirms the worldwide "profound ideological influence" of this chronicle of the "apostasy and spiritual bankruptcy of the bourgeois intelligentsia."

11 _____, ed. Gor'kovskie chteniia: K 100-letiiu so dnia rozhdeniia pisatelia [Readings in Gorky: For the 100th anniversary of the writer's birth]. Moscow: Nauka, 422 pp.
    Contains the following materials:
    1. Gorky's correspondence with A.N. Aleksin.
    2. Gorky's correspondence with L.V. Sredin.
    Contains the following articles:
    1. B.A. Piradov, "Delo No. 31" [Case No. 31]. See 1968.94.
    2. L.M. Farber, "Revoliutsionnoe okruzhenie A.M. Gor'kogo v Nizhnem Novgorode (1901-1904)" [A.M. Gorky's revolutionary environment in Nizhny Novgorod (1901-1904)]. See 1968.38.
    3. V.A. Maksimova, "Leninskaia Iskra i Gor'kii" [Lenin's Iskra and Gorky]. See 1968.68.
    4. E. Dubnova, "M. Gor'kii i teatr V.F. Komissarzhevskoi" [M. Gorky and V.F. Komissarzhevskaia's theater]. See 1968.29.

5. L.N. Iokar, "A.M. Gor'kii i S.A. Tolstaia" [A.M. Gorky and S.A. Tolstaia]. See 1968.53.
6. I.V. Koretskaia, "Gor'kii i Andrei Belyi" [Gorky and Andrei Belyi]. See 1968.59.
7. T. Akhumian, "Istoriia odnogo pis'ma" [The history of a letter].
8. "Istoriia odnoi fotografii--A.M. Gor'kii i F.I. Shaliapin [The history of one photograph--A.M. Gorky and F.I. Shaliapin].
9. V. Zemskov, "Vstrechi M. Gor'kogo i S. Esenina" [Meetings of M. Gorky and S. Esenin]. See 1968.127.
10. R.M. Vul', "Pervoe redaktorstvo A.M. Gor'kogo" [A.M. Gorky's first editorship]. See 1968.126.
11. K.D. Muratova, "M. Gor'kii i zhurnal Sovremennik" [M. Gorky and the journal Sovremennik]. See 1968.79.
12. L.N. Iokar, "Gor'kii v izdatel'stve Academia" [Gorky in the Academia press]. See 1968.54.
13. A. Sigorskii, "A.M. Gor'kii i Nizhegorodskaia gubernskaia uchenaia arkhivnaia komissiia" [A.M. Gorky and the Nizhny Novgorod provincial academic archival commission].
14. G.A. Mendelevich, "Gor'kii i Assotsiatsiia dlia razvitiia i rasprostraneniia polozhitel'nykh nauk" [Gorky and the Association for the Development and Dissemination of the Positive Sciences].
15. A.A. Borisov, "A.M. Gor'kii--organizator pervogo Doma uchenykh" [A.M. Gorky--the organizer of the first Academic house].
16. N.A. Zaburdaev, "Babushka i otets A.M. Gor'kogo" [A.M. Gorky's grandmother and father].
17. M.N. Elizarova, "U istokov tvorchestva M. Gor'kogo" [At the sources of M. Gorky's work].
18. R.G. Beislekhem and R.M. Vul', "Zametki o stranstviiakh Gor'kogo" [Notes on Gorky's wanderings].
19. A.V. Sobolev, "Neizvestnoe pis'mo S.T. Grigor'eva" [An unknown letter of S.T. Grigorev].
20. I.V. Nikitina, "Iu.A. Bolotova i drugie" [Iu.A. Bolotova and others].
21. M.I. Polonskii, "Ego imia na znameni goroda" [His name is on the banner of the city].
22. N.A. Zaburdaev, "Rukopisnyi zhurnal starykh nizhegorodtsev-gor'kovchan" [The manuscript journal of the old citizens of Nizhny Novgorod-Gorky].
23. E. Mirova-Florin, "Maksim Gor'kii v Germanii" [Maksim Gorky in Germany]. See 1968.74.
24. I.V. Koretskaia, "Stat'ia Marselia Kashena o Gor'kom" [Marcel Kashen on Gorky].
25. Marsel' Kashen, "Prizyv Maksima Gor'kogo" [The call of Maksim Gorky].

12 BIALIK, BORIS. "Luka: Un personaje clave para entender el sentido de la obra." Translated by Amaya Lacasa. Primer Acto (Madrid), no. 94:52-53.

See 1968.97. Corrects "mistaken" interpretations of the character Luka in The Lower Depths [Na dne].

13 _____. "Maxim Gorki über Probleme der Literatur." Kunst und Literatur 16, no. 2:171-180.
Gorky versus modernism and the idea that art is independent of life.

14 _____. "Neischerpaemye vozmozhnosti realizma" [Inexhaustible possibilities of realism]. Voprosy literatury 12, no. 3: 36-49.
A counterattack against claims by "bourgeois" critics who do not like Gorky's role in forming socialist realism. Argues against Pablo Neruda who sees the possibility of several avenues of literary development, for example, realist, experimentalist.

15 _____. "Rossiia v 90-e gody" [Russia of the 1890s]. In Russkaia literatura kontsa XIX-nachala XXv.--devianostye gody [Russian literature at the end of the 19th-early 20th century--1890s]. Moscow: Nauka, pp. 45-91.
Sees Gorky as an important socioliterary phenomenon of the 1890s. Puts his development in the perspective of socioeconomic developments of the period.

16 _____. Sud'ba Maksima Gor'kogo [The fate of Maksim Gorky]. Moscow: Khud. lit., 389 pp.
Gorky's personality and personal fate is seen as a "prism" that refracts the central artistic and intellectual movements of the twentieth century. An attempt to draw conclusions based on his lifelong work on Gorky.

17 BOGUSLOVSKII, A.O. "Neissiakaemyi istochnik vdokhnoveniia: Gor'kovskaia kontseptsiia cheloveka i sovremennaia dramaturgiia" [An inexhaustible source of inspiration: Gorky's concept of human nature and contemporary drama]. Voprosy literatury 12, no. 8 (August):23-40.
For Gorky the main criterion for defining the human self [lichnost'] are the ideas of revolution and socialism, and the reality they transform. In each person is a "builder" and a "master." Analyzes The Petit Bourgeois [Meshchane]. Notes Gorky's influence on Brecht, Wolf, and an echo in works of Arthur Miller, Dürrenmatt, Frisch.

18 BORRAS, F.M. Maxim Gorky and Lev Tolstoy. Leeds, England: University of Leeds Press, 19 pp.
Popular lecture. Contrasts Tolstoy and Gorky as social types; analyzes Gorky's rebellion against Tolstoyanism.

19 BRECHT, BERTOLT. "Gorkis Einfluß auf die Literatur." In Mit der Menschheit auf du und du. Edited by R. Schröder. Berlin: Kultur und Fortschritt, pp. 98-99.
See 1968.102. Written around 1936. Gorky is a model who "turned [other] writers into readers."

20 BROD, MAX. "Das Licht des Geistes in ein lichtloses Leben." In Mit der Menschheit auf du und du. Edited by R. Schröder. Berlin: Kultur und Fortschritt, pp. 100-101.
   See 1968.102. Written in 1928. Sketch of Gorky's moral character. His greatest asset as a writer and person is his bravery, his trust, his ability to reveal human goodness.

21 BUENO, SALVADOR. Bibliografia de Maximo Gorki. Havana: Biblioteca Nacional Jose Marti, 24 pp.
   Bibliography. Contains holdings of the Jose Marti National Library on Gorky and information on Gorky and cinema.

22 BURSOV, B.I. "Izbrannik istorii" [The chosen of history]. Neva, no. 6:175-78.
   Gorky is the "friend of all humanity." He is known as a "fervent revolutionary, a resolute, indomitable fighter for freedom." He loves humanity as a heroic creative force: everyone can be a hero.

23 CASALI, RENZO. "Gorki o la ética como presupuesto de creación." Primer Acto (Madrid), no. 93:14-17.
   See 1968.96. Discusses Gorky's concern with morality in The Petit Bourgeois [Meshchane] and The Lower Depths [Na dne].

24 CZIKOWSKY, E., IDZIKOWSKI, I., and SCHWARZ, G. Maxim Gorki in Deutschland: Bibliographie 1899 bis 1965. Berlin: Akademie, 386 pp.
   East German bibliography of primary and secondary works in German, largely in leftist publications. Deals with Gorky's reception in Germany.

25 DARONIAN, S.K. Gor'kii i Armeniia [Gorky in Armenia]. Erevan: MITK, 702 pp.
   Contains letters, articles by Gorky, and memoirs. Includes a letter to A.I. Mikoian, a letter from the memoirist G.M. Tumanov, and Tumanov's reminiscences of Gorky.

26 DAVIES, R. "Gorky: The End of the Beginning." In The Great Books of Russia. Norman: University of Oklahoma Press, pp. 364-92.
   Gorky had "narrative power" although he lacked the "genius" and "artistry" of other Russian writers. His work helped legitimize the proletariat in the mind of the Russian intellectual. Finds his reminiscences and The Life of Klim Samgin to be among his best works.

27 DESNIZKI, W. "Gorki und Majakowski zum gleichen Thema." Kunst und Literatur 16, no. 3:244-53.
   Tells about a writing competition between Gorky and Maiakovsky on the cruel death of a dray horse. Both works appeared in Novaia zhizn' in 1918.

28 _____. "Lenin und Gorki." Kunst und Literatur 16, no. 4: 391-410.
   The friendship of the politician and the artist is "symbolic" of the early struggle of the proletariat for socialism: it "proves" the creative powers of the working class. Tells the usual story. Smooths over the rough spots of 1908-9, 1917-18.

29 DUBNOVA, E. "M. Gor'kii i teatr V.F. Komissarzhevskoi" [M. Gorky and V.F. Komissarzhevskaia's theater]. In Gor'kovskie chteniia. Moscow: Nauka, pp. 152-75.
   See 1968.11. Gives an account of the production of Gorky's plays, Summer Folk [Dachniki] and Children of the Sun [Deti solntsa], in Kommissarzhevskaia's theater in St. Petersburg during the years 1904-6.

30 ELISEEV, A.I., ed. M. Gor'kii v vospominaniiakh nizhegorodtsev [Gorky in the memoirs of people from Nizhny Novgorod]. Gorky: Volgoviat. knizh. izd-vo., 312 pp.
   Contains memoir material on Gorky before 1900.

31 EREMENKO, V. Posle universitetov: M. Gor'kii v Nizhnem Povolzh'e [After the universities: M. Gorky in the lower Volga region]. Volgograd: Nizhne-Volzhskoe knizh. izd-vo., 126 pp.
   Biographical material. Studies Gorky's work on the railway in 1888 and 1889. Finds this an important period in the formation of his political views.

32 ERMAKOV, I.I., et al., eds. Gor'kovskii sbornik [A Gorky collection]. Gorky: Volgo-viat. knizh. izd-vo., 311 pp.
   Contains the following articles:
      1. I.A. Baskevich, "Iz istorii otnoshenii pisatelia i kritika" [From the history of the relationship between writer and critic].
      2. D.T. Chirov, "O partiinosti romana M. Gor'kogo Mat'" [On the idea of party loyalty in M. Gorky's novel Mother].
      3. S.I. Sukhikh, "Spory 20-kh godov o romane i A.M. Gor'kii" [A.M. Gorky and arguments of the 1920s about the novel].
      4. D.A. Balika, "Filosofskie interesy molodogo M. Gor'kogo" [The philosophical interests of the young M. Gorky]. See 1968.7.
      5. A.M. Ladyzhenskii, "Esche raz o 'Makare Chudre' i 'Starukhe Izergil'" [Once more about "Makar Chudra" and "Old Woman Izergil'"].
      6. A.A. Tikhovodov, "Protsess 'vylamyvaniia' v Voskresenii L. Tolstogo i Fome Gordeeve M. Gor'kogo" [The process of breaking off in L. Tolstoy's Resurrection and M. Gorky's Foma Gordeev]. See 1968.117.
      7. E.F. Mishina, "O nekotorykh antonimicheskikh protivopostavleniiakh v rannem tvorchestve M. Gor'kogo" [On certain antonymic juxtapositions in M. Gorky's early work].

8. V.V. Osnovin, "M. Gor'kii i L. Tolstoi" [M. Gorky and L. Tolstoy]. See 1968.85.
9. A.N. Orfanova, "M. Gor'kii o Saltykove-Shchedrine" [M. Gorky on Saltykov-Shchedrin].
10. A.S. Lipovetskii, "M. Gor'kii o P.I. Mel'nikove-Pecherskom" [M. Gorky on Melnikov-Pechersky].
11. M.Ia. Ermakova, "Problema cheloveka v tvorchestve M. Gor'kogo i L. Andreeva" [The problem of human nature in works of M. Gorky and L. Andreev]. See 1968.33.
12. V.V. Smirenskii, "M. Gor'kii i K. Fofanov" [M. Gorky and K. Fofanov].
13. V.V. Kharchev, "M. Gor'kii i A. Grin" [M. Gorky and A. Grin].
14. A.D. Zaidman, "M. Gor'kii i N. Nikitin" [M. Gorky and N. Nikitin].
15. G.M. Parshina, "M. Gor'kii i A. Platonov" [M. Gorky and A. Platonov]. See 1968.89.
16. B.V. Kir'ianov, "D'iakon Ipat'evskii."
17. I.V. Nikitina, "Marina Zotova."
18. T.A. Marakhova, "Iskusstvo vospominanii M. Gor'kogo o zhizni, o liudiakh" [M. Gorky's art of reminiscing about life and people].
19. S.A. Cherviakovskii, "Portretnye kharakteristiki v Fome Gordeeve" [Qualities of portraiture in Foma Gordeev].
20. Z.E. Libinzon, "O gor'kovskom vospriiatii Shillera" [On Gorky's reception of Schiller].
21. Iu.S. Iazikova, "Obrazy i poniatiia religii v povesti Gor'kogo V liudiakh" [Images and concepts of religion in Gorky's novel My Apprenticeship]. See 1968.51.
22. L.L. Trube, "Imia A.M. Gor'kogo na karte strany" [Gorky's name on the national map].
Contains also A.V. Iarovitskii's letters on Gorky, 1899-1903.

33 ERMAKOVA, M.IA. "Problema cheloveka v tvorchestve M. Gor'kogo i L. Andreeva" [The problem of human nature in works of M. Gorky and L. Andreev]. In Gor'kovskii sbornik. Gorky: Volgoviat. knizh. izd-vo., pp. 176-89.
See 1968.32. Juxtaposes Andreev's "Story about Sergei Petrovich" ["Rasskaz o Sergee Petroviche," 1900] and Gorky's "Man" ["Chelovek," 1904]; Andreev's philosophical relativism and Gorky's "historicist" optimism.

34 ERMOLAEV, GERMAN. Review of The Bridge and the Abyss: The Troubled Friendship of Maxim Gorky and V.I. Lenin, by Bertram D. Wolfe. Novyi zhurnal, no. 91:295-98.
Wolfe gives impartial picture of a relationship that has been overidealized by Soviet historians.

35 ERPENBEK, FRITS. "Skhola revoliutsionnykh idei i gumanizma" [The school of revolutionary ideas and humanism]. Voprosy literatury 12, no. 3:95-98.

Legend making. In praise of Gorky and his works in German translation.

36 EVENTOV, I. "Perepiska i vstrechi" [Correspondence and encounters]. Zvezda 45, no. 1:168-72.
About Gorky and Nadezhda Krupskaia.

37 FARBER, LEONID M. A.M. Gor'kii v Nizhnem Novgorode: Ocherk zhizni i tvorchestva, 1889-1904 [Gorky in Nizhny Novgorod: A sketch of his life and work, 1889-1904]. 2d ed. Gorky: Volgo-Viat. knizh. izd-vo., 248 pp.
Biography. Gorky's life in Nizhny was important because the city allowed him to see capitalist exploitation firsthand and because the city was a center of political-economic unrest. Analyzes the social and cultural life of Nizhny in the 1890s.

38 _____. "Revoliutsionnoe okruzhenie A.M. Gor'kogo v Nizhnem Novgorode (1901-1904)" [The revolutionary ambience surrounding M. Gorky in Nizhny Novgorod (1901-1904)]. In Gor'kovskie chteniia. Moscow: Nauka, pp. 99-128.
See 1968.11. Treats Gorky's involvement with student radicals who had been exiled to Nizhny Novgorod for political activities in the two capitals. Discusses Gorky's early political development. Analyzes these radicals as prototypes for Gorky's revolutionary protagonists in works such as Mother [Mat'].

39 FEDIN, KONSTANTIN. Gor'kii sredi nas [Gorky among us]. Moscow: Sovetskii pisatel', 382 pp.
Memoir. Important source for Gorky in the 1920s.

40 FEUCHTWANGER, LION. "Es war das Volk selber, das Stimme bekommen hatte." In Mit der Menschheit auf du und du. Edited by R. Schröder. Berlin: Kultur und Fortschritt, pp. 152-54.
See 1968.102. Written in 1954. Gorky's view of society. He opened to the world the "underworld" of Russian life.

41 FINK, L.A., and IVANOV-PAIMEN, V.Z., eds. Maksim Gor'kii i Samara [Maksim Gorky and Samara]. Kuibyshev: Kuib. knizh. izd-vo., 431 pp.
Contains memoirs, letters, and stories printed in Samara.

42 GANDHI, MAHATMA K. "Maxim Gorky." Indian Literature 11, no. 1:49-50.
A note written in 1905 in Indian Opinion reports on Gorky's participation in social unrest. Says that he is thought of as a "great champion of the people's rights."

43 GEI, N.K. "Gor'kii i russkaia klassika: Khudozhestvennoe osveshchenie meniaiushchegosia mira" [Gorky and Russian classical literature: Artistic illumination of the changing world]. In Slavianskie literatury: Doklady sovetskoi delegatsii [Slavic literatures: Papers of the Soviet delegation]. Sixth

International Conference of Slavists. Moscow: Nauka, pp. 378-99.
Analyzes how a changing conception of "reality" is accommodated in experimentation with new aspects of novelistic form. Uses examples ranging from Gorky's memoirs of Tolstoy to The Life of Klim Samgin [Zhizn' Klima Samgina].

44 GILENSON, B. "Gor'kii i peredovaia amerikanskaia obshchestvennost' v 1918-1921 godakh: Po novym materialam" [Gorky and progressive American social thought, 1918-1921: New materials]. Voprosy literatury 12, no. 6 (June):247-50.
Surveys Gorky's literary and political relations with Americans from 1906 to the 1920s. Mentions John Reed, Upton Sinclair, Isaac McBride.

45 GIN, M.M. "Neizvestnoe pis'mo N.K. Mikhailovskogo o M. Gor'kom" [An unknown letter of N.K. Mikhailovsky on Gorky]. Russkaia literatura 11, no. 3:158-60.
The letter deals with Gorky's arrest in 1898.

46 GOLUBEVA, O.D. "Dva izdatelia (I.D. Sytin i M. Gor'kii)" [Two publishers (I.D. Sytin and M. Gorky)]. In M. Gor'kii i ego sovremenniki. Leningrad: Nauka, pp. 184-95.
See 1968.78. Analyzes Sytin and Gorky as promoters of literature of "writers from the people" [samorodki].

47 GRECHNEV, V. Gor'kii v Peterburge-Leningrade [Gorky in Petersburg-Leningrad]. Leningrad: Lenizdat, 223 pp.
Partial biography. Recounts Gorky's activities in St. Petersburg and his response to the intellectual life of the city in the 1890s, before 1905, and during the Revolution.

48 GRISHIN, DMITRY. "K piatidesiatiletiiu 'Nesvoevremennykh myslei' A.M. Gor'kogo" [On the 50th anniversary of Gorky's Untimely Thoughts]. Melbourne Slavonic Studies 2:13-20.
Sees Untimely Thoughts [Nesvoevremennye mysli] as the key to understanding Gorky's view of the October Revolution and his postrevolutionary literary activity. Analyzes Gorky's reasons for considering socialist revolution "premature."

49 GUSEVA, ZINAIDA A. Svidanie na Kapri [Encounter on Capri]. Moscow: Sovetskaia Rossiia, 220 pp.
Gives fictionalized account of Lenin's trip to visit Gorky on Capri in 1908.

50 HACKETT, FRANCIS. "Night Lodging." In Invisible Censor. Freeport, N.Y.: Books for Libraries, pp. 101-5.
Reprinted from 1921 edition. Review of Arthur Hopkins's production of The Lower Depths [Na dne]. Gorky's play is great. His critics are "mentally inelastic."

51 IAZIKOVA, IU.S. "Obrazy i poniatiia religii v povesti Gor'kogo V liudiakh" [Images and concepts of religion in Gorky's novel My Apprenticeship]. In Gor'kovskii sbornik. Gorky: Volgo-viat. knizh. izd-vo., pp. 289-96.
    See 1968.32. Discusses Gorky's treatment of the role of the church in the aesthetic ennoblement of people. Analyzes religious imagery in My Apprenticeship.

52 IDZIKOWSKI, ILSE. "Maxim Gorki in der DDR und in Westdeutschland." Kunst und Literatur 16, no. 1:3-18.
    Gorky's reception in East Germany. Reaffirms the link between East German literature and the literary tradition of Gorky. The attitude to Gorky is a "touchstone" for one's "humanistic consciousness." In West Germany, Gorky's work has been suppressed despite a desire on the part of readers to know more about him.

53 IOKAR, L.N. "A.M. Gor'kii i S.A. Tolstaia: Pomety na knigakh lichnoi biblioteki Gor'kogo" [A.M. Gorky and S.A. Tolstaia: Remarks in books of Gorky's personal library]. In Gor'kovskie chteniia. Moscow: Nauka, pp. 176-88.
    See 1968.11. Analyzes Gorky's attempt to correct the view of Tolstoy's followers that Tolstoy was a "hero" and his wife, his "tormentor."

54 _____. "Gor'kii v izdatel'stve Academia" [Gorky in the Academia press]. In Gor'kovskie chteniia. Moscow: Nauka, pp. 289-306.
    See 1968.11. Treats Gorky's editorial activity in the 1930s.

55 KELDYSH, V.A., et al., eds. M. Gor'kii i literatury zarubezhnogo vostoka: Sbornik stat'ei [M. Gorky and the literatures of the East: A collection of articles]. Moscow: Nauka, 343 pp.
    Contains the following articles:
    1. K. Rekho, "Nasledie Gor'kogo i iaponskaia literatura" [Gorky's heritage and Japanese literature].
    2. V.N. Li, "Gor'kii i koreiskaia proletarskaia literatura 20-30-kh godov" [Gorky and Korean proletarian literature of the 1920s and 1930s].
    3. M.E. Shneider, "Gor'kii i kitaiskaia literatura" [Gorky and Chinese literature].
    4. I.P. Zimonina, "Gor'kii i demokraticheskie pisateli V'etnama" [Gorky and democratic writers of Vietnam].
    5. G.I. Mikhailov, "M. Gor'kii i mongol'skie pisateli" [Gorky and Mongolian writers].
    6. N.M. Smurova, "Perevody proizvedenii Gor'kogo v Indonezii" [Translations of Gorky's works in Indonesia].
    7. E.A. Zapadova, "M. Gor'kii i birmanskaia literatura 50-kh godov" [M. Gorky and Burmese literature of the 1950s].

8. E.P. Chelyshev, "Gor'kii i indiiskaia literatura" [Gorky and Indian literature].
9. V.A. Novikova, "O perevodakh proizvedenii Gor'kogo v Bengalii" [On translations of Gorky's work in Bengal].
10. A.S. Gerasimova, "Gor'kii v Afganistane" [Gorky in Afghanistan].
11. A. Ostovar, "Gor'kii v persidskikh perevodakh i osnovnye populiarizatory gor'kovskogo tvorchestva v Irane" [Gorky in Persian translations and the main popularizers of Gorky's work in Iran].
12. S.N. Uturgauni, "Gor'kii i turetskaia literatura" [Gorky and Turkish literature].
13. A.A. Dolinina, "Pervyi sbornik proizvedenii M. Gor'kogo na arabskom iazyke" [The first collection of Gorky's work in Arabic].
14. D.I. Belkin, "Vostok v dorevoliutsionnom tvorchestve M. Gor'kogo" [The East in Gorky's prerevolutionary work].
15. A.A. Bodrova, "Deiatel'nost' vostochnoi kollegii Vsemirnoi literatury pod rukovodstvom M. Gor'kogo" [The work of the eastern section of World Literature under Gorky's directorship].
16. N.A. Vishnevskaia, "Indologicheskie knigi v lichnoi biblioteke M. Gor'kogo" [Indological books in Gorky's personal library].
17. V.M. Alekseev, "Gor'kii v Kitae" [Gorky in China].

The volume also contains a conversation of Nobori Siomu with Gorky and a bibliography of works about Gorky in the East.

56 KHODASEVICH, VALENTINA. "Takim ia znala Gor'kogo" [Gorky as I knew him]. Novyi mir 44, no. 3:11-66.

Memoirs of the artist (Vladislav Khodasevich's niece) and her work as illustrator and costume designer. Focuses on years from 1919 to 1936. Contains letters from Gorky to Valentina Khodasevich.

57 KHVATOV, A.I. "M. Sholokhov i M. Gor'kii" [M. Sholokhov and M. Gorky]. In M. Gor'kii i ego sovremenniki. Leningrad: Nauka, pp. 255-72.

See 1968.78. Considers the question of "reverse influence" in the case of Gorky and Sholokhov.

58 KLINE, GEORGE. "The 'God-Builders': Gorki and Lunacharski." In Religious and Anti-Religious Thought in Russia. Chicago: University of Chicago Press, pp. 103-26.

Says that Gorky coined the term God-building. Analyzes "Man" [Chelovek] and Confession [Ispoved'].

59 KORETSKAIA, I.V. "Gor'kii i Andrei Belyi" [Gorky and Andrei Belyi]. In Gor'kovskie chteniia. Moscow: Nauka, pp. 189-206.

See 1968.11. Discusses each author's views of the other. Koretskaia sees Belyi of 1910 as a typical "bourgeois-liberal" critic who distinguishes (wrongly) Gorky's "talent" from his "world view," but who senses in Gorky the "poet of limitless and rebellious Rus'." Discusses Belyi's cooperation with Gorky after 1919.

60   KOSTELIANETS, B. "Spor o cheloveke" [The argument about man]. Neva, no. 3:165-77.
      Gorky's view of human nature grows from nineteenth-century Russian literature by way of his polemics with Dostoevsky, Tolstoy, Chekhov. Gorky sees a person mainly as a "participant in sharp social collisions." The Lower Depths [Na dne] was a crucial link in the development of Gorky's worldview.

61   KOVALEV, V.A. "L. Leonov i M. Gor'kii" [L. Leonov and M. Gorky]. In M. Gor'kii i ego sovremenniki. Leningrad: Nauka, pp. 215-54.
      See 1968.78. On Gorky's influence. Looks at the question of appropriation of literary themes by a younger literary generation from an older one.

61A KOVTUN, L.S., ed. Slovoupotreblenie i stil' M. Gor'kogo [Word usage and style of M. Gorky]. Leningrad: Izd. LGU, 194 pp.
      Continuation of 1962.8. Contains the following articles:
      1. L.S. Kovtun, "Slovarnoe opisanie semantiko-stilisticheskoi sistemy pisatelia (o Slovare M. Gor'kogo)" [The description in the dictionary of the writer's semantic-stylistic system (on the Gorky dictionary)].
      2. Iu.S. Iazikova, "Semanticheskoe svoeobrazie leksiki M. Gor'kogo" [The semantic originality of M. Gorky's lexicon].
      3. V.A. Sirotina, "O vidakh semanticheskoi dvuplanovosti v satiricheskikh proizvedeniiakh M. Gor'kogo . . ." [On the types of semantic bileveling in M. Gorky's satirical works . . .].
      4. M.B. Borisova, "Stilisticheskie kontrasty v dramaturgii M. Gor'kogo" [Stylistic contrasts in M. Gorky's dramatic works].
      5. O.N. Semenova, "O edinstve semantiko-stilisticheskoi sistemy Skazok ob Italii M. Gor'kogo" [On the unity of the semantic-stylistic system in M. Gorky's Tales of Italy].
      6. M.A. Karpenko, "Gor'kovskie slova-simvoly v proizvedeniiakh pisatelia i v sovremennom literaturnom iazyke" [Gorky's word-symbols in his own works and in contemporary literary language].
      7. G.A. Lilich, "Razvitie obobshchenno-simvolicheskogo znacheniia u slov griaz', griaznyi v proizvedeniiakh M. Gor'kogo" [The development of a generalized symbolic meaning for the words dirt, dirty in Gorky's works].
      8. I.L. Gorodetsskaia, "Evfemisticheskie inoskazaniia v avtobiograficheskoi trilogii M. Gor'kogo" [Euphemisms in M. Gorky's autobiographical trilogy].
      9. N.M. Svetlichnaia, "O sistemnosti slovoupotrebleniia pisatelia" [On the systemic nature of the writer's word usage].

10. D.M. Potsepnia, "Sinonimiia goria i skorbi v avtobiograficheskoi trilogii M. Gor'kogo [The synonymic character of misery and mourning in M. Gorky's autobiographical trilogy].
11. O.I. Trofimkina, "Prirodnye i stikhiinye zvuki v avtobiograficheskoi trilogii M. Gor'kogo [Natural and elemental sounds in M. Gorky's autobiographical trilogy].
12. E.V. Agarkova, "O prieme olitsetvoreniia v avtobiograficheskoi trilogii M. Gor'kogo [On the device of personification in M. Gorky's autobiographical trilogy].
13. O.I. Foniakova, "Semantiko-stilisticheskii analiz glagolov s pristavkami u M. Gor'kogo" [The semantic-stylistic analysis of prefixed verbs in M. Gorky's works].
14. P.M. Alekseev and E.A. Belousova, "Kolichestvennye kharakteristiki slovaria avtobiograficheskoi trilogii M. Gor'kogo [Quantitative characteristics of the dictionary of M. Gorky's autobiographical trilogy].
15. B.A. Larin, L.S. Kovtun, et al., "Printsipy sostavleniia Slovaria M. Gor'kogo" [Principles by which the Gorky dictionary was compiled].

62 KUPRIIANOVSKII, P.V. "M. Gor'kii i zhurnal Severnyi vestnik" [M. Gorky and the journal Severnyi vestnik]. In M. Gor'kii i ego sovremenniki. Leningrad: Nauka, pp. 21-50.
    See 1968.78. Looks at Gorky's attitudes to modernism and symbolism through the prism of his work in Severnyi vestnik. Asks what role the relationships that were formed there played in creating Gorky's later attitudes to modernism.

63 LIBINZON, Z.E. "O gor'kovskom vospriiatii Shillera" [On Gorky's reception of Schiller]. In Gor'kovskii sbornik. Gorky: Volgo-viat. knizh. izd-vo., pp. 281-288.
    See 1968.32. Deals with Gorky's article of 1919 on Schiller, "A Difficult Question" ["Trudnyi vopros"].

64 LUDWIG, NADEZHDA. Maxim Gorki: Sein Leben und Werk. Berlin: Volk und Wissen, 302 pp.
    A biography of Gorky as the "shining and enduring model for a generation of new socialist writers."

65 LUNACHARSKY, ANATOLY. "A Portrait." Soviet Literature, no. 3:139-46.
    Legend making. Reprint of Lunacharsky's speech at Gorky's sixtieth birthday party in 1928.

66 MAGUIRE, ROBERT A. Red Virgin Soil: Soviet Literature in the 1920's. Princeton: Princeton University Press, pp. 26-31, 171-81.
    Discusses the relationship between Gorky and Voronsky, the founder of the journal Red Virgin Soil.

67 MAKSIMOV, P. Vospominaniia o Gor'kom: Perepiska i vstrechi [Memoirs about Gorky: Correspondence and encounters]. 4th ed. Rostov-on-Don: Rostovskoe knizh. izd-vo., 182 pp.
    Contains thirty letters from Gorky to Maksimov. Attention given to Gorky and collectivization in the Rostov region.

68 MAKSIMOVA, V.A. "Leninskaia Iskra i Gor'kii" [Lenin's The Spark and Gorky]. In Gor'kovskie chteniia. Moscow: Nauka, pp. 129-51.
    See 1968.11. Discusses Gorky's earliest contact with Lenin's newspaper.

69 MANN, HEINRICH. "Das Nachtasyl." In Mit der Menschheit auf du und du. Edited by R. Schröder. Berlin: Kultur und Fortschritt, pp. 155-58.
    See 1968.102. Written around 1930. The Lower Depths [Na dne] first seemed like the original naturalist drama, a study of misery. With Piscator's production in Berlin, 1926, it took on universal, symbolic meaning as the ultimate in social drama. Separate portraits of wretchedness became whole frescoes of human suffering. Gorky has lasted so long because he could see into the future and show its roots.

70 MANN, THOMAS. "Ein Organ des öffentlichen Gewissens." In Mit der Menschheit auf du und du. Edited by R. Schröder. Berlin: Kultur und Fortschritt, pp. 83-84.
    See 1968.102. Written in 1928. Deals with Gorky's moral view. Gorky is a "moral leader," an "organ of public conscience." Mann sees his work as a "bridge between Nietzsche and socialism."

71 MARKOV, VLADIMIR. Russian Futurism: A History. Berkeley: University of California Press, pp. 281-83.
    Recounts Gorky's defense of the futurists in 1915 and his proclamation at the Stray Dog that "They've got something!" Discusses his article "About Futurism."

72 MIKHAILOVA, A.N. "Iz izdatel'skoi deiatel'nosti M. Gor'kogo" [From M. Gorky's editing activity]. In M. Gor'kii i ego sovremenniki. Leningrad: Nauka, pp. 196-203.
    See 1968.78. Treats Gorky's efforts to publish minority literature, particularly Georgian, Armenian, Jewish. Most attention is given to Jewish literature.

73 MIKHAL'SKII, E.N. "M. Gor'kii o khudozhestvennom masterstve I. Bunina" [M. Gorky on I. Bunin's artistic mastery]. In Velikii rodonachal'nik sotsialisticheskoi literatury. Kiev: Izd. KGU, pp. 83-93.
    See 1968.125. Deals with Gorky's judgments of Bunin's style.

74 MIROVA-FLORIN, E. "Maksim Gor'kii v Germanii" [Maksim Gorky in Germany]. In Gor'kovskie chteniia. Moscow: Nauka, pp. 400-416.
    See 1968.11. On Gorky's reception in Germany. Reviews history of translations of Gorky's works into German, productions of his plays, reviews in the German press. Reports on Gorky's visits to Germany. The focus is on Gorky's impact as a revolutionary proletarian writer.

75 MITROPAN, PETR. "M. Gor'kii v Iugoslavii" [Gorky in Yugoslavia]. Izvestiia AN SSSR, otdelenie literatury i iazyka 27, no. 2:127-33.
    Gorky's reception in Serbia and Croatia.

76 MOHRENSCHILDT, DIMITRI VON, ed. "Gorky--The Humanitarian (Two Letters by Maxim Gorky)." Russian Review, no. 27:351-53.
    Two letters from the civil war years to Henri Barbusse and Anatole France.

77 MURATOVA, K.D. "Gor'kovedenie 1960-kh godov" [Gorky studies in the 1960s]. Russkaia literatura 11, no. 1:6-22.
    Overview of the history of Soviet Gorky studies from the 1930s: the opening and organization of the personal archive, comparison of Gorky and various prerevolutionary writers, his aesthetic views, his role in the development of Soviet literature, basic bibliographies of Gorky's works. In the 1930s a group of literary critics was assigned to study life and works (V. Desnitsky, S. Balukhatyi, I. Gruzdev, B. Bialik, S. Kastorsky, K. Muratova, I. Iuzovsky, N. Piksanov). The second generation emerged in the late 1940s and early 1950s: B.V. Mikhailovsky, E.B. Tager, B.I. Bursov, A.I. Ovcharenko, and others. They discussed Gorky's place in the broader context of world literature. In the 1950s and 1960s, studies were devoted to separate works, particularly drama. Now by Gorky's one-hundredth birthday Soviet Gorky studies have established an "image of Gorky the litterateur and ardent revolutionist" and have documented his place in the Revolution. Notes a need to study Gorky's aesthetic views in comparison to other views of the 1900s, especially Nietzsche's. Calls for study of Gorky as critic.

78 MURATOVA, K., ed. M. Gor'kii i ego sovremenniki [Gorky and his contemporaries]. Leningrad: Nauka, 302 pp.
    Contains the following articles:
    1. B.N. Dvinianinov, "Tvorcheskie pereklichki (M. Gor'kii i P. Iakubovich)" [Creative resonances (M. Gorky and P. Iakubovich)].
    2. P.V. Kupriianovskii, "M. Gor'kii i zhurnal Severnyi vestnik" [Gorky and the journal Severnyi vestnik]. See 1968.62.
    3. K.D. Muratova, "Soputniki (V. Veresaev i M. Gor'kii)" [Traveling companions (V. Veresaev and M. Gorky)]. See 1968.80.

4. L.K. Dolgopolov, "Vokrug Detei solntsa" [Around Children of the Sun].
5. N.A. Trifonov, "A.V. Lunacharskii i M. Gor'kii (k istorii literaturnykh i lichnykh otnoshenii do Oktiabria)" [A.V. Lunacharsky and M. Gorky (toward a history of their literary and personal relations before October)]. See 1968.118.
6. V.V. Timofeeva, "Ob odnom neosushchestvlennom zamysle M. Gor'kogo (vstrechi i sud'by)" [On one of M. Gorky's unrealized plans (meetings and fates)].
7. O.D. Golubeva, "Dva izdatelia (I.D. Sytin i M. Gor'kii)" [Two publishers (I.D. Sytin and M. Gorky)]. See 1968.46.
8. A.N. Mikhailova, "Iz izdatel'skoi deiatel'nosti M. Gor'kogo" [From M. Gorky's publishing activity]. See 1968.72.
9. V.P. Vil'chinskii, "D. Rizov i M. Gor'kii" [D. Rizov and M. Gorky].
10. V.A. Kovalev, "L. Leonov i M. Gor'kii" [L. Leonov and M. Gorky]. See 1968.61.
11. A.I. Khvatov, "M. Sholokhov i M. Gor'kii" [M. Sholokhov and M. Gorky]. See 1968.57.
12. V.A. Shoshin, "N. Tikhonov i M. Gor'kii" [N. Tikhonov and M. Gorky].

79 MURATOVA, K.D. "M. Gor'kii i zhurnal Sovremennik" [M. Gorky and the journal, The Contemporary]. In Gor'kovskie chteniia. Moscow: Nauka, pp. 247-88.
    See 1968.11. Good overview of Gorky's activities as editor, publisher, and literary entrepreneur. Focus is on Gorky's work on the moderate leftist journal Sovremennik, 1911-13.

80 _____. "Soputniki (V. Veresaev i M. Gor'kii)" [Fellow travelers (V. Veresaev and M. Gorky)]. In M. Gor'kii i ego sovremenniki. Leningrad: Nauka, pp. 51-78.
    See 1968.78. Treatment of Veresaev and Gorky includes information about St. Petersburg literary life around 1900, the early Marxist press, and Marxist editors and critics such as V.A. Posse and E.A. Solovev.

81 NEMIROVICH-DANCHENKO, VLADIMIR. My Life in the Russian Theater. Translated by J. Cournos. New York: Theater Arts Books, pp. 227-46, 257-58.
    Reprint of 1936 edition. Describes Gorky's explosive impact on the theatergoing audience around 1905.

82 NINOV, A. "Lenin i Gor'kii: Iz istorii zhurnala Prosveshchenie" [Lenin and Gorky: From the history of the journal Enlightenment]. Neva, no. 1:177-81.
    Discusses Gorky's role in reorganizing Prosveshchenie in 1912.

83   OJETTI, UGO. "Gorki Twenty Years Ago." In As They Seemed to Me. Translated by H. Furst. Freeport, N.Y.: Books for Libraries Press, pp. 95-100.
      Memoir. First printed in 1927. Notes Gorky's contradictory remarks, even on such topics as the Russian peasant.

84   OPREA, AL. "Panait Istrati, Maxim Gorki, Nikos Kazantzakis." Secolul XX 111:91-95.
      See 1968.105. In Romanian. About a comment of Kazantsakis on Gorky.

85   OSNOVIN, V.V. "M. Gor'kii i L. Tolstoi" [M. Gorky and L. Tolstoy]. In Gor'kovskii sbornik. Gorky: Volgo-viat. knizh. izd-vo., pp. 134-47.
      See 1968.32. Polemicizes with N.K. Piksanov on the relative value of Gorky's earliest impressions of Tolstoy (1900) and a later one (1908).

86   OVCHARENKO, A. "Maksim Gor'kii i literaturnye iskaniia XX stoletiia" [Maksim Gorky and literary searchings of the 20th century]. Znamia 38, no. 4:217-32; 38, no. 5:205-24.
      Gorky is above any one style or school: he is unique. Discusses short works of the 1920s, stories, and Fragments from My Diary. Explains why Gorky is not "modernist." Mentions James Joyce.

87   PANKOV, VIKTOR. M. Gor'kii i sovetskaia deistvitel'nost' [M. Gorky and Soviet reality]. Moscow: Moskovskii rabochii, 350 pp.
      Expanded version of 1955.8.

88   PANTELEEVA, R., ed. "Zapisnaia knizhka M. Gor'kogo: Fevral' 1906-Mart 1908, Berlin, Amerika, Italiia" [Gorky's notebook: February 1906-March 1908, Berlin, America, Italy]. Voprosy literatury 12, no. 3 (March):99-120.
      Contains abundant explanatory notes by the editor to the notebooks.

89   PARSHINA, G.M. "M. Gor'kii i A. Platonov" [M. Gorky and A. Platonov]. In Gor'kovskii sbornik. Gorky: Volgo-viat. knizh. izd-vo., pp. 217-24.
      See 1968.32. Sees a philosophical similarity between Gorky in his Italian stories (1911-13) and Platonov in his works (1927-50).

90   PEL'T, V.D. Gor'kii-zhurnalist (1928-1936) [Gorky the journalist, 1928-1936]. Moscow: Izd. MGU, 426 pp.
      Deals with Gorky's journalistic activity after his reentry into Soviet life in 1928. Sees him as a "passionate propagator of truth about the Soviet Union within our country and abroad [who] tirelessly fought with the enemies of working people, against all kinds of petit bourgeois, against imperialism, against fascism and wars." Studies his propagandistic journalism

in Our Achievements [Nashi dostizheniia], The USSR on the Building Site [SSSR na stroike], his efforts to reach peasant readers with The Collective Farmer [Kolkhoznik], his anti-imperialist propaganda in Abroad [Za rubezhom], and his educational work Literary Study [Literaturnaia ucheba].

90A PERTSOV, V. "Trailblazers: On the Creative Techniques of Gorky and Mayakovsky." Soviet Studies in Literature 4, no. 4 (Fall):54-64.
Translated from Literaturnaia gazeta, no. 17 (1968). Summarizes the similarities of the two writers.

91 PÉRUS, JEAN. Gorki en France. Paris: Presses universitaires de France.
Bibliography. Contains French translations of Gorky's primary works as well as secondary literature about him, 1899-1939.

92 _____. Romain Rolland et Maxime Gorki. Paris: Les éditeurs français réunis, 367 pp.
Calls into question the political-revolutionary legend about Gorky and Rolland as fighters for international socialism. Finds the basis for their friendship in their similar worldviews: both had a clear, honest vision of the moral, philosophical, and political upheaval of their age, and both had confidence in the future of humanity. Bases this study on the correspondence between Gorky and Rolland. Finds each more concerned with affirming his own point of view than grasping that of the other.

93 PIKSANOV, N.K. "Grazhdanskaia patetika rannego Gor'kogo v iunosheskom vospriiatii" [Civic pathos of the early Gorky as perceived by an adolescent]. Russkaia literatura 11, no. 3:232-34.
Memoirs from the Gorkyist Piksanov's university days, 1898-1902.

94 PIRADOV, B.A. "Delo No. 31" [File No. 31]. In Gor'kovskie chteniia. Moscow: Nauka, pp. 58-98.
See 1968.11. Political activity. Deals with Gorky's arrest in May 1898 and his role in the Fedor Afanasev affair.

95 PLOTKIN, L. "Gumanizm bortsa" [The humanism of a fighter]. Zvezda 45, no. 3:146-53.
Distinguishes two kinds of "individualism": petit bourgeois and heroic.

96 Primer Acto 93 (February).
This number is devoted to Gorky's centenary celebration. Contains:
1. Juan Eduardo Zúñiga, "En torno a Gorki."
2. Juan Eduardo Zúñiga, "Fechas en la vida de Máximo Gorki."

3. Renzo Casali, "Gorki o la ética como presupuesto de creación." See 1968.23.
4. Constantin Stanislavski, "Cómo ambienté 'Los Bajos Fondos.'"
5. Vl. Nemirovich-Danchenko, "Una carta de Nemirovich-Danchenko a Stanislavski."
6. Ricardo R. Budet, "Gorki, por primera vez."

97 Primer Acto 94 (March).
This number has three articles on Gorky:
1. José Monleón, "Gorki, ahora."
2. Eduardo Zúñiga, "Tres reseñas del estreno."
3. Boris Bialik, "Luká, un personaje clave." See 1968.12.

98 RADÓ, GYÖRGY. "The Death of Maxim Gorki: Word by Word." Texas Quarterly 11, no. 3:138-42.
Biographical note. An account of Gorky's dying words.

99 "Reminiscences by Gorky's Contemporaries." Soviet Literature, no. 3:153-64.
Memoirs. Kornei Chukovsky speaks of two Gorkies. Vsevolod Ivanov shows Gorky as guardian angel. Veniamin Kaverin presents him as the "severe but kindly" teacher who would rather not be thought of as a teacher.

99A RIURIKOV, BORIS. "The Maxim Gorky Tradition and Contemporary Literature." Soviet Literature, no. 11:138-56.
A speech given in Gorky, June 1968, at a joint meeting of the boards of the Soviet and Russian writers' unions by the secretary of the board of the Soviet Writers' Union. Reaffirms the Soviet legend of Gorky.

100 ROMANOVICH, I. "Obyknovennoe neschast'e, Na dne M. Gor'kogo" [Routine unhappiness, Gorky's The Lower Depths]. Teatr 29, no. 9 (September):33-36.
Remarks on the "bare-minimum" staging. Luka is basically a "positive" figure.

101 ROSHAL', A.A. "M. Gor'kii i A.F. Pisemskii" [M. Gorky and A.F. Pisemsky]. Russkaia literatura 11, no. 3:155-58.
Reports Gorky's marginalia on Pisemsky's works.

102 SCHRÖDER, RALF, ed. Mit der Menschheit auf du und du: Schriftsteller der Welt über Gorki. Berlin: Kultur und Fortschritt, 494 pp.
Contains Schröder's lengthy introduction (see 1968.103) and essays and memoirs of writers including the following German writers:
1. Johannes R. Becher, "Die realistisch-zeitgenössische Vervollkommnung des klassischen Ideals"; "Die Unteilbarkeit von Leben und Dichtung"; "Das Zeitenlose und höchst Zeitgemäße widerspruchslos vereint." See 1968.8; 1968.9.

2. Willi Bredel, "Im Sinne Goethes: Unser Befreier."
3. Thomas Mann, "Ein Organ des öffentlichen Gewissens"; "Mittler zwischen den Werten der Vergangenheit und dem Willen zur Zukunft." See 1968.70.
4. Gerhart Hauptmann, "Das aus den Tiefen der russischen Volksseele kommende Weltgenie."
5. Bertolt Brecht, "Gorkis Einfluß auf die Literatur." See 1968.19.
6. Max Brod, "Das Licht des Geistes in ein lichtloses Leben." See 1968.20.
7. Stefan Zweig, "In ihm allein wird die künftige Geschichte dokumentarisch ablesen können, daß jener Aufstand in Rußland ein organisch Volksgeschaffenes war"; see 1968.132. "Das Werk der Artamonows." See 1968.131.
8. Lion Feuchtwanger, "Es war das Volk selber, das Stimme bekommen hatte." See 1968.40.
9. Heinrich Mann, "Das Nachtasyl." See 1968.69.
10. Arnold Zweig, "Maxim Gorkis Weg zur Höhe."
11. Anna Seghers, "Die Tendenz in der reinen Kunst."

103 SCHRÖDER, RALF. "Gorki und die Erlösung der Kunst." In <u>Mit der Menschheit auf du und du</u>. Edited by R. Schröder. Berlin: Kultur und Fortschritt, pp. 7-54.
See 1968.102. Sees Gorky as a great figure in the history of world literature whose reading of classics and whose impact on twentieth-century literature are of the first magnitude of importance. Ranked with Goethe. Sees his basic theme as the whole of "bourgeois" culture.

104 SECHIN, V. "Gor'kii 'po-staromu'" [Gorky old style]. <u>Teatr</u> 29, no. 5 (May):16-26.
Looks at traditional productions of Gorky plays and asks what is attractive about them for the contemporary theatergoer.

105 <u>Secolul 20: Revistă de literatură universală</u> (Bucharest) 3.
In Romanian. Contains four articles commemorating Gorky's centenary:
1. György Radó, "Amurgul, deliral şi moartea lui Gorki--în româneşte de R. Locusteanu."
2. Tamara Motiliova, "O prietenie memorabilă: Rolland şi Gorki" [A memoir: Rolland and Gorky].
3. Konstantin Fedin, "Gorki şi Fraţii Serapion" [Gorky and the Serapion Brothers].
4. Al. Oprea, "Panait Istrati, Maxim Gorki şi Nikos Kazantzakis" [Panait Istrati, Maksim Gorky, and Nikos Kazantzakis]. See 1968.84.

106 SHAGINIAN, MARIETTA. "Rozhdestvo v Sorrento" [Christmas in Sorrento]. <u>Druzhba narodov</u>, no. 11:3-54.
Memoirs. Reflects on Gorky's relationship to Lenin, and their respective concepts of the artist.

107 SHELDON, RICHARD R. "Šklovskij, Gor'kij and the Serapion Brothers." SEEJ 12, no. 1:1-13.
   Gorky provided the setting in which the writers who made up the Serapion Brothers first met and joined in a group. Analyzes the hostile relationship of V. Shklovsky and Gorky and its effect on the Serapions.

108 SHISHKINA, A.N. "O kontsepsii kharaktera v tvorchestve M. Gor'kogo dooktiabr'skogo perioda" [On the conception of character in Gorky's prerevolutionary work]. Russkaia literatura 11, no. 1:49-61.
   Uses Gorky's article "The Destruction of Personality" ["Razrushenie lichnosti"] (1908) as the point of departure for an analysis of Gorky's conception of character.

109 SKOROBOGATOV, K. "Moi Gor'kii" [My Gorky]. Neva, no. 11: 193-99.
   Memoirs of an actor; remembers roles in Gorky plays, especially Luka in The Lower Depths [Na dne].

110 SLADE, JOSEPH W. "Markham and Gorky." Markham Review, no. 1:1-2.
   Recounts Edwin Markham's fondness for Gorky and his efforts to help him in 1906.

111 SMIRNOVA, A.D. "Pomety M. Gor'kogo na knigakh I.S. Turgeneva" [M. Gorky's marginalia on the books of I.S. Turgenev]. Russkaia literatura 11, no. 4:65-73.
   Gorky's earliest marginalia date from 1907-8 when he was preparing lectures for the Capri school; the latest were made in the 1930s.

112 SÖTÉR, ISTVÁN. "Gorkij." Kritika (Budapest) 6, no. 5:3-10.
   In Hungarian. A tribute to Gorky.

113 Soviet Literature, no. 3.
   This number is devoted to Gorky. Contains:
   1. Selections from Gorky's work: "Song of the Stormy Petrel," "Makar Chudra," "A Man Is Born," The Life of Klim Samgin, Egor Bulychev and Others, "Vladimir Ilych Lenin."
   2. Letters: Gorky to Russian writers, foreign writers to Gorky.
      3. Articles:
         a. A. Lunacharsky, "A Portrait."
         b. B. Byalik, "A Great Epopee."
      4. Reminiscences by K. Chukovsky, Vsev. Ivanov, V. Kaverin.
         5. Articles on producing Gorky's work:
            a. B. Schukin, "My work on Egor Bulychev."
            b. L. Pogozheva, "Screen Versions of Gorky's Work."
            c. E. Mnatsakanova, "'Death and the Maiden'--an Oratorio by Herman Galynin."

114 STAUCHE, ILSE, ed. Maxim Gorki, Drama und Theater. Berlin: Henschel Verlag, 466 pp.
   Contains German translations of Soviet articles on Gorky's dramatic works and a chronicle of productions of Gorky's plays on the German stage. The largest part is Stauche's analysis of Gorky's plays in Germany, in the period after World War II, his reception in East Germany.

115 TAGER, E.B. "Revoliutsionnyi romantizm Gor'kogo" [Gorky's revolutionary romanticism]. In Russkaia literatura kontsa XIX-nachala XX veka [Russian literature in the late 19th-early 20th century]. Vol. 1. Moscow: Nauka, pp. 213-43.
   Sees the essence of Gorky's "revolutionary romanticism" as the "poeticization of the creative will to transform actuality."

116 Teatr 29, no. 3 (March).
   This issue is devoted to Gorky's centenary. Contains:
   1. G. Tovstonogov, "Moi Gor'kii" [My Gorky].
   2. B. Babochkin, "Zametki o Dachnikakh" [Notes on Summer Folk].
   3. Isidor Shtok, "Vstrecha" [Meeting].
   4. L. Shchepilova, "'. . . i ne khochet oboitis' bez geroia' (o Gor'kovskoi traditsii v sovremennoi drame)" ["He doesn't want to do without a hero" (on the tradition of Gorky in contemporary drama)].
   5. T. Kulova, "Novaia pravda o cheloveke (M. Gor'kii i dooktiabr'skaia dramaturgiia)" [A new truth about man (M. Gorky and prerevolutionary dramaturgy)].
   6. I. Sudakova, "Na studencheskoi stsene (N.M. Gorchakov repetiruet p'esu Gor'kogo Deti)" [On the student stage (N.M. Gorchakov rehearses Gorky's play Children)].
   7. E. Dubnova, "Nakanune revoliutsii 1905 goda (k istorii pervoi postanovki Dachnikov)" [On the eve of the 1905 revolution (On the history of the first production of Summer Folk)].

117 TIKHOVODOV, A.A. "Protsess 'vylamyvaniia' v Voskresenii L. Tolstogo i Fome Gordeeve M. Gor'kogo" [The process of breaking off in L. Tolstoy's Resurrection and M. Gorky's Foma Gordeev]. In Gor'kovskii sbornik. Gorky: Volgo-viat. knizh. izd-vo., pp. 106-26.
   See 1968.32. Finds "polemic" hidden in these two works. This polemical dialogue centers on the themes of search for truth, the yearning for "existential beauty" and social equality.

118 TRIFONOV, N.A. "A.V. Lunacharskii i M. Gor'kii (k istorii literaturnykh i lichnykh otnoshenii do Oktiabria)" [A.V. Lunacharsky and M. Gorky (toward a history of their literary and personal relations before October)]. In M. Gor'kii i ego sovremenniki. Leningrad: Nauka, pp. 110-57.
   See 1968.78. Analyzes the mutual influence of Gorky and Lunacharsky in the prerevolutionary period. Devotes significant attention to Confession [Ispoved'] and God-building.

119   . "Soratniki (Lunacharskii i Gor'kii posle Oktiabria)" [Fellows-at-arms (Lunacharsky and Gorky after October)]. Russkaia literatura 11, no. 1:23-48.
   Deals with relations between A. Lunacharsky and Gorky, starting with the debacle around Novaia zhizn' [New Life] in 1918 and ending with the start of the biographical series, "The Life of Remarkable People."

120   UDONOVA, Z. Gor'kii v bor'be s dekadentami [Gorky's struggle with the decadents]. Moscow: Sovetskaia Rossiia, 192 pp.
   Popularized treatment of Gorky's polemic with "modernism" and "decadence." Seen as an attempt to look beyond the disintegration of "bourgeois" society and its reactionary values.

121   VAINBERG, I. "Vsled za gor'kovskoi strokoi (poiski i nabliudeniia)" [On the trail of Gorky's line: Explorations and observations]. Voprosy literatury 12, no. 3 (March): 50-67.
   Argues for a full commentary to The Life of Klim Samgin [Zhizn' Klima Samgina]. Analyzes some instances of quotation and significant misquotation in Klim Samgin.

122   VOLKOV, A. "Velikoe sodruzhestvo" [The great community]. Voprosy literatury 12, no. 3 (March):19-35.
   Asks what kind of impact early Soviet literature had on Gorky. Looks at his criticism and further development of "revolutionary romanticism," particularly the problem of a hero with the "right" kind of personality, ideals, inner life. Discusses Olesha's Envy [Zavist'], Fedin's Cities and Years [Goroda i gody], Gorky's The Life of Klim Samgin, and Sholokhov's Quiet Flows the Don [Tikhii Don].

123   VOROB'EV, V.F. "Glashatai partiinosti" [The herald of party loyalty]. Zvezda 45, no. 1:173-78.
   Argues that Gorky understood and insisted on the connection between politics and literature. Responds to the "bourgeois" view that art and politics should be separate. Uses articles from late 1920s and early 1930s. Notes a "contradictory" view in the early 1920s.

124   . "K publikatsii pis'ma V.I. Lenina A.M. Gor'komu ot 15 sentiabria 1919 goda" [On the publication of a letter from V.I. Lenin to A.M. Gorky dated 15 September 1919]. Russkaia literatura 11, no. 2:134-38.
   The publication of this letter in Lenin's Complete Works, volume 49, sheds new light on Gorky's role as a politician and Lenin's attitudes to literature.

125   VOROB'EV, V.F., et al., eds. Velikii rodonachal'nik sotsialisticheskoi literatury [The great progenitor of socialist letters]. Kiev: Izd. KGU, 187 pp.

Collection. Contains the following articles:
1. N.I. Zhuk, "A.M. Gor'kii-drug ukrainskogo naroda" [A.M. Gorky, the friend of the Ukrainian people].
2. P.P. Kononenko, "A.M. Gor'kii i problema novogo cheloveka" [A.M. Gorky and the problem of the new man].
3. L.P. Aleksandrova, "M. Gor'kii i voprosy istorizma v literature sotsialisticheskogo realizma" [M. Gorky and questions of historicism in socialist realist literature]. See 1968.3.
4. V.E. Prozhogin, "Chelovek--tvorets 'vtoroi prirody'" [Man as the creator of a "second nature"].
5. V.F. Vorob'ev, "Neutomimyi vospitatel' novykh talantov" [The tireless educator of new talents].
6. I.R. Semenchuk, "Problemy khudozhestvennogo masterstva" [Problems of artistic mastery].
7. E.N. Mikhal'skii, "M. Gor'kii o khudozhestvennom masterstve I. Bunina" [M. Gorky on I. Bunin's artistic mastery]. See 1968.73.
8. V.A. Sirotina, "Khudozhestvennaia emkost' gor'kovskogo slova" [The artistic capacity of Gorky's word].
9. M.A. Karpenko, "Stil' i slovoupotreblenie M. Gor'kogo poeta" [Style and word use of M. Gorky the poet].
10. E.I. Samokhvalova, "Sistemnost' formirovaniia obrazov na osnove znachenii odnogo slova v proizvedeniiakh M. Gor'kogo" [The systemic character of the formation of images on the basis of the meaning of one word in Gorky's works].
11. A.V. Shvets, "Perenosnoe i obraznoe upotreblenie v sisteme narechii" [Abstract and figurative usage in the system of adverbs].
12. A.I. Mamalyga, "Ideino-esteticheskoe svoeobrazie leksiki truda v khudozhestvennoi rechi M. Gor'kogo" [the ideational-aesthetic peculiarity of the lexicon of labor in Gorky's artistic language].
13. V.I. Masal'skii, "Na putiakh poznaniia khudozhestvennogo slova A.M. Gor'kogo" [Toward cognition of A.M. Gorky's artistic word].
14. N.S. Zaritskii, "Sostavlenie slovaria A.M. Gor'kogo i problema sootnosheniia slova, poniatiia i znacheniia v leksikografii" [The compilation of a Gorky dictionary and the problem of the interrelationship of word, concept, and meaning in lexicography].

126 VUL', R.M. "Pervoe redaktorstvo A.M. Gor'kogo" [A.M. Gorky's first editorship]. In Gor'kovskie chteniia. Moscow: Nauka, pp. 224-46.
See 1968.11. Discusses Gorky's experience as editor of Samarskaia gazeta.

127 ZEMSKOV, V. "Vstrechi M. Gor'kogo i S. Esenina" [Meetings of M. Gorky and S. Esenin]. In Gor'kovskie chteniia. Moscow: Nauka, pp. 210-23.

See 1968.11. Presents new material on the relationship between Gorky and Esenin. Stresses Gorky's desire to save the poet and man Sergei Esenin from the bad reputation of eseninshchina.

128 ZERNITSKAIA, E.I. Gor'kii i teatr [Gorky and the theater]. Moscow: Min. kul't. SSSR, Gos. Tsent. Teatr. Bibl., 101 pp.
Selected bibliography on Gorky and the theater. Organized by play.

129 ZHURAVLEV, I.K. "Tvorchestvo M. Gor'kogo v otsenke sotsialisticheskoi kritiki SShA (1901-1917 gody)" [Gorky's work in the evaluation of socialist criticism of the U.S.A. (1901-1917)]. Russkaia literatura 11, no. 2:212-18.
Reviews Gorky's early reception among socialist intellectuals in the United States.

130 ZIMINA, SERAFIMA. "Arkhiv velikogo pisatelia--iz arkhiva A.M. Gor'kogo" [The archive of a great writer--from the archives of Gorky]. Russkaia literatura 11, no. 2:3-35.
Surveys the contents of publications of the Gorky Archive. Publishes material of Gorky on Tolstoy, Dostoevsky, and Leskov.

131 ZWEIG, STEFAN. "Das Werk der Artamonows." In Mit der Menschheit auf du und du. Edited by R. Schröder. Berlin: Kultur und Fortschritt, pp. 191-96.
See 1968.102. Written 1927. A review of The Artamonov Business [Delo Artamonovykh]. This novel is written in a naturalist style through which emanates a symbolic vision, a view of three generations in the prerevolutionary period.

132 _____. "In ihm allein wird die künftige Geschichte dokumentarisch ablesen können, daß jener Aufstand in Rußland ein organisch Volksgeschaffenes war." In Mit der Menschheit auf du und du. Edited by R. Schröder. Berlin: Kultur und Fortschritt, pp. 127-38.
See 1968.102. Written in 1931. Gorky is a miracle in Russian culture: for the first time in its thousand-year history the Russian "people" found its voice in him.

1969

1 ADLING, WILFRIED. "Gorki und Shakespeare: Zur Shakespeare-Rezeption im dramatischen Spätwerk Maxim Gorkis." Shakespeare-Jahrbuch (Weimar) 105:89-103.
Shakespeare is for Gorky a standard of classic art. Reviews Gorky's reception of Shakespeare. Compares Gorky's "historical" dramas, especially Egor Bulychev, with Shakespeare's King Lear.

2   AIKHENVAL'D, IULII [ISAEVICH]. "Maksim Gor'kii." Siluety russkikh pisatelei [Silhouettes of Russian writers]. 4th ed. The Hague: Mouton, pp. 223-35.

   Reprinted from 1923 edition (Berlin: Slovo). Gorky's "Thought" from "Man" ["Chelovek"] enslaves and ties down more than it liberates. Gorky is too much the moralist and didact. "Gorky is apparently more a personality than an author."

3   BELEN'KII, E.I. "O povesti M. Gor'kogo Leto" [On M. Gorky's novella Summer]. Russkaia literatura 12, no. 3: 190-95.

   Although Summer is not a first-rate work, it is valuable as a treatment of rural life and as a continuation of the ideological and artistic principles of Mother [Mat'].

4   BERBEROVA, NINA. The Italics Are Mine. Translated by P. Radley. New York: Harcourt, Brace, & World, pp. 171-97. Translation of 1967.1. See 1972.1.

5   BIALIK, BORIS. "'Revoliutsiia est' udel sil'nykh'" [Revolution is the lot of the strong]. Znamia 39, no. 9:225-40; 39, no. 10:217-35.

   On Lenin and Gorky. Analyzes works of each which show how close they were in their views of art, politics, and the process of social change. Wants to show that socialist realism was not the result of a "directive from above," but rather that it developed organically.

6   BORISOVA, M.B. "Ideologicheskaia struktura slova v dramaturgii M. Gor'kogo (ob upotreblenii slova dobryi)" [The ideological structure of the word in Gorky's plays (on the use of the word kind)]. In Voprosy teorii i istorii iazyka. Edited by N.A. Meshcherskii. Leningrad: Izd. LGU, pp. 27-38.

   Studies Gorky's ethical values by discussing how he used the word kind in his plays and autobiographical trilogy.

7   EVENTOV, I.S. "O nekotorykh osobennostiakh dramaturgii M. Gor'kogo (komicheskoe i tragicheskoe)" [On certain peculiarities of Gorky's plays (the comic and the tragic)]. Russkaia literatura 12, no. 4:57-74.

   Although Gorky's plays give accurate pictures of their period, contemporary mores, social relations, their essence lies in the conflict of ideas and the ideological treatment of "life" questions.

8   FONIAKOVA, O.I. "O polisemii glagolov, vvodiashchikh priamuiu rech' v avtobiograficheskoi trilogii M. Gor'kogo" [On the polysemic quality of verbs that introduce direct speech in Gorky's autobiography]. In Voprosy teorii i istorii iazyka. Edited by N.A. Meshcherskii. Leningrad: Izd. LGU, pp. 124-30.

Distinguishes the "social" and the "individual" use of vocabulary in Gorky's trilogy. Shows some aspects of Gorky's stylistic innovation.

9   GARNETT, EDWARD. "Maxim Gorky." Introduction to "Twenty-Six Men and a Girl," and Other Stories by Maxim Gorky. Translated by E. Jakowleff and D.B. Montefiore. Freeport, N.Y.: Books for Libraries Press, pp. vii-xvi.
    Reprinted from 1902 edition. Gorky's reception in England. Asks why Gorky should be so popular in Russia now (1902). Points out some differences between English and Russian literary taste. Predicts that Gorky will not be popular in England. He is great, however, because he analyzes human nature without falsifying it.

10 GORELOV, ANATOLII. "Pered burei" [Before the storm]. In Podvig russkoi literatury. The Hague: Mouton, pp. 353-402.
    See 1969.11. Analyzes Gorky's treatment of his women characters.

11 _____. Podvig russkoi literatury. [The heroic deed of Russian literature]. The Hague: Mouton, pp. 317-402, 459-71.
    Reprinted from 1957 edition (Leningrad). Contains three chapters on Gorky:
    1. "Revoliutsionnyi zapev" [Revolutionary song]. See 1969.12.
    2. "Pered burei" [Before the storm]. See 1969.10.
    3. "Vozrozhdenie lichnosti" [The rebirth of selfhood]. See 1969.13.

12 _____. "Revoliutsionnyi zapev" [Revolutionary song]. In Podvig russkoi literatury. The Hague: Mouton, pp. 317-52.
    See 1969.11. Gorky is a voice of optimism in the 1890s, a period of pessimism. Notes romanticism in Gorky's outlook.

13 _____. "Vozrozhdenie lichnosti" [The rebirth of selfhood]. In Podvig russkoi literatury. The Hague: Mouton, pp. 459-71.
    See 1969.11. Gorky gives Russian literature a new kind of artistic consciousness, different from the "bourgeois" aesthetic consciousness, which divides, analyzes, takes apart.

14 GOR'KII, M. Khudozhestvennye proizvedeniia, stat'i, zametki [Artistic works, articles, notes]. Edited by E.B. Tager et al. Arkhiv A.M. Gor'kogo, vol. 12. Moscow: Nauka, 434 pp.
    Contains fifteen belletristic works, fifty articles, eleven notes--including notes on N. Leskov, F. Dostoevsky, L. Tolstoy--thirty-three sketches for portraits--including B. Zaitsev; Iu. Aikhenval'd; E. Zamiatin; G. Hauptmann; Kn. Hamsun; B. Savinkov; Vl. Khodasevich; E. Azef; A. Aleksin; S. Zweig; F. Shaliapin; V. Maiakovsky; V. Briusov.

15 "Gor'ky, Maksim." In The Penguin Companion to European Literature. Edited by A. Thorlby. New York: McGraw-Hill; Harmondsworth: Penguin, pp. 324-26.
  Outline of life and literary direction. Gorky is characterized as a natural rebel and a convinced humanist.

16 GRIGOR'EV, A.L. "Nemetskaia kniga o dramakh i teatre Gor'kogo" [A German book on the drama and theater of Gorky]. Russkaia literatura 12, no. 4:217-19.
  Review of Ilse Stauche, ed., Maxim Gorki: Drama und Theater. Welcomes this book as the product of collaboration between Soviet and East German Gorky specialists.

17 GUZHIEVA, N.V. "Russkaia realisticheskaia dramaturgiia 1910-kh godov" [Russian realist drama of the 1910s]. Russkaia literatura 12, no. 3:36-54.
  Survey of developments in realist theater in the 1910s with special emphasis on Gorky (especially Vassa Zheleznova) and Leonid Andreev.

18 IVANOV, ANATOLII S. Gor'kii v muzyke [Gorky in music]. Moscow: Sovetskii kompozitor, 79 pp.
  Bibliography. Contains lists of works reflected in musical compositions, premieres of operas and ballets, comments of composers and conductors about their work, and a bibliography of secondary sources.

19 IVANOV, VSEVOLOD. Perepiska s A.M. Gor'kim: Iz dnevnikov i zapisnykh knizhek [Correspondence with Gorky: From diaries and notebooks]. Moscow: Sovetskii pisatel', 447 pp.
  Contains letters from the years 1916-36.

20 KOZ'MIN, M.B., and KORITSKAIA, N.F., eds. A.M. Gor'kii v izobrazitel'nom iskusstve, 1868-1968 [A.M. Gorky in representational art, 1868-1968]. Moscow: Nauka, 578 pp.
  The fullest available description of materials collected at the Gorky Museum at the Institute of World Literature in Moscow.

21 KUŹMICZOW, IWAN. "Gorki i problem poetyzacji myśli" [Gorky and the problem of poeticization of thought]. Slavia Orientalis 18, no. 2:143-62.
  In Polish. Analyzes Gorky's literary innovations.

22 Maxime Gorki. Les bibliographies du Centre national de bibliographie, no. 69.01. Brussels: Mundaneum, 15 pp.
  Contains a list of major primary works in French and a selected bibliography of secondary works in French, Russian, German.

23 MIASNIKOV, A.S. V.I. Lenin i M. Gor'kii [V.I. Lenin and M. Gorky]. Moscow: Znanie, 62 pp.

Pamphlet. Lenin was the first to discover Gorky as a "great proletarian writer." Concentrates largely on Lenin's and Gorky's views of the social-political role of art.

24 MIKHAILOVSKII, B.V. "Avtobiograficheskaia trilogiia M. Gor'kogo" [M. Gorky's autobiographical trilogy]. In Izbrannye stat'i o literature i iskusstve. Moscow: Izd. MGU, pp. 292-352.
See 1969.28. Looks at the autobiography as an "idiosyncratic continuation" of Mother, written at the advice of Lenin. Compares it with Tolstoy's autobiographical works.

25 _____. "Gor'kii i Gogol'" [Gorky and Gogol]. In Izbrannye stat'i o literature i iskusstve. Moscow: Izd. MGU, pp. 132-74.
See 1969.28. Discusses Gorky's interest in Gogol's "heroic-romantic" works such as Taras Bulba and "The Terrible Vengeance" ["Strashnaia mest'"]. Deals with Gorky's lecture on Gogol on Capri in 1909.

26 _____. "Gor'kii i Ibsen" [Gorky and Ibsen]. In Izbrannye stat'i o literature i iskusstve. Moscow: Izd. MGU, pp. 247-91.
See 1969.28; 1958.44. Gorky's socialist realist drama presented and responded to social issues of the day in a way that brought him into close contact with the point of view and dramatic style of Henrik Ibsen.

27 _____. "Iz etiudov o romantizme rannego Gor'kogo (iumor i ego sviaz' s literaturnoi traditsiei)" [From studies on the romanticism of the early Gorky (humor and its connection with literary tradition)]. In Izbrannye stat'i o literature i iskusstve. Moscow: Izd. MGU, pp. 175-246.
See 1969.28. Gorky's romanticism of the mid-1890s has no Marxist overtones. Rather it reflects the impact of "utopian socialism" and populism. Although he does not yet see the revolutionary proletariat as his "positive hero," he senses "positive characteristics" in his central protagonists. His "task": "to show the positive hero in the conditions of the actual social environment." Discusses a large number of stories from this period.

28 _____. Izbrannye stat'i o literature i iskusstve [Selected articles on literature and art]. Moscow: Izd. MGU.
Contains the following articles on Gorky:
1. "Tvorcheskie iskaniia molodogo Gor'kogo (osobennosti realizma)" [The creative explorations of the young Gorky (particularities of realism)]. See 1969.29.
2. "Gor'kii i Gogol'" [Gorky and Gogol]. See 1969.25.
3. "Iz etiudov o romantizme rannego Gor'kogo (iumor i ego sviaz' s literaturnoi traditsiei)" [From studies on the romanticism of the early Gorky (humor and its connection with literary tradition)]. See 1969.27.

4. "Gor'kii i Ibsen" [Gorky and Ibsen]. See 1969.26.

5. "Avtobiograficheskaia trilogiia M. Gor'kogo" [The autobiographical trilogy of M. Gorky]. See 1969.24.

29 _____. "Tvorcheskie iskaniia molodogo Gor'kogo (osobennosti realizma)" [The creative explorations of the young Gorky (particularities of realism)]. In Izbrannye stat'i o literature i iskusstve. Moscow: Izd. MGU, pp. 61-131.
See 1969.28. Analyzes Gorky's early style in the context of realist prose of the 1880s and 1890s.

30 MIKHAILOVSKII, B.V., and TAGER, E.B. Tvorchestvo M. Gor'kogo [The creative work of M. Gorky]. 3d ed. Moscow: Prosveshchenie, 335 pp.
Devoted to Gorky's belletristic work. Mikhailovsky deals with work up to 1917, and Tager, from 1917 on. Does not deal with Confession [Ispoved'].

31 MORAVTSEVICH, NICHOLAS. "Gorky and the Western Naturalists: Anatomy of a Misalliance." Comparative Literature 21, no. 1:63-75.
Analyzes stylistic influences that helped shape Gorky's dramatic technique. Finds Gorky a very doubtful naturalist.

32 MURATOVA, K.D. "M. Gor'kii vo Frantsii i v Germanii" [M. Gorky in France and Germany]. Russkaia literatura 12, no. 2:226-30.
Review of work done both in the USSR and abroad on the theme of Gorky's impact on French and German literature. Notes the need for better bibliographies.

33 "Pis'ma pisatelei" [Letters of writers]. Novyi zhurnal, no. 95:216-31.
Contains two letters, one dated 3 March 1924 to Emma Voitinskaia, one dated 22 February 1925 to V.S. Voitinsky.

34 POPOVA, N.V. "Nizhegorodskii dialekt v povesti M. Gor'kogo Detstvo" [The Nizhny Novgorod dialect in Gorky's Childhood]. Russkaia rech' 3, no. 5:26-32.
On Gorky's style. Although it reflects the living language, Gorky's usage of dialect often embellishes existing vocabulary. Shows the "larger context" rather than the immediate "superficial" meaning of the word.

35 RELINGER, JEAN. "Sur un livre de Jean Pérus: Romain Rolland et Maxime Gorki." La pensée: Revue du rationalisme moderne, no. 144 (April):100-111.
A long review of Pérus's book. Finds it the highest quality of work using comparativist techniques. An interesting view of the problem of influence.

36 RUEHLE, JUERGEN. Literature and Revolution: A Critical Study of the Writer and Communism in the Twentieth Century. Translated by J. Steinberg. New York: Frederick A. Praeger, pp. 8-12, 20-34, 236-37, 336-37.
  Discusses The Life of Klim Samgin as a "key" to understanding contemporary Russia.

37 SCHRÖDER, R. "Maksim Gor'kii unter der Optik Thomas Manns." In Slawisch-deutsche Wechselbeziehungen in Sprache, Literatur und Kultur. Edited by W. Krauss et al. Vol. 44. Berlin: Akademie, pp. 446-59.
  Explains why Thomas Mann saw in Gorky's work a "global literary renewal."

38 SEMENOVSKII, O. Marksistskaia kritika o Gor'kom [Marxist criticism on Gorky]. Kishinev: Izd. Kartia Moldoveniaske, 188 pp.
  Deals with early Marxist Gorky criticism in the context of its debate with the modernists. Treats Gorky criticism up to 1907 and the debate around Mother [Mat'].

39 SIROTININA, O.B., ed. Voprosy stilistiki. Vol. 3. Saratov: Izd. SGU.
  Contains the following articles on Gorky's literary style:
  1. L.S. Kovtun, "Razgovornyi iazyk v khudozhestvennom tekste" [Conversational language in the artistic text]. Deals with spoken language as "model" of living language.
  2. N.A. Kirsanova and E.M. Nozhkina, "Sredstva sozdaniia ekspressii v iazyke dramaturgii M. Gor'kogo" [Means of creating expression in the language of Gorky's drama]. Looks at Egor Bulychev, Dostigaev, Somov.
  3. N.I. Bakhmutova, "Ob ekspressivnom komponente znacheniia slova" [On the expressive component in the meaning of a word]. Looks at use of slovo, rech', mysl', duma, and their levels of meaning and nuance in Gorky's work.

40 SKOBELEV, V.P. "Spor M. Gor'kogo i K. Fedina o muzhike v 20-e gody (k probleme 'vlasti zemli' i revoliutsii)" [The argument of M. Gorky and K. Fedin about the peasant in the 1920s (on the problem of the "power of the earth" and revolution)]. Russkaia literatura 12, no. 1:17-27.
  Influence must be viewed as a "complex system of mutual attractions and repulsions." Previous studies of Gorky and Soviet writers have pictured a teacher-student relationship. This study analyzes a real difference of opinion between the two writers and its implications.

41 TETENI, MARIIA. "Delo Artamonovykh M. Gor'kogo i Gospoda Golovlevy M. Shchedrina" [Gorky's The Artamonov Business and Shchedrin's The Golovlev Family]. Studia Slavica Academiae Scientiarum Hungaricae (Budapest) 15:119-29.

Analyzes The Artamonov Business in the light of the genre of the family novel. Compares with Western family novels—for example, Galsworthy's Forsythe Saga and Mann's Buddenbrooks.

42 THOMSON, R.D.B. Introduction to Foma Gordeyeff. Translated by I.F. Hapgood. Geneva, Switzerland: Edito-Service S.A., pp. ix-xvi.
Notices parallels between the life and character of Foma Gordeev and his creator: orphans, physically very strong, emotionally sensitive. This novel shows a path Gorky could have taken.

42A VOLKOV, A.A. Put' khudozhnika: M. Gor'kii do Oktiabria [The way of the artist: M. Gorky before October]. Moscow: Khud. lit., 407 pp.
Analysis is devoted to epic elements of style, imagery, and worldview in Gorky's prerevolutionary work. Concerned with demonstrating the originality of Gorky's art.

43 YARMOLINSKY, AVRAHM. "Maxim Gorky—Soviet Laureate." In The Russian Literary Imagination. New York: Funk & Wagnalls, pp. 111-30.
Gorky is a flawed writer of short stories: he indulges in "bathos," "sophomoric commentary." Concentrates on his novels, especially Mother [Mat'] and the autobiographies.

1970

1 BIALIK, BORIS. "Lenin and Gorky: Notes on Their Correspondence." Soviet Literature, no. 3:110-41.
Part of the Lenin-Gorky correspondence. Introductory notes present Gorky as fallible and often mistaken about the Revolution, ideological points, and politics. Lenin is the wiser of the two.

2 _____. Vlastiteli dum i chuvstv: V.I. Lenin i M. Gor'kii [Rulers of thoughts and feelings: V.I. Lenin and M. Gorky]. Moscow: Sovetskii pisatel', 248 pp.
Presents Lenin and Gorky's political-literary relationship. It is viewed as the "supreme example of the beneficial effect of Lenin's ideas on art" and as the "embodiment of party loyalty (partiinost) in literature." Written as an answer to Wolfe (1967.18) and Levin (1965.8). The chronicle of Lenin and Gorky's relationship passes over the difficult times of 1908-9 with just two pages of discussion and does not mention 1918 at all. A second chapter deals with these crises from the point of view that Lenin was the wiser of the two.

3 BORISOVA, M.B. Slovo v dramaturgii M. Gor'kogo [The word in Gorky's drama]. Saratov: Izd. SGU, 198 pp.

An analysis of Gorky's dramatic style with special emphasis on the ideological coloration of his work.

4   BRODSKAIA, S.IA. "O nekotorykh zarubezhnykh kritikakh Gor'kogo" [On some of Gorky's foreign critics]. Izvestiia ANSSSR 29, no. 3:236-44.
    A review of Gorky's critical reception in the United States. Notes that not all critics are "hostile."

5   EL'KIND, P.S. Otrazhenie leninskikh idei v pravovykh vozzreniiakh A.M. Gor'kogo [The reflection of Lenin's ideas in Gorky's legal views]. Leningrad: Izd. LGU, 40 pp.
    An analysis of Gorky's legal views shows Gorky's "high aesthetic mastery" and his "party-minded [partiinyi] passion."

6   GIPPIUS, ZINAIDA N. "Vybor meshka" [Taking sides]. In Literaturnyi dnevnik [Literary diary]. Munich: W. Fink, pp. 171-86.
    Reprinted from 1908.4. Gorky as a writer has faded. As a social phenomenon he is a touchstone for the "honesty of convictions" of an intellectual: if one dislikes Gorky, it means one likes repression, censorship, and so on.

7   HERLING-GRUDZIŃSKI, GUSTAW. "The Seven Deaths of Maksim Gorky." In Kultura Essays. Edited by L. Tyrmand. London: Collier-Macmillan; New York: Free Press, pp. 151-73.
    Biographical material. Shows the lack of agreement of official versions of Gorky's death. Gives a new reading of Gorky's exile years and the reasons for his return to the USSR. Argues that Gorky showed neither "strength" nor "incorruptibility," and that behind a façade of "false modesty" was hidden a "mania for greatness."

8   KOSING, EVA. "Lenin and Gorki im Zerrspiegel des Antikommunismus." Kunst und Literatur (Berlin) 18, no. 11:1156-73.
    Review of B.D. Wolfe's book (1967.18). Predictably negative: Wolfe uses no new sources; his method, however, is "new"; quotes and translates incorrectly; quotes in a distorting way. Denies Wolfe's argument. Calls the whole thing a "fabrication" by the "worst of hecklers."

9   KOSTKA, EDMUND. "Maksim Gorky: Russian Writer with a Western Bent." Rivista di letterature moderne e comparate, no. 23: 5-20.
    Discusses Gorky's affinity for Byron, Nietzsche, Hauptmann.

10 KROPOTKIN, PRINCE PETER. Ideals and Realities in Russian Literature. Westport, Conn.: Greenwood, pp. 249-60.
    Reprinted from 1915 edition. Gorky's tales are appealing because of the "interesting, original, and new characters."

11   LUKIRSKAIA, K.P., MILLER, O.V., and MORSHCHIKHINA, A.S.
     Literatura o M. Gor'kom: Bibliografiia, 1961-1965 [Literature
     on M. Gorky: Bibliography, 1961-1965]. Edited by K.D.
     Muratova. Leningrad: Biblioteka ANSSSR, 291 pp.
         An updated bibliography of secondary works. See 1965.11.

12   MURATOVA, KSENIIA DM. "Über den russischen Nationalcharakter
     im Schaffen Gor'kijs." Wissenschaftliche Zeitschrift der
     Universität Berlin 19, no. 3:271-76.
         Gorky brought out the active, strong-willed aspects of the
     Russian character. He felt that if people believed they were the
     creators of the world, they could conceive a "'new person and a
     new history.'"

13   NIKOLIUKIN, A.N. "Gor'kii i SShA (po neopublikovannym
     materialam)" [Gorky and the U.S.A. (from unpublished
     materials)]. In Gor'kii i sovremennost'. Moscow: Nauka,
     pp. 440-45.
         See 1970.18. Shows Gorky's attitude to America in a
     brighter light. Positive response to I. Weil (1965.18).

14   OVCHARENKO, A.I. "Iazyk i stil' povesti M. Gor'kogo Mat'"
     [Language and style in Gorky's novel Mother]. Russkaia rech'
     4, no. 2:96-101.
         Gorky's style in Mother combines "realist" epithets and
     images with "romantic" metaphors and similes.

15   PETROSIAN, A.A., et al., eds. Gor'kii i literatura narodov
     sovetskogo soiuza [Gorky and the national literatures of the
     Soviet Union]. Erevan: Izd. EGU, 627 pp.
         Contains papers from the conference in 1968 on Gorky's
     impact on national literatures of the Soviet Union.

16   SAMVELIAN, G.K. Nekotorye voprosy iazyka i stilia
     proizvedenii A.M. Gor'kogo, 1909-1914 gg. [Some questions of
     language and style in Gorky's works, 1909-1914]. Erevan:
     Luis, 52 pp.
         Analyzes two aspects of Gorky's style: the process of
     metaphorization and the use of the dash.

17   SCHRÖDER, JORG. "Die amerikanische Literatur im Urteil
     Gor'kiis." Wissenschaftliche Zeitschrift der Universität
     Berlin 19, no. 3:311-15.
         Sketches Gorky's views on American literature, his meeting
     with Mark Twain, his opinion of Bret Harte, O. Henry, Dos Passos,
     W. Whitman, J. London.

18   SHCHERBINA, V.R., et al., eds. Gor'kii i sovremennost' [Gorky
     and the present]. Moscow: Nauka, 463 pp.
         Devoted to Gorky's aesthetics and his international influ-
     ence. Contains the following articles:

1. M.B. Khrapchenko, "Gor'kii i nashe vremia" [Gorky and our time].
2. V.R. Shcherbina, "M. Gor'kii: Kontseptsiia mira i iskusstva" [M. Gorky: The view of the world and art].
3. R.M. Samarin and L.M. Iur'eva, "M. Gor'kii i mirovoi literaturnyi protsess" [M. Gorky and the world literary process].
4. A.I. Ovcharenko, "M. Gor'kii i literaturnye iskaniia XX stoletiia" [M. Gorky and literary searchings of the 20th century].
5. L.I. Timofeev, "M. Gor'kii i mnogonatsional'naia sovetskaia literatura" [M. Gorky and multinational Soviet literature].
6. B.A. Bialik, "Neischerpaemye vozmozhnosti realizma" [The inexhaustible possibilities of realism].
7. A.S. Miasnikov, "M. Gor'kii i voprosy sovremennoi estetiki" [Gorky and questions of contemporary aesthetics].
8. Ia.E. El'sberg, "Stil' Gor'kogo i stilevye iskaniia sovetskoi prozy" [Gorky's style and stylistic explorations in Soviet prose].
9. D.V. Zatonskii, "Zhizn' Klima Samgina i nekotorye problemy sovremennogo zarubezhnogo romana" [The Life of Klim Samgin and certain problems of the contemporary foreign novel].
10. A.O. Boguslavskii, "Gor'kovskaia kontseptsiia cheloveka i sovremennaia dramaturgiia" [Gorky's concept of man and contemporary drama].
11. V.V. Novikov, "O novykh formakh khudozhestvennogo obobshcheniia" [On new forms of artistic generalization].
12. Khristo Dudevskii, "Maksim Gor'kii--zhivoi uchastnik sovremennogo literaturnogo protsessa Bolgarii" [Maksim Gorky--a living participant in Bulgaria's present literary life].
13. Vasil Kolevskii, "Gumanizm Gor'kogo" [Gorky's humanism].
14. Gabor Tolnai, "Vliianie tvorchestva M. Gor'kogo na vengerskuiu literaturu" [The influence of Gorky's work on Hungarian literature].
15. O.K. Rossiianov, "Sovremennost' Gor'kogo" [Gorky's contemporaneity].
16. I. Idtsikovski, "Maksim Gor'kii v Germanskoi Demokraticheskoi Respublike" [Maksim Gorky in East Germany].
17. E.Ia. Mirova-Florin, "Aktual'nye problemy literaturovedeniia GDR i 100-letie iubilei M. Gor'kogo" [Actual problems of literary criticism in East Germany and the 100th anniversary of Gorky].
18. N. Tun, "Preodolenie otchuzhdeniia v avtobiograficheskoi trilogii Gor'kogo [Overcoming alienation in Gorky's autobiographical trilogy].
19. S. Luvsanvandan, "Printsip aktivnosti i deiatel'naia svoboda" [The principle of activism and active freedom].
20. Ia.S. Givin, "P'esa M. Gor'kogo Na dne na pol'skikh stsenakh" [Gorky's play The Lower Depths on the Polish stage].

21. T. Nikolesku, "Tvorchestvo M. Gor'kogo i rumynskaia obshchestvennost' XX veka" [Gorky's work and 20th-century Romanian social consciousness].
22. S.I. Belza, "Tvorchestvo Gor'kogo i slovatskaia literatura" [Gorky's work and Slovak literature].
23. A. Flaker, "Khorvatskie vstrechi s Maksimom Gor'kim" [Croatian meetings with Maksim Gorky].
24. N.B. Iakovleva, "M. Gor'kii i peredovaia literatura Iugoslavii" [M. Gorky and progressive literature of Yugoslavia].
25. A.P. Sarukhanian, "Gor'kii i O'Keisi" [Gorky and O'Casey].
26. Iannis Mochos, "Traditsii Maksima Gor'kogo v grecheskoi literature" [Gorkian traditions in Greek literature].
27. Madan Lal Madkhu, "Gor'kii i Indiia" [Gorky and India].
28. E.P. Chelyshev, "Gor'kii v segodniashnei Indii" [Gorky in India of today].
29. Z.G. Osmanova, "Gor'kovskie traditsii v sovremennoi literature Irana" [Gorkian traditions in contemporary Iranian literature].
30. Z.M. Potapova, "Gor'kii i Italiia" [Gorky and Italy].
31. A. Bibilashvili, "Rol' M. Gor'kogo v tvorcheskoi sud'be meksikanskogo pisatelia Khose Mansisidora" [Gorky's role in the creative career of the Mexican writer Jose Mansisidor].
32. L.G. Grigor'ev, "Po gor'kovskomu puti (norvezhskii 'rabochii' roman XX v.)" [On Gorky's way (the 20th-century Norwegian worker's novel].
33. A.N. Nikoliukin, "Gor'kii i SShA" [Gorky and the U.S.A.]. See 1970.13.
34. N.F. Rzhevskaia, "Dramaturgiia Gor'kogo v sovremennoi Frantsii" [Gorky's plays in present-day France].
35. K. Rekho, "M. Gor'kii v poslevoennom tvorchestve iaponskikh pisatelei" [M. Gorky in postwar Japanese belles lettres].

18A SUKHAREV, G.M. "Gor'kii i Bal'mont (iz istorii ikh literaturnykh sviazei)" [Gorky and Balmont (from the history of their literary ties]. <u>Uchenye zapiski Ivanovskogo pedagogicheskogo instituta</u> (Ivanovo) 73:73-82.
   Deals with Gorky's view of Balmont and decadent art. Gives account of their first acquaintance and ensuing dealings.

19 VAINBERG, I. "Dostovernost' fakta i pravda iskusstva (v tvorcheskoi laboratorii M. Gor'kogo: <u>Zhizn' Klima Samgina</u>)" [Plausibility of fact and truth of art (in Gorky's creative laboratory: <u>The Life of Klim Samgin</u>)]. <u>Voprosy literatury</u> 14, no. 10:131-52.
   Treats the text as a series of clues to a past "reality." The concrete document is Gorky's literary material. <u>The Life of Klim Samgin</u> is a kind of "encyclopedia of the typical in art." By studying these "clues" we can come to a reading of the novel.

20 VIL'CHINSKII, V.P. "Neizvestnaia stat'ia o M. Gor'kom" [An unknown article on Gorky]. Russkaia literatura 13, no. 3: 136-39.
    An article by S.S. Gouloushev about Gorky's support in April-May 1917 of a new association for the popularization of the sciences.

21 WEGNER, MICHAEL. "Rosa Luxemburg und Maxim Gorki." Wissenschaftliche Zeitschrift der Friedrich-Schiller Universität Jena 19, no. 4:671-78.
    Shows Gorky's influence on Luxemburg's views on cultural politics and aesthetic theory.

22 ZAMIATIN, EVGENII. "Maxim Gorky." In A Soviet Heretic. Translated by M. Ginsburg. Chicago: University of Chicago Press, pp. 246-58.
    Translation of 1936.9; 1967.19. Describes Gorky in the early years after the Revolution: Gorky as "unofficial minister of culture" and as critic of his own work. Discusses Gorky's relationship to Lenin and Stalin, his role in the Gumilev and Zamiatin cases.

23 ZELINSKY, KORNELY. "Maxim Gorky." In Soviet Literature: Problems and People. Moscow: Progress, pp. 49-57.
    Memoir of Gorky. Compares him to Leonardo da Vinci in the "range of his interests" and his "insatiable curiosity."

1971

1 ERMOLAEV, G. "Vvedenie" [Introduction] to Nesvoevremennye mysli [Untimely Thoughts]. Paris: Editions de la Seine, pp. 7-18.
   The period of Gorky's work on the "internationalist" newspaper Novaia zhizn' [New Life], 1917-19, was among Gorky's most fruitful. Recounts Gorky's polemic with Lenin during these years carried on through the newspaper and the group Culture and Freedom [Kul'tura i svoboda].

2 EVENTOV, I.S. "Tragikomediia ukhodiashchego mira: O dramaturgicheskoi epopee M. Gor'kogo" [The tragicomedy of the departing world: On Gorky's dramatic epic]. Russkaia literatura 14, no. 2:36-52.
   Analyzes Gorky's view of comedy and why it is suitable as a way of treating the events of the war and the Revolution.

3 GOR'KII, A.M. M. Gor'kii i syn: Pis'ma, vospominaniia [Gorky and his son: Letters, memoirs]. Edited by B.A. Bialik et al. Arkhiv A.M. Gor'kogo, vol. 13. Moscow: Nauka, 319 pp.
   Correspondence. Contains all Gorky's letters to his son, Maksim Peshkov, and selected letters from Peshkov to Gorky. Also includes memoirs of Maksim Peshkov's wife and others.

4   HABERMANN, GERHARD. Maksim Gorki. Translated by E. Schlant. New York: Ungar, 105 pp.
    Biography. Emphasizes Gorky's political formation and his social activity.

5   LAVRIN, JANKO. "Maxim Gorky." In From Pushkin to Mayakovsky. Westport, Conn.: Greenwood, pp. 192-219.
    Reprinted from 1948 edition. Compares Gorky to L.N. Tolstoy and H.G. Wells. The "artist" and social "reformer" in him strengthen each other.

6   LO GATTO, ETTORE. Russi in Italia dal secolo XVII ad oggi. Rome: Editori Riuniti, pp. 233-41.
    Biographical material. Gorky's life and work in Italy.

7   MIKHAILOVSKII, B.V. "Stanovlenie sotsialisticheskogo realizma v tvorchestve A.M. Gor'kogo" [The rise of socialist realism in the creative work of A.M. Gorky]. In Russkaia literatura kontsa XIX-nachala XX v., 1901-1907 [Russian literature of the end of the 19th-early 20th century, 1901-1907]. Moscow: Nauka, pp. 58-91.
    Discusses the formation of socialist realist principles in Gorky's early drama and in Mother [Mat'].

8   MUCHNIC, HELEN. Russian Writers. New York: Random House.
    Contains essays and review articles on Gorky:
        1. "About Tolstoi, Chekhov, Gorky." See 1971.9.
        2. "Maxim Gorky." See 1971.11.
        3. "Circe's Swine: Plays by Gorky and O'Neill." See 1951.10; 1961.19.
        4. "Gorky from Chaliapin to Lenin." See 1971.10.

9   _____. "About Tolstoi, Chekhov, Gorky." In Russian Writers. New York: Random House, pp. 194-99.
    See 1971.8. Review of Filia Holtzman, The Young Maxim Gorky: 1868-1902. First appeared in The Russian Review 4 (1949). Finds that Gorky, "without question, one of the most curious figures of modern times," is here given "naive" treatment.

10 _____. "Gorky from Chaliapin to Lenin." In Russian Writers. New York: Random House, pp. 249-57.
    See 1971.8. Review of Maxim Gorky, Chaliapin: An Autobiography, trans. and ed. N. Froud and J. Hanley; Gorky, Untimely Thoughts, trans. H. Ermolaev; Bertram D. Wolfe, The Bridge and the Abyss. First appeared in the New York Review of Books, 27 March 1969. Contains some biographical material. Shows Gorky during the tumultuous period between 1916, when he wrote Shaliapin's autobiography, through the Revolution and Lenin's death. Seen as strongly, selflessly concerned with issues of national culture, individual rights, political justice, which

made him the figurehead of the Revolution but often put him at odds with it.

11 _____. "Maxim Gorky." Russian Writers. New York: Random House, pp. 231-32.
See 1971.8. Review of Richard Hare, Maxim Gorky, in Russian Review 2 (April 1963). Finds Hare's book a needed, sane judgment of Gorky: Hare is "[n]either a hagiographer nor an apologist."

12 MURATOVA, K.D. M. Gor'kii na Kapri, 1911-1913 [Gorky on Capri, 1911-1913]. Leningrad: Nauka, 275 pp.
Partial biography. Sees the period just before Gorky's return to Russia as a period of healing after the debacle between Lenin and Bogdanov. Analyzes Gorky's editorial, political, and creative activities during this time. Discussion is devoted to his work in the journal Sovremennik [The Contemporary], the founding of the Russo-Italian Society, as well as his polemic against "decadence" in literature.

13 OBERLÄNDER, ERWIN, et al., eds. Russia Enters the Twentieth Century, 1894-1917. New York: Schocken Books, pp. 282-84.
Gorky's prerevolutionary works are characterized by moral relativism.

14 OLGIN, MOISSAYE J. "Maxim Gorky." In A Guide to Russian Literature (1820-1917). New York: Russell & Russell, pp. 222-29.
Reprinted from 1920 edition. Gorky's literary career developed in three stages: (1) he was a "herald of a coming era" (1892-1905), (2) he struggled to keep pace with reality (1905-9), (3) he recorded the past. Accordingly his style evolves from romantic to realist.

15 OVCHARENKO, A. M. Gor'kii i literaturnye iskaniia XX stoletiia [Gorky and literary searchings of the 20th century]. Moscow: Sovetskii pisatel', 286 pp.
See 1968.86; 1970.18. A defense of socialist realism against literary critics from capitalist countries. Discusses Gorky's major works from the 1920s and 1930s, The Artamonov Business [Delo Artamonovykh] and The Life of Klim Samgin [Zhizn' Klima Samgina].

16 REILLY, A.P. "Four Early Impressions: Gorky, Mayakovsky, Pilnyak, Ilf and Petrov." In America in Contemporary Soviet Literature. New York: New York University Press, pp. 3-45.
Gorky is one of five writers who helped mold the negative Soviet image of America. Pages 4 to 12 deal with Gorky's "The City of the Yellow Devil" ["Gorod zheltogo d'iavola"] which Reilly sees as a possible "accident of fate."

17 SCHRÖDER, RALF. Gorkis Erneuerung der Fausttradition: Faustmodelle im russischen geschichtsphilosophischen Roman. Berlin: Rütten und Loening, 416 pp.
    The Life of Klim Samgin [Zhizn' Klima Samgina] can be seen as the last of a series of assimilations of the Faust myth in Russian literature. Schröder discusses Tolstoy, Dostoevsky, Bulgakov. The Faust myth is at base a bourgeois myth. Klim Samgin discredits it through parodic techniques and opens the way for a proletarian socialist myth. Klim Samgin is opposed to Thomas Mann's Doktor Faustus, which remains in the tradition of bourgeois "critical realism."

18 SIMMONS, ERNEST J. An Outline of Modern Russian Literature (1880-1940). Westport, Conn.: Greenwood, pp. 15-17.
    Reprinted from 1945 edition. Gorky "liberated" Russian realism from its conservative, "Victorian" traditions. Outlines Gorky's development.

19 SIROTINA, V.A. "'More smeialos''" ["The Sea Laughed"]. Russkaia rech' 5, no. 1:19-26.
    Deals with Gorky's view of stylistic exactness.

20 VAINBERG, IOSIF. "Zhizn' Klima Samgina" M. Gor'kogo: Istoriko-literaturnyi kommentarii [Gorky's The Life of Klim Samgin: Historical literary commentary]. Moscow: Prosveshchenie, 381 pp.
    A guide to events, figures, books mentioned in The Life of Klim Samgin.

21 VOGÜE, E.M. de. "Maxime Gorky: L'oeuvre et l'homme." In Le roman Russe, augmenté d'un article sur Maxime Gorki. Montreux: Ganguin, pp. 307-53.
    First published as an article in Revue des deux mondes (August 1901), and included in Vogüe's study of the Russian novel in 1905. Gorky is emerging as a rival to Chekhov. His appearance on the literary social scene shows how little Europeans understand Russia. Sees Gorky as a "romantic."

22 WEISS, EDGAR. "Das Verhältnis und die Beziehungen J.R. Bechers zu Maksim Gor'kij." In Becher und die sowjetische Literaturentwicklung, (1917-1933). Edited by H.H. Bielfeldt. Veröffentlichungen des Instituts für Slawistik, no. 53. Berlin: Akademie, pp. 46-59.
    Discusses J.R. Becher's "discovery" of Gorky in the early 1920s.

23 ZYTARUK, GEORGE J. "D.H. Lawrence's Hand in the Translation of Maksim Gorki's 'Reminiscences of Leonid Andreev.'" Yale University Library Gazette, no. 46:29-34.
    Discusses Lawrence's revision of the Mansfield-Koteliansky translation.

1972

1 BERBEROVA, NINA. Kursiv moi: Avtobiografiia [The italics are mine: An autobiography]. Munich: W. Fink, pp. 196-98, 200-230, 325-27.
See 1961.4; 1967.1; 1969.4. Biographical material. About Gorky in Petrograd, Berlin, and Sorrento from the viewpoint of someone who dismisses him as a writer but knew him well as a person in exile.

2 BIALIK, B.A., and KELDYSH, V.A. "Sotsialisticheskii realizm na novom etape" [Socialist realism at a new stage]. In Russkaia literatura kontsa XIX-nachala XX v., 1908-1917 [Russian literature of the end of the 19th-early 20th century, 1908-1917]. Moscow: Nauka, pp. 27-74.
Authors discuss new currents in Gorky's literary "method." Focus on The Town of Okurov [Gorodok Okurov], The Life of Matvei Kozhemiakin [Zhizn' Matveia Kozhemiakina], Confession [Ispoved'], Around Russia [Po Rusi].

3 BRAUN, EDWARD. Introduction to Enemies. Translated by K. Hunter-Blair and J. Brooks. New York: Viking.
Enemies [Vragi] is still relevant because of its look at relations between workers and industrialists.

4 BROOKS, JEREMY. Preface to Enemies. Translated by K. Hunter-Blair and J. Brooks. New York: Viking, pp. xiv-xviii.
Enemies is an important social play, which shows a great deal of understanding about the nature of social oppressors.

5 BUDBERG, MOURA. Preface to Fragments from My Diary. London: Penguin, pp. vii-xiv.
Reprinted from 1940 edition. Biographical material by a close friend of Gorky in the 1920s. A flavorful picture of Gorky's energetic character, lively style, and enthusiastic love of knowledge and books.

6 BYKOVTSEVA, L. Gor'kii v Moskve, 1931-1936 [Gorky in Moscow, 1931-1936]. 2d ed. Moscow: Moskovskii rabochii, 320 pp.
Biographical material. Analyzes the city of Moscow as an important aspect of Gorky's literary geography. Moscow was one of the few places Gorky thought of as home. Spends several pages describing the Riabushinsky house where Gorky lived in the 1930s.

7 EVENTOV, I.S. "Ob odnoi p'ese M. Gor'kogo" [On one play of Gorky's]. Neva, no. 3:177-80.
Deals with Gorky and satire.

8 FRANKEL, TOBIA. The Russian Artist: The Creative Person in Russian Culture. New York: Macmillan; London: Collier-Macmillan, pp. 92-95, 113-14, 129-30.

At the turn of the century, Gorky was a "hero of our times." Discusses Gorky and Shaliapin's friendship.

9   KARPENKO, MARGARITA A. M. Gor'kii i russkii literaturnyi iazyk sovetskoi epokhi [M. Gorky and Russian literary language of the Soviet era]. Kiev: Izd. KGU, 216 pp.
    Studies the interrelationship between Gorky's literary language and the standard literary language of Russia in the 1920s and 1930s. Studies story cycles--for example, "Around the Union of Soviets" ["Po soiuzu sovetov"], "Stories of Heroes" ["Rasskazy o geroiakh"], sketches, plays, publicistic essays, and The Life of Klim Samgin [Zhizn' Klima Samgina].

10 KOSIN, IGOR. Introduction to The Petit Bourgeois. Translated by I. Kosin. N.p.: Washington State University Press, pp. 1-8.
    Outlines Gorky's attitude to the Russian petit bourgeois (meshchanin) both as a social group and as a mentality. This play is about the "generation gap."

10A L[ASKY], M.J. "Maxim Gorky: The Shame and the Glory." Encounter 38, no. 3 (March):92-94.
    Review of Untimely Thoughts [Nesvoevremennye mysli], ed. H. Ermolaev. Finds reason to rehabilitate Gorky from his Stalinist ignominy.

11 MANDEL'SHTAM, NADEZHDA. Vtoraia kniga [Second book]. Paris: YMCA Press, pp. 74-76.
    Recounts in acerbic tones Mandelshtam's and Akhmatova's experiences with Gorky in 1920.

12 MATLAW, MYRON. Modern World Drama: An Encyclopedia. New York: E.P. Dutton, pp. 309-10, 481-82.
    Gorky is one of the "greatest practitioners of naturalism." Only The Lower Depths [Na dne] has achieved international acclaim. Surveys briefly Gorky's other plays. The Lower Depths is a "Lumpenproletariat analogue of Chekhov's The Cherry Orchard."

13 ROMANOVA, E.S., ed. Proizvedeniia sovetskikh pisatelei v perevodakh na inostrannye iazyki, 1965-1970 [The works of Soviet writers in foreign translation, 1965-1970]. Moscow: Kniga, pp. 40-49.
    Bibliography. Continuation of 1966.19.

14 SHKLOVSKY, VIKTOR. Mayakovsky and His Circle. Translated by L. Feiler. New York: Dodd, Mead & Co., pp. 108-10.
    Discusses Gorky and Maiakovsky's relations.

14A TURNER, C.J.G. "'Iconoclasm' as a Structural Device in Three of Gorky's Stories." Modern Language Journal 67, no. 1 (January):143-50.

Analyzes "Twenty-Six and One" ["Dvadtsat' shest' i odna"], "Boles'," and "Varenka Olesova." Sees "iconoclasm," or the reversal of character images, as a major device used by Gorky in the construction of his short stories.

15 VENGEROV, S.A., ed. Russkaia literatura XX veka [Russian literature of the 20th century]. Munich: W. Fink, 1:188-234, 2:170-79.
    Reprint from 1915.5.

16 VOLKOV, A.A. Lenin i Gor'kii [Lenin and Gorky]. Moscow: Sovremennik, 287 pp.
    Studies how Lenin as thinker and Gorky as artist complemented each other's worldview. Arrives at a view of creative personality that is more sophisticated than earlier works on this theme. Shows the relationship more as a debate between equals than as a teacher-student situation. Traces Lenin's effort to form Gorky's philosophical and political principles.

1973

1   BABAIAN, E. Rannii Gor'kii [The early Gorky]. Moscow: Khud. lit., 231 pp.
    Traces Gorky's evolution to proletarian literature.

1A BARTKOVICH, JEFFREY. "Maxim Gorky's 'Twenty-six Men and a Girl': The Destruction of an Illusion." Studies in Short Fiction 10:287-88.
    Sees this story as a study in nihilism.

2   BIALIK, BORIS. Sud'ba Maksima Gor'kogo [The fate of Maksim Gorky]. 2d ed. Moscow: Khud. lit., 364 pp.
    Gorky's life story is a kind of "crystal ball" through which we can see the important points of aesthetic and intellectual development of our time. Talks about his life in religious terms: his life is a "trial in hell" [khozhdenie po mukam], his "resurrection" consists of the fact that he is still "alive" as writer and teacher. Concentrates on "significant" moments in his political development, his participation in revolutionary circles, his discovery of Marxism, his relationship with Lenin.

2A BLAIR, KITTY HUNTER. "Gorky on Gorky." Theatre Quarterly 3, no. 9:27-30.
    See 1973.9A. Translations of Gorky's and actors' comments on Enemies and The Lower Depths.

3   BRAUN, EDWARD. "Introduction to The Lower Depths. Translated by K. Hunter-Blair and J. Brooks. New York: Viking, pp. xi-xiv.

Originally appeared in Flourish 1 (1972). Gives a brief review of the censors' treatment of The Lower Depths [Na dne] and its initial productions.

3A BROOKS, JEREMY. "Translating Gorky." Theatre Quarterly 3, no. 9:24-26.
    See 1973.9A. The literary manager of the Royal Shakespeare Company discusses the problems of translating Gorky's plays.

4   BYALIK, BORIS. Preface to Childhood. Translated by M. Wettlin. Moscow: Progress, pp. 5-16.
    Childhood brings into relief key themes in Gorky's work--for example, spiritual rebirth and the disintegration of the self.

5   ERMAKOVA, M.IA. Romany Dostoevskogo i tvorcheskie iskaniia v russkoi literature XX veka (L. Andreev, M. Gor'kii) [Dostoevsky's novels and creative searchings in 20th-century Russian literature (L. Andreev, M. Gorky)]. Gorky: Volgoviat. knizh. izd-vo., pp. 257-318.
    One of the clearest discussions of Gorky's attitudes to Dostoevsky. Treats Gorky's estimation of Dostoevsky, Gorky's response in the Okurov cycle to Dostoevsky's psychological views, Gorky's development of the Dostoevskian tradition in the novel.

5A ESSLIN, MARTIN. "Plumbing the Lower Depths." Theatre Quarterly 3, no. 9:6-11.
    See 1973.9A. Analyzes eighteen reviews of one performance of The Lower Depths. Asks what the role of reviewing should be.

6   EVENTOV, I.S. Sila sarkazma: Satira i iumor v tvorchestve M. Gor'kogo [The force of sarcasm: Satire and humor in M. Gorky's work]. Leningrad: Sovetskii pisatel', 431 pp.
    The first study devoted to Gorky's use of satire. Compares Gorky to Anatole France, G.B. Shaw, Mark Twain, Jaroslav Haszek. Differs from Eventov's earlier work (1962) in that he analyzes satire from a theoretical standpoint and discusses its function in the whole range of literary, dramatic, and publicistic genres used by Gorky. This book is intended to help contemporary writers and critics better to understand and use satire and humor.

7   IMENDÖRFER, HELENE. Die perspektivische Struktur von Gor'kijs Roman "Žizn' Klima Samgina." Osteuropa Institut, Freie Univ. Berlin. Wiesbaden: Otto Harrassowitz, 176 pp.
    Analyzes the hero's perception and interpretation of "reality" in The Life of Klim Samgin, and defines the relationship of the "whole reality of the novel" to the hero's consciousness.

7A JONES, DAVID. "Directing Gorky." Theatre Quarterly 3, no. 9:12-23.
    See 1973.9A. Interview with the English director of Enemies and The Lower Depths. Talks about what attracted him,

particularly to a relatively rarely staged play like <u>Enemies</u>, and how he transmitted his insight to the actors and prepared them for their roles.

7B RISCHBIETER, HENNING. <u>Maxim Gorki</u>. Hannover: Friedrich Verlag, 145 pp.
    Devoted to an analysis of all Gorky's plays and their major productions. Gives background of Gorky's political development and its impact on his career as a dramatist.

8   ROZANOV, IVAN N. "Maksim Gor'kii." In <u>Putevoditel' po sovremennoi russkoi literature</u> [A guide to contemporary Russian literature]. Leipzig: Universitätsbibliothek Leipzig, pp. 235-51.
    Reprinted from 1929 edition (Moscow). Gorky is the "brightest name" in twentieth-century Russian literature, and he is a "great organizer of Russian letters." Discusses editing and organizing work. Gives short primary and secondary bibliographies.

8A SIMON, JOHN. "Theater Chronicle." <u>Hudson Review</u> 26, no. 1:187-91.
    A very negative review of Ellis Rabb's staging of <u>Enemies</u> [<u>Vragi</u>] with the Lincoln Center Repertory Company.

9   STRUVE, GLEB. "Gorky in the Soviet Period." In <u>Major Soviet Writers</u>. Edited by E.J. Brown. Oxford: Oxford University Press, pp. 197-201.
    Reprinted from G. Struve, <u>Russian Literature under Lenin and Stalin, 1917-1953</u>. Points out the ambivalence of Gorky's attitude to the Soviet regime in its earliest years.

9A <u>Theatre Quarterly</u> 3, no. 9:6-30.
    Four articles devoted to Gorky:
    1. Martin Esslin, "Plumbing the Lower Depths." See 1973.5A.
    2. David Jones, "Directing Gorky." See 1973.7A.
    3. Jeremy Brooks, "Translating Gorky." See 1973.3A.
    4. Kitty Hunter Blair, "Gorky on Gorky." See 1973.2A.

10 USPENSKAIA, V.E. <u>M. Gor'kii v pechati rodnogo kraia, 1959-1968: Ukazatel' literatury</u> [M. Gorky in his hometown press, 1959-1968: Literary index]. Gorky: Gor. Obl. Bibl. im. V.I. Lenina, 121 pp.
    Bibliography of books and articles written by and about Gorky in the Gorky press for 1959 to 1968.

11 ZHELEZNOV, PAVEL IL'ICH. <u>Maksim Gor'kii, Vladimir Maiakovskii: Poemy-vospominaniia</u> [Maksim Gorky, Vladimir Maiakovsky: Poems-memoirs]. Moscow: Nauka, 103 pp.
    A collection of poetry devoted to Gorky and Maiakovsky.

1974

1. BRIGGS, ANTHONY D. "Gorky's 'Burevestnik': Problems of Definition and Origin." Forum for Modern Language Studies 10, no. 2 (April):147-55.
    Shows that "The Stormy Petrel" is actually a poem, not prose, and analyzes its heritage in Longfellow's Hiawatha.

2. BYKOVTSEVA, L. "Gor'kii v Italii" [Gorky in Italy]. Znamia 44, no. 3:178-209; 44, no. 8:203-26.
    Biographical material. First part is an account of Gorky's life on Capri, 1906-13. Second part tells about his life in Sorrento, 1924-33. More about daily life than about issues. Sentimental tone. Sees Gorky's life as a "narrative poem."

3. DALLIN, DAVID J. Forced Labor in Soviet Russia. New York: Octagon Books, pp. 242-43.
    Explains Gorky's support of the volume on the Belomor Canal by his "childish naïveté."

4. ELISEEV, A. A.M. Gor'kii v N. Novgorode [Gorky in Nizhny Novgorod]. Gorky: Volgo-Viat. knizh. izd-vo., 110 pp.
    Biographical material. Gives a short account of Gorky's life in Nizhny Novgorod. Gives addresses of places Gorky lived and worked.

5. ISAEV, G.G. "A.M. Gor'kii o znachenii traditsii Dostoevskogo dlia tvorchestva L. Leonova" [A.M. Gorky on the meaning of the Dostoevskian tradition for the work of L. Leonov]. In Voprosy gor'kovedeniia. Vol. 1. Gorky: Izd. GGU, pp. 208-21.
    See 1974.7. Discusses Gorky's and L. Leonov's differing views of Dostoevsky.

6. IUREVA, LIDIA. "Die Tradition Gor'kijs und die deutschen Schriftsteller des Sozialistischen Realismus (Brecht, Becher, Seghers)." Wissenschaftliche Zeitschrift der Friedrich-Schiller Universität Jena 23, no. 1:45-52.
    Analyzes Gorky's influence upon Becher's aesthetic views, on Brecht's reworking of Mother [Mat'] into a play, Tolstoy's and Gorky's impact on Seghers's "Die Rettung," "Die Toten bleiben jung."

7. KUZ'MICHEV, I.K., ed. In Voprosy Gor'kovedeniia. Vol. 1. Gorky: Izd. GGU, 228 pp.
    Devoted to Mother [Mat']. Contains the following articles (titles are shortened in some cases):

1. N.I. Khomenko, "O poeticheskoi idee materinstva v tvorchestve M. Gor'kogo" [On the poetic idea of motherhood in Gorky's work].
2. N.D. Baranova and V.I. Baranov, "Povest' Mat' i tvorchestvo Gor'kogo 20-kh godov" [The novel Mother and Gorky's work of the 1920s].
3. L.N. Dar'ialova, "Khudozhestvennyi istorizm i struktura povesti Mat'" [Artistic historicism and the structure of the novel Mother].
4. E.F. Mishina and Zh.N. Laletina, "Upotreblenie leksiki mysli . . ." [The use of the lexicon of thought . . .].
5. M.G. Kireeva, "Epitet v strukture obraza Nilovny" [The epithet in the structure of the image of Nilovna].
6. O.A. Saltaeva, "Graficheskie i zvukovye sredstva izobrazheniia narodnoi massy . . ." [Graphic and sound media in the depiction of the masses of the people . . .].
7. N.Iu. Rusova, "O nekotorykh osobennostiakh postroeniia predlozheniia . . ." [On certain peculiarities in the construction of the sentence . . .].
8. M.T. Pinaev, "Tvorcheskii opyt narodnicheskoi literary i . . . Mat'" [The creative experience of populist literature and . . . Mother].
9. Iu.F. Shal'nov, "Glumovy, Gde luchshe? F. Reshetnikova i Mat' . . ." [The Glumovs and Where Is It Better? by F. Reshetnikov and Mother . . .].
10. I.V. Nikitina, "O nizhegorodskikh prototipakh zhenshchin-revoliutsionerok . . ." [On Nizhny Novgorod prototypes of women revolutionaries . . .].
11. V.N. Morokhin, "Fol'klor v povesti . . ." [Folklore in the novel . . .].
12. G.G. Isaev, "A.M. Gor'kii o znachenii traditsii Dostoevskogo dlia tvorchestva L. Leonova" [Gorky on the meaning of the Dostoevskian tradition for the work of L. Leonov]. See 1974.5.
Also contains a review of S.I. Sukhikh of K.D. Muratova's book Gor'kii na Kapri, 1911-1913.

8 LARIN, B.A. Slovar' avtobiograficheskoi trilogii M. Gor'kogo [Dictionary of M. Gorky's autobiographical trilogy]. Vol. 1. Leningrad: Izd. LGU, 315 pp.
Covers the letters "A" to "vsevidiashchii." The first of six volumes.

9 _____. "Zametki o iazyke p'es M. Gor'kogo i ego teatral'noi interpretatsii" [Notes on the language of Gorky's plays and its dramatic interpretation]. In Estetika slova i iazyk pisatelia [The aesthetics of the word and the language of the writer]. Leningrad: Khud. lit., pp. 196-213.
Discusses use of intonation and levels of style in Gorky's plays.

10 MIRSKY, PRINCE DMITRY S. Modern Russian Literature. New York: Haskell House, pp. 92-96, 103-7.
    Some of Gorky's stories--for example, "Twenty-six and One" ["Dvadtsat' shest' i odna"]--are excellent. Foma Gordeev shows promise: "great power of detailed and sagacious observation." His plays are "all very bad."

11 PROZHOGIN, V. Problematika v tvorchestve M. Gor'kogo i sovremennost' [Problems in Gorky's work and our time]. Kiev: Vysshaia shkola, 271 pp.
    Legend making. Written in response to the Twenty-fourth Party Congress with the goal of raising the revolutionary consciousness of Soviet people. Makes Gorky relevant to the issues of contemporary life.

12 SADOVSKII, IA. Stil' dramaturga i problema perevoda [The dramatist's style and the problem of translation]. Baku: Azerneshr, 124 pp.
    Discusses problems of translating distinct speech patterns of characters in a drama.

13 SCHOOLFIELD, GEORGE C. "Rilke, Gorki, and Others: A Biographical Diversion." In Views and Reviews of Modern German Literature: Festschrift für Adolf D. Klarmann. Edited by K.S. Weimar. Munich: Delp, pp. 105-20.
    Tells about Rilke's encounter with Gorky on Capri. Comments on what Rilke's concept of "Russian-ness" meant with regard to Gorky.

14 STACY, R.H. Russian Literary Criticism: A Short History. Syracuse: Syracuse University Press, pp. 187-88, 199-201, 206-7.
    Discusses Gorky's role in the formation of socialist realist doctrine. Finds his comments on literature "in no sense original or illuminating," but revealing as to the links between nineteenth-century "critical realism" and the "Soviet brand of realism."

15 ZUBAREVA, K.A. "Genrikh Mann i Maksim Gor'kii" [Heinrich Mann and Gorky]. Zeitschrift für Slawistik 19:1-14.
    Analyzes influence of Gorky on H. Mann. Compares the treatment of the lower middle class in the work of each writer.

1975

1 BIALIK, B.A. "Rozhdenie tvorcheskikh printsipov sotsialisticheskogo realizma" [The birth of creative principles of socialist realism]. In Literaturno-esteticheskie kontseptsii v Rossii kontsa XIX-nachala XX v. [Literary-aesthetic concepts in Russia at the end of the 19th

and beginning of the 20th centuries]. Moscow: Nauka, pp. 7-65.

Analyzes Gorky's work as foundation of socialist realism. The Lower Depths [Na dne], The Petit Bourgeois [Meshchane] are Gorky's first socialist realist works. Here Gorky creates a new kind of hero, which Chekhov called a "worker-turned-intellectual." Bialik asks how Gorky could have written "God-seeking" works such as Mother [Mat'] after founding socialist realism. He attributes this development to personal confusion and depression after the revolt of 1905.

2   BIRMAN, SERAFIMA. "Life's Gift of Encounters." Soviet Literature, no. 3:74-119.

Excerpts from the actress Birman's memoirs, including "My Vassa Zhelezhova." Liked this part because of the power and moral complexity of Vassa's character.

3   BYKOVTSEVA, L. Gor'kii v Italii [Gorky in Italy]. Moscow: Sovetskii pisatel', 384 pp.

Popularized biography. Italy was a setting in which Gorky did some of his most important work and in which his friendship with Lenin matured. Presents some new documents on Gorky's sojourn in Italy. Reads like a travelogue, with descriptions of Italian sites.

4   DÉLANO, LUIS ENRIQUE. "Manuel Rojas, el Gorky chileno." Revista de Bellas Artes (Mexico), no. 23:2-8.

The Chilean writer Manuel Rojas is compared with Gorky as a "vibrant and sensitive" writer.

5   FISCHER, JAN O. "'Les Fous' de Béranger cités chez Gorki." Babel (International Journal of Translation) 21, no. 2:61-68.

The Actor quotes part of this poem in The Lower Depths [Na dne] and uses it to bolster his failed self-esteem.

6   GIGOLOV, G.M. Dramaturgiia M. Gor'kogo 1902-1906 gg. v sovremennoi kritike i publitsistike [Gorky's plays from 1902 to 1906 in contemporary criticism and publicistic writing]. Tbilisi: Izd. TGU, 320 pp.

An attempt to discredit non-Soviet and nonleftist critical approaches to Gorky. Analyzes critical reception of Gorky's early plays as a prism for distinguishing major social and cultural issues of the period around 1905.

7   Gor'kovskie chteniia: 1974 [Readings in Gorky: 1974]. Gorky: Volgo-viat. knizh. izd-vo., 159 pp.

Papers are devoted to Gorky's influence on journalistic writing throughout the Soviet Union.

8   "Iz epistoliarnogo naslediia M. Gor'kogo" [From Gorky's epistolary legacy]. In Literaturno-esteticheskie kontseptsii

v Rossii kontsa XIX-nachala XX v. [Literary-aesthetic conceptions in Russia at the end of the 19th-early 20th century]. Moscow: Nauka, pp. 348-72.

Contains nineteen letters from Gorky to A.L. Volynsky, L.Ia. Gurevich, and the editorial board of Severnyi vestnik, and one letter to A.V. Lunacharsky.

9   KALUSTOVA, N.G. Izobrazhenie zhenshchiny-materi v tvorchestve M. Gor'kogo 1912-1917 godov: Ocherki [The depiction of women as mothers in Gorky's works from 1912 to 1917: Sketches]. Grozny: Checheno-ingushskoe knizh. izd-vo., 94 pp.

Analyzes motherhood as a symbol of developing revolutionary feeling, social renewal, and personal rebirth. Concentrates on Eccentrics [Chudaki], Stories about Italy [Skazki ob Italii], Childhood [Detstvo], Around Russia [Po Rusi].

10 KELDYSH, V.A. Russkii realizm nachala XX veka [Russian realism of the early 20th century]. Moscow: Nauka, 280 pp.

A typology of "critical realism" in relationship to other literary developments, especially modernism and socialist realism.

11 KOSTKA, E.K. "Maksim Gorky: Russian Writer with a Western Bent." In Glimpses of Germanic-Slavic Relations from Pushkin to Heinrich Mann. Lewisburg, Pa.: Bucknell University Press, pp. 38-54.

Reprinted from 1970.9.

12 KOTOVSKOV, V.IA. "Gor'kovskii impul's" [The Gorkian impulse]. In Tvorchestvo Mikhaila Sholokhova: Stat'i, soobshcheniia, bibliografiia. Edited by V.A. Kovalev and A.I. Khvatov. Leningrad: Nauka, pp. 245-49.

Gorky saw M. Sholokhov as one of a few successful "proletarian" writers.

13 KUZ'MICHEV, I. M. Gor'kii i khudozhestvennyi progress [Gorky and artistic progress]. Gorky: Volgo-Viat. knizh. izd-vo., 192 pp.

Analyzes the question of whether progress in art is possible.

14 LARIN, B.A. Slovar' avtobiograficheskoi trilogii M. Gor'kogo [Dictionary of M. Gorky's autobiographical trilogy]. Leningrad: Izd. LGU, 104 pp.

See 1974.8. An appendix to the six-volume dictionary. Covers proper names.

15 LENGYEL, B. "Gorkij über Rilke--Rilke über Gorkij." Studia Slavica Academiae Scientiarum Hungaricae 21:191-98.

Recounts the meetings and impressions of these opposed artistic natures.

16 MATHEWSON, R.W. "Lenin and Gorky: The Turning Point." In The Positive Hero in Russian Literature. 2d ed. Stanford: Stanford University Press, pp. 156-76.

Lenin's article "Party Organization and Party Literature" and Gorky's novel Mother mark a watershed in the history of Russian thought: the start of a new tradition and a "death sentence" to the old. This pair of works is a first collaboration in "Soviet literary partisanship."

17 REGNAUT, MAURICE. "Gorki." In Sur: Adamov, Artaud, Brecht, Genet, Gorki, Racine, Weiss. Paris: Oswald, pp. 137-45.

Deals with The Lower Depths [Na dne]. The underworld is a mime of the aristocratic life, the world of power. The upper world has power and is organized according to a strict code. The underworld has illusory, empty freedom.

18 SHARYPKIN, D.M. Russkaia literatura v skandinavskikh stranakh [Russian literature in Scandinavian countries]. Leningrad: Nauka, pp. 47-48, 86-89, 138-41.

Summarizes Gorky's reception in Scandinavian literatures. Discusses his relationship to Knut Hamsun.

19 SURGANOV, V. "Seiateli: Gor'kii i tema krest'ianstva" [The sowers: Gorky and the theme of the peasantry]. Voprosy literatury 19, no. 3 (March):58-89.

Finds Gorky's attack on peasants in his early stories to be at most "relative." Analyzes other stories from the period that are "real peasant stories"--for example, "Shary" or "Kirilka" about peasants who have become self-aware and socially and morally conscious.

20 YEDLIN, TOVA. "Maxim Gorky: His Early Revolutionary Activity and His Involvement in the Revolution of 1905." Canadian Slavonic Papers 17:76-105.

Reexamines Gorky's literary-political activity before 1905 and puts it in a fresh perspective. Reviews his relationship to populist and Marxist activists and his own development as a political activist.

21 ZERNOV, NIKOLAI. "Osnovopolozhnik i zavershitel' sotsrealizma: Gor'kii i Sholokhov" [The founder and the perfector of socialist realism: Gorky and Sholokhov]. Novyi zhurnal, no. 121:82-90.

Blames Gorky for changing the course of Russian literature, making it monotonous and bringing it in line with political power. Calls him the "ideologue of socialist realism." Discusses Gorky and Lenin's relationship. Gorky was in perfect agreement with the Bolshevik line. He believed in the "elevating lie."

22 ZIMINA, SERAFIMA, ed. "From the Correspondence of Maxim Gorky." Soviet Literature 10:164-67.

A letter to the historian Pokrovsky.

1976

1 BARAKHOV, V.S. Iskusstvo literaturnogo portreta: Gor'kii o V.I. Lenine, L.N. Tolstom, A.P. Chekhove [The art of the literary portrait: Gorky on V.I. Lenin, L.N. Tolstoy, A.P. Chekhov]. Moscow: Nauka, 184 pp.
   Studies Gorky's literary portraits on the basis of a lengthy theoretical discussion of the literary portrait as a form of memoir writing. Views portrait writing as one of the most effective ways a writer can capture the spirit of his time. Finds Lenin the "continuator of Russian history" after Tolstoy and a new kind of leader. He is Gorky's ideal "Man." Barakhov compares the 1924 and 1930 editions of the portrait of Lenin.

2 BAZANOV, V.V. "O zhanre literaturnogo portreta v tvorchestve Gor'kogo" [On the genre of the literary portrait in Gorky's work]. Russkaia literatura 19, no. 4:233-47.
   A bibliographical review of studies on Gorky's literary portraits.

3 BURIAN, IAROSLAV. "Tvorchestvo M. Gor'kogo i pervaia russkaia revoliutsiia, 1905-1907 gg" [Gorky's works and the first Russian revolution, 1905-1907]. Československá Rusistika 21, no. 1:1-4.
   The rise of revolutionary feeling among the masses in the period before 1905 gave Gorky inspiration for his "leading heroes of the epoch," for example, Nil in The Petit Bourgeois [Meshchane]. Gorky's work impressed Lenin as the embodiment of "free literature" and influenced his article "Party Organization and Party Literature."

4 CALDER, ANGUS. Russia Discovered: Nineteenth-century Fiction from Pushkin to Chekhov. London: Heinemann, pp. 276-80.
   Values Gorky for his reminiscences and documents of the past.

5 "Conversation with Sophie Dubinov." Yale/Theater 7, no. 2: 54-55.
   See 1976.35. An admiring memoir.

6 DIKUSHINA, N.I. "Problema kul'tury i revoliutsii v estetike A.M. Gor'kogo i A.V. Lunacharskogo" [The problem of culture and revolution in the aesthetic views of A.M. Gorky and A.V. Lunacharsky]. In Gor'kovskie chteniia, 1975. Gorky: Volgo-viat. knizh. izd-vo., pp. 52-58.
   See 1976.13. Discusses Gorky's correspondence with Lunacharsky and their common "fight with the philosophy of individualism."

7 DONCHIN, G. "Gorky." In Russian Literary Attitudes from Pushkin to Solzhenitsyn. Edited by R. Freeborn, G. Donchin, and N.J. Anning. New York: Barnes & Noble, pp. 79-98.

Gorky's art is motivated by the feelings and values that motivated his actions in life. Feels that belles lettres should create an illusion that will spur its reader to action. Literature should be a "'well-aimed shaft.'"

8   EVSELEVSKII, L.I. "Neopublikovannoe pis'mo Gor'kogo" [An unpublished letter of Gorky]. Russkaia literatura 19, no. 1:207-8.
    A letter from 1935 to N.N. Popov of the Central Committee on the history of Russian factories.

9   FOMENKO, L.P. "A.M. Gor'kii--kritik Andreia Platonova" [A.M. Gorky as critic of Andrei Platonov]. In Gor'kovskie chteniia, 1975. Gorky: Volgo-viat. knizh. izd-vo., pp. 140-45.
    See 1976.13. Deals with the history of Platonov's novel Chevengur (1929) and Gorky's response to it.

10 GEROULD, DANIEL. "Gorky, Melodrama, and the Development of Early Soviet Theatre." Yale/Theater 7, no. 2:33-44.
    See 1976.35. Discusses the revival of the melodramatic form after the Revolution and its use as a popular form. Describes a "melodrama contest" from 1919.

11 GLICKSBERG, C.I. "Gorky and the Conflict between Art and Politics." In The Literature of Commitment. Lewisburg, Pa.: Bucknell University Press, pp. 412-18.
    Analyzes how the clash over freedom of art arose between Gorky, the first "practitioner of socialist realism," and Lenin. Reevaluates Gorky's artistic personality. Quotes Wolfe (1967.18) and Ermolaev (1971.1).

12 GOR'KII, M. Neizdannaia perepiska [Unpublished correspondence]. Edited by B.A. Bialik et al. Arkhiv A.M. Gor'kogo, vol. 14. Moscow: Nauka, 531 pp.
    Includes correspondence with A.V. Lunacharsky, M.N. Pokrovsky, A.S. Bubnov, N.E. Burenin, E.K. Malinovskaia, D.A. Lutokhin, P.P. Kriuchkov.

13 Gor'kovskie chteniia, 1975 [Readings in Gorky, 1975]. Gorky: Volgo-viat. knizh. izd-vo., 159 pp.
    Devoted to Gorky as a literary critic. See 1976.6, 1976.9.

14 JUIN, HERBERT. "London et Gorki." Europe 54, nos. 561-562 (January-February):72-75.
    Compares Jack London and Gorky, their ideas of culture and their feelings toward their countries.

15 KANDEL', B.L., FEDIUSHINA, L.M., and BENINA, M.A. Russkaia khudozhestvennaia literatura i literaturovedenie [Russian belles lettres and literary criticism]. Moscow: Kniga, pp. 328-40.

Contains a list of basic Soviet indexes; bibliographies; works devoted to Gorky's style, genre; memoirs; "kraevedenie"; translations; reception in other literatures; archive list.

16   KHODASEVICH, VLADISLAV. "Khodasevich's Gorky." Translated by R. Reeder. Yale/Theater 7, no. 2:8-24.
     See 1976.35. English translation of Khodasevich's memoir (1939.5). Discusses the conflict in Gorky's character between an overt love of truth and a covert quest for the "comforting lie." Among the most sympathetic memoirs on Gorky from the émigré community. Defends Gorky against rumors of extravagance.

17   KOLOBAEVA, LIDIIA. "'Tochka zreniia' geroini v romane M. Gor'kogo Mat'" [Point of view of the heroine in Gorky's novel Mother]. Vestnik MGU 30, no. 4:3-9.
     Points out the need for concrete textual and stylistic analysis of Mother, especially how publicistic material was worked successfully into a novel. Analyzes the point of view of the mother as an organizing principle.

18   KUPCHENKO, V.P. "M. Gor'kii i M. Voloshin" [M. Gorky and M. Voloshin]. Russkaia literatura 19, no. 2:144-51.
     On Gorky's acquaintance with the modernist poet Maksimilian Voloshin in 1917.

19   LANDESMAN, ROCCO. "The Grand Illusionist." Yale/Theater 7, no. 2:4-7.
     See 1976.35. On Gorky's reception in the West. Notes a Gorky revival. Finds the reason for the revival, in part, in the "dramatic politicization" of Western cultures in the late 1960s.

20   LANE, ANN M. "Nietzsche in Russian Thought, 1890-1917." Ph.D. diss., University of Wisconsin, pp. 560-78.
     Outlines Nietzsche's impact on Gorky during his formative years. Emphasizes the theme of the strong person.

21   LATRELL, CRAIG. "Gorky as Apologist: The White Sea Canal Project." Yale/Theater 7, no. 2:88-94.
     See 1976.35. Argues that Gorky sold out to Stalin to save his "biography."

22   LAWSON, STEPHEN R. "Caught in the Middle: The Ironies of Enemies." Yale/Theater 7, no. 2:78-87.
     See 1976.35. Remarks on Gorky's secret sympathy for the spiritual malaise of the Bardin family.

23   LENGYEL, BÉLA. "Gemeinsame Züge in der Wertung Nietzsches und Gorkis." Acta Litteraria Academiae Scientiarum Hungaricae 18:157-90.
     Notes that almost every great writer of the turn of the twentieth century was inspired by Nietzsche. Discusses Gorky's early reception across Europe as a "Nietzschean." Discusses

Gorky's and Nietzsche's intertwined influences on Hungarian literature.

24 LEONOV, LEONID. Literatura i vremia [Literature and time]. Moscow: Moskovskii rabochii, pp. 15-20, 126-29, 313-29.
Contains three memoiristic essays devoted to Gorky.

25 LIUBUSHIN, V.I. "Printsipy inoskazatel'nosti v poezii M. Gor'kogo" [Principles of allegory in Gorky's poetry]. Vestnik MGU 30, no. 5:3-12.
Analyzes use of allegory in Gorky's verse.

26 MARAMZIN, VLADIMIR. "Gorky vs. Pushkin." Translated by Barry Rubin. Yale/Theater 7, no. 2:45-53.
See 1976.35. A view of Gorky delivered by someone who grew up in the Soviet Union. Opposes Pushkin and Gorky and finds Pushkin infi-nitely higher.

27 MOULIK, ACHALA. "Maksim Gorky." In Silhouettes of Russian Literature: Pushkin to Yevtushenko. Mysore, India: Wesley Press, pp. 117-31.
Gorky occupies a special place in Russian literature as both the creator of a new kind of literature and the preserver of the old.

28 REMIZOV, ALEKSEY. "Gorky: A Memoir." Yale/Theater 7, no. 2:95-105.
See 1976.35. From a 1950 memoir. Praises Gorky.

29 ROMANOVA, E.S., ed. Proizvedeniia sovetskikh pisatelei v perevodakh na inostrannye iazyki, 1971-1975 [Works by Soviet writers in foreign-language translation, 1971-1975]. Moscow: Kniga, pp. 36-43.
Bibliography. Continuation of 1972.13.

30 ROUGLE, CHARLES. "Maksim Gor'kii." In Three Russians Consider America: America in the Works of Maksim Gor'kij, Aleksandr Blok, and Vladimir Majakovskij. Stockholm: Almquist & Wiksell International, pp. 13-58.
Considers Gorky's three impressions of New York, "The City of the Yellow Devil," "The Kingdom of Ennui," "Mob"; the satirical portraits in "My Interviews" and the short story "Charley Men." Notes a heavy, embellished, repetitive style which makes for a "narcotic" quality. Compares Gorky's view of America with Dostoevsky's view of France.

31 SEGEL, HAROLD. "Gorky's Major Plays." Yale/Theater 7, no. 2:56-77.
See 1976.35. Contrasts Chekhov's and Gorky's development as dramatists. Discusses the ideological nature of Gorky's plays. Compares The Lower Depths [Na dne] to O'Neill's The Iceman Cometh. Discusses Gorky's other plays.

32 VAINBERG, IOSIF. Za gor'kovskoi strokoi: Real'nyi fakt i pravda iskusstva v romane "Zhizn' Klima Samgina" [Beyond Gorky's line: Real fact and the truth of art in the novel The Life of Klim Samgin]. 2d ed. expanded. Moscow: Sovetskii pisatel', 480 pp.
    A popularized discussion of Gorky's last novel.

33 Voprosy gor'kovedeniia [Questions in Gorky studies]. Vol. 2. Gorky: Izd. GGU, 112 pp.
    Contains the following articles devoted to aspects of The Life of Klim Samgin (titles are shortened):
    1. S.I. Sukhikh, "Problema zhanra Zhizni Klima Samgina v literaturovedenii 70-kh godov" [The problem of the genre of The Life of Klim Samgin in literary criticism of the 1970s].
    2. A.V. Barmin, "Apokrif" [The apocrypha].
    3. G.S. Zaitseva, "Krest'ianskaia tema" [The peasant theme].
    4. N.G. Kalustova, "Problema zhenshchiny-materi" [The problem of woman as mother].
    5. O.A. Saltaeva, "'Peizazh za oknom'" ["The landscape outside the window"].
    6. V.K. Krasunov, "Nachal'naia stranitsa kriticheskoi letopisi" [The first page of the critical history].
    7. S.A. Cherviakovskii, "Iz portretnoi galerei" [From the portrait gallery].
    Also contains a bibliography by S.I. Sukhikh of criticism on The Life of Klim Samgin from 1966 to 1975.

34 WEGNER, MICHAEL. "Tradition und Neubeginn: Maxim Gorki." Schriftsteller und literarisches Erbe: Zum Traditionsverhältnis sozialistischer Autoren. Edited by Hans Richter. Berlin: Aufbau, pp. 13-90.
    In the process of literary creation, the literary reworking of "life," the artist in Gorky's view must also respond to literary models. Discusses My Universities [Moi universitety], essays, the sketch of L. Tolstoy.

35 Yale/Theater 7, no. 2.
    The whole issue is devoted to Gorky. Contains:
    1. Rocco Landesman, "The Grand Illusionist." See 1976.19.
    2. Vladislav Khodasevich, "Khodasevich's Gorky" (translated by R. Reeder). See 1976.16.
    3. "Gorky on Playwriting" (translated by R. Reeder).
    4. Daniel Gerould, "Gorky, Melodrama, and the Development of Early Soviet Theatre." See 1976.10.
    5. Vladimir Maramzin, "Gorky vs. Pushkin." See 1976.26.
    6. "Conversation with Sophie Dubinov." See 1976.5.
    7. Harold Segel, "Gorky's Major Plays." See 1976.31.
    8. Stephen R. Lawson, "Caught in the Middle: The Ironies of Enemies." See 1976.22.
    9. Craig Latrell, "Gorky as Apologist: The White Sea Canal Project." See 1976.21.
    10. Aleksey Remizov, "Gorky: A Memoir" (translated by R. Reeder). See 1976.28.

11. Russell Vandenbroucke, "Bitter Dregs: A Review of Steve Tesich's Gorky."
12. Henning Rischbieter, "Peter Stein's Gorky: A Review of Summer Folk in West Berlin" (translated by J. Zipes).
Also contains a selected bibliography of theater reviews and magazine articles. An attempt at an assessment of Gorky's theater and his political-social concerns. Great faults and great merits are juxtaposed.

36 ZABURDAEV, N.A. V sem'e Kashirinykh: Dokumental'nye ocherki [In the Kashirin family: Documentary sketches]. Gorky: Volgo-viat. knizh. izd-vo., 184 pp.
Family biography. Popularized work on the history of family in Nizhny Novgorod.

1977

1 APONIUK, NATALIA. "From Critic to Proselyte: A Study of the Development of Gor'ky's Political and Literary Views, 1921-1928." Ph.D. diss., University of Toronto.
DAI 37:7782A. Shows how Gorky, during his European exile in the 1920s, underwent a transformation of political and philosophical views that allowed him to reconcile himself to the Soviet regime.

1A BIALIK, B. M. Gor'kii--dramaturg [M. Gorky the playwright]. 2d ed. Moscow: Sovetskii pisatel', 639 pp.
The Soviet classic on Gorky's dramaturgy. First edition came out partly as a response to flagging interest in Gorky's plays. Divides plays into early period (1901-6), middle period (1908-17), late period (1931-36). Shows close relationship between political plays (for example, Enemies [Vragi] or Dostigaev and Others [Dostigaev i drugie]) and philosophical drama (for example, The Lower Depths [Na dne] and Counterfeit Money [Fal'shivaia moneta]). Ranks Gorky with Shakespeare.

2 DOLGOPOLOV, L.K. "M. Gor'kii i problema Detei solntsa: 1900-e gody" [M. Gorky and the problem of Children of the Sun: The 1900s]. In Na rubezhe vekov [At the turn of the century]. Leningrad: Sovetskii pisatel', pp. 60-95.
Views Gorky as a modernist who uses sun imagery to symbolize strong will, hope, energy. Analyzes "Old Woman Izergil" ["Starukha Izergil"], "Malva," and Children of the Sun [Deti solntsa]. Compares Gorky's use of sun imagery with Balmont's and Belyi's.

3 FODOR, I. "Précisions sur un échange de lettres entre Barbusse et Gor'kii." Studia Slavica Academiae Scientiarum Hungaricae 23:171-73.
Contains two letters, one from H. Barbusse to Gorky (8 January 1928) and one from Gorky to Barbusse (20 January 1928). A note on Gorky's relationship to this French leftist.

4   FORTUNATOVA, V.A. "Stsenicheskaia obrabotka Bertol'dom Brekhtom romana A.M. Gor'kogo Mat'" [Bertold Brecht's dramatization of A.M. Gorky's novel Mother]. In Gor'kovskie chteniia. Gorky: Volgo-viat. knizh. izd-vo., pp.157-63.
   See 1977.7. Analyzes the use of the chorus in Brecht's play.

5   GEI, N.K. "Mnogogolosie zhizni i khudozhestvennyi mir M. Gor'kogo" [The polyphony of life and Gorky's artistic world]. Izvestiia ANSSSR 36, no. 5:406-15.
   Looks at the "grand artistic controversy" in Gorky's work.

6   "Gor'kii i sovremennost'" [Gorky and the present]. Novyi mir, no. 1 (January):230-52.
   At the request of Novyi mir, present-day writers, critics, literary historians tell about the "place of Gorky in their creative development." Bialik tells about wanting to write his dissertation in the early 1930s on "Gorky's aesthetic views" and having it almost be turned down. Gorky did not want him to do it. Ovcharenko: "We need Gorky."

7   Gor'kovskie chteniia, 1976 [Readings in Gorky, 1976]. Gorky: Volgo-viat. knizh. izd-vo., 200 pp.
   Devoted to Gorky and the theater. Contains the following articles:
   1. A.N. Alekseeva, "Sovremennye problemy stsenicheskoi interpretatsii dramaturgii A.M. Gor'kogo" [Present-day problems in interpretation for the staging of A.M. Gorky's plays].
   2. S.I. Sukhikh, "A.M. Gor'kii-kritik M. Gor'kogo-dramaturga" [A.M. Gorky the critic of M. Gorky the dramatist].
   3. E.L. Zhavoronkova, "Gor'kii o tragedii" [Gorky on tragedy].
   4. V.N. Morokhin, "A.M. Gor'kii ob ustnoi narodnoi drame" [A.M. Gorky on the oral folk drama].
   5. E.I. Komkova, "'Narodnye deistva' v otsenke A.M. Gor'kogo" [Folk plays in A.M. Gorky's estimation].
   6. G.S. Zaitseva, "Krest'ianskaia tema v nabroskakh A.M. Gor'kogo k 'p'ese o kulake'" [The peasant theme in A.M. Gorky's sketches for "The play about the Rich Peasant"].
   7. V.I. Baranov, "K kharakteristike khudozhestvennykh iskanii M. Gor'kogo (p'esa Vragi v sisteme tvorchestva pisatelia)" [Toward a characterization of M. Gorky's artistic explorations (the play Enemies in the writer's creative system)].
   8. B.V. Vidishchev, "O zhanrovoi strukture gor'kovskoi dramy" [On the generic structure of Gorky's drama].
   9. A.M. Minakova, "Drama A.M. Gor'kogo ob intelligentsii 1905-1907 godov Deti solntsa i p'esy ego sovremennikov" [A.M. Gorky's play about the intelligentsia 1905-1907, Children of the Sun, and the plays of his contemporaries]. See 1977.12.
   10. L. Farber, "Kompozitsionnoe svoeobrazie Na dne M. Gor'kogo" [The originality of composition in M. Gorky's The Lower Depths].

11. I.A. Reviakina, "K itogam tekstologicheskogo izucheniia dramaturgii A.M. Gor'kogo (Iz opyta podgotovki Polnogo sobraniia sochinenii pisatelia)" [Some conclusions from the textual study of A.M. Gorky's drama (From the experience of preparing the writer's complete works)].

12. A.A. Tikhovodov, "Tema ukhoda 'ot zla zhizni' v p'esakh L. Tolstogo i M. Gor'kogo" [The theme of retreat "from the evil of life" in the plays of L. Tolstoy and M. Gorky].

13. L.F. Garanina, "Problema otvetstvennosti khudozhnika v dramaturgii A.M. Gor'kogo posleoktiabr'skogo perioda" [The problem of the artist's responsibility in A.M. Gorky's post-revolutionary drama].

14. S.A. Cherviakovskii, "Sotsial'naia funktsiia rechi personazhei v p'esakh Egor Bulychev i drugie i Dostigaev i drugie" [The social function of characters' speech in the plays Egor Bulychev and Others and Dostigaev and Others].

15. S.G. Pynzaru, "P'esy Gor'kogo na stsene kishinevskikh teatrov v gody pervoi russkoi revoliutsii" [Gorky's plays on the Kishinev stage during the first Russian revolution].

16. B.A. Piradov, "Dramaturgiia A.M. Gor'kogo i gruzinskii teatr" [A.M. Gorky's drama and the Georgian theater].

17. R.M. Saburova, "A.M. Gor'kii i sovetskaia uzbekskaia dramaturgiia" [A.M. Gorky and Soviet Uzbek drama].

18. D.N. Nuraliev, "A.M. Gor'kii i sovetskaia turkmenskaia dramaturgiia" [A.M. Gorky and Soviet Turkmen drama].

19. V.Z. Davletshina, "P'esy A.M. Gor'kogo na stsene tatarskogo teatra" [A.M. Gorky's plays on the Tatar stage].

20. B.B. Remizov, "Teatr M. Gor'kogo i poiski polozhitel'nogo geroia v dooktiabr'skoi dramaturgii B. Shou" [M. Gorky's drama and B. Shaw's search in his prerevolutionary drama for a positive hero]. See 1977.13.

21. V.A. Fortunatova, "Stsenicheskaia obrabotka Bertol'dom Brekhtom romana A.M. Gor'kogo Mat'" [Bertold Brecht's dramatization of A.M. Gorky's novel Mother]. See 1977.4.

22. I.V. Kireeva, "Gor'kii i amerikanskii teatr 30-kh godov" [Gorky and the American theater of the 1930s]. See 1977.9.

23. A.N. Svobodov, "M. Gor'kii--teatral'nyi retsenzent" [M. Gorky--theater critic].

24. I.V. Nikitina, "Arzamasskii prototipicheskii material v p'ese Varvary" [Prototypic material from Arzamas in the play Barbarians].

25. N.A. Zaburdaev, "Detstvo A.M. Gor'kogo v instsenirovkakh" [A.M. Gorky's Childhood on stage].

26. T.A. Ryzhova, "Muzei-propagandist dramaturgii A.M. Gor'kogo" [The museum as advertiser for A.M. Gorky's drama].

8   KHETSO [Kjetsaa], GEIR. "Maksim Gor'kii v Norvegii" [Gorky in Norway]. Russkaia literatura 20, no. 2:152-62.

Gorky's reception in Norway started in 1899. Enumerates articles on Gorky, translations, productions of plays, his impact on writers such as J. Falkberget, K. Hamsun, F. Nansen.

9   KIREEVA, I.V. "Gor'kii i amerikanskii teatr 30-kh godov" [Gorky and the American theater of the 1930s]. In Gor'kovskie chteniia. Gorky: Volgo-viat. knizh. izd-vo., pp. 164-70.
    See 1977.7. Outlines Gorky's reception in the United States in the 1930s.

10 LARIN, B.A. Slovar' avtobiograficheskoi trilogii M. Gor'kogo [Dictionary of M. Gorky's autobiographical trilogy]. Vol. 2. Leningrad: Izd. LGU, 299 pp.
    Continuation of 1974.8. Covers the letters "vsegda" to "zhdat'."

11 LOE, MARY L. "Maxim Gorky and the Sreda Circle, 1899-1905." Ph.D. diss., Columbia University, 369 pp.
    Analyzes Gorky's role in shaping the literary-ideological character of the Sreda group.

12 MINAKOVA, A.M. "Drama A.M. Gor'kogo ob intelligentsii 1905-1907 godov" [The drama of A.M. Gorky on the intelligentsia during 1905-1907]. In Gor'kovskie chteniia, 1976. Gorky: Volgo-viat. knizh. izd-vo.
    See 1977.7. Devoted to Children of the Sun [Deti solntsa].

13 REMIZOV, B.B. "Teatr M. Gor'kogo i poiski polozhitel'nogo geroia v dooktiabr'skoi dramaturgii B. Shou" [M. Gorky's drama and B. Shaw's search in his prerevolutionary drama for a positive hero]. In Gor'kovskie chteniia, 1976. Gorky: Volgo-viat. knizh. izd-vo., pp. 148-56.
    See 1977.7. Discusses the impact of Gorky's drama on Shaw's view of social change, 1906-11. Discusses Shaw's play Misalliance (1909-10).

14 SALISBURY, HARRISON E. Black Night, White Snow: Russia's Revolutions, 1905-1917. New York: Doubleday, pp. 554-57.
    Popularized description of Gorky's polemic in Novaia zhizn' [New Life] in 1917. Mentions Gorky's relationship to Z. Gippius.

15 SCHULTZE, BRIGITTE. "Zur Problematik der Gestalt des Luka in M. Gor'kij's Na dne." Zeitschrift für slavische Philologie 39:298-319.
    Shows through detailed textual analysis that Luka in The Lower Depths is neither "positively" nor "negatively" characterized: he is an ambivalent figure.

16 SMIRNOVA, L.N. "Stranitsy tvorcheskoi druzhby: Chekhov i Gor'kii" [Pages of a creative friendship: Chekhov and Gorky]. In Chekhov i ego vremia [Chekhov and his time]. Edited by L.D. Opul'skaia et al. Moscow: Nauka, pp. 176-83.

Although the relationship between Gorky and Chekhov appeared to be one of student to teacher, it was sustained by ongoing argument and polemic. Gorky puts Chekhov's stylistic advice to use only in the late 1900s.

17 "Sovremennaia sovetskaia literatura i khudozhestvennyi opyt Gor'kogo" [Contemporary Soviet literature and Gorky's artistic experiment]. Voprosy literatury 21, no. 9:14-91.
   Speeches by several writers and critics in honor of Gorky and the sixtieth anniversary of the Bolshevik Revolution. Bialik notices a lack of interest in Gorky in the younger generation.

18 TROTSKY, LEON. "Maxim Gorky." In Leon Trotsky on Literature and Art. Edited by P.N. Siegel. New York: Pathfinder, pp. 217-20.
   First published in Biulleten' oppozitsii [Bulletin of the Opposition] (July 1936) on the occasion of Gorky's death. The integrity of Gorky's character lies in his concern for public education and the broadening and preservation of high culture. His consistent effort in these areas explains the changing, seemingly contradictory phases of his relationship to revolutionaries and the Revolution.

19 Voprosy gor'kovedeniia [Questions in Gorky studies]. Vol. 3. Gorky: Izd. GGU, 142 pp.
   Devoted to discussion of The Lower Depths [Na dne]. Contains a selected bibliography of criticism from 1925 to 1976.

20 VUL', R.M. V kontore advokata [In the lawyer's office]. Gorky: Volgo-viat. knizh. izd-vo., 144 pp.
   Traces Gorky's experience in Lenin's legal office in Nizhny Novgorod and analyzes the impact of this experience on a variety of works including The Three of Them [Troe], Summer Folk [Dachniki], Mother [Mat'], The Life of Klim Samgin [Zhizn' Klima Samgina].

21 WALTER, RON. "Gorky and Soviet Children's Literature." Children's Literature 6:182-87.
   Argues that Gorky is responsible for the richness of Soviet children's literature. Discusses the relationship of his theory of children's literature with the theory of socialist realism. Contains a selected bibliography of Russian works on Gorky and children's literature.

22 WEGNER, M. "Gor'kii und das literarische Experiment." Zeitschrift für Slawistik 22:95-101.
   Gorky was stylistically innovative, especially in his stories from 1922 to 1925. Analysis focuses on the stories "The Story of a Certain Romance" and "About Cockroaches."

23 WILLIAMS, ROBERT C. Artists in Revolution: Portraits of the Russian Avant-garde, 1905-1925. Bloomington and London: Indiana University Press, pp. 42-45, 49-51, 69-70.
   Discusses Gorky's relations with Lunacharsky and his editing and publishing work.

24 ZHEGALOV, NIKOLAI. "The Correspondence of Maxim Gorky." Soviet Literature 11:16-38.
   Contains sixteen letters to and from Gorky. Includes Stefan Zweig, George Bernard Shaw, H.G. Wells, John Galsworthy, Upton Sinclair, Sherwood Anderson, Theodore Dreiser.

1978

1 BARANOVA, N.D. M. Gor'kii--master kriticheskoi prozy [M. Gorky--A master of critical prose]. Gorky: Volgo-viat. knizh. izd-vo., 142 pp.
   Sees Gorky the critic as an ally and later a continuator of Marxist literary traditions established by Plekhanov, Vorovsky, and Lunacharsky. Studies Gorky's critical method and essayistic style.

2 BARRATT, ANDREW. "Maksim Gorky and the Russian Revolution: The Crisis of 1910." New Zealand Slavonic Journal, no. 2: 59-74.
   Gorky's "crisis" in 1910 caused him to reevaluate his activity as writer and revolutionary. Sees the Capri incident as Gorky's final attempt to engage in politics. Sees a change in his literary orientation from "utopianism" to "critical realism."

3 BIALIK, B. "Gumanizm podlinnyi i mnimyi: P'esa Na dne segodnia" [Authentic and false humanism: The Lower Depths today]. Znamia 48, no. 7:215-27.
   Notes that young people today are very interested in The Lower Depths. Important debates about ethics arise in the classroom when discussion turns to the character of Luka.

4 BIRIUKOV, FEDOR. "Zaveshchano Maksimom Gor'kim" [Bequeathed by Maksim Gorky]. Nash sovremennik 15, no. 5:166-78.
   More legend building: Gorky was one of the "titans" in the greatest moment in Russian history. He laid the foundations for a new socialist literary culture.

5 ELISEEV, A.I., ed. Gor'kii nizhegorodskikh let: Vospominaniia [Gorky of the Nizhny Novgorod years: Memoirs]. Gorky: Volgo-viat. knizh. izd-vo., 335 pp.
   Memoirs by O.Iu. Kamenskaia, Z.V. Vasileva, E.P. Peshkova, the Metlins, V.A. Posse, A.E. Bogdanovich, I.I. Semenov, among others. Kamenskaia's, Vasileva's, and the Metlins' memoirs are published here for the first time.

6   GITEL'MAN, L. "Narodnyi teatr i M. Gor'kii" [Folk theater and M. Gorky]. In Russkaia klassika na frantsuzskoi stsene [Russian classics on the French stage]. Leningrad: Iskusstvo, pp. 134-53.
    Discusses Gorky's reception on the French stage.

7   GRÜSS, NOE. Tolstoi, Tchekhov, Gorki au contact des juifs. Paris: Association des médecins israélites de France, 36 pp.
    Sees Gorky's efforts to fight discrimination against Jews after as well as before the Revolution as part of his general struggle against social injustice. Traces Jewish motifs in Gorky's work, his relationship to specific Jewish writers--for example, Sholom Aleichem and Bialik--and his social work on behalf of Jews.

7A KASIK, JOHN PHILLIP. "The Work and World of Ivan Olbracht: A Study of the Parallel and Divergent Influences of Maxim Gor'kij in Romanticism and Socialist Realism. A Typological Analysis." Ph.D. diss., Brown University, 156 pp.
    Deals with Czech writer Ivan Olbracht and Gorky's impact upon him. In particular, discusses Gorky's archetype of the tramp.

8   KRUTIKOVA, N.E. V nachale veka: Gor'kii i simvolisty [At the beginning of the century: Gorky and the symbolists]. Kiev: Naukova dumka, 306 pp.
    Concentrates on specific topics and problems--for example, Gorky's participation in Severnyi vestnik and the "reactionary legend" of Gorky's Nietzscheanism. Discusses Gorky's own search for an aesthetic view.

9   KULESHOV, V.I. "Maksim Gor'kii." Istoriia russkoi kritiki XVIII-XIX vekov [The history of Russian criticism of the 18th and 19th centuries]. 2d ed. Moscow: Prosveshchenie, pp. 506-17.
    Deals with Gorky's pre-1917 critical work, especially his concept of "active romanticism" and his analysis of "realism." Focuses on Gorky's attitudes toward nineteenth-century Russian classics, particularly Dostoevsky.

10 KUZ'MICHEV, I.K., ed. M. Gor'kii i voprosy literaturnykh zhanrov [M. Gorky and questions of literary genres]. Gorky: Izd. GGU, 162 pp.
    Contains the following articles:
        1. S.I. Sukhikh, "Zhizn' Klima Samgina M. Gor'kogo i Filosofiia obshchego dela N.F. Fedorova" [Gorky's Life of Klim Samgin and N.F. Fedorov's Philosophy of the Common Cause]. See 1978.22.
        2. G.S. Zaitseva, "Kontseptiia krest'ianskogo kharaktera v Zhizni Klima Samgina" [The conception of the peasant in The Life of Klim Samgin].

3. A.V. Barmin, "Plasticheskie i groteskye formy v epopee XX veka (Zhizn' Klima Samgina)" [Plastic and grotesque forms in the 20th-century epic (The Life of Klim Samgin)].

4. A.N. Sabat, "Satiricheskii portret v romane M. Gor'kogo Zhizn' Klima Samgina kak sredstvo sotsial'noi tipizatsii" [The satiric portrait in Gorky's Life of Klim Samgin as a means of social typologization].

5. V.Iu. Polyskalov, "Ob"ektivnoe i sub"ektivnoe v khudozhestvennoi sisteme Zhizni Klima Samgina" [The objective and subjective in the artistic system of The Life of Klim Samgin].

6. A.V. Rasskazov, "O nekotorykh osobennostiakh perevoda romana A.M. Gor'kogo Zhizn' Klima Samgina (1 ch.) v Germanii" [On some peculiarities of the German translation of the first part of Gorky's Life of Klim Samgin].

7. M.P. Shustov, "K probleme skazochnosti stilia M. Gor'kogo ('Makar Chudra')" [On elements of the fairy tale in Gorky's style ('Makar Chudra')].

8. V.K. Krasunov, "O svoeobrazii konflikta skazki A.M. Gor'kogo 'Devushka i smert'" [On the peculiarity of the conflict of Gorky's fairy tale "The Girl and Death"].

9. V.P. Vladimirtsev, "Kto i kogda nazval Gor'kogo Burevestnikom?" [Who called Gorky a stormy petrel and when?].

10. O.G. Vavilycheva, "M. Gor'kii o stile Barsukov L. Leonova" [M. Gorky on the style of L. Leonov's Badgers].

11. V.N. Morokhin, "Ustnye rasskazy ob A.M. Gor'kom" [Oral accounts of A.M. Gorky].

11 LUNACHARSKY, ANATOLY. "A Portrait." Translated by A. Miller. In Collected Works in Ten Volumes by Maxim Gorky. Vol. 1. Moscow: Progress, pp. 1-32.
Excerpts from speech given on the occasion of Gorky's sixtieth birthday (1928). Compares Gorky's life story to a "vertically soaring line."

12 MAKSIMOVA, V.A. "M. Gor'kii i bol'shevistskaia pechat'" [M. Gorky and the Bolshevik press]. In Revoliutsiia 1905-1907 godov i literatura [The revolution of 1905-1907 and literature]. Edited by B.A. Bialik. Moscow: Nauka, pp. 43-53.
Discusses Gorky's financial and publicistic contributions to Bolshevik newspapers and publishing houses.

13 MIROVA-FLORIN, E. "'Skazki deistvitel'nosti' M. Gor'kogo: problema zhanra" [Gorky's "Tales of reality": The problem of genre]. Zeitschrift für Slawistik 23:221-28.
Analyzes Gorky's literary folk tales in the light of their folkloric inheritance. Focuses on story cycles from the 1910s' Tales of Italy [Skazki ob Italii] and Around Russia [Po Rusi].

14 NOVIKOV, VASILII. "'Priznaem li my za iskusstvom pravo preuvelichivat' . . .' (Gor'kii o novykh formakh khudozhestvennogo obobshcheniia)" ["Do we acknowledge along with art the right to exaggerate . . ." (Gorky on new forms of

artistic generalization)]. <u>Voprosy literatury</u> 22, no. 3 (March):3-28.

Socialist realism is not the same as revolutionary romanticism. The revolutionary romantic sees real life as dull and gray; he embroiders on it, making it heroic, lofty. Socialist realism is not limited to any <u>one</u> form or <u>one</u> style. What Gorky wanted was for writers to be "chroniclers" and also to see into the future, to innovate and thus to "aid in the transformation of life."

15 _____. "Traditsii Gor'kogo segodnia" [Gorkian traditions today]. <u>Znamia</u> 48, no. 4:227-38.

Gorky heralded the union of labor and high culture brought about by the Revolution. Mentions K. Fedin, L. Leonov, F. Gladkov, V. Kataev, M. Shaginian. Says that these traditions are alive today, but does not mention any well-known contemporary writers.

16 OSMANOVA, Z.A. "Tvorchestvo M. Gor'kogo i sud'by sovetskogo romana" [Gorky's works and the fates of the Soviet novel]. In <u>Sovetskii roman: Novatorstvo, poetika, tipologiia</u> [The Soviet novel: innovation, poetics, typology]. Edited by N. Vorob'eva et al. Moscow: Nauka, pp. 90-115.

Reviews critical approaches to the topic of Gorky's influence upon the national literatures of the Soviet Union and concludes with topics that require more research, such as Gorky's impact as a publicist and the influence of his view of women.

17 OSTROVSKAIA, S. "Gor'kii i molodye pisateli" [Gorky and young writers]. <u>Russkii iazyk za rubezhom</u>, no. 2:112-16.

Reaffirms Gorky's role as model for younger writers.

18 OVCHARENKO, A.I. <u>M. Gor'kii i literaturnye iskaniia XX stoletiia</u> [Gorky and literary searchings of the 20th century]. 2d ed. Moscow: Sovetskii pisatel', 510 pp.

See 1971.15. This edition includes more material on <u>The Life of Klim Samgin</u> [<u>Zhizn' Klima Samgina</u>].

19 _____. "M. Gor'kii i mirovaia literatura: Itogi khudozhestvennykh iskanii" [Gorky and world literature: Conclusions of artistic searchings]. <u>Moskva</u>, no. 1:195-209; no. 2:192-204; no. 3:183-98.

Deals with Gorky's treatment of the Russian "bourgeoisie" in <u>The Artamonov Business</u> [<u>Delo Artamonovykh</u>] and compares Gorky's treatment with analogous treatments by Thomas Mann, among others.

20 PICKERING, JERRY V. "Maxim Gorky." In <u>Theatre: A History of the Art</u>. St. Paul, Minn.: West Publishing Co., pp. 487-90.

Gives a brief biography and a short history of his plays.

21 "Pis'ma A.M. Gor'kogo k V.V. Rozanovu i ego pomety na knigakh Rozanova" [Letters of Gorky to V.V. Rozanov and his markings on

Rozanov's books]. In Kontekst 1978 [Context 1978]. Moscow: Nauka, pp. 297-342.

Contains seven letters from Gorky to Rozanov from November 1905 to April 1912 and marginalia by Gorky on Rozanov's books. Abundant notes.

22 SUKHIKH, S.I. "Zhizn' Klima Samgina M. Gor'kogo i Filosofiia obshchego dela N.F. Fedorova" [Gorky's Life of Klim Samgin and N.F. Fedorov's Philosophy of the Common Cause]. In M. Gor'kii i voprosy literaturnykh zhanrov. Gorky: Izd. GGU, pp. 3-38.

See 1978.10. Traces the response to Nikolai Fedorov's ethics in Gorky's Life of Klim Samgin.

23 TEIXIDÓ, RAUL. "Las Memorias de Gorki o La Escuela de la Vida." In La Vida Redimida. Barcelona: Tipoform, pp. 13-48.
Analyzes Gorky's autobiographies.

24 VOLKOV, A.A. Khudozhestvennyi mir Gor'kogo (sovetskie gody) [The artistic world of Gorky (the Soviet years)]. Moscow: Sovremennik, 366 pp.

Shows how Gorky's artistic treatment of the revolutionary era led to generic "innovation." Deals with the stories of the 1920s, the literary portraits, the plays, and the epic novels.

25 WOLFE, BERTRAM D. "V.I. Lenin and Maxim Gorky: Study of a Stormy Friendship." In Society and History: Essays in Honor of Karl August Wittfogel. Edited by G.L. Ulmen. The Hague: Mouton, pp. 281-309.

Reuses the metaphors of bridge and abyss to characterize Gorky and Lenin's relationship: real friendship and admiration versus equally real differences in temperament, philosophical outlook, politics. Analyzes their differences in outlook.

1979

1 BARON, PHILIPPE. "Čehov et Gor'kii sur la scène française en 1902." Revue de littérature comparée 53, no. 2:246-52.
About Lidia Yavorskaia and her role in Franco-Russian theater connections.

2 BENOIST, JEAN-PIERRE. Les fonctions de l'ordre des mots en russe moderne: Romans et nouvelles de Gorki. Paris: Institut d'études slaves, 373 pp.
A stylistic analysis of Gorky's prose.

3 BIALIK, BORIS. "Politika trusov vsegda politika zhestokosti" [The politics of cowards is always the politics of cruelty]. Znamia 49, no. 12:234-44.

In response to the directive from the Central Committee that ideological education be improved. Suggests using materials from Gorky, the "founder" of Soviet literature. What Gorky has to say about capitalism and the bourgeois mentality sounds very relevant today. Quotes Richard Nixon.

3A   DIENES, L. "An Unpublished Letter by Maksim Gor'kij. Or, Who Is Gajto Gazdanov?" Die Welt der Slaven 24, no. 1:39-54.
   Contains a letter from Gorky to Russian émigré writer G. Gazdanov.

4   ERSHOVA, L.V. "Peizazh v povestiakh okurovskogo tsikla M. Gor'kogo" [Landscape in Gorky's Okurov cycle]. Vestnik MGU 34, no. 2:60-67.
   Through use of landscape imagery Gorky evaluates events and provides a way of seeing into characters' inner life.

5   FORMAN, BETTY YETTA. "Nietzsche and Gorky in the 1890's: The Case for an Early Influence." In Western Philosophical Systems in Russian Literature: A Collection of Critical Studies. Edited by A. Mlikotin. Series in Slavic Humanities. Vol. 3. Los Angeles: University of Southern California Press, pp. 153-64.
   Reviews Soviet discussion of Nietzsche's impact on Gorky. Gives a brief survey of Gorky's reading of Nietzsche. Focuses discussion on the story "The Song of the Falcon" ["Pesnia o sokole"].

5A   GRECHNEV, V.IA. "Gor'kii-novellist" [Gorky as writer of the novella]. In Russkii rasskaz kontsa XIX-XX veka (problematika i poetika zhanra) [The Russian story of the end of the 19th-early 20th centuries: The problems and poetics of the genre]. Leningrad: Nauka, pp. 154-96.
   Finds two elements in Gorky's work that set him apart from his precursors Garshin and Chekhov: a heightened, romanticized view of humanity and a harsh, realistic view of existing social conditions.

6   IL'INICH, K.M. "A.M. Gor'kii i A.V. Lunacharskii [A.M. Gorky and A.V. Lunacharsky]. In M. Gor'kii i voprosy zhanra i stilia. Gorky: Izd. GGU, pp. 3-18.
   See 1979.11. Discusses Gorky and Lunacharsky's earliest acquaintance.

7   IMENDÖRFER, HELENE. "Die Rezeption Maksim Gor'kijs in der Formulierungsphase des sozialistischen Realismus (1928-34)." In Von der Revolution zum Schriftsteller Kongress. Edited by G. Erler et al. Wiesbaden: Harrassowitz, pp. 391-421.
   Notes the strong variation in Gorky's reception in Russia: Although he is today revered as the father of socialist realism, in the 1920s he stood on the periphery of literary life as a "fellow traveler." Finds the period 1928-34 particularly important as a turning point in Gorky's Soviet reception.

8   KHLEBOSTROEVA, I.V. "L. Tolstoi i M. Gor'kii: Filosofiia iskusstva i zhizni (1890-1910)" [L. Tolstoi and M. Gorky: Philosophy of art and life (1890-1910)]. In Revoliutsiia, zhizn', pisatel' [Revolution, life, writer]. Voronezh: Izd. VGU, pp. 3-34.
    Deals with Tolstoy's and Gorky's separate "confessions," with their unique ways of searching for higher meaning in existence. Devoted several pages to Gorky's Confession [Ispoved'].

9   KIREEVA, I.V. "Amerikanskaia literatura XIX-XX veka v otsenke A.M. Gor'kogo" [A.M. Gorky's evaluation of 19th- and 20th-century American literature]. In M. Gor'kii i voprosy zhanra i stilia. Gorky: Izd. GGU, pp. 69-84.
    See 1979.11. Gorky's interpretation of American literature helped him work out his own new literary method and lay the groundwork for socialist realism. Discusses Soviet American literature studies, Gorky's view of J.F. Cooper, H.B. Stowe, H.W. Longfellow, Walt Whitman, E.A. Poe, among others.

10 KLÜGE, ROLF-DIETER. "Maxim Gor'kii, Die Mutter." In Der russische Roman. Edited by Bodo Zelinsky. Düsseldorf: Bagel, pp. 242-64.
    Gives a formal analysis of Mother and discusses its critical reception and its impact upon the idea of socialist realism. Mentions the sharp differences of opinion in literary criticism without coming to his own evaluation.

11 KUZ'MICHEV, I.K. M. Gor'kii i voprosy zhanra i stilia [M. Gorky and questions of genre and style]. Gorky: Izd. GGU, 157 pp.
    Contains the following articles:
    1. K.M. Il'inich, "A.M. Gor'kii i A.V. Lunacharskii (o pervoi vstreche)" [Gorky and Lunacharsky (on their first meeting)]. See 1979.6.
    2. L.N. Dar'ialova, "Ob ideino-esteticheskoi funktsii avtora v zhanre literaturnogo portreta M. Gor'kogo (ocherk 'V.I. Lenin')" [On the ideational-aesthetic function of the author in the genre of the literary portrait of M. Gorky (the sketch "V.I. Lenin")].
    3. M.P. Shustov, "K probleme skazochnosti stilia M. Gor'kogo ('Devushka i Smert'')" [On the problem of elements of the fairy tale in Gorky's style ("The Girl and Death")].
    4. V.Iu. Polyskalov, "Tochka zreniia povestvovatelia v kompozitsii Zhizni Klima Samgina M. Gor'kogo" [The narrator's point of view in the composition of Gorky's The Life of Klim Samgin].
    5. V.N. Morokhin, "Fol'klor v Zhizni Klima Samgina" [Folklore in The Life of Klim Samgin].
    6. A.T. Lipatov, "Slovo serdtse v upotreblenii M. Gor'kogo" [Gorky's use of the word heart].
    7. G.M. Atanov, "Gor'kii o literature i fol'klore" [Gorky on literature and folklore].

8. I.V. Kireeva, "Amerikanskaia literatura XIX-XX veka v otsenke A.M. Gor'kogo" [A.M. Gorky's evaluation of 19th- and 20th-century American literature]. See 1979.9.
9. Z.E. Libinzon, "A. Kurella i M. Gor'kii" [A. Kurella and M. Gorky].
10. L.S. Kaufman, "Gor'kii v literaturnoi sud'be G. Veizenborn" [Gorky in G. Veizenborn's literary career].
11. N.G. Kalustova, "Zhenshchina-mat' v tvorchestve Gor'kogo i Rollana" [The image of woman as mother in Gorky's and Rolland's work].
12. M.M. Savchenko, "Gor'kii na Kubani" [Gorky in the Kuban].
13. N.V. Skoblo, "Na dne M. Gor'kogo v zarubezhnoi kritike (1903-1978, na russkom iazyke)" [Gorky's Lower Depths in foreign criticism (1903-1978, in Russian)]. Sources are Soviet publications.
14. A.D. Zaidman, "Gumanizm tvorchestva M. Gor'kogo (ukazatel' osnovnoi literatury za 1968-1977 gg.)" [The humanism of Gorky's work (a bibliography of basic secondary literature, 1968-1977)].

12 LENGYEL, BÉLA. Gorkii és Nietzsche [Gorky and Nietzsche]. Budapest: Akadémiai Kiadó, 282 pp.
In Hungarian. The longest existing treatment of Gorky's literary-philosophical relationship with Nietzsche.

13 _____. "Napoleon's Folklore-Bild in Gorki's Meine Kindheit: Glosse zur Möglichkeit einer internationalen Forschung." Acta Litteraria Academiae Scientiarum Hungaricae 21, nos. 1-2:161-64.
Discusses folk consciousness in Childhood [Detstvo].

14 NEMIROVICH-DANCHENKO, VLADIMIR. Izbrannye pis'ma v dvukh tomakh [Selected letters in two volumes]. Vol. 1. Moscow: Iskusstvo, pp. 216, 284-302, 317-18, 347, 369-72.
Contains a great deal on Gorky and the Moscow Art Theater, on his relationship to S.T. Morozov and M.F. Andreev, on the reception of his plays, The Petit Bourgeois [Meshchane] and Summer Folk [Dachniki].

15 NIKULINA, N.I. "Filosofiia soznaniia v romane M. Gor'kogo Zhizn' Klima Samgina" [The philosophy of consciousness in Gorky's Life of Klim Samgin]. In Ot Griboedova do Gor'kogo: Iz istorii russkoi literatury [From Griboedov to Gorky: From the history of Russian literature]. Edited by N.I. Sokolov. Leningrad: Izd. LGU, pp. 124-36.
Argues for a redefinition of the genre of The Life of Klim Samgin on the grounds that previous critics have not taken into account the narrative function of Samgin's consciousness.

16 NOVIKOV, V. "M. Gor'kii i sovremennost'" [Gorky and the present]. In Dvizhenie istorii--dvizhenie literatury:

Nasledie i stilevoe bogatstvo sovremennoi sovetskoi literatury [The course of history is the course of literature: The legacy and stylistic richness of contemporary Soviet literature]. Moscow: Sovetskii pisatel', pp. 133-238.

Analyzes Gorky's influence upon Soviet writers in the 1930s.

17   SCHERR, BARRY. "Gor'kij's Childhood: The Autobiography as Fiction." SEEJ 23, no. 3:333-45.

Analyzes Childhood [Detstvo] in terms of the literary devices Gorky uses to reshape his autobiography. Compares Childhood with notes for an autobiography started in 1893. Argues that Gorky focuses more on growth of his own consciousness than on external social realities.

18   SEGEL, HAROLD B. Twentieth-Century Russian Drama: From Gorky to the Present. New York: Columbia University Press, pp. 1-49.

Contains two chapters on Gorky, one on his prerevolutionary plays, one on his Soviet plays. Expanded from 1976, compares Gorky with Chekhov: their development as dramatists, their dramatic technique. The second chapter focuses largely on Egor Bulychev and Dostigaev.

19   SOKOLOV, A.G. "Formirovanie metoda sotsialisticheskogo realizma v tvorchestve M. Gor'kogo 1892-1907 gg." [The formation of the socialist realist method in M. Gorky's work from 1892 to 1907]. In Istoriia russkoi literatury kontsa XIX-nachala XX veka. Moscow: Vysshaia shkola, pp. 107-51.

See 1979.20. Gorky as the first "proletarian" writer and the founder of a "new socialist art." Surveys Gorky's early literary development in connection with his "revolutionist" activities. Finds in them some of the principles of socialist realism: optimism, social activism, national character. Surveys early stories, novels, plays; ends with Mother [Mat'].

20   _____. Istoriia russkoi literatury kontsa XIX-nachala XX veka [The history of Russian literature of the end of the 19th and beginning of the 20th century]. Moscow: Vysshaia shkola, pp. 107-51, 275-99.

Contains two chapters on Gorky:
1. "Formirovanie metoda sotsialisticheskogo realizma v tvorchestve M. Gor'kogo 1892-1907 gg." [The formation of the socialist realist method in M. Gorky's work from 1892 to 1907]. See 1979.19.
2. "Tvorchestvo M. Gor'kogo 1908-1917 gg." [M. Gorky's work from 1908 to 1917]. See 1979.21.

21   _____. "Tvorchestvo M. Gor'kogo 1908-1917 gg." [M. Gorky's work from 1908 to 1917]. In Istoriia russkoi literatury kontsa XIX-nachala XX veka. Moscow: Vysshaia shkola, pp. 275-99.

See 1979.20. Surveys Gorky's God-building period, his relationship to Lenin, novels and story cycles of the middle period, autobiographical works.

22 WILKS, RONALD. Introduction to My Universities. Harmondsworth: Penguin, pp. 5-9.
    Gorky's "universities" were revolutionary circles in Kazan.

23 ZAIKA, S.V. "V predoshchushchenii novogo iskusstva: Korolenko i Gor'kii v literaturnom dvizhenii 'Rubezha vekov'" [Prescience of a new art: Korolenko and Gorky in the literary movement "Turn of the century"]. Russkaia literatura 22, no. 3:45-60.
    Discusses similarities of theme between V. Korolenko and Gorky--for example, their shared interests in the life of social pariahs. Sees a difference in mood. Discusses their long literary interaction over fifteen years.

24 ZHELTOVA, N.I. "M. Gor'kii i khudozhestvennaia kul'tura nachala XX veka" [Gorky and artistic culture of the early 20th century]. Russkaia literatura 22, no. 4:204-9.
    Review of N.E. Krutikova, V nachale veka: Gor'kii i simvolisty (1978.8).

1980

1 CHIKIN, VALENTIN. "Pervoprokhodtsy novogo mira: V.I. Lenin v tvorcheskoi biografii A.M. Gor'kogo" [The first pioneers of the new world: V.I. Lenin in the creative biography of A.M. Gorky]. Nash sovremennik, no. 4:145-60.
   Concentrates on the discordant periods in Gorky and Lenin's relationship: the God-building period and the Untimely Thoughts period. More detail than usual, but standard interpretation.

2 DAR'IALOVA, L.N. "Zhanrovaia osobennost' tsikla rasskazov 1922-1924 gg. M. Gor'kogo" [The generic particularity of Gorky's story cycle of 1922-1924]. In Zhanr i kompozitsiia literaturnogo proizvedeniia [Genre and composition of the literary work]. Vol. 5. Kaliningrad: Izd. Kal. GU, pp. 79-90.
   Sees this cycle as a renewal of epic form and a polemic against the "existentialist" philosophy of Nietzsche, Bergson, Berdiaev.

3 The Diary of Valery Bryusov (1893-1905). Edited and translated by J.D. Grossman. Berkeley: University of California Press, pp. 104-7.
   First published Moscow: Sabashnikovy, 1927. Description of a meeting with Gorky in 1900.

4   GABLE, CHRIS. "Maxim Gorky and the Theme of Unrest in Bulgarian Literature (1900-1944)." Ph.D. diss., New York University, 591 pp.
    DAI 41:2634A. Examines Gorky's influence on the Bulgarian writers, Dimitar Poljanov, Xristo Smirnenski, Nikola Vapcarov, Krum Velkov. Pays particular attention to their treatment of the theme of revolution.

5   IL'INICH, K.M. "A.V. Lunacharskii ob Ispovedi A.M. Gor'kogo" [A.V. Lunacharsky on A.M. Gorky's Confession]. In Gor'kovskie chteniia. Gorky: Volgo-viat. knizh. izd-vo., pp. 70-77.
    See 1980.8. Traces Lunacharsky's attitude to Confession. From Lunacharsky's discussion the author derives ideas about "'freedom of thought and creativity' within the party."

6   KOTLIAROV, IU.F. "Utochnenie k napechatannomu: Gor'kii i Shaliapin" [An addition to what has already been published: Gorky and Shaliapin]. Russkaia literatura 23, no. 4:182.
    Redates a letter from Gorky to Shaliapin. Asks where missing letters from Gorky to Shaliapin are.

7   KRIUKOVA, A. "K istorii otnoshenii Gor'kogo i Bloka" [Toward a history of the relationship of Gorky and Blok]. Voprosy literatury 24, no. 10 (October):197-227.
    Concentrates on Aleksandr Blok and Gorky's relationship during the civil war and Gorky's remarks about Blok in the years after his death (1921). Finds grounds for a reinterpretation of Blok on Gorky's part in the mid-1930s.

8   KUZ'MICHEV, I.K., et al., eds. Gor'kovskie chteniia, 1980: Materialy k konferentsii 'A.M. Gor'kii i roman XX veka' [Readings in Gorky, 1980: Materials from the conference "A.M. Gorky and the 20th-century novel"]. Gorky: Volgo-viat. knizh. izd-vo., 189 pp.
    Contains the following papers:
    1. I.K. Kuz'michev, "M. Gor'kii i roman XX veka" [Gorky and the 20th-century novel].
    2. A.I. Ovcharenko, "A.M. Gor'kii i razvitie sovetskogo romana" [A.M. Gorky and the development of the Soviet novel].
    3. V.V. Shakhov, "A.M. Gor'kii i razvitie russkoi realisticheskoi prozy na rubezhe XIX-XX vv." [A.M. Gorky and the development of Russian realist prose at the turn of the 20th century].
    4. A.V. Barmin, "Funktsii dialoga v epopee XX veka" [The functions of dialogue in the 20th-century epic].
    5. L.A. Evstigneeva, "A.M. Gor'kii i A.V. Amfiteatrov" [A.M. Gorky and A.V. Amfiteatrov].
    6. L.M. Farber, "Roman o partii" [The novel about the party].
    7. K.M. Il'inich, "A.V. Lunacharskii ob Ispovedi A.M. Gor'kogo" [A.V. Lunacharsky on A.M. Gorky's Confession]. See 1980.5.

8. A.M. Minakova, "A.M. Gor'kii i sovetskaia filosofskaia proza 20-30-kh godov" [A.M. Gorky and Soviet philosophical prose of the 1920s and 1930s].
9. V.N. Morokhin, "A.M. Gor'kii o znachenii fol'klora dlia razvitiia literatury" [A.M. Gorky on the meaning of folklore for the development of literature].
10. S.A. Cherviakovskii, "Gor'kovskie traditsii v romane i stsenarii A.S. Serafimovicha Gorod v stepi" [Gorkian traditions in the novel and scenarios of A.S. Serafimovich, The City in the Steppe].
11. L.F. Garanina, "Traditsii A.M. Gor'kogo v romane G.I. Konovalova Istoki" [Traditions of A.M. Gorky in G.I. Konovalov's novel, Sources].
12. V.A. Khanov, "A.M. Gor'kii i V. Astaf'ev" [A.M. Gorky and V. Astafev].
13. E.I. Prokhorov, "Nekotorye cherty tvorcheskoi raboty M. Gor'kogo" [Certain aspects of M. Gorky's creative work].
14. D.N. Nuraliev, "A.M. Gor'kii i voprosy stilia turkmenskogo romana" [A.M. Gorky and questions of the style of the Turkmen novel].
15. R.M. Saburova, "A.M. Gor'kii i razvitie uzbekskogo sovetskogo romana" [A.M. Gorky and the development of the Uzbek Soviet novel].
16. V.I. Mamedova, "A.M. Gor'kii i stanovlenie Azerbaidzhanskogo sovetskogo romana" [A.M. Gorky and the development of the Azerbaijani Soviet novel].
17. B.A. Piradov, "A.M. Gor'kii i roman L. Kiacheli Tariel golua [A.M. Gorky and L. Kiacheli's novel, Tariel golua].
18. L.Ia. Garanin, "A.M. Gor'kii i problema filosofskikh iskanii v romanakh K. Chornogo" [A.M. Gorky and the problem of philosophical searchings in K. Chornyi's novels].
19. V.A. Vavere, "Maksim Gor'kii i Andrei Upit" [Maksim Gorky and Andrei Upit].
20. I.V. Kireeva, "Amerikanskii roman XX veka v otsenke A.M. Gor'kogo" [The 20th-century American novel in A.M. Gorky's evaluation].
21. Iu.I. Sokhriakov, "A.M. Gor'kii i literatura SShA 20-30-kh godov" [A.M. Gorky and American literature of the 1920s and 1930s].
22. E.A. Leonova, "Traditsii A.M. Gor'kogo v antivoennom romane GDR" [The traditions of A.M. Gorky in the East German antiwar novel].
23. B.B. Remizov, "A.M. Gor'kii i avtobiograficheskie romany A. Kronina 40-50-kh godov" [A.M. Gorky and the autobiographical novels of A. Cronin in the 1940s and 1950s].
24. L.S. Kaufman, "Roman A.M. Gor'kogo Mat' i nemetskaia antifashistskaia literatura 30-40-kh godov" [Gorky's novel Mother and German antifascist literature of the 1930s and 1940s].

9   READ, CHRISTOPHER. Religion, Revolution and the Russian Intelligentsia, 1900-1912: The "Vekhi" Debate and Its Intellectual Background. New York: Harper & Row, pp. 85-86.
    Discusses Confession as a God-building novel. Sees it as an attempt to introduce into Bolshevism a religious-philosophical aspect.

10 RINNE, MATTI. "Nastoiashchee zoloto gumanizma: Gor'kii v Finliandii" [The genuine gold of humanism: Gorky in Finland]. Voprosy literatury 24, no. 2 (February):299-303.
    Outlines Gorky's reception in Finland.

11 ROUGLE, CHARLES. "Intellectuals Organize: Gor'kii's 'Culture and Freedom' Society of 1918." Scando-slavica (Copenhagen) 26:85-103.
    Gorky's attempt in 1918 to unite Petrograd intellectuals behind a shared interest in the cultural enlightenment of peasants and workers is seen as the intelligentsia's last concerted effort to establish a cultural bond with the people.

11A SETZER, HEINZ. "Die Bedeutung der Energielehre für die Literaturkonzeption Maksim Gor'kijs nach der ersten russischen Revolution." Die Welt der Slaven 25, no. 2:394-427.
    Looks at the foundation of God-building in thermodynamic theory. Gorky comes to a new understanding of literary cognition. Analyzes the Okurov cycle and the articles published just before World War I.

12 SUKHIKH, S.I. "M. Gor'kii i N.F. Fedorov" [M. Gorky and N. F. Fedorov]. Russkaia literatura 23, no. 1:160-68.
    Analyzes Gorky's response to Fedorov's philosophy in publicistic articles, "More on Mechanic Citizens" and "About Women," and in The Life of Klim Samgin.

13 TOPER, P. "V gor'kovskoi perspektive: M. Gor'kii i literaturnyi protsess v sotsialisticheskikh stranakh: K postanovke voprosa" [In a Gorkian perspective: Gorky and the literary process in socialist countries: Posing the question]. Voprosy literatury 24, no. 12 (December):15-39.
    Sees the belles lettres of socialist countries coming closer, growing together under the influence of Gorky's ideas and works.

14 VAINBERG, I.I. Stranitsy bol'shoi zhizni [Pages from a great life]. Moscow: Det. lit., 240 pp.
    Collection of memoirs.

15 WEBSTER, C.D. "Gorky's 'Nilushka': Autism Case Report." Journal of Autism and Development Disorders (Washington) 10, no. 2:227-29.
    Sees Gorky's sketch, "Nilushka," as an accurate description of autism.

1981

1   BIALIK, B.A. "Moi Gor'kii" [My Gorky]. In <u>Velikoe slovo</u> [The great word]. Moscow: Sovetskii pisatel', pp. 220-43.
    A profession of faith by a leading Soviet Gorky specialist.

2   BUNIN, IVAN. "Gor'kii." In <u>Vospominaniia</u> [Memoirs]. Paris: Lev, pp. 118-29.
    Reprinted from 1950.2A.

3   BYKOVTSEVA, L.P., et al., <u>Lichnaia biblioteka A.M. Gor'kogo v Moskve: Opisanie</u> [Gorky's personal library in Moscow: Description]. Two vols. Moscow: Nauka, vol. 1, 412 pp.; vol. 2, 228 pp.
    Organized according to subject for books located in the library. Those located outside the library are listed according to room. Includes a listing of N.A. Peshkova's and E.P. Peshkova's libraries. Has indexes by name, title, books with Gorky's marginalia, books with inscriptions from the author to Gorky.

4   CHUVAKOV, VADIM. "An Unknown Letter from Maxim Gorky." <u>Soviet Literature</u>, no. 12:68-69.
    A letter from 1910-13 on "pure art" and "tendentiousness" in art.

5   CLARK, KATERINA. <u>The Soviet Novel: History as Ritual</u>. Chicago: University of Chicago Press, pp. 27-30, 52-67, 118-19, 147-55.
    Deals with Gorky's role in formulating the concept of socialist realism. Discusses <u>On Literature, Mother, Life of Klim Samgin</u>. Discusses Gorky's God-building as a prefiguration of Stalinist "high" culture of the 1930s.

6   CLOWES, EDITH W. "A Philosophy 'For All and None': The Early Reception of Friedrich Nietzsche's Thought in Russian Literature, 1892-1912." Ph.D. diss., Yale University, pp. 117-65.
    Shows Nietzsche's influence on Gorky's moral and aesthetic views. Discusses early stories, including "Chelkash," "The Mistake" ["Oshibka"], "The Reader" ["Chitatel'"], Gorky's first novel, <u>Foma Gordeev</u>, and the prose poem "Man" ["Chelovek"].

7   FROST, EDGAR L. "Maksim Zorkij, or the Tale of the Sharp-Eyed, Self-Taught Writer from Nizhny Novgorod." <u>Russian Language Journal</u> 35, nos. 121-122:163-71.
    Argues for a more positive and broader evaluation of Gorky in Western criticism. He wrote more of value than just "Twenty-six and One" ["Dvadtsat' shest' i odna"] and his portraits. Analyzes "A Man Is Born" ["Rozhdenie cheloveka"] for its verbal texture and the structure of its imagery.

8   KALINA, E.I., ed. Proizvedeniia sovetskikh pisatelei v perevodakh na inostrannye iazyki, 1976-1980 [Works by Soviet writers in foreign-language translation, 1976-1980]. Moscow: Kniga, pp. 38-46.
    Bibliography. Continuation of 1976.29.

9   KELDYSH, V.A. "Zhizn'" [Life]. In Literaturnyi protsess i russkaia zhurnalistika kontsa XIX-nachala XX veka [The literary process and Russian journalism of the end of the 19th and early 20th centuries]. Moscow: Nauka, pp. 231-308.
    Discusses Gorky and Vladimir Posse's collaboration on Zhizn' (1898-1901).

9A KOLOBAEVA, L.A. "Avtor i geroi v romane M. Gor'kogo Mat'" [Author and hero in M. Gorky's novel Mother]. In Aktual'nye problemy sotsialisticheskogo realizma [Current problems in socialist realism]. Moscow: Nauka, pp. 188-97.
    A close reading of the text with attention to narrative point of view, structure of the fabula, stylistic device.

10 KOVAL', L.M. Russko-ital'ianskie obshchestvennye sviazi [Russo-Italian social ties]. Moscow: Nauka, pp. 64-74.
    Biographical note. Summarizes Gorky's life in Italy, particularly the Capri period. Discusses Gorky's library on Capri.

11 KUZ'MICHEV, I.K. M. Gor'kii i proza XX veka [M. Gorky and 20th-century prose]. Gorky: Izd. GGU, 102 pp.
    Devoted to study of Gorky's influence on the Soviet novel. Contains the following articles:
    1. K.S. Nikolaeva, "A.M. Gor'kii i stanovlenie sovetskogo romana 20-kh godov" [A.M. Gorky and the emergence of the Soviet novel in the 1920s].
    2. A.I. Vaniukov, "Moi universitety M. Gor'kogo i russkaia sovetskaia povest' 20-kh godov" [My Universities by M. Gorky and the Russian Soviet novel of the 1920s].
    3. A.I. Kupriianovskii, "Romany D.A. Furmanova v svete otsenok A.M. Gor'kogo i gor'kovskikh traditsii" [The novels of D.A. Furmanov in the light of A.M. Gorky's evaluation and of Gorkian traditions].
    4. G.S. Zaitseva, "M. Gor'kii i krest'ianskii roman kontsa 20-kh-nachala 30-kh godov" [M. Gorky and the peasant novel of the late 1920s-early 1930s].
    5. K.K. Vasin, "Traditsii M. Gor'kogo i stanovlenie mariiskogo istoriko-revoliutsionnogo romana" [Gorkian traditions and the emergence of the Marian historical-revolutionary novel].
    6. L.M. Slobozhaninova, "Gor'kii i Bazhov (izobrazhenie cheloveka truda v sovetskoi proze 30-40-kh gg.)" [Gorky and Bazhov (the depiction of the person of labor in Soviet prose of the 1930s and 1940s)].
    7. V.A. Khanov, "Traditsii M. Gor'kogo v povesti N. Kochina Iunost'" [Gorkian traditions in N. Kochin's novel Youth].

8. M.P. Shustov, "Stilevye osobennosti rasskaza M. Gor'kogo 'Khan i ego syn'" [Stylistic features of M. Gorky's story, "The Khan and His Son"].
9. A.F. Tsirulev, "Mnogolikaia istina" [Many-sided truth].
10. V.Iu. Polyskalov, "Sopostavlenie kak stilisticheskii priem v Zhizni Klima Samgina" [Juxtaposition as a stylistic device in The Life of Klim Samgin].
11. S.A. Cherviakovskii, "Povest' Zhizn' nenuzhnogo cheloveka" [The novel The Life of a Superfluous Man].
12. K.M. Il'inich, "A.M. Gor'kii i A.V. Lunacharskii v period kapriiskoi shkoly i gruppy 'Vpered'" [A.M. Gorky and A.V. Lunacharsky in the period of the Capri School and the "Forward" group].
13. V.A. Zlobin, "Maksim Gor'kii i Dzhuzeppe Madzini" [Maksim Gorky and Giuseppe Mazzini].

12 Maksim Gor'kii v vospominaniiakh sovremennikov [Maksim Gorky in the memoirs of contemporaries]. Edited by I.S. Eventov and A.A. Krundyshev. 2 vols. Moscow: Khud. Lit., vol. 1, 445 pp.; vol. 2, 445 pp.
    Contains reprints of memoirs of writers and political activists.

13 MURATOVA, K.D. M. Gor'kii: Seminarii [M. Gorky: A seminar]. Moscow: Prosveshchenie, 206 pp.
    Bibliography. Includes a lengthy introduction outlining the history of Gorky's critical reception and of scholarly approaches to the study of Gorky in the USSR. Gives an involved chronology of Gorky's life and work. The bibliography is divided into themes such as Gorky and literary movements of the beginning of the twentieth century, Gorky and his contemporaries, Gorky and world literature. Listings are all Soviet sources.

14 NABOKOV, VLADIMIR. "Maxim Gorki (1868-1936)." New York Review of Books 28, no. 14 (24 September):49-52.
    Gives a brief literary-political biography. Gorky's political activity, relations to the Moscow Art Theater, relation to the Bolsheviks. Finds him a "colorful phenomenon in the social structure of Russia." Analyzes "On the Rafts" ["Na plotakh"]. Notes "schematic characters," "mechanical structure," similar to the medieval fabliaux or moralité.

15 _____. "Maxim Gorki." In Lectures on Russian Literature. New York: Harcourt, pp. 297-306.
    Reprint of 1981.14.

15A NIKITINA, I.V. Po sledam geroev M. Gor'kogo [On the tracks of M. Gorky's heroes]. Gorky: Volgo-viat. knizh. izd-vo., 191 pp.
    Finds prototypes for Gorky's merchant and revolutionary characters among his acquaintances in Nizhny Novgorod. Discusses Mother [Mat'], Barbarians [Varvary], Egor Bulychev, Dostigaev, The Life of Klim Samgin [Zhizn' Klima Samgina].

16 OVSIANNIKOV, NIKOLAI. "Okurovskii tsikl Gor'kogo" [Gorky's Okurov cycle]. Voprosy literatury 25, no. 5 (May):193-207.
   Analyzes The Town of Okurov [Gorod Okurova] and The Life of Matvei Kozhemiakin [Zhizn' Matveia Kozhemiakina] as part of Gorky's continuing struggle against decadence. Discusses his response to Landmarks [Vekhi].

17 ZHELTOVA, N.I. "Gor'kovedenie 1970-ikh godov" [Gorky studies in the 1970s]. Russkaia literatura, no. 3:179-84.
   Gorky studies bring innovative theoretical and historical methods to literary criticism because of the great and ever relevant literary material they treat. Mentions the publications of new materials, analyses of Gorky's influence on present literature, and studies of historical sources.

1982

1 BAUMANN, WINFRIED. Erinnerung und Erinnertes in Gor'kijs Kindheit. Frankfurt: Peter Lang, 192 pp.
   Analyzes Childhood [Detstvo] from pedagogical, psychological, sociological, and critical points of view. The purpose is to gain insight into the creative impulse of memory by studying what is remembered and how it is shaped.

1A BERBEROVA, N.N. Zheleznaia zhenshchina, 1892-1974 [The iron woman, 1892-1974]. 2d ed. New York: Russica, pp. 111-43, 157-72, 184-94, 295-305, 334-42.
   Biography of Baroness M.I. Budberg. Contains enormous amount of material on Gorky: the early Soviet years, exile, relations with H.G. Wells, relations with Stalin, death.

2 DAR'IALOVA, L.N. "Zhizn' Klima Samgina M. Gor'kogo kak novyi tip romana-epopei (roman filosofskii i roman 'potoka soznaniia')" [Gorky's The Life of Klim Samgin as a new type of epic novel (the philosophical novel and the "stream-of-consciousness" novel)]. In M. Gor'kii i voprosy poetiki. Gorky: Izd. GGU, pp. 27-37.
   See 1982.10. Sees in Gorky's stream-of-consciousness style a necessary device for unfolding his philosophical polemic with Nikolai Berdiaev and others.

3 ELIZAROVA, R., and KHOROSHUKHIN, E. "Lev Tolstoi v otsenkakh S. Tsveiga i M. Gor'kogo" [Lev Tolstoy as evaluated by S. Zweig and M. Gorky]. In Iskusstvo slova [Verbal art]. Tashkent: Tash. gos. ped. in-t., pp. 36-42.
   Compares Stefan Zweig's and Gorky's works on L.N. Tolstoy. Sheds light on the lack of comment on Tolstoy as artist in Gorky's work.

4 An End to Silence: Uncensored Opinion in the Soviet Union from Roy Medvedev's Underground Magazine "Political Diary."

Edited by S.F. Cohen. Translated by G. Saunders. New York and London: W.W. Norton, pp. 76, 119.
Insight into Gorky's relationship to Stalin.

5 FREEBORN, RICHARD. "Proletarian Heroism and Intelligentsia Militancy." In The Russian Revolutionary Novel. Cambridge: Cambridge University Press, pp. 39-64.
Juxtaposes Mother [Mat'] and Andrei Belyi's Petersburg as response to the revolution of 1905: both show alienation from the urban, capitalist environment. Both in their own way didactic. Analyzes Mother as a conscious effort to prod and encourage revolution. Despite doubtful aesthetic value, the figure of the mother is captivating: Gorky imagines in idealized form the mother he lacked.

6 _____. "The Revolutionary Epic." In The Russian Revolutionary Novel. Cambridge: Cambridge University Press, pp. 174-79.
On The Life of Klim Samgin. Sees it as a bildungsroman, an "enormous chronicle." Helps set the "dilemma of a Dr. Zhivago" in context. Samgin's life is an "epic of futility."

7 GALENKO, O.K., et al., eds. M. Gor'kii v pechati rodnogo kraia, 1969-1977 [M. Gorky in his hometown press, 1969-1977]. Gorky: Volgo-viat. knizh. izd-vo., 144 pp.
Bibliography of books and articles on Gorky printed in the city of Gorky.

7A HIELSCHER, KARLA. "Zum Verhältnis der Poetik Gor'kijs und Čechovs." Wiener Slawischer Almanach 9:151-63.
Analyzes Gorky's relationship to Chekhov as a polemic. Gives most attention to "The Reader" ["Chitadel'"] as an answer to Chekhov's aesthetic views.

7B KHODASEVICH, VLADISLAV. "Belyi koridor" [The white corridor]. In Izbrannaia proza [Selected prose]. New York: Russica, pp. 303-4.
Reprinted from 1954. Memoir of Gorky, the World Literature publishing house, and the hostility between Gorky and the Kamenevs.

8 KIREEVA, I.V. "Gor'kovskaia kontseptsiia amerikanskogo realizma XX veka" [Gorky's concept of 20th-century American realism]. In M. Gor'kii i voprosy poetiki. Gorky: Izd. GGU, pp. 69-81.
See 1982.10. Gorky saw in American realism the danger of overexperimentation with formal device and lack of attention to social problems.

9 _____. "Iz istorii vospriiatiia dramaturgii Gor'kogo v Amerike (20-30 gody)" [From the reception of Gorky's plays in America (1920s and 1930s)]. In Literaturnye sviazi i problema vzaimovliianiia [Literary connections and the problem of mutual influence]. Gorky: Izd. GGU, pp. 3-17.
Studies the popularization of Gorky's plays in the United States in the 1930s.

10 KUZ'MICHEV, I.K., et al., eds. M. Gor'kii i voprosy poetiki [M. Gorky and questions of poetics]. Gorky: Izd. GGU, 87 pp. Contains the following articles:
  1. S.I. Sukhikh, "Problemy poetiki Zhizni Klima Samgina (po materialam zarubezhnoi pechati)" [Problems in the poetics of The Life of Klim Samgin (with materials from the foreign press)]. See 1982.24.
  2. L.N. Dar'ialova, "Zhizn' Klima Samgina M. Gor'kogo kak novyi tip romana-epopei (roman filosofskii i roman 'potoka soznaniia')" [Gorky's The Life of Klim Samgin as a new type of epic novel (the philosophical novel and the "stream-of-consciousness" novel)]. See 1982.2.
  3. V.Iu. Polyskalov, "O prirode zhanra Zhizni Klima Samgina" [On the generic nature of The Life of Klim Samgin].
  4. V.I. Zhil'tsov, "Voprosy kompozitsii Zhizni Klima Samgina v kriticheskikh rabotakh 20-kh godov" [Questions of the composition of The Life of Klim Samgin in critical works of the 1920s].
  5. M.P. Shustov, "Kompozitsionnaia struktura 'Valashskoi skazki o malen'kom fee i molodom chabane' M. Gor'kogo" [The compositional structure of "The Valashian Tale of the Small Fairy and the Young Shepherd" of M. Gorky].
  6. L.V. Liapaeva, "O stilizatsii v Skazkakh ob Italii M. Gor'kogo" [On stylization in M. Gorky's Tales of Italy].
  7. A.F. Tsirulev, "O putiakh analiza nravstvennogo stanovlenii lichnosti (avtobiograficheskaia trilogiia M. Gor'kogo)" [On the ways of analyzing the moral development of personality (M. Gorky's autobiographical trilogy)].
  8. I.V. Kireeva, "Gor'kovskaia kontseptsiia amerikanskogo realizma XX veka" [Gorky's concept of 20th-century American realism]. See 1982.2.
  Also contains A.F. Tsirulev's select bibliography of works dating from 1914 to 1981 on Gorky's autobiography.

11 LANTSUZSKII, V.A. "Lunacharskii-kritik Gor'kogo: o stat'e Lunacharskogo 'Dachniki'" [Lunacharsky as a critic of Gorky: on Lunacharsky's article, "Summer Folk"]. In Iskusstvo slova [Verbal art]. Tashkent: Tash. gos. ped. in-t., pp. 43-52.
  Lunacharsky's article played an important role in the formation of his aesthetic theory and had an impact on Russian Marxist criticism.

12 LARIN, B.A. Slovar' avtobiograficheskoi trilogii M. Gor'kogo [Dictionary of M. Gorky's autobiographical trilogy]. Vol. 3. Leningrad: Izd. LGU, 269 pp.
  Continuation of 1974.8 and 1977.8. Covers the letters from "zhe" to "kiparisovyi."

13 LAZAREV, V.A. "Roman M. Gor'kogo Delo Artamonovykh v zarubezhnoi pechati i kritike 30-kh godov" [Gorky's novel The Artamonov Business in the foreign press and criticism of the 1930s]. In Ideino-stilevoe mnogoobrazie sovetskoi literatury

[The ideational-stylistic variety of Soviet literature]. Moscow: Mos. gos. ped. in-t., pp. 160-93.
Reviews the reception of The Artamonov Business in the West.

14 LUKER, NICHOLAS. "Maxim Gorky (1868-1936)." In An Anthology of Russian Neo-Realism: The "Znanie" School of Maxim Gorky. Ann Arbor: Ardis, pp. 233-35.
A brief outline of Gorky's literary life.

15 MATVEICHUK, N.F. V tvorcheskoi masterskoi M. Gor'kogo [In M. Gorky's creative workshop]. Lvov: Izd. L'vov. GU, 159 pp.
Analyzes Gorky's appropriation of folkloric materials and folk language.

16 MIKHAILOV, OLEG N. "Po Rusi (zametki o predrevoliutsionnom tvorchestve M. Gor'kogo)" [Around Russia (notes on Gorky's prerevolutionary work)]. In Stranitsy russkogo realizma (zametki o russkoi literature XX veka) [Pages of Russian realism (notes on Russian literature of the 20th century)]. Moscow: Sovremennik, pp. 263-80.
Analyzes Gorky's autobiographical trilogy and the cycle of stories, Around Russia. Notes Gorky's novel image of childhood. Compares Gorky's autobiographical form with older forms, the lubok (popular illustrated literature) view of life, the saint's life.

17 NIVAT, GEORGE MICHEL. Vers la fin du mythe russe: Essais sur la culture russe de Gogol à nos jours. Lausanne: L'age d'homme, pp. 150-54, 181-83.
Defines "mythemes" of Russian literature and looks for mythic structures that have survived in modern Russian and Soviet culture. Sees The Three of Them and the Okurov cycle as echoes of Dostoevsky. Compares them to contemporary novels of Belyi.

18 NOVIKOV, V. Dvizhenie istorii-dvizhenie literatury [The course of history is the course of literature]. Moscow: Sovetskii pisatel', pp. 128-207.
Contains the following articles on Gorky:
1. "M. Gor'kii i sovetskaia literatura" [M. Gorky and Soviet literature].
2. "'Luchshaia radost' na zemle . . .--byt' blizkim narodu svoemu'" [The best joy on earth is to be near one's own people].
3. "M. Gor'kii o novykh formakh khudozhestvennogo obobshcheniia" [M. Gorky on new forms of artistic generalization].

19 O'TOOLE, L.M. "Plot." In Structure, Style, and Interpretation in the Russian Short Story. New Haven: Yale University Press, pp. 128-41.

A narrative analysis of "Twenty-six and One" ["Dvadtsat' shest' i odna"] and comparison with Pushkin's "The Shot."

20 OVCHARENKO, A.I. M. Gor'kii i literaturnye iskaniia XX stoletiia [M. Gorky and literary explorations of the 20th century]. 3d ed., expanded. Moscow: Khud. lit., 590 pp.
    See 1971.15. Compares Gorky with a broad spectrum of Western writers.

21 _____. Ot Gor'kogo do Shukshina [From Gorky to Shukshin]. Moscow: Sovremennik, 494 pp.
    Some of Ovcharenko's conclusions from a career of studying Gorky, Soviet literature, and the "new person." Deals with Lidia Seifullina, Konstantin Fedin, Mikhail Sholokhov, Vasilii Shukshin, among others.

22 SADOVSKII, IA.G. "Slovo Gor'kogo-publitsista" [The style of Gorky the publicist]. Russkaia rech' 16, no. 1:48-53.
    Analyzes Gorky's attack in 1932 on capitalist culture in "What Side Are You On, 'Masters of Culture'? An Answer to American Correspondents" ["S kem vy, 'mastera kultury'? Otvet amerikanskim korrespondentam"].

23 SESTERHENN, RAIMUND. Das Bogostroitel'stvo bei Gor'kij und Lunačarskij bis 1909: Zur ideologischen und literarischen Vorgeschichte der Parteischule von Capri. München: Otto Sagner, 366 pp.
    Argues that God-building was more than just a short-lived aberration. Shows the roots deep in both Lunacharsky's and Gorky's earlier work and its parallels in Western European socialism. Looks at implications of God-building for Gorky's image as "father of socialist realism."

24 SUKHIKH, S.I. "Problemy poetiki Zhizni Klima Samgina (po materialam zarubezhnoi pechati)" [Problems in the poetics of The Life of Klim Samgin (with materials from the foreign press)]. In Gor'kii i voprosy poetiki. Gorky: Izd. GGU, pp. 3-27.
    See 1982.10. Reviews Western criticism of The Life of Klim Samgin. Largely a positive review of H. Imendörffer's book (1973.7).

25 VORONSKII, A[LEKSANDR]. Izbrannye stat'i o literature [Selected articles on literature]. Moscow: Khud. lit., pp. 31-69.
    Contains two articles on Gorky:
    1. "O Gor'kom" [On Gorky]. Reprinted and expanded from 1926.5. See also 1929.4.
    2. "Vstrechi i besedy s Maksimom Gor'kim" [Meetings and conversations with Maksim Gorky]. See 1982.26.

26   _____. "Vstrechi i besedy s Maksimom Gor'kim" [Meetings and conversations with Maksim Gorky]. Izbrannye stat'i o literature. Moscow: Khud. lit., pp. 48-69.
   See 1982.25. First written in 1936 shortly after Gorky's death. Printed in part in Novyi mir 6 (1966). Deals with Gorky's support for Krasnaia nov' and the Serapion Brothers. Records conversations in which Gorky claimed he still had "not achieved true mastery as a writer."

27   VUL'F, V. Ot Brodveia nemnogo v storonu [Off Broadway]. Moscow: Iskusstvo, pp. 249-53.
   Mentions stage productions of Summer Folk [Dachniki], The Lower Depths [Na dne], among others, in the 1970s and discusses American plays written about Gorky.

28   ZAIKA, S.V. M. Gor'kii i russkaia klassicheskaia literatura kontsa XIX-nachala XX veka [M. Gorky and Russian classical literature of the end of the 19th and the early 20th century]. Moscow: Nauka, 143 pp.
   Discusses Gorky's appropriation of themes and values from L. Tolstoy, A. Chekhov, V. Korolenko.

1983

1   BETHEA, DAVID M. Khodasevich: His Life and Art. Princeton: Princeton University Press, pp. 262-72.
   Finds in the failure of Khodasevich's and Gorky's relationship the "failure of Soviet and émigré literature to find a common ground." Recounts their efforts at the joint Soviet-émigré venture, the journal Beseda [Conversation].

2   FLEISHMAN, LAZAR; RAEFF, MARC; and RAEVSKY-HUGHES, O., eds. "Iz perepiski Maksima Gor'kogo" [From Maksim Gorky's correspondence]. In Russkii Berlin, 1921-1923: Po materialam arkhiva B.I. Nikolaevskogo v guverovskom institute [Russian Berlin, 1921-1923: From materials in the archive of B.I. Nikolaevsky at the Hoover Institute]. Paris: YMCA, pp. 337-404.
   Contains twenty-four letters from Gorky to Nikolaevsky and Z.I. Grzhebin and one letter from Nikolaevsky to Gorky. Lengthy introduction and full notes. Illuminates the early years of Gorky's second emigration as well as Russian literary life in Berlin in the early 1920s. Contains information on Gorky's relationship to the industrialist Savva Morozov.

3   FORMAN, BETTY YETTA. "The Early Prose of Maksim Gorky. 1892-1899." Ph.D. diss., Harvard University, 619 pp.
   The first full-length Western treatment of the early Gorky. Analyzes Gorky's effort to shape his public literary personality through the calculated selection and publication of his first

collected works. Focuses on the influence of Korolenko and
Nietzsche on the young writer.

4   GALAGAN, G.IA. "L. Tolstoi 1900-kh godov i roman M. Gor'kogo
    Mat'" [L. Tolstoy in the 1900s and M. Gorky's novel Mother].
    Russkaia literatura 26, no. 1:152-58.
        Discusses Tolstoy's literary response to Mother in sketches
    for folktales.

5   GUTSCHE, GEORGE. "The Role of the 'One' in Gor'kij's 'Twenty-
    six and One.'" In Studies in Honor of Xenia Gąsiorowska.
    Edited by L.G. Leighton. Columbus, Ohio: Slavica,
    pp. 145-55.
        Treats the moral view implicit in the story. Suggests that
    Tania represents a new mode of moral valuation.

6   HENRY, PETER. "Imagery of podvig and podvizhnichestvo in the
    Works of Garshin and the Early Gor'ky." SEER 61, no. 1
    (January):139-59.
        Compares Gorky's and Garshin's moral consciousness with
    respect to the ethos of revolutionary struggle.

7   PROKHOROV, E.I. Tekstologiia khudozhestvennykh proizvedenii
    M. Gor'kogo [Textology of M. Gorky's literary works]. Moscow:
    Nauka, 279 pp.
        Analyzes the special problems and issues in making a crit-
    ical edition of Gorky's work. Suggests areas of further textual
    work.

8   ZAIKA, S.V. "Mir prirody v gumanisticheskoi kontseptsii
    Gor'kogo" [The world of nature in Gorky's humanist concep-
    tion]. Izvestiia ANSSSR 42, no. 6:531-39.
        Shows how descriptions of nature help Gorky form his "hu-
    manistic ideal" in his earliest works.

1984

1   FEN'VESHI, I. "Gor'kii i Vengriia" [Gorky and Hungary].
    Zvezda, no. 11:171-83.
        Memoirs. Three interviews with Gorky by Hungarians taken
    between 1902 and 1910. Three descriptions of meetings of Gorky
    with Hungarian intellectuals between 1912 and 1924.

1A FLEISHMAN, LAZAR'. Boris Pasternak v tridtsatye gody [Boris
    Pasternak in the 1930s]. Jerusalem: Magnes Press, pp. 23-36,
    45-47, 82-89, 117-43, 158-60, 190-205, 209-19, 224-30, 237-44,
    263-66, 335-37, 348-64.
        Presents an enormous amount of valuable material on Gorky
    in the 1930s.

2   LARIN, B.A. Slovar' avtobiograficheskoi trilogii M. Gor'kogo [Dictionary of M. Gorky's autobiographical trilogy]. Vol. 4. Leningrad: Izd. LGU, 310 pp.
    Continuation of 1974.8; 1977.8; 1982.11. Covers the letters from "kipenie" to "naiavu."

3   OSTROVSKAIA, S. "Pered dokladom (pomety M. Gor'kogo na knigakh ego lichnoi biblioteki)" [Before the speech (Gorky's notes in books from his personal library)]. Voprosy literatury, no. 8:152-173.
    Discusses Gorky's preparations for his speech, "Soviet Literature," given at the First Congress of the Writers' Union, 17 August 1934. Uses marginalia as evidence of his developing ideas. Shows influence of Lenin's Materialism and Empiriocriticism and Engels's Anti-Dühring.

4   RUCKMAN, JO ANN. The Moscow Business Elite: A Social and Cultural Portrait of Two Generations, 1840-1905. DeKalb: Northern Illinois University Press, pp. 169-71, 179-80.
    Characterizes friendship between Gorky and Savva Morozov as one of "rare warmth and mutual understanding" between a businessman and an intellectual.

5   TSVETAEVA, ANASTASIIA. Vospominaniia [Memoirs]. 3d ed. Moscow: Sovetskii pisatel', pp. 643-708.
    Personal impressions, meetings with Gorky after 1927. Contains five letters.

6   ZHEGALOV, N. "Velikoe, vechno zhivoe . . . (traditsiia russkoi klassiki v tvorchestve Gor'kogo)" [The great, the eternally living (the Russian classical tradition in Gorky's work)]. Voprosy literatury, no. 8:53-89.
    Analyzes the impact of late nineteenth-century prose on the formation of Gorky's "new literary method." Concentrates on Gorky's reassessment of the image of the people in relation to works of Pomialovsky, Leskov, Gleb Uspensky, and Korolenko.

6A ZHELTOVA, N.I., and SAVINKOVA, T.V. "Gor'kovedenie segodnia" [Gorky studies today]. Russkaia literatura 27, no. 3:202-10.
    Reviews the status of Soviet research on Gorky. Looks forward to the publication of the complete letters and articles of Gorky. Notes a reticence among critics concerning Gorky's relevance for the present day.

1985

1   BARAKHOV, V.S. "Nasledie A.M. Gor'kogo i voprosy kul'tury" [A.M. Gorky's heritage and questions of culture]. Russkaia literatura 28, no. 3:43-57.

Concerned with the question of Gorky's relevance for the present day. Draws attention to dangers of "automatizing" Gorky's reception.

2   DROBYSHEVA, M.N. "Ranniaia dramaturgiia M. Gor'kogo v Khorvatii nachala XX veka" [M. Gorky's early drama in Croatia at the beginning of the 20th century]. Russkaia literatura 28, no. 3:176-82.
    Deals with the staging and critical reception of Gorky's earliest plays in Croatia. Concentrates particularly on The Petit Bourgeois [Meshchane] and The Lower Depths [Na dne]. Contains useful bibliographical sources.

3   GANELIN, R.SH. "Iz vospominanii A.V. Liverovskogo (o prebyvanii M. Gor'kogo v Arzamase)" [From the memoirs of A.V. Liverovsky (on M. Gorky's sojourn in Arzamas)]. Russkaia literatura 28, no. 4:227.
    Notes the passages on Gorky in the memoirs of the engineering professor A.V. Liverovsky.

4   LOE, MARY LOUISE. "Maksim Gor'kii and the Sreda Circle: 1899-1905." Slavic Review 44, no. 1 (Spring):49-66.
    Examines why Gorky was accepted as moral leader of the Sreda group before 1905 and analyzes the debate within the circle about the role of the intellectual in bringing about social and political change.

5   LUKIRSKAIA, K.P., and MORSHCHIKHINA, A.S., eds. Literatura o Gor'kom: Bibliografiia 1966-1970 [Literature on Gorky: Bibliography 1966-1970]. Moscow and Leningrad: Nauka.
    Third volume. Continuation of the Gorky bibliography series. See 1965.11; 1970.11.

6   OSTROVSKAIA, S. Rukoi Gor'kogo: Sovetskaia russkaia proza v lichnoi biblioteke A.M. Gor'kogo [By Gorky's hand: Soviet Russian prose in the personal library of A.M. Gorky]. Moscow: Sovetskii pisatel', 238 pp.
    Analyzes Gorky's literary connections and influence on writers in the early Stalinist era.

7   TERRAS, VICTOR. "Gorky." In Handbook of Russian Literature. Edited by Victor Terras. New Haven: Yale University Press, pp. 180-82.
    Gorky has had an enormous influence on literature of socialist orientation. His high place in the literary hierarchy is incommensurate with his talent.

8   ZHELTOVA, N.I. "Roman Gor'kogo Mat' i stat'ia V.I. Lenina 'Predislovie k russkomu perevodu pisem K. Marksa k L. Kugel'manu'" [Gorky's novel Mother and V.I. Lenin's article, "Foreword to the Russian Translation of K. Marx's Letters to L. Kugelman"]. Russkaia literatura 28, no. 4:108-10.

Relates Lenin's views on Mother to his views on the 1905 revolt.

1986

1. GOR'KII, MAKSIM. Iz literaturnogo naslediia: Gor'kii i evreiskii vopros [From the literary heritage: Gorky and the Jewish question]. Edited by M. Agurskii and M. Shklovskaia. Jerusalem: Hebrew University, Center for Research and Documentation of East European Jewry, 535 pp.
   Contains Gorky's correspondence, articles, and belles lettres relevant to the Jewish question. Many published works are here republished for the first time. Organized chronologically.

2. PAKLIN, N.A. "Neizvestnye pis'ma M. Gor'kogo" [Unknown letters of M. Gorky]. Novyi mir, no. 1 (January):183-92.
   Contains ten letters from Gorky to Shaliapin from 1922 to 1930.

3. TERRY, GARTH M. Maxim Gorky in English: A Bibliography, 1868-1936-1986. Nottingham, England: Astra Press, 28 pp.
   Bibliography of English-language sources.

4. WEIL, IRWIN. "Aleksei Maksimovich Gorky." In The Modern Encyclopedia of Russian and Soviet Literature. Edited by H. Weber. Gulf Breeze, Fla.: Academic International Press.
   A biographical sketch. Draws attention to major issues in the study of Gorky: his social and moral views, his attitude to Dostoevsky, his relationship to the symbolists, his relationship with Lenin and Stalin. Themes highlighted in Gorky's belles lettres include the father figure, sex, the individual.

FORTHCOMING

1. LOE, MARY LOUISE. "Gorky and Nietzsche: The Quest for a Russian Superman." In Nietzsche in Russia. Edited by B.G. Rosenthal. Princeton: Princeton University Press.
   Analyzes why the young Gorky found Nietzsche appealing and how his vision of the new man differs from Nietzsche's superman.

2. LUKER, NICHOLAS, ed. Fifty Years On: Gorky and His Time. Nottingham, England: Astra Press.
   Contains articles on all aspects of Gorky's literary work.

Author Index

ABRAHAM, P., 1960.7
ADAMOVIC, G., addendum 5
ADLING, W., 1968.2; 1969.1
AGAPOW, B., 1956.1
AIKHENVAL'D, I., 1969.2
AIZMAN, D.IA., 1936.3
AKHUMIAN, T., 1968.11
AKHUNDOVA, B., 1966.1, 23
AKIMOV, IU.L., 1961.1
ALEKSANDROV, V., 1937.5
ALEKSANDROVA, L.P., 1968.3, 125
ALEKSANDROVICH, I., 1908.1
ALEKSEEV, I.A., 1959.12
ALEKSEEV, K.S. [K.S. Stanislavskii], 1928.10; 1952.5; 1958.9; 1963.1; 1968.96
ALEKSEEV, V.M., 1968.55
ALEKSEEVA, A.N., 1977.7
ALEKSIN, A.N., 1951.8
ALEKSINSKAIA, T., 1968.4
ALEXANDROVA, V., 1963.2
ALEXINSKY, G., 1950.1
AMFITEATROV, A., 1904.1; 1908.2; 1922.1; 1934.2
AMSTERDAM, A., 1956.2, 13
ANDREEV, L.N., 1916.1; 1934.2; 1965.10
ANDREEVA, M.F. See ZHELIABUZHSKAIA, M.
ANDREEVICH. See SOLOV'EV, E.
ANISIMOV, I.I., 1965.1
ANNENSKII, I., 1906.1
APLETIN, M.IA., 1954.1; 1959.1
APONIUK, N., 1977.1
APOSTOLOV, N.N., 1928.1
ARAGON, L., 1955.1-2
ARIF, M., 1949.1

ARNAUTOVA, M., 1961.2
ARSKII, R., 1928.10
ASEEV, N., 1928.10
ASHUKIN, N.S., 1928.2
ASTAF'EV, A., 1966.2, 23
ATANOV, G.M., 1979.11

BABAIAN, E.I., 1973.1
BABEL', I., 1966.3
BABOCHKIN, B., 1968.116
BAIN, R.N., 1902.1
BAKHMUTOVA, N.I., 1969.39
BAKHUNET'EV, VL., 1951.9
BAKSHY, A., 1959.2
BALATOVA, E.G., 1964.2
BALIKA, D.A., 1938.1; 1968.7, 32
BAL'MONT, K., 1934.2
BALUKHATYI, S.D., 1934.1-2; 1936.1-3; 1938.2-3; 1940.3; 1941.1-3
BARAKHOV, V.S., 1959.3; 1976.1; 1985.1
BARANOV, V.I., 1974.7; 1977.7
BARANOVA, N.D., 1974.7; 1978.1
BARBUSSE, H., 1960.10
BARMIN, A.V., 1976.33; 1978.10; 1980.8
BARON, P., 1979.1
BARRATT, A., 1978.2
BARTEL, M., 1928.10
BARTKOVICH, J., 1973.1A
BASKEVICH, I.Z., 1968.32
BATIUSHKOV, F.D., 1898.1; 1936.3
BATOURENSKY, V., 1915.2
BAUMANN, W., 1982.1
BAZANOV, V.V., 1976.2
BECHER, J.R., 1960.10; 1964.1; 1968.8-9, 102

197

BEERBOHM, Sir M., 1954.2
BEISLEKHEM, R.G., 1964.2; 1968.11
BELIN'KII, E.I., 1961.3; 1969.3
BELKIN, D.I., 1968.55
BELKINA, N.P., 1949.1; 1951.5
BELOUSOV, I.A., 1928.10
BELOZEROV, A., 1926.1
BELYI, A. See BUGAEV, B.
BELZA, S.I., 1970.18
BENINA, M.A., 1976.15
BENOIST, J.-P., 1979.2
BERBEROVA, N.N., 1961.4; 1967.1; 1969.4; 1972.1; 1982.1
BEREZARK, I., 1938.3A, 6A; 1940.3; 1956.14
BESPALOV, I.M., 1928.3-4; 1929.1
BETHEA, D.M., 1983.1
BIALIK, B.A., 1938.3B, 6B; 1939.1; 1947.1-2; 1948.1; 1951.5; 1954.9; 1958.1-2, 19, 42; 1959.3-5; 1960.1-2, 7; 1964.2; 1967.2; 1968.10-16, 97; 1969.5; 1970.1-2, 18; 1972.2; 1973.2; 1975.1; 1977.1A; 1978.3; 1979.3; 1981.1. See also BYALIK, B.
BIBILASHVILI, A., 1970.18
BILL, V.T., 1959.6
BIRIUKOV, F., 1978.4
BIRMAN, S., 1975.2
BLAGOI, D.D., 1949.1
BLAIR, K.H., 1973.2A, 9A
BLOCH, J.-R., 1960.3-4, 7
BLOK, A., 1907.1
BOBROVA, E.I., 1941.4
BOCHAROV, S.G., 1960.5
BOCHAROVA, I.A., 1962.6
BODROVA, A.A., 1968.55
BOGATYREV, SH.SH., 1959.3
BOGDANOVICH, A., 1898.2; 1901.1
BOGUSLOVSKII, A.O., 1958.3, 19; 1968.17; 1970.18
BONCH-BRUEVICH, V., 1928.5
BORDON, M., 1936.4
BORISOV, A.A., 1968.11
BORISOVA, M.B., 1962.8; 1969.6; 1970.3
BORRAS, F.M., 1967.3; 1968.18
BORSHCHUKOV, V., 1957.12
BOTSIANOVSKII, V.F., 1901.3; 1903.1

BOTURA, M., 1961.24
BOURNE, R.S., 1956.3
BOWEN, E., 1950.2; 1963.3
BRANDES, G., 1901.2
BRAUN, E., 1972.3; 1973.3
BRECHT, B., 1968.19, 102
BREDEL, W., 1968.102
BRIGGS, A.D., 1974.1
BRINTON, C., 1905.1
BRIUSOV, V.IA., 1934.2; 1958.9
BROD, M., 1968.20, 102
BRODSKAIA, S.IA., 1957.2; 1959.3, 7; 1962.1, 6; 1963.4; 1967.4; 1970.4
BRODSKII, N.L., 1949.1; 1955.3
BROOKS, J., 1972.4; 1973.3A, 9A
BROWN, B.W., 1938.4
BUDBERG, M., 1972.5
BUDET, R., 1968.96
BUENO, S., 1968.21
BUGAEV, B. [A. Belyi], 1908.3; 1910.1; 1911.1; 1922.2
BUGROV, B.S., 1964.2-3
BUNIN, I.A., 1936.3; 1950.2A; 1958.9, 11; 1961.18; 1981.2
BURIAN, I., 1976.3
BURMISTRENKO, O.I., 1961.5
BURNS, J., 1903.2
BURSOV, B.I., 1951.2; 1952.1; 1968.22
BUSHKANETS, E.G., 1954.9
BUSHMIN, A.S., 1951.4; 1953.2
BYALIK, B., 1968.113; 1973.4. See also BIALIK, B.A.
BYKHOVSKII, N.IA., 1925.1
BYKOVTSEVA, L.P., 1972.6; 1974.2; 1975.3; 1981.3

CALDER, A., 1976.4
CASALI, R., 1968.23, 96
CHANDLER, F.W., 1931.1
CHEKHOV, A.P., 1936.3; 1951.7
CHELYSHEV, E.P., 1968.55; 1970.18
CHEMERISKII, I.A., 1965.2
CHEREMNOV, A.S., 1958.11
CHERVIAKOVSKII, S.A., 1968.32; 1976.33; 1977.7; 1980.8; 1981.11
CHESTERTON, G.K., 1906.2
CHIKIN, V., 1980.1
CHIRIKOV, E.M., 1916.2
CHIROV, D.T., 1968.32

Author Index

CHITADZE, S., 1964.2, 4
CHOLODOW, JE., 1953.1
CHRISTIAN, R.F., 1964.5
CHUKOVSKII, K., 1909.1; 1928.10; 1962.2; 1968.113
CHUVAKOV, V., 1966.23; 1981.4
CHUZHAK, N., 1926.2; 1928.6
CLARK, B.H., 1938.5; 1947.3; 1951.3
CLARK, K., 1981.5
CLOWES, E.W., 1981.6
COOKE, G.W., 1905.2
CZIKOWSKY, E., 1965.3; 1968.24

DALLIN, D.J., 1974.3
DANILOVA, S.S., 1959.12
DAN'KO, E., 1938.5A, 6A
DAR'IALOVA, L.N., 1974.7; 1979.11; 1980.2; 1982.2, 10
DARONIAN, S.K., 1968.25
DAVIES, R., 1968.26
DAVLETSHINA, V.Z., 1977.7
DELANO, L.E., 1975.4
DEMENT'EV, A., 1964.6
DEMIDOV, A., 1928.10
DERMAN, A., addendum 2
DESNITSKII, V.A., 1928.10; 1934.2; 1936.3; 1941.2; 1951.4; 1953.2; 1959.8. See also DESNIZKI, W.
DESNIZKI, W., 1968.27-28. See also DESNITSKII, V.A.
DEWEY, V., 1924.1
DIENES, L., 1979.3A
DIKUSHINA, N.I., 1976.6
DILLON, E.J., 1902.2
DIVIL'KOVSKII, A., 1905.3
DMITRAKOV, I.P., 1953.2
DOLGOPOLOV, L.K., 1968.78; 1977.2
DOLININA, A.A., 1968.55
DONCHIN, G., 1976.7
DOROVATOVSKII, N.S., 1928.7
DROBYSHEVA, M.N., 1985.2
DUBNOVA, E., 1968.11, 29, 116
DUBNOVA-ERLIKH, S.S., 1963.5
DUDEVSKII, K., 1970.18
DUKES, A., 1967.5
DUN, A., 1960.6
DVINIANINOV, B.N., 1968.78

EASTMAN, M., 1934.3
EGOLIN, A.M., 1949.1; 1951.5

EIKHENBAUM, B., 1929.1A
ELISEEV, A., 1968.30; 1974.4; 1978.5
ELIZAROV, S.S., 1957.1-2, 12
ELIZAROVA, M.N., 1968.11
ELIZAROVA, R., 1982.3
EL'KIND, P.S., 1970.5
ELLIS. See KOBYLINSKII, L.
ELPATEVSKII, S.IA., 1928.10
EL'SBERG, IA.E., 1940.1; 1949.1; 1970.18
EMEL'IANOV, B., 1937.5
EOFF, S.H., 1961.6
EREMENKO, V., 1968.31
ERIKSON, E., 1963.6
ERMAKOV, I.I., 1968.32
ERMAKOVA, M.IA., 1968.32-33; 1973.5
ERMILOV, VL., 1936.5; 1941.5. See also JERMILOV, W.
ERMOLAEV, G., 1968.34; 1971.1
ERPENBEK, F., 1968.35
ERSHOVA, L.V., 1979.4
ESSLIN, M., 1973.5A, 9A
EVENTOV, I.S., 1951.4; 1955.4; 1956.4, 14; 1968.36; 1969.7; 1971.2; 1972.7; 1973.6
EVSELEVSKII, L.I., 1976.8
EVSTIGNEEVA, L.A., 1980.8

FARBER, L.M., 1960.8; 1961.7; 1964.2; 1968.11, 37-38; 1977.7; 1980.8
FAST, H., 1947.4
FEDIN, K.A., 1951.6, 9; 1956.1; 1968.39, 105
FEDIUSHINA, L.M., 1976.15
FEDORENKO, N.T., 1951.5
FEDOROV, A., 1956.14
FEN'VESHI, I., 1984.1
FETISOV, M.I., 1954.9
FEUCHTWANGER, L., 1968.40, 102
FILOSOFOV, D., 1903.3; 1904.2; 1907.2
FINK, L.A., 1968.41
FISCHER, J.O., 1975.5
FISH, G., 1951.9
FLAKER, A., 1970.18
FLEISHMAN, L., 1983.2; 1984.1A
FLEKSER, A. [A.L. Volynskii], 1898.3
FODOR, I., 1977.3
FOMENKO, L.P., 1976.9

FOMIN, A.G., 1915.3, 6
FOMINA, M.I., 1961.8, 23
FONIAKOVA, O.I., 1969.8
FORMAN, B.Y., 1979.5; 1983.3
FORSH, O., 1928.10
FORTUNATOVA, V.A., 1977.4, 7
FRANK, V.S., 1964.7
FRANKEL, T., 1972.8
FREDERIKSEN, N., 1964.2, 8
FREEBORN, R., 1982.5-6
FREEDLEY, G., 1947.3
FRENKEL, L., 1928.10
FREY, D., 1963.7
FRICHE, V., 1928.8
FRIED, J., 1946.1
FROST, E.L., 1981.7

GABLE, C., 1980.4
GAK, A.M., 1964.2
GALAGAN, G.IA., 1983.4
GALENKO, O.K., 1982.7
GALKINA-FEDORCHUK, E.M., 1961.23
GAMARRA, P., 1960.7, 9
GANDHI, M.K., 1968.42
GANELIN, R.SH., 1958.4; 1985.3
GARANIN, L.IA., 1980.8
GARANINA, L.F., 1977.7; 1980.8
GARNETT, E., 1969.9
GASSNER, J., 1954.3
GEI, N.K., 1968.43; 1977.5
GEKKER, N., 1901.3
GEL'ROT, M., 1903.4
GERASIMOV, M.P., 1934.2
GERASIMOVA, A.S., 1968.55
GERMANOVICH, A.I., 1962.8
GEROULD, D., 1976.10, 35
GERRERO, L., 1964.2, 9
GIFFORD, H., 1964.10
GIGOLOV, G.M., 1975.6
GILENSON, B., 1968.44
GIN, M.M., 1968.45
GIPPIUS, V., 1934.2
GIPPIUS, Z.N. [Anton Krainii],
  1908.4; 1912.1; 1923.1;
  1934.2; 1970.6
GIROD, M., 1965.4; 1966.4
GITEL'MAN, L., 1978.6
GIUSTI, W., 1959.9
GIVIN, IA.S., 1970.18
GLICKSBERG, C.I., 1976.11
GLINKA, A.S. [Volzhskii], 1906.3
GOLOVINA, S.A., 1964.2

GOLUBEV, V.Z., 1941.2
GOLUBEVA, O.D., 1968.46, 78
GORBOV, D.A., 1928.9
GORCHAKOV, N.A., 1957.3
GORELOV, A., 1969.10-13
GORKI, M., 1960.7. See also
  GOR'KII, A.M.
GOR'KII, A.M., 1936.7; 1937.5;
  1939.2; 1941.6; 1951.7-8;
  1953.10; 1954.4; 1955.5;
  1957.2, 4-5; 1959.10;
  1960.10; 1961.9; 1963.8;
  1964.5, 11-13, 30; 1965.5,
  15; 1966.4, 6; 1968.76;
  1968.88; 1969.14; 1971.3;
  1976.12; 1977.3-3A; 1986.1-2.
  See also GORKI, M.;
  GORKY, M.
GORKY, M., 1954.9; 1958.11. See
  also GOR'KII, A.M.
GORNFEL'D, A.G., 1908.4A
GORODETSKAIA, I.L., 1962.8
GORODETSKII, B.P., 1934.2
GOSSE, Sir E.W., 1922.3
GOURFINKEL, N., 1960.11
GRECHNEV, V.IA., 1958.5;
  1964.14; 1968.47; 1979.5A
GRIGOR'EV, A.L., 1969.16
GRIGOR'EV, L.G., 1970.18
GRIGOR'EV, M.A., 1947.5
GRIGOR'IAN, K.N., 1951.4
GRINBERG, S., 1901.3
GRINBERG, Z.G., 1940.2
GRISHIN, D., 1968.48
GROMOV, P., 1956.5, 14
GRUSS, N., 1978.7
GRUZDEV, I.A., 1928.10; 1930.1;
  1938.5B, 6A; 1946.2; 1959.3,
  12; 1960.12; 1961.10; 1966.4
GUSEVA, Z.A., 1968.49
GUTSCHE, G., 1983.5
GUZHIEVA, N.V., 1969.17

HABERMANN, G., 1971.4
HACKETT, F., 1968.50
HAMILTON, C.M., 1920.1
HAMSUN, K., 1960.10
HAPGOOD, I., 1901.4; 1902.3
HARE, R., 1962.3
HARRIS, F., 1923.2
HARVEY, W.F., 1910.2

Author Index

HAUPTMANN, G., 1934.2; 1960.10; 1968.102
HELLENS, F., 1960.7, 13
HENRY, P., 1983.6
HERLING-GRUDZINSKI, G., 1970.7
HIELSCHER, K., 1982.7A
HINGLEY, R., 1967.6
HOGARTH, C.J., 1932.1
HOLTZMAN, F., 1948.2; 1949.2
HUFF, N.K., 1932.4
HUNEKER, J., 1908.5
HUXLEY, A., 1939.3

IAKOVLEV, N.V., 1957.6
IAKOVLEVA, N.B., 1970.18
IAKUBOVICH, P., 1936.3
IAZIKOVA, IU.S., 1962.8; 1968.32, 51
IDZIKOWSKI, I., 1964.15; 1967.7; 1968.24, 52; 1970.18
IGNATOV, I., 1901.3
ILEK, B., 1965.6
ILIE, P., 1961.11
IL'INICH, K.M., 1979.6, 11; 1980.5, 8; 1981.11
IL'INSKII, A., 1937.1
IMENDÖRFER, H., 1973.7; 1979.7
INBER, V., 1951.9; 1958.6
IOKAR, L.N., 1964.2; 1966.7, 23; 1968.11, 53-54
IONOV, I.I., 1964.12
ISAEV, G.G., 1974.5, 7
ISSAKOWSKII, M., 1956.1
IUNOVICH, M., 1961.12
IUR'EVA, L.M,., 1958.7, 19; 1965.7; 1970.18; 1974.6
IUZOVSKII, IU., 1937.4; 1940.3; 1947.5; 1959.11. See also YOUZOVSKY, J.
IVANOV, A.S., 1969.18
IVANOV, VS., 1928.10; 1950.3; 1968.113; 1969.19
IVANOV-PAIMEN, V.Z., 1968.41
IVANOV-RAZUMNIK, R., 1907.3

JACKSON, R.L., 1958.8
JERMILOV, W., 1950.4. See also ERMILOV, VL.
JONES, D., 1973.7A, 9A
JUIN, H., 1962.5; 1976.14
JÜNGER, H., 1966.8

KALAUSHIN, M.M., 1946.3
KALEPS, B.A., 1963.9
KALINA, E.I., 1981.8
KALININ, N.F., addendum 4
KALIUZHNYI, A., 1934.2
KALUSTOVA, N.G., 1975.9; 1976.33; 1979.11
KANAEV, F.F., 1951.4
KANDEL', B.L., 1976.15
KARASIK, Z.M., 1951.5; 1957.2; 1958.9, 44; 1959.3
KARPENKO, M.A., 1968.125; 1972.9
KARPOV, P.I., 1934.2
KASATKINA, I.M., 1959.3
KASHEN, M., 1968.11
KASIK, J.P., 1978.7A
KASTORSKII, S.V., 1940.4; 1941.2, 7; 1951.4; 1956.6-7, 14; 1957.7; 1958.10-12; 1959.12; 1960.13A; 1961.13-14; 1963.10-11
KAUFMAN, L.S., 1979.11; 1980.8
KAUN, A.S., 1928.11; 1930.2-4; 1931.2; 1937.2; 1939.4; 1942.1; 1960.10
KAVERIN, V., 1968.113
KAZIN, A., 1955.6
KELDYSH, V.A., 1959.3; 1960.14, 18; 1962.6; 1964.2, 16; 1968.55; 1972.2; 1975.10; 1981.9
KERZHENTSEV, P., 1928.10
KESICH, L.W., 1967.8
KHALATOV, A.B., 1964.12
KHANOV, V.A., 1980.8; 1981.11
KHARCHEV, V.V., 1968.32
KHETSO [KJETSAA], G., 1977.8
KHLEBOSTROEVA, I.V., 1979.8
KHLODOVSKII, R.I., 1961.24
KHODASEVICH, VAL., 1968.56
KHODASEVICH, VL.F., 1937.3; 1939.5; 1940.5; 1953.6; 1976.16, 35; 1982.7B
KHOLODOV, E. See CHOLODOW, JE.
KHOMENKO, N.I., 1974.7
KHOROSHUKHIN, E., 1982.3
KHRAPCHENKO, M.B., 1970.18
KHVATOV, A.I., 1968.57, 78
KIM, L., 1964.2, 17
KINLOCH, A., 1904.3
KIREEVA, I.V., 1977.7, 9; 1979.9, 11; 1980.8; 1982.8-9

KIREEVA, M.G., 1974.7
KIR'IANOV, B.V., 1968.32
KIRSANOVA, N.A., 1969.39
KLINE, G.L., 1968.58
KLÜGE, R.-D., 1979.10
KOBYLINSKII, L. [Ellis], 1908.7
KOCHETOVA, I.P., 1959.3
KOGAN, P.S., 1928.10, 12
KOLEVSKII, V., 1970.18
KOLOBAEVA, L., 1976.17; 1981.9A
KOLTSOV, M., 1938.6
KOMKOVA, E.I., 1977.7
KONI, A.F., 1936.3
KONONENKO, P.P., 1968.125
KONSTANTINOVA, M.S., 1964.2
KORABEL'NIKOVA, L.Z., 1964.2
KORETSKAIA, I.V., 1966.9, 23; 1968.11, 59
KORITSKAIA, N.F., 1962.7; 1964.2; 1969.20
KOROLENKO, V. [Zhurnalist], 1904.4; 1957.4
KOROLITSKII, M., 1916.2A
KOSING, E., 1970.8; 1972.10
KOSTELIANETS, B., 1956.8, 14; 1968.60
KOSTKA, E.K., 1970.9; 1975.11
KOTLIAROV, IU.F., 1980.6
KOTOVSKOV, V.IA., 1975.12
KOVAL', L.M., 1981.10
KOVALEV, V.A., 1953.2-3; 1961.23; 1967.9; 1968.61, 78
KOVTUN, L.S., 1962.8; 1968.61A; 1969.39
KOZHEVNIKOV, IU.A., 1959.3
KOZ'MIN, M.B., 1969.20
KRAINII, A. See GIPPIUS, Z.N.
KRANIKHFEL'D, VL., addendum 1
KRASIN, P., 1907.4
KRASUNOV, V.K., 1976.33; 1978.10
KRENDEL', R.N., 1959.3
KRIUKOVA, A., 1980.7
KROPOTKIN, Prince P., 1967.10; 1970.10
KRUTIKOVA, N.E., 1958.42; 1978.8
KUBLANOV, I., 1941.8
KULESHOV, V.I., 1978.9
KULOVA, T., 1968.116
KUNITZ, J., 1929.2
KUPCHENKO, V.P., 1976.18
KUPRIIANOVSKII, A.I., 1981.11
KUPRIIANOVSKII, P.V., 1968.62, 78

KUSKOVA, E.K., 1928.13-14; 1936.6; 1954.5
KUZ'MICHEV, I.K., 1960.8; 1974.7; 1975.13; 1978.10; 1979.11; 1980.8; 1981.11; 1982.10. See also KUZMICZOW, I.
KUZMICZOW, I., 1969.21. See also KUZ'MICHEV, I.K.

LADYZHENSKII, A.M., 1968.32
LAMM, M., 1953.4
LANDESMAN, R., 1976.19, 35
LANE, A.M., 1976.20
LANINA, V.N., 1949.1; 1954.9; 1960.15, 18; 1961.18
LANTSUZSKII, V.A., 1982.11
LARIN, B.A., 1962.8; 1974.8-9; 1975.14; 1977.10; 1982.12; 1984.2
LASKY, M.J., 1972.10A
LATRELL, C., 1976.21, 35
LAVRENT'EV, I.E., 1934.2
LAVRETSKII, A., 1937.4
LAVRIN, J., 1947.6; 1954.6; 1971.5
LAWSON, S.R., 1976.22, 35
LAZAREV, L., 1964.18
LAZAREV, V.A., 1982.13
LAZAREV, V.N., 1934.2
LEE, R., 1930.5
LEGRAS, J., 1936.7
LEKTORSKII, A., 1957.12
LEMOS, N., [n.d.].1
LENGYEL, B., 1975.15; 1976.23; 1979.12-13
LENIN, V.I., 1924.2; 1961.9. See also UL'IANOV, V.I.
LEONOV, L., 1976.24
LEONOVA, E.A., 1980.8
LESNÁKOVA, S., 1961.15
LEVIN, D., 1965.8-9
LEVIN, F., 1966.10
LEVIN, J.D., 1957.8
LEVIN, M.B., 1947.5
LEVITINA, V.B., 1961.18
LEWIS, A., 1962.9
LEWISOHN, L., 1922.4
LI, V.N., 1968.55
LIAPAEVA, L.V., 1982.10
LIBINZON, Z.E., 1968.32, 63; 1979.11

Author Index

LIDIN, VL., 1928.10
LILICH, G.A., 1962.8
LIPATOV, A.T., 1979.11
LIPOVETSKII, A.S., 1968.32
LITVINOV, V.V., 1961.23
LIUBUSHIN, V.I., 1976.25
LIVANOVA, T., 1957.8A
LOBIKOVA, N.M., 1962.6, 10
LOE, M.L., 1977.11; 1985.4; forthcoming.1
LO GATTO, E., 1924.3; 1971.6
LONDON, J., 1955.7
LONDON, K., 1937.6
LOURIE, O., 1905.5. See also OSSIP-LOURIE, M.
LUDWIG, N., 1968.64
LUKACS, G., 1952.2; 1964.19
LUKER, N., 1982.14; forthcoming 1
LUK'IANOV, A.A., 1958.11
LUKIRSKAIA, K.P., 1965.11; 1970.11; 1985.5
LUNACHARSKII, A.V., 1903.5; 1905.6; 1906.4; 1909.2; 1924.4; 1927.1; 1928.15; 1931.3; 1933.1; 1938.7-9; 1963.12; 1964.20; 1968.65, 113; 1978.11; addendum 3
LUTOKHIN, D., 1928.10
LUVSANVANDAN, S., 1970.18
LUZHSKII, V.V., 1928.10
L'VOV-ROGACHEVSKII, V.L., 1915.4, 6

MADKHU, M., 1970.18
MAGUIRE, R.A., 1968.66
MAIAKOVSKII, V.V., 1927.2
MAIMIN, E.A., 1961.23
MAKAROVA, IU.I., 1957.2
MAKSIMOV, P., 1937.5; 1968.67
MAKSIMOVA, V.A., 1949.1; 1951.5; 1954.8; 1957.2; 1962.6, 11; 1968.11, 68; 1978.12
MALAMUD, I.T., 1938.10
MALYSHEV, S.V., 1934.2
MAMALYGA, A.I., 1968.125
MAMEDOVA, V.I., 1980.8
MANDEL'SHTAM, N., 1972.11
MANN, H., 1968.69, 102
MANN, TH., 1960.10; 1968.70, 102
MANNING, C.A., 1934.4
MANUKHIN, I.I., 1967.11
MARAKHOVA, T.A., 1968.32

MARAMZIN, V., 1976.26, 35
MARCHESE, R., 1958.13
MARKOV, V., 1968.71
MARSHAK, S., 1928.10; 1960.16
MASAL'SKII, V.I., 1968.125
MASHIROV, M., 1918.1
MATHEWSON, R.W., 1958.14; 1975.16
MATLAW, M., 1972.12
MATSAI, A., 1964.21
MATVEICHUK, N.F., 1982.15
MEIERHOLD, V.E., 1958.9
MEILAKH, B., 1958.15-16
MEKHLIS, L.Z., 1964.12
MENDELEVICH, G.A., 1968.11
MEN'SHIKOV, M., 1901.3, 6
MEREZHKOVSKII, D.S., 1906.5; 1916.3
MIASNIKOV, A.S., 1958.17; 1969.23; 1970.18
MIERAU, F., 1966.11
MIKHAILOV, G.I., 1968.55
MIKHAILOV, N., 1956.1
MIKHAILOV, O.N., 1966.12, 23; 1982.16
MIKHAILOVA, A.N., 1968.72, 78
MIKHAILOVSKII, B.V., 1946.4; 1949.1; 1951.5, 10; 1954.9; 1957.2; 1958.18-19, 44; 1960.17-18; 1961.16-18, 24; 1962.6, 12; 1964.22; 1965.12; 1969.24-30; 1971.7
MIKHAILOVSKII, N.K., 1901.3, 7
MIKHAL'SKII, E.N., 1968.73, 125
MIKOLAITIS, J., 1965.13
MILLER, N.B., 1924.5
MILLER, O.V., 1970.11
MINAKOVA, A.M., 1977.7, 12; 1980.8
MINSKII, N., 1901.3, 8
MIROLIUBOV, V.S., 1941.2
MIROVA-FLORIN, E.IA., 1968.11, 74; 1970.18; 1978.13. See also MIROWA, E.
MIROWA, E., 1962.13. See also MIROVA-FLORIN, E.IA.
MIRSKY, Prince D.S., 1926.3; 1974.10
MISHINA, E.F., 1968.32; 1974.7
MITROKHINA, V.I., 1961.22
MITROPAN, P., 1968.75
MNATSAKANOVA, E., 1968.113

MOCHOS, I., 1970.18
MOHRENSCHILDT, D. VON, 1968.76
MONLEON, J., 1968.97
MORACHEVSKII, N.IA., 1934.2
MORAVTSEVICH, N., 1969.31
MOROKHIN, V.N., 1974.7; 1977.7; 1978.10; 1979.11; 1980.8
MORSHCHIKHINA, A.S., 1965.11; 1970.11; 1985.5
MOTILIOVA, T., 1968.105. See also MOTYLEVA, T.L.; MOTYLJOVA, T.
MOTYLEVA, T.L., 1958.20. See also MOTILIOVA, T.; MOTYLJOVA, T.
MOTYLJOVA, T., 1947.7. See also MOTILIOVA, T.; MOTYLEVA, T.
MOULIK, A., 1976.27
MUCHNIC, H., 1951.11; 1961.19-20; 1971.8-11
MURATOVA, K.D., 1938.3; 1941.3; 1951.4; 1953.2, 5; 1956.9; 1957.9; 1958.21-22; 1959.12; 1965.10, 14; 1966.13; 1968.11, 77-80; 1969.32; 1970.12; 1971.12; 1981.13

NABOKOV, V.V., 1981.14-15
NAKORIANOV, N.N., 1964.12
NARBUT, V.I., 1964.12
NATHAN, G.J., 1948.3
NAUMOV, E., 1958.23; 1966.14
NAZAREVSKII, B. [Ben], 1912.2
NEDELJKOVIC, D., 1958.24
NEIMAN, B., 1940.3; 1960.18
NEMIROVICH-DANCHENKO, VL.I., 1928.10; 1958.9; 1968.81, 96; 1979.14
NEMUDROV, N., 1966.23
NIKITIN, N., 1928.10
NIKITINA, I.V., 1968.11, 32; 1974.7; 1977.7; 1981.15A
NIKOLAEVA, K.S., 1981.11
NIKOLAEVSKII, B.I., 1921.1
NIKOLESKU, T., 1970.18
NIKOLIUKIN, A.N., 1970.13, 18
NIKULINA, N.I., 1956.10; 1979.15
NILSSON, N.A., 1958.25
NINOV, A.A., 1956.14; 1964.23; 1965.16; 1966.15-16, 23; 1968.82
NIVAT, G.M., 1982.17

NORES, D., 1959.13
NOVICH, I.S., 1965.17
NOVIKOV, I., 1928.10
NOVIKOV, V.V., 1965.18-19; 1970.18; 1978.14-15; 1979.16; 1982.18
NOVIKOVA, V.A., 1968.55
NOZHKINA, E.M., 1969.39
NURALIEV, D.N., 1977.7; 1980.8

OBERLÄNDER, E., 1971.13
OBOLENSKII, L.E., 1901.3
OJETTI, F., 1965.20
OJETTI, U., 1968.83
OLGIN, M.J., 1933.2; 1971.14
OLIVA, L.J., 1967.12
OPREA, A., 1968.84, 105
ORFANOVA, A.N., 1968.32
ORLOV, A., 1953.6
ORLOVA, V.IA., 1957.2
OSMANOVA, Z.G., 1970.18; 1978.16
OSNOVIN, V.V., 1968.32, 85
OSSIP-LOURIE, M., 1905.7. See also LOURIE, O.
OSTOVAR, A., 1968.55
OSTROVSKAIA, S., 1978.17; 1984.3; 1985.6
OSTWALD, H., 1907.5
O'TOOLE, L.M., 1982.19
OVCHARENKO, A.I., 1951.5; 1954.9; 1956.11; 1957.2; 1959.3; 1963.13; 1965.21-22; 1968.86; 1970.18; 1971.15; 1978.18-19; 1980.8; 1982.20-21
OVNAN, G., 1949.1
OVSIANNIKOV, N., 1981.16

PACHMUSS, T., 1965.23
PAKLIN, N.A., 1986.2
PALEI, A.R., 1934.2
PANKOV, V., 1955.8; 1968.87
PANTELEEVA, R., 1968.88
PARAF, P., 1960.7, 19
PARKHOMENKO, M.N., 1949.1
PARSHINA, G.M., 1968.32, 89
PASCAL, R., 1960.20
PAWLENKO, P., 1953.7
PEISAKHOVICH, M., 1967.13
PEL'T, V.D., 1968.90
PERIUS, ZH., 1958.26. See also PERUS, J.

Author Index

PERSKY, S.M., 1913.2
PERTSOV, P.P., 1933.3
PERTSOV, V.O., 1964.24; 1968.90A
PERTSOV, V.V., 1927.3
PÉRUS, J., 1958.27; 1961.21; 1965.24; 1968.91-92. See also PERIUS, ZH.
PESHKOVA, E.P., 1958.9
PETROSIAN, A.A., 1970.15
PETROV, S.M., 1949.1; 1951.5; 1954.9; 1967.14
PETROVA, M.G., 1960.18; 1961.18; 1966.18, 23
PHELPS, W.L., 1911.2
PICKERING, J.V., 1978.20
PIKSANOV, N.K., 1932.2A; 1938.10A: 1948.4; 1961.22; 1968.93
PIMENOV, VS., 1949.3
PINAEV, M.T., 1974.7
PINKEVICH, A., 1928.10
PIRADOV, B.A., 1957.10, 12; 1964.2; 1968.11, 94; 1977.7; 1980.8
PLATONOV, A., 1937.5, 7
PLEKHANOV, G.V., 1907.6; 1909.2A; 1927.4; 1958.28
PLOTKIN, L., 1956.12, 14; 1968.95
POGODIN, N., 1951.9
POGOZHEVA, L., 1968.113
POLIANSKAIA, L.I., 1941.9
POLONSKII, M.I., 1968.11
POLYSKALOV, V.IU., 1978.10; 1979.11; 1981.11; 1982.10
POOLE, E., 1944.1
POPOVA, E.V., 1961.23
POPOVA, N.V., 1969.34
PORTNOFF, G., 1932.3
POSSE, V., 1901.3, 9; 1929.3
POTAPOVA, Z.M., 1970.18
POZNER, V., 1957.11; 1960.7, 21-22
PRISHVIN, M., 1928.10
PRITCHETT, V.S., 1964.25
PROKHOROV, E.I., 1980.8; 1983.7
PROOST, K.F., 1952.3
PROSHOGIN, W., 1950.5. See also PROZHOGIN, V.E.
PROTOPOPOV, S., 1928.10

PROZHOGIN, V.E., 1968.125; 1974.11. See also PROSHOGIN, W.
PSICHARI, L., 1960.7, 23
PUKHOV, IU.S., 1956.12A
PUSHKAREV, V.A., 1958.29
PYNZARU, S.G., 1977.7

RADÓ, G., 1967.15; 1968.98, 105
RAEFF, M., 1983.2
RAEVSKY-HUGHES, O., 1983.2
RAIGUEL, G.E., 1932.4
RAK, O.I., 1962.8
RASSKAZOV, A.V., 1978.10
READ, C., 1980.9
REEVE, F.D., 1962.14
REGNAUT, M., 1975.17
REILLY, A.P., 1971.16
REKHO, K., 1968.55; 1970.18
RELINGER, J., 1969.35
REMIZOV, A., 1976.28, 35
REMIZOV, B.B., 1977.7, 13; 1980.8
REMPEL, M., 1959.14
REVIAKINA, I.A., 1960.18; 1977.7
REZNIKOV, L.IA., 1960.24, 26
RINNE, M., 1980.10
RISCHBIETER, H., 1973.7B; 1976.35
RIURIKOV, B., 1968.99A
ROLLAND, R., 1960.7, 10, 25
ROMANOVA, E.S., 1966.19; 1972.13; 1976.29
ROMANOVICH, I., 1968.100
ROSHAL', A.A., 1968.101
ROSKIN, A., 1946.5
ROSSIIANOV, O.K., 1959.3; 1970.18
ROUGLE, C., 1976.30; 1980.11
ROZANOV, I.N., 1973.8
RUCKMAN, J.A., 1984.4
RUDNEV, V.V., 1928.17
RUEHLE, J., 1969.36
RÜHLE, I., 1959.15
RUSOVA, N.IU., 1974.7
RUSSELL, C.E., 1921.1
RYZHOVA, T.A., 1977.7
RZHEVSKAIA, N.F., 1970.18

SABAT, A.N., 1978.10
SABUROV, A.A., 1951.5

SABUROVA, R.M., 1977.7; 1980.8
SADOF'EV, I.I., 1934.2
SADOVSKII, IA.G., 1974.12; 1982.22
SALGALLER, E., 1959.16; 1962.15
SALISBURY, H.E., 1977.14
SALTAEVA, O.A., 1974.7; 1976.33
SAMARIN, R.M., 1961.24; 1964.2; 1970.18
SAMOKHVALOVA, E.I., 1968.125
SAMVELIAN, G.K., 1970.16
SARUKHANIAN, A.P., 1961.24-25; 1970.18
SAVCHENKO, M.M., 1979.11
SAVINKOVA, T.V., 1984.6A
SAYLER, O.M., 1920.2
SCHERR, B., 1979.17
SCHNITTKIND, H.T., 1920.3
SCHOOLFIELD, G.C., 1974.13
SCHRÖDER, J., 1970.17
SCHRÖDER, R., 1967.16; 1968.102-3; 1969.37; 1971.17
SCHUKIN, B., 1968.113
SCHULTZE, B., 1977.15
SCHWARZ, G., 1968.24
SCOTT-JAMES, R.A., 1958.30
SECHIN, V., 1968.104
SEGEL, H.B., 1976.31, 35; 1979.18
SEGHERS, A., 1960.10; 1968.102
SEMASHKO, N., 1928.10
SEMENCHUK, I.R., 1968.125
SEMENOVA, G.P., 1967.17
SEMENOVSKII, D.M., 1938.11
SEMENOVSKII, O., 1969.38
SEREBROV, A. [A.N. Tikhonov], 1966.20
SERGEEV-TSENSKII, S., 1928.10; 1941.10; 1951.9
SERGIEVSKII, I.V., 1937.5; 1951.12
SERGIJEWSKIJ, A., 1948.5
SESTERHENN, R., 1982.23
SETZER, H., 1980.11A
SHAGINIAN, M., 1968.106
SHAKHOV, V.V., 1980.8
SHALIAPIN, F.I., 1954.9
SHAL'NOV, IU.F., 1974.7
SHARYPKIN, D.M., 1975.18
SHATKOV, G.V., 1961.24, 26
SHAW, G.B., 1934.2; 1960.10
SHCHEPILOVA, L., 1968.116

SHCHERBAKOV, A.S., 1964.12
SHCHERBINA, V.R., 1958.19, 31; 1963.14; 1970.18
SHEGALOW, N., 1958.32.
See also ZHEGALOV, N.
SHELDON, R.R., 1968.107
SHISHKINA, A.N., 1968.108
SHISHKOV, V., 1928.10
SHKAPA, I., 1966.21
SHKLOVSKII, V., 1924.6; 1926.4; 1928.10; 1972.14
SHMARINOV, D.A., 1954.9
SHNEERSON, M.A., 1956.13
SHNEIDER, M.E., 1968.55
SHOPTERIANU, V., 1963.15
SHOSHIN, V.A., 1968.78
SHTOK, I., 1968.116
SHUB, D.K., 1958.33
SHUMSKII, A.M., 1958.34; 1962.16
SHUSTOV, M.P., 1978.10; 1979.11; 1981.11; 1982.10
SHVETS, A.V., 1968.125
SIGORSKII, A.V., 1964.2; 1968.11
SIMMONS, E.J., 1971.18
SIMON, J., 1973.8A
SINCLAIR, U., 1960.10
SINIAVSKII, A.D., 1958.19, 35; 1960.18, 26
SIROTINA, V.A., 1968.125; 1971.19
SIROTININA, O.B., 1969.39
SKABICHEVSKII, A., 1901.3, 10
SKOBELEV, V.P., 1969.40
SKOBLO, N.V., 1979.11
SKOROBOGATOV, K., 1968.109
SLADE, J.W., 1968.110
SLOBOZHANINOVA, L.M., 1981.11
SLONIM, M.L., 1958.36; 1961.27
SLONIMSKII, M., 1941.11
SMIRENSKII, V.V., 1968.32
SMIRNOV, S.V., 1959.17
SMIRNOVA, A.D., 1968.111
SMIRNOVA, L.N., 1977.16
SMUROVA, N.M., 1968.55
SNOW, C.P., 1961.28
SOBOLEV, A.V., 1968.11
SOISSONS, C. de, 1902.5
SOKHRIAKOV, IU.I., 1980.8
SOKOLOV, A.G., 1979.19-21
SOKOLOVA, I.I., 1959.3
SOKRUTENKO, JE.JU., 1961.29
SOLOGUB, F., 1934.2

Author Index

SOLOV'EV, E. [Andreevich], 1900.1
SOLOV'EV, G., 1957.12
SÖTER, I., 1968.112
SOUVARINE, B., 1964.27; 1965.25
SPARGO, J., 1906.5A
SPECTOR, I., 1952.4
SREDIN, L.V., 1958.9
STACY, R.H., 1974.14
STANISLAVSKII, K.S. See ALEKSEEV, K.S.
STAUCHE, I., 1964.28; 1968.114
STECH'KIN, N.IA., 1904.5
STRANNIK, I., 1902.6
STRAUKAITE, D., 1962.17
STROKOV, P., 1962.18
STRUNSKY, R., 1916.4-5
STRUVE, G., 1935.1; 1973.9
SUDAKOVA, I., 1968.116
SUKHAREV, G.M., 1970.18A
SUKHIKH, S.I., 1968.32; 1974.7; 1976.33; 1977.7; 1978.10, 22; 1980.12; 1982.10, 24
SURGANOV, V., 1975.19
SURKOW, E., 1949.4
SURPIN, M.L., 1961.18; 1966.23
SVOBODOV, A.N., 1925.2; 1927.5-6; 1977.7

TACHELOV, I.I., 1934.2
TAGER, E.B., 1949.1; 1958.19, 37-38; 1960.18; 1961.18; 1962.6, 19; 1964.29; 1966.23; 1968.115; 1969.30
TARARAEV, A.IA., 1954.9; 1957.2; 1959.3; 1961.18
TARASOV, E.M., 1958.11
TARASOVA, A.A., 1960.18, 27; 1962.6, 20
TEIXIDO, R., 1978.23
TELESHOV, N.D., 1958.9, 39
TERRAS, V., 1985.7
TERRY, G.M., 1986.3
TETENI, M., 1969.41
THOMSON, R.D.B., 1969.42
THORGEVSKY, I., 1945.1
TIKHOVODOV, A.A., 1968.32, 117; 1977.7
TIMOFEEV, L.I., 1958.19, 40; 1970.18
TIMOFEEVA, V.V., 1953.2, 8; 1968.78

TOLNAI, G., 1970.18
TOLSTOI, A., 1928.10
TOPER, P., 1980.13
TOVSTONOGOV, G., 1968.116
TRENEV, K.A., 1934.2
TRIFONOV, N.A., 1968.78, 118-19
TRIFONOVA, S.V., 1962.8
TROTSKY, L., 1977.18
TRUBE, L.L., 1968.32
TSIMBAL, S.L., 1956.14
TSIRULEV, A.F., 1981.11; 1982.10
TSVETAEVA, A., 1984.5
TUIKOV, N.S., 1964.2
TUMANOV, G.M., 1905.8
TUN, N., 1970.18
TURNER, C.J.G., 1972.14A
TYNIANOV, IU., 1938.6A, 11A

UDONOVA, Z., 1968.120
ULAM, A.B., 1965.26
UL'IANOV, V.I., 1909.3. See also LENIN, V.I.
UL'RIKH, L.N., 1962.6
UMBRASAS, K., 1949.1
USPENSKAIA, V.E., 1973.10
USPENSKII, I.N., 1954.9
UTKIN, I., 1964.2
UTURGAUNI, S.N., 1968.55

VAINBERG, I.I., 1961.18; 1963.16; 1966.23-24; 1968.121; 1970.19; 1971.20; 1976.32; 1980.14
VALENTINOV, N., 1965.27
VANDENBROUCKE, R., 1976.35
VAN DOREN, M., 1942.2; 1946.6
VAN GYSEGHEM, A., 1943.1
VANIUKOV, A.I., 1981.11
VASIL'EV, F.P., 1953.2
VASIN, K.K., 1981.11
VAVERE, V.A., 1980.8
VAVILYCHEVA, O.G., 1978.10
VDOVICHENKO, V., 1957.12
VENGEROV, S.A., 1915.5-6; 1941.2; 1972.15
VENGROV, N., 1947.8; 1959.3, 18
VERRET, G., 1958.41
VERTSMAN, I., 1937.5
VESHNEV, V.G., 1927.7
VIDISHCHEV, B.V., 1977.7
VIL'CHINSKII, V.P., 1968.78; 1970.20

Author Index

VISHNEVSKAIA, N.A., 1968.55
VLADIMIRTSEV, V.P., 1978.10
VOGT, H., 1958.43
VOGUÉ, E.M., 1971.21
VOLKHOVSKY, F., 1902.7
VOLKOV, A.A., 1951.5; 1955.8A; 1962.6; 1968.122; 1969.42A; 1972.16; 1978.24
VOL'NOV, I.E., 1934.2
VOL'SKII, N.V., 1965.27
VOLYNSKY, A.L. 1958.9. See also FLEKSER, A.
VOLZHSKII. See GLINKA, A.S.
VON ENGELHARDT, A., 1899.1
VOROB'EV, V.F., 1968.123-25
VORONOV, I.K., 1958.11
VORONSKII, A.K., 1926.5; 1929.4; 1965.5; 1982.25-26
VOROVSKII, V.V., 1964.12
VUL', R.M., 1966.23; 1968.11, 126; 1977.20
VUL'F, V., 1982.27

WALTER, R., 1977.21
WEBSTER, C.D., 1980.15
WEGNER, M., 1970.21; 1976.34; 1977.22
WEIL, I.A., 1960.28-29; 1964.29A; 1965.28; 1966.25; 1986.4
WEISS, E., 1971.22
WELLS, H.G., 1906.7; 1960.10
WERNER, M.R., 1949.5
WIENER, L., 1924.7
WILCZKOWSKI, C., 1949.6
WILKS, R., 1966.26; 1979.22
WILLCOX, L.C., 1906.8
WILLIAMS, R.C., 1977.23
WILSHIRE, G., 1906.9
WILSON, E., 1953.9
WINKEL, H.-J., 1964.30
WOLFE, B.D., 1967.18; 1978.25

YAKOBSON, S., 1953.10
YARMOLINSKY, A., 1941.12; 1969.43
YEDLIN, T., 1975.20
YERSHOV, P., 1958.45-46
YOUZOVSKY, J., 1936.8. See also IUZOVSKII, IU.

ZABURDAEV, N.A., 1952.6; 1959.3; 1968.11; 1976.36; 1977.7
ZAIDMAN, A.D., 1968.32; 1979.11
ZAIKA, S.V., 1979.23; 1982.28; 1983.8
ZAITSEVA, G.S., 1976.33; 1977.7; 1978.10; 1981.11
ZAKHAROVA, V.A., 1956.15
ZAMIATIN, E., 1936.9; 1967.19; 1970.22
ZAMOSHKIN, N.I., 1964.31
ZAPADOVA, E.A., 1968.55
ZARITSKII, N.S., 1968.125
ZASURSKII, IA.N., 1964.32
ZATONSKII, D.V., 1970.18
ZAVALISHIN, V., 1958.47
ZDOBNOV, N.V., 1940.2
ZELINSKII, K.L., 1958.19, 48; 1960.30; 1970.23
ZEMSKOV, V., 1968.11, 127
ZERNITSKAIA, E.I., 1968.128
ZERNOV, N., 1975.21
ZHAVORONKOVA, E.L., 1977.7
ZHEGALOV, N.N., 1958.44, 49; 1961.18; 1965.29; 1977.24; 1984.6. See also SHEGALOW, N.
ZHELEZNOV, P.I., 1973.11
ZHELIABUZHSKAIA, M. [M.F. Andreeva], 1963.17
ZHELTOVA, N.I., 1965.30-31; 1979.24; 1981.17; 1984.6A; 1985.8
ZHIL'TSOV, V.I., 1982.10
ZHUK, N.I., 1968.125
ZHURAVLEV, I.K., 1968.129
ZHURAVLEVA, M.V., 1934.2
ZIMINA, S.S., 1958.42; 1968.130; 1975.22
ZIMONINA, I.P., 1968.55
ZIUZENKOV, I., 1958.44
ZLOBIN, V.A., 1981.11
ZLOBIN, V.N., 1953.2
ZLOTNITSKII, D., 1956.14
ZOZULIA, E., 1928.10
ZUBAREVA, K.A., 1974.15
ZUNIGA, E., 1968.96-97
ZWEIG, A., 1968.102
ZWEIG, S., 1959.19; 1960.10; 1968.102, 131-32
ZYTARUK, G.J., 1971.23

Subject Index

acmeism, 1954.7
Aikhenval'd, Iu., 1969.14
Aizman, D., 1964.3
Akhmatova, A.A., 1972.11
Aleksin, A.N., 1968.11; 1969.14
Amateur Show, 1965.1
Amfiteatrov, A., 1980.8
Anderson, S., 1964.32; 1977.24
Andreev, L.N., 1911.2; 1938.10; 1958.45-46; 1959.8, 16; 1964.3; 1965.14; 1968.32-33; 1969.17; 1971.23
-Gorky on, 1955.6; 1957.5; 1964.25; 1965.10
Andreeva, M.F., 1906.5A, 9; 1940.5; 1958.42; 1962.4; 1963.17; 1979.14
"And Still More on the Devil," 1960.26
Aragon, L., 1958.7
Around Russia, 1959.3; 1972.2; 1978.13; 1982.16
-motherhood in, 1975.9
-style, 1916.2A
Around the Union of Soviets, 1951.5; 1955.8
-style, 1972.9
The Artamonov Business, 1926.2; 1928.4, 6; 1935.1; 1949.1; 1958.37; 1963.10; 1971.15
-as epic, 1956.12
-as family chronicle, 1961.14; 1969.14
-foreign reception, 1982.13
-merchant in, 1959.6; 1978.19
-structure, 1926.4

-style, 1968.131
-variants, 1966.23
Artsybashev, M., 1963.16
Astafev, V., 1980.8
autobiography, 1923.2; 1936.7; 1940.1; 1956.3, 10; 1959.8; 1964.25; 1966.26; 1969.6, 24; 1970.18; 1978.23; 1982.10
-childhood, 1982.16
-dictionary of, 1968.125; 1974.8; 1975.14; 1977.10; 1982.12; 1984.2
-folklore, 1956.15
-positive hero, 1949.1
-structure, 1982.16
-style, 1968.61A; 1969.8
-See also Genres; Childhood; My Apprenticeship; My Universities
Azef, E., 1969.14

Babel, I., 1963.8; 1966.16
Balmont, K.D., 1925.2; 1948.5; 1957.1, 12; 1970.18A; 1977.2
Balukhatyi, S., 1968.77
Balzac, H., 1952.2; 1964.19
Barbarians, 1908.7; 1938.9; 1954.9; 1964.20; 1965.19; 1977.7
-characterization, 1981.15A
-society, 1906.4
-style, 1907.2
-variants, 1962.6
Barbusse, H., 1958.7, 32; 1968.76; 1977.3

Baroja, P., 1961.6
Becher, J.R., 1965.7; 1971.22; 1974.6
"Beglye zametki," 1960.17
Belinsky, V.G., 1928.15
Belomor Canal, 1964.7; 1974.3; 1976.21
Belousov, I.D., 1959.10
Belyi, A., 1968.11, 59; 1977.2; 1982.17
-Gorky on, 1957.5
-Petersburg, 1982.5
Berdiaev, N., 1980.2; 1982.2
Bergson, H., 1980.2
Beseda, 1953.10; 1983.1
Bialik, B., 1968.77; 1977.6, 17
bibliographies, 1915.3; 1926.3; 1934.1; 1936.1; 1938.3; 1940.2; 1941.3; 1954.1; 1956.9; 1958.20; 1959.1; 1960.8; 1965.11; 1966.19; 1967.4; 1970.11; 1972.13; 1973.8, 10; 1976.2, 15, 29, 33, 35; 1977.19; 1979.11; 1981.8, 13; 1982.7; 1985.5; addendum 4
-autobiography, works on, 1982.10
-cinema, 1968.21
-English, 1986.2A
-foreign, 1963.9
-French, 1968.91; 1969.22
-German, 1968.6, 24
-Indian, 1968.5
-music, Gorky in, 1969.18
-Spanish, 1932.3
-theater, 1968.128
-Ukrainian, 1959.3
Bjornson, B.M., 1961.16
Blok, A., 1924.1; 1929.1; 1940.5; 1959.11
-Gorky on, 1955.6; 1980.7
-Gorky's impact on, 1959.3, 18
Bobryshev, V.T., 1965.5
Bogdanov, A., 1958.16; 1971.12
Bogdanovich, A.E., 1978.5
"Boles," 1972.14A
Bolotova, Iu.A., 1968.11
"Bol'shaia liubov'." See "A Great Love"
Bolshevism, 1915.4; 1928.8; 1960.29

-Gorky and, 1908.6; 1928.5, 14; 1951.4, 10; 1957.2; 1980.9; 1981.14
bourgeoisie, 1904.1-2; 1908.2; 1928.8
-Gorky on, 1951.8
Bourne, R., 1964.32
Brecht, B., 1958.7; 1965.7; 1968.17; 1977.4
-and Mother, 1963.7; 1974.6; 1977.7
Briusov, V.Ia., 1925.2; 1928.8; 1937.1; 1948.5; 1957.1; 1969.14; 1980.3
Bubnov, A.S., 1976.12
Budberg, Baroness M.I., 1982.1A
Bulgakov, M.A., 1971.17
Bunin, I., 1956.6; 1964.23; 1966.15-16, 23; 1967.1; 1968.73, 125
-"The Country," 1966.12;
-Gorky on, 1966.12; 1968.73
Burenin, N.E., 1954.9; 1957.2; 1976.12
"Burevestnik." See "Song of the Stormy Petrel"
Bursov, B., 1968.77
Byron, G., 1907.4; 1970.9

capitalism, 1933.1; 1949.4; 1968.37
-Gorky on, 1982.22
Capri school, 1928.8; 1938.7; 1939.2; 1958.16; 1965.16; 1967.18; 1968.4, 111; 1978.2; 1981.11
censorship, 1940.3; 1941.2, 9; 1964.27; 1965.25; 1973.3
Cervantes, Don Quixote, 1960.17
Chagin, P.I., 1965.5
Chekhov, A.P., 1900.1; 1904.2; 1906.5; 1943.1; 1949.1; 1951.7, 12; 1961.28; 1962.14; 1967.5; 1968.60; 1971.21; 1972.12; 1976.1, 31; 1979.1, 5A, 18; 1982.7A, 28
-as critical realist, 1951.1
-and drama, 1959.11; 1961.2; 1963.11
-Gorky on, 1925.2; 1936.3; 1955.6; 1957.5

Subject Index

(Chekhov, A.P.)
-and style, 1977.16
"Chelkash," 1902.5; 1966.9
"Chelovek." See "Man"
Childhood, 1923.2; 1951.4;
  1952.6; 1960.20; 1961.23;
  1964.10; 1966.26; 1973.4;
  1977.7; 1979.17; addendum 2
-film of, 1963.6
-folklore in, 1956.15; 1979.13
-and memory, 1982.1
-motherhood in, 1975.9
-religious view in, 1915.1;
  1916.3
-style in, 1969.34
Children of the Sun, 1931.1;
  1934.2; 1937.5; 1941.2;
  1957.3; 1961.12; 1964.4;
  1968.29, 78; 1977.7, 12
-style in, 1977.2
Chirikov, E., 1964.3
"Chitatel'." See "The Reader"
Chornyi, K., 1980.8
Chudaki. See Eccentrics
"The City of the Yellow Devil,"
  1956.1; 1976.30
Committee for Aid to the Hungry,
  1928.13; 1965.2
Communist party, 1928.15;
  1947.1; 1958.23
"Comrades," 1913.1
The Confession, 1908.3; 1909.2,
  2A; 1910.1; 1911.1; 1916.5;
  1924.4; 1927.1; 1965.8;
  1967.2, 17; 1968.58, 118;
  1972.2; 1979.8; 1980.5, 8-9;
  addendum 1, 3
-and God-seeking, 1908.6
-and romantic realism, 1910.2
Cooper, J.F., 1979.9
Counterfeit Money, 1965.1;
  1977.1A
"Criminals," 1941.6
critical realism, style of,
  1951.2; 1961.27; 1965.7;
  1968.3; 1971.17; 1974.14;
  1975.10; 1978.2
Cronin, A., 1980.8
"Cursory Notes," 1960.17

Dachniki. See Summer Folk
Dante, 1939.1
-Divine Comedy, 1965.22

decadence, 1937.5, 7; 1948.5;
  1949.1; 1957.4; 1958.44, 49;
  1961.18; 1966.24; 1971.12
-Gorky on, 1966.23; 1968.120;
  1981.16
Dekhterev, B., 1958.29
Delo Artamonovykh. See The
  Artamonov Business
Desnitsky, V.A., 1959.12;
  1968.77
Deti solntsa. See Children of
  the Sun
Detstvo. See Childhood
"Devushka i smert'." See "The
  Girl and Death"
Dickens, C., 1908.5; 1920.3;
  1962.12
-Oliver Twist, 1902.1
-theme of labor, 1950.5
Divilkovsky, A.A., 1957.2
Dobin, E.S., 1965.5
Dobroliubov, N.A., 1958.2
Dorovatovsky, S.P., 1928.7
Dos Passos, J., 1970.17
Dostigaev and Others, 1953.1;
  1957.3; 1960.18; 1962.8;
  1965.19; 1969.39; 1977.1A, 7;
  1979.18
-characterization in, 1981.15A
Dostoevsky, F.M., 1901.2;
  1902.4; 1906.1; 1941.5;
  1951.5; 1967.16; 1968.60;
  1969.14; 1971.17; 1974.5, 7;
  1976.30; 1978.9; 1982.17;
  1986.3; addendum 5
-Gorky on, 1948.1; 1953.3;
  1968.130; 1973.5
-moral view, 1901.7; 1915.2
-as naturalist, 1932.1
-Notes from the House of the
  Dead, 1905.5
-Notes from the Underground,
  1958.8
-political view, 1948.1
drama, 1938.5; 1959.2; 1968.116;
  1975.6; 1979.14, 18
-naturalist, 1924.5
-realist, 1920.2; 1961.27;
  1964.3; 1969.17
-Soviet, 1938.6A; 1958.3;
  1959.12; 1968.104; 1971.7;
  1976.10; 1977.7

(drama)
—See also Genres: drama;
   individual plays
Dreiser, T., 1958.7; 1977.24
Dürrenmatt, F., 1968.17
"Dvadtsat' shest' i odna." See
   "Twenty-six and One"

Eccentrics, 1975.9
Egor Bulychev i drugie, 1936.8;
   1938.4; 1953.1; 1957.3;
   1961.27; 1962.8-9; 1969.1;
   1977.7; 1979.18
—characterization in, 1981.15A
—style, 1969.39
Enemies, 1907.6; 1908.7; 1927.4;
   1951.10; 1957.3; 1964.2;
   1966.13; 1972.3-4; 1976.22;
   1977.1A, 7
Engels, F., 1984.3
Erenburg, I., 1956.12
Ermolaev, G., 1971.10
Esenin, S., 1956.4; 1968.11
—Eseninism, 1968.127
existentialism, 1980.2
"Evgraf Bukeev," 1941.6

Fadeev, A., 1951.4
Falkberget, J., 1977.8
Fal'shivaia moneta. See
   Counterfeit Money
Faust, myth of, 1967.16; 1971.17
Fedin, K., 1963.8; 1969.40;
   1978.15; 1982.21
—Cities and Years, 1968.122
Fedorov, N.F., 1978.10, 22;
   1980.12
Filosofov, D., 1908.4A, 6;
   1912.2; 1957.1
First Congress of Soviet
   Writers, 1947.1; 1984.3
Flaubert, G., 1958.24
Fofanov, K., 1968.32
folklore, 1941.1; 1951.8;
   1953.2; 1956.14; 1961.26;
   1974.7; 1977.7; 1978.13;
   1979.11; 1980.8; 1982.15-16
—in Foma Gordeev, 1956.13
—in Gorky's autobiography,
   1956.15
—influence on Gorky, 1932.2A;
   1938.10A; 1947.2; 1961.3

—in Mother, 1961.5
Foma Gordeev, 1900.1; 1902.4;
   1907.5; 1961.18; 1962.6;
   1965.12; 1968.117; 1969.42;
   1974.10; 1981.6
—capitalism in, 1955.7; 1966.9
—characterization in, 1938.3B;
   1968.32
—editions of, 1962.20
—folklore in, 1956.13
—merchants in, 1901.10
—moral view, 1901.4; 1961.6
Forsh, O., 1963.8
Fox, R., 1958.7
Fragments from My Diary, 1924.6;
   1968.32, 86; 1976.4
France, A., 1958.26; 1960.23;
   1965.24; 1968.76; 1973.6
Frisch, M., 1968.17
Furmanov, D.A., 1981.11
futurism, 1927.2; 1928.6;
   1968.71

Galsworthy, J., 1961.16;
   1962.14; 1964.5; 1977.24
—Forsythe Saga, 1969.41
Garin-Mikhailovsky, N., 1966.7,
   23
Garshin, V.M., 1979.5A; 1983.6
Gazdanov, G., 1979.3A
genres, 1967.4; 1976.15, 34;
   1979.9, 11, 15
—autobiography, 1915.5; 1923.2;
   1926.5; 1934.4; 1940.1;
   1949.1; 1951.4; 1952.6;
   1956.3; 1962.8; 1964.26;
   1966.26; 1967.6; 1969.24,
   28, 43; 1978.13; 1979.17,
   21; 1982.10
—bildungsroman, 1933.1; 1964.26;
   1982.6
—diary, 1924.6
—drama, 1908.2, 7; 1924.5;
   1936.8; 1938.5; 1947.3;
   1951.5, 10; 1956.13; 1958.3,
   37; 1959.2, 11; 1960.18;
   1961.2, 16, 18, 24; 1963.11;
   1964.2; 1965.18-19; 1967.17;
   1968.29; 1969.6; 1970.3;
   1971.7; 1972.9; 1974.12;
   1976.35; 1977.1; 1978.20, 24

212

Subject Index

(genres)
-epic, 1951.8; 1956.12-13; 1958.19, 35, 38; 1962.18; 1969.42A; 1978.24; 1980.2, 8; 1982.2
-family chronicle, 1961.14
-historical novel, 1951.4; 1968.3; 1981.11
-literary criticism, 1925.1
-memoirs, 1945.1
-novel, 1924.6; 1926.4; 1928.6; 1941.2; 1951.8; 1960.15, 18, 28; 1963.16; 1968.32, 43; 1973.5; 1974.7; 1978.16; 1979.21; 1980.8; 1981.11
-novella, 1960.14, 18
-polemics, 1927.5; 1928.15
-portraiture, 1924.6; 1931.3; 1955.6; 1956.7; 1958.5, 17; 1960.14, 18; 1962.16; 1964.14, 25; 1966.7; 1967.6; 1976.1-2; 1978.24; 1979.11
-short story, 1899.1; 1903.1; 1907.5; 1908.7; 1924.3; 1926.3-4; 1934.4; 1950.2; 1951.8; 1963.3; 1968.86; 1977.22; 1980.2
-social drama, 1906.1; 1962.9; 1968.69; 1972.4
-social novel, 1905.5; 1961.17
-tragedy, 1922.4
Gippius, Z.N., 1963.16; 1965.23; 1977.14
"The Girl and Death," 1978.10; 1979.11
Gladkov, F., 1956.12A; 1963.8; 1978.15
God-building, 1909.2; 1915.4; 1924.4; 1967.2; 1968.58, 118; 1979.21; 1980.1, 9; 1981.5; 1982.23; addendum 3
-science and, 1980.11A
God-seeking, 1908.6
Goethe, J.W., 1940.1
-Faust, 1965.22; 1967.16
Gogol, N.V., 1908.5; 1949.1
-Dead Souls, 1905.5
-and romanticism, 1969.28
-Taras Bulba, 1969.25
-"Terrible Vengeance," 1969.25
Goncharov, I.A., 1957.5
Gorbunov, K.Ia., 1965.5
Gorchakov, N.M., 1968.116

Gorky, Maksim
-aesthetic views, [n.d.].1; 1916.4-5; 1937.4; 1938.8; 1939.1, 4; 1941.12; 1947.1; 1953.8; 1956.8-9; 1958.15, 33-34; 1961.20; 1966.14; 1968.77, 106; 1969.13; 1970.18; 1975.13; 1976.7, 11; 1977.5; 1978.8; 1981.6; 1982.7A
-on American literature, 1979.9, 11; 1980.8; 1982.8, 10. See also individual authors
-on Andreev, L.N., 1955.6; 1957.5; 1964.25; 1965.10
-and Andreeva, M.F., 1963.17
-archive, 1936.2; 1968.77, 130; 1976.15
-his autobiographical stories, 1915.5; 1954.9
-his autographs, 1959.3
-on Belyi, A., 1957.5
-biographical material, 1901.3, 5-6; 1902.1-2; 1903.1-2; 1931.2; 1933.2; 1946.2, 5; 1951.8; 1952.3; 1958.1, 18; 1959.4; 1960.11-12, 21; 1965.8-9, 20; 1966.11, 23, 26; 1967.15; 1968.47, 49, 64, 98; 1970.7; 1971.6, 10, 12; 1972.1, 5; 1975.3; 1976.21; 1978.20; 1986.3
--in civil war, 1928.14; 1936.9; 1941.11; 1955.8; 1957.11; 1960.30; 1962.2; 1965.27; 1967.11; 1968.87
--cultural activity, 1918.1; 1937.6; 1970.21
--death, 1953.6; 1968.98; 1970.7
--early life, 1926.1; 1929.3; 1936.7; 1948.2; 1949.2; 1957.10; 1966.23; 1968.11, 30-31; 1976.86; 1977.20; 1978.5
--in 1880s, 1925.1; 1933.3; addendum 4
--in 1890-1905, 1901.5; 1917.1; 1921.1; 1941.8; 1959.8; 1968.11, 37, 45; 1974.4
--exile, 1927.1; 1938.9; 1951.3; 1957.11; 1959.9; 1966.15; 1967.1, 11; 1968.4, 88, 106;

213

(Gorky, Maksim, biographical material)
1971.6; 1972.7; 1974.2; 1981.10; 1982.1A
--family background, 1936.7; 1952.6
--as journalist, 1959.3; 1962.3; 1963.5; 1964.12; 1965.21; 1966.16; 1968.90; 1975.7; 1981.9; 1982.22
--literary development, 1929.3; 1945.1; 1964.21-22; 1966.25; 1968.15; 1976.36
--as literary organizer, 1905.8; 1926.3; 1936.9; 1956.7; 1958.39; 1964.7
--under police surveillance, 1921.1; 1965.3
--political activity, 1902.7; 1918.1; 1925.1; 1926.3; 1927.2; 1928.5, 17; 1929.3; 1930.3; 1936.6; 1939.5; 1950.1; 1954.5; 1955.3, 8A; 1956.9; 1961.7; 1962.3-4; 1965.27; 1968.38, 42, 94; 1971.4; 1973.2; 1975.20; 1978.2; 1981.14
 -in 1905, 1930.4; 1955.4, 8A
 -in 1906-17, 1930.2
--Revolution, role in, 1928.14
--social activity, 1927.6; 1928.8; 1965.2; 1971.4; 1978.7
--social-literary development, 1908.4; 1929.1
--in Soviet period, 1930.5; 1936.6, 9; 1937.2; 1940.5; 1949.6; 1954.3; 1961.4; 1967.1; 1982.1A
--in Stalin period, 1936.9; 1960.1, 25; 1965.27; 1966.21; 1972.6; 1976.21; 1984.1A
--in theater, 1938.5B; 1968.81, 109; 1975.2
--in United States, 1906.5A, 9; 1911.2; 1931.2; 1944.1; 1957.2; 1962.4; 1965.3; 1967.12; 1968.110
--in World War I, 1957.11
--See also Autobiography
-on Blok, A., 1955.6; 1980.7
-in Bolshevik press, 1978.12

-and Bolshevism, 1908.6; 1928.5, 14; 1951.4, 10; 1957.2; 1980.9; 1981.14
-on bourgeoisie, 1951.8
-on Bunin, I., 1966.12; 1968.73
-on capitalism, 1982.22
-in Capri, 1927.1; 1967.11
-his Capri school, 1928.8; 1938.7; 1939.2; 1958.16; 1965.16; 1967.18; 1968.4, 111; 1978.2; 1981.11
-on Chekhov, A.P., 1925.2; 1936.3; 1955.6; 1957.5
-and children's literature, 1964.12; 1977.21
-and collectivization, 1968.67
-correspondence, 1934.2; 1936.3; 1941.2; 1958.9; 1959.7, 10; 1963.8; 1964.11, 13, 30; 1965.5, 15; 1967.4; 1968.11, 25, 41, 113; 1969.19, 33; 1970.1; 1971.3; 1975.22; 1976.6, 8, 12; 1977.24; 1981.4; 1983.2
--with Andreev, L.N., 1958.46; 1965.10
--with Andreeva, M.F., 1963.17
--with Babel, I., 1963.8; 1966.3
--with Barbusse, H., 1977.3
--with Batiushkov, F.D., 1936.4
--with Briusov, V., 1928.2
--with Bunin, I., 1936.4; 1961.18
--with Chekhov, A.P., 1936.3; 1951.7
--with Dorovatovsky, N.S., 1928.7
--with Fedin, K., 1963.8
--foreign, 1958.32; 1960.10
--with Forsh, O., 1963.8
--with Gladkov, F., 1963.8
--with Gruzdev, I.A., 1966.5
--with Ivanov, Vs., 1950.3; 1969.19
--with Kaverin, V., 1963.8
--with Khodasevich, Vl., 1953.10; 1968.56
--with Korolenko, V.G., 1957.4
--with Lenin, V.I., 1924.2; 1958.42; 1961.9
--with Leonov, L., 1963.8
--with Lunacharsky, A.V., 1976.6
--with Maksimov, P., 1968.67
--with Mikhailovsky, N.K., 1968.45
--with Miroliubov, V.S., 1941.2

Subject Index

(Gorky, Maksim, correspondence)
--with Nikolaevsky, B.I., 1983.2
--with Novitsky, A.N., 1960.22
--with Ovsianiko-Kulikovskii,
   D.N., 1941.2
--with Pasternak, B., 1963.8;
   1966.17
--with Peshkova, E.P., 1955.5;
   1966.6
--with Piatnitsky, K.P., 1954.4
--with Pilniak, B., 1963.8
--with Platonov, A., 1963.8
--with Plekhanov, G., 1958.28
--with Rozanov, V.V., 1923.3;
   1978.21
--with Sergeev-Tsenskii, S.,
   1941.10
--with Shaliapin, F., 1954.9;
   1986.2
--with Sholokhov, M., 1963.8
--with Soviet editors, 1964.12;
   1965.5
--with Soviet writers, 1963.8
--from Third World writers,
   1962.7
--with Tsvetaeva, A., 1984.5
--with Tynianov, Iu., 1963.8
--with Vengerov, S.A., 1941.2
--with Vinogradov, A.K., 1968.1
--with Zoshchenko, M., 1963.8
-as critic, 1925.2; 1942.1;
   1951.8; 1968.32, 77;
   1976.13; 1977.7; 1978.1, 9;
   1980.11A
-cultural views, 1918.1; 1923.1;
   1938.2; 1946.4; 1977.18
-on decadence, 1966.23;
   1968.120; 1981.16
-as dissenter, 1937.2; 1960.29
-on Dostoevsky, F.M., 1948.1;
   1953.3; 1968.130; 1973.5
-as editor, 1937.5; 1954.8;
   1960.27; 1964.6, 12, 31;
   1965.5; 1968.11, 54, 72, 78-
   79, 82, 126; 1977.23;
   1982.7A
-as educator, 1958.48; 1968.125;
   1977.18. See also Gorky,
   Maksim: his Capri school
-as fellow traveler, 1979.7
-film adaptations, of his work,
   1942.2; 1963.6; 1968.21
-on Goncharov, I.A., 1957.5

-illustrations of works, 1958.29
-his impact
--cultural, 1952.2; 1958.21;
   1970.21
--literary, 1925.1; 1928.6;
   1938.11; 1953.3; 1956.2, 7,
   12A; 1958.7; 1960.3;
   1964.32; 1965.7; 1967.9;
   1969.35, 40; 1975.7;
   1978.15-16; 1985.6
--political, 1937.6; 1941.1
--social, 1936.4; 1948.5;
   1952.2; 1955.2-3; 1961.2;
   1977.13
--See also Gorky, Maksim: his
   reception
-and intelligentsia, 1900.1;
   1908.2; 1928.8, 13; 1929.1A;
   1933.2; 1947.6; 1954.5;
   1965.15; 1968.26; 1980.11;
   1981.15A; 1985.4
-on Ivanov, Viach., 1957.5
-on Korolenko, V.G., 1957.1
-as legend, 1928.16; 1932.2;
   1936.9; 1946.2; 1950.2A;
   1951.1, 6, 9; 1953.10;
   1955.3; 1959.8; 1961.1, 28;
   1967.1; 1968.32, 35, 65,
   99A; 1973.2; 1974.11;
   1978.1, 4
-and Lenin, 1934.3; 1947.2;
   1958.17, 42; 1965.27;
   1967.2; 1970.2
-and Leonov, L.M., 1953.3;
   1961.3; 1968.61; 1974.5
-on Lermontov, M.Iu., 1949.1
-on Leskov, N.S., 1962.17;
   1968.130
-his library, 1959.3; 1981.3,
   10; 1984.3; 1985.6
-on *Life of Klim Samgin*, 1951.5
-literary techniques, 1969.30;
   1978.24
--allegory, 1928.3; 1976.25
--characterization, 1924.1;
   1960.5, 15, 18; 1961.3;
   1962.18; 1965.18; 1966.4;
   1968.108; 1979.4
--characters, 1898.3; 1901.3, 7;
   1902.2; 1905.3; 1906.1;
   1907.4-5; 1909.1; 1912.1;
   1937.5; 1960.17; 1961.29;
   1966.5; 1968.108; 1970.10

(Gorky, Maksim, literary
   techniques, characters)
   —epic heroes, 1958.38
   —mass heroes, 1960.15;
   1962.18
   —positive heroes, 1949.1;
   1950.4; 1956.11; 1958.14;
   1960.14; 1968.125; 1969.27
   —tramp-heroes, 1898.3;
   1900.1; 1901.1, 3, 7;
   1902.2; 1904.3; 1913.2;
   1916.3; 1961.29
   —women, 1901.2; 1969.10;
   1974.7; 1975.9; 1978.16
   —workers, 1956.5, 11
--comedy, 1969.7; 1971.2
--folklore, 1932.2A; 1938.10A;
   1947.2; 1956.13, 15; 1961.3,
   5; 1983.4
--imagery, 1928.3; 1959.9;
   1961.18; 1968.51; 1977.2;
   1979.4; 1981.7; 1983.8
--irony, 1961.8; 1976.22
--music, 1957.8A
--narrative devices, 1934.3;
   1950.2; 1960.14; 1962.17;
   1965.6; 1968.26; 1979.15;
   1982.19
--naturalism, 1957.3; 1969.31
--satire, 1956.14; 1957.2, 6, 9;
   1960.18, 26; 1961.8;
   1968.61A; 1972.7; 1973.6
--style, 1907.5; 1912.1;
   1941.52; 1961.3, 23; 1962.8;
   1965.12; 1968.32, 61A;
   1969.6, 21, 29, 31, 34, 39;
   1970.3, 16; 1971.19; 1974.9;
   1976.15; 1977.22; 1979.2, 9,
   11; 1982.10; 1982.16
   -avant-garde, 1924.6
   -decadent, 1937.5; 1939.1;
   1957.1
   -impressionist, 1902.2
   -modernist, 1968.86;
   1976.18; 1977.2
   -naturalist, 1898.1; 1908.5;
   1910.2; 1913.1; 1931.1;
   1932.1; 1957.1; 1968.69,
   131; 1972.12
   -realist, 1898.1; 1906.1;
   1910.1-2; 1920.2; 1923.2;
   1928.3; 1931.1; 1932.1;
   1935.1; 1937.5; 1938.3B;
   1939.1, 4; 1949.1; 1958.47;
   1959.5; 1960.5, 13A; 1962.5,
   9; 1963.14; 1965.12;
   1967.10; 1968.1; 1970.14,
   18; 1971.14, 18; 1978.9;
   1979.5A; 1980.8; 1982.8
   -romantic, 1898.1; 1910.2;
   1935.1; 1938.3B; 1939.1, 4;
   1945.1; 1954.5; 1960.17-18;
   1961.23; 1965.12; 1967.14;
   1968.115, 122; 1969.12, 27;
   1970.14; 1971.14, 21;
   1978.9, 14; 1979.5A
   -symbolist, 1906.1; 1910.1;
   1968.131
--tragedy, 1922.4; 1969.7;
   1977.7
-Luxemburg, R., impact on,
   1970.21
-Mann, H., impact on, 1974.15
-and minorities, 1978.7
-as modernist, 1906.2; 1924.6;
   1968.86; 1977.2
-on modernism, 1956.4; 1963.14;
   1968.13, 62, 120
-moral views, 1901.7; 1902.2;
   1905.3, 6; 1906.6; 1907.4;
   1910.1; 1912.1; 1915.2;
   1916.3; 1927.7; 1936.7;
   1939.3; 1953.5; 1958.5;
   1961.13, 20; 1966.26;
   1968.20, 23, 60, 70, 95;
   1969.2, 6-7, 15; 1971.13;
   1975.2; 1976.7, 16; 1978.22;
   1981.6; 1982.10; 1983.5;
   1985.1; 1986.3
--cruelty, 1958.30
--dualism, 1909.1
--"great lie," 1903.3; 1906.3;
   1939.5; 1964.10; 1967.18;
   1975.21
--Jewish question, 1929.2;
   1965.25; 1986.1
--prophecy, 1934.4
-museum, 1957.8; 1959.3;
   1969.20; 1977.7
-and nihilism, 1973.1A
-his notebooks, 1968.88
-as personality, 1901.6; 1902.7;
   1906.2; 1908.4; 1922.2;
   1932.2; 1956.8; 1962.14;

Subject Index

(Gorky, Maksim, personality)
1968.22, 35, 64, 112;
1969.2; 1981.1
-philosophical views, 1901.3;
1906.6; 1938.1; 1968.7, 32-
33, 89; 1982.2
-on Pisemsky, A.F., 1968.101
-on Platonov, A., 1976.9
-poetry writing, 1958.10-11, 15;
1964.16; 1974.1A; 1976.25
-political views, 1930.5;
1945.1; 1968.31; 1973.9;
1977.1; 1979.3
-and populism, 1915.4; 1967.8;
1969.27; 1974.7; 1975.20
-portraits of, 1946.3; 1965.30;
1969.20
-as proletarian writer, 1901.9;
1907.6; 1908.2; 1927.4;
1928.12; 1946.2; 1947.6;
1954.6; 1958.36; 1962.3;
1973.1
-as publicist, 1927.5; 1928.15;
1953.2, 5; 1954.9; 1956.1;
1957.2, 6; 1959.3, 17;
1965.21; 1978.16
-on Pushkin, A.S., 1949.1
-reception of, 1915.5; 1969.35;
1976.15; 1980.13; 1985.1, 3
--Afghanistan, 1968.55
--Arabs, 1968.55
--Argentina, 1964.2, 9
--Armenia, 1949.1; 1968.25
--Asia, 1968.55
--Azerbaijan, 1949.1
--Bengal, 1968.55
--bourgeoisie, 1904.1; 1909.3
--Bulgaria, 1959.3; 1961.15;
1970.18; 1980.4
--Burma, 1968.55
--China, 1951.5; 1968.55
--Croatia, 1968.75; 1970.18;
1985.2
--Czechoslovakia, 1959.3;
1961.15, 24; 1978.7A
--Denmark, 1904.2A
--early, 1975.6
--East Germany, 1964.15; 1967.7;
1968.52, 114; 1969.16;
1970.18; 1980.8
--Eastern Europe, 1961.15;
1970.18

--England, 1904.2A; 1954.2;
1961.24-25; 1969.9; 1973.9A;
1977.13
--Finland, 1980.10
--foreign, 1904.2A; 1930.1;
1941.2; 1958.7, 19; 1959.3;
1962.1; 1962.6; 1963.4;
1967.3; 1969.32; 1982.13
--France, 1904.2A; 1955.2;
1958.27; 1969.32; 1970.18;
1978.6; 1979.1
--Georgia, 1977.7
--Germany, 1930.1; 1958.43;
1962.13; 1964.1, 28; 1965.7;
1968.11, 19, 24, 35, 74,
102; 1969.32; 1980.8
--Hungary, 1959.3; 1970.18
--India, 1968.42, 55; 1970.18
--Indonesia, 1968.55
--Iran, 1968.55; 1970.18
--Italy, 1904.2A; 1959.3;
1961.24; 1970.18
--Japan, 1964.2, 17; 1968.55;
1970.18
--Korea, 1968.55
--Lithuania, 1949.1
--mass readers, 1929.1
--Mexico, 1970.18
--Mongolia, 1968.55
--Norway, 1964.2, 8; 1970.18;
1977.8
--peasant readers, 1968.90
--Poland, 1961.15; 1970.18
--proletarian readers, 1925.2;
1928.6, 9
--Rumania, 1959.3; 1963.15;
1970.18
--Russia, 1901.9; 1904.1, 5;
1952.5; 1968.81; 1980.8.
See also Soviet Union below
--Scandinavia, 1961.24, 26;
1975.18
--Serbia, 1968.75
--Slovakia, 1970.18
--Slovenia, 1961.15
--Soviet Union, 1953.2; 1954.8;
1956.1-2, 9, 11; 1958.19,
21-22, 36, 40; 1961.1;
1964.6; 1967.3; 1968.35, 65,
92; 1974.11; 1977.6, 17;
1978.4, 17; 1979.7, 16;

(Gorky, Maksim, reception of)
    1981.11; 1982.18. See also
    Russia above
--Spain, 1904.2A; 1932.3
--Sweden, 1904.2A
--Third World, 1956.11; 1962.7
--Turkey, 1968.55
--Turkmenia, 1977.7
--Ukraine, 1949.1
--United States, 1906.7-9;
    1911.2; 1941.4; 1944.1;
    1947.4; 1948.3; 1949.4-5;
    1951.3; 1958.4; 1962.4;
    1964.32; 1968.44, 129;
    1970.4; 1973.8A; 1977.7, 9;
    1982.9, 27
--Uzbekistan, 1977.7
--Vietnam, 1968.55
--West, 1976.19
--Yugoslavia, 1961.14; 1968.75;
    1970.18
-religious views, 1915.1;
    1916.3; 1959.14; 1968.32, 51
-on Russia, Russians, 1916.1-2,
    5; 1933.1
-Russian culture, place in,
    1906.5; 1923.1; 1928.11
-Russian literature
--place in, 1905.7; 1906.2;
    1912.2; 1932.4; 1936.4;
    1947.1; 1949.1; 1958.2, 21;
    1959.19; 1966.23; 1968.8,
    60, 103; 1976.27
--views on, 1939.2; 1949.1, 6
-on Saltykov-Shchedrin, M.E.,
    1968.32
-on Schiller, F., 1968.32, 63
-and science, 1948.4; 1961.12;
    1964.11; 1968.11; 1970.20;
    1980.11A
-sexual views, 1923.2; 1959.14;
    1986.3
-Shaw, G.B., impact on, 1977.13
-as social historian, 1964.19
-social impact of, 1904.3;
    1905.1-2; 1908.4; 1916.4;
    1923.1; 1928.9; 1970.6;
    1978.7
-and socialism, 1907.1; 1941.12;
    1962.15; 1980.13
-and socialist realism, 1937.4;
    1941.7; 1954.7; 1956.2, 11;
    1960.3; 1968.64; 1974.14

-social views, 1950.5; 1968.40
-Soviet writers
--impact on, 1926.5; 1953.2, 7;
    1956.2, 5, 14; 1958.21, 23,
    40; 1963.14; 1977.17;
    1978.17; 1979.16; 1982.18,
    21; 1985.6
--influence of, 1962.6; 1968.57,
    122
--views on, 1963.8; 1964.13
-and Stalin, J., 1947.2;
    1958.33; 1965.27
-studies on, 1958.22, 31;
    1964.29A; 1969.16; 1981.17;
    1984.6A; 1985.1
-on symbolism, 1968.62
-on theater, 1938.3A; 1962.11;
    1964.11; 1965.13; 1973.9A;
    1976.35
-and Tolstoy, L.N., 1922.3;
    1926.5; 1928.1; 1929.4;
    1946.6; 1951.3; 1955.6;
    1958.5; 1959.5; 1961.22;
    1964.25; 1968.85, 130;
    1971.8
-translations of works, 1956.14;
    1968.35, 55; 1973.3A;
    1974.12
-on United States, 1906.5A;
    1965.15; 1967.12; 1970.13,
    17; 1971.16; 1976.30;
    1982.9, 22
-unpublished works of, 1934.2;
    1936.3; 1951.8
-world literature, place in,
    1956.11; 1958.7; 1961.16,
    24; 1965.12; 1970.18;
    1982.20
Gorodok Okurov. See The Town of
    Okurov
"Gorod zheltogo d'iavola." See
    "The City of the Yellow
    Devil"
"A Great Love," 1951.8; 1959.3
Grigorev, S.T., 1968.11
Grin, A., 1968.32
Grivsky, I., 1966.1
Gruzdev, I., 1968.77
Grzhebin, Z.I., 1983.2
Gumilev, N., 1940.5; 1970.22
Gurevich, L.Ia., 1975.8
Gurovich, A.S., 1965.5
Gusev, V., 1961.3

Subject Index

Hamsun, K., 1969.14; 1975.18; 1977.8
Hare, R., 1963.4; 1971.11
Harte, B., 1970.17
Haszek, J., 1973.6
Hauptmann, G., 1959.11, 14; 1961.16; 1965.7; 1969.14; 1970.9
–The Weavers, 1924.7; 1953.4
Henry, O., 1923.2; 1957.5; 1970.17
Herzen, A.I., 1940.1; 1958.2
Hillquit, M., 1962.6
Hitler, A., 1963.6
Holtzman, F., 1971.9
Hoover, H., 1965.15
Hopkins, A., 1922.4
Hugo, V., 1898.1; 1965.12
humanism, Communist, 1950.4; 1963.13; 1968.95

"Iakov Bogomolov," 1941.6
Iakubovich, P., 1968.78
Iarovitskii, A.V., 1968.32
Ibsen, H., 1901.8; 1958.44; 1959.11; 1961.16; 1965.12; 1969.2, 28
"I eshche o cherte." See "And Still More on the Devil"
Imendörffer, H., 1982.24
industrialization, 1901.1; 1966.9
intellectual movements, prerevolutionary, 1968.11; 1979.24
Ispoved'. See The Confession
Iushkevich, S., 1964.3
Iuzovsky, I., 1968.77
Ivanov, Viach., 1957.5
Ivanov, Vsev., 1969.19

Jerome, J.K., Passing of the Third Floor Back, 1920.3; 1931.1
Joyce, J., 1968.86

"Kain i Artem," 1929.2; 1961.11
Kamegulov, A.D., 1965.5
Kamenev, L.B., 1924.2; 1940.5; 1982.7A
Kamenskaia, O.Iu., 1978.5
"Karamora," 1958.8

Karo, E., 1938.1
Kashen, M., 1968.11
Kastorsky, S., 1968.77
Kataev, V., 1978.15
Kaverin, V., 1963.8
Kazakov, Iu., 1966.25
Kazantzakis, N., 1968.84, 105
"The Khan and His Son," 1981.11
Kharlamov, A.A., 1949.3
Khodasevich, Vlad., 1961.4; 1969.14; 1983.1
"Khristofor Bukeev," 1941.6
Kiacheli, L., 1980.8
"Kirilka," 1901.10; 1975.19
"Knight's Move," 1941.6
Kochin, N., 1981.11
Kolkhoznik, 1965.5
Kol'tsov, M.E., 1965.5
Kol'tsov, N.K., 1965.5
Komissarzhevskaia, V.F., 1968.11, 29
Konovalov, G.I., 1980.8
Korolenko, V.G., 1958.2; 1961.29; 1982.28; 1983.3; 1984.6
–Gorky on, 1957.1
–social view, 1979.23
Kostrov, T., 1965.5
Krasnaia nov', 1965.5; 1968.66
Kriuchkov, P.P., 1976.12
Krokodil, 1957.9
Krupskaia, N.K., 1958.42; 1968.36
Kukryniksov, 1958.29
Kuprin, A.I., 1959.10; 1966.23
–Moloch, 1966.9
Kurella, A., 1979.11

Ladyzhnikov, I.P., 1959.10
"The Last Ones," 1908.7; 1957.2
Lawrence, D.H., 1971.23
Lenin, V.I., 1928.15; 1940.5; 1946.1-2; 1955.8; 1958.14, 16, 23; 1960.30; 1964.11; 1965.16, 21, 26-27; 1966.14; 1967.18; 1968.28, 34, 82, 106; 1969.23-24; 1970.5, 22; 1971.1, 8, 10, 12; 1972.16; 1973.2; 1975.3, 16, 21; 1976.1, 3, 11; 1978.25; 1979.21; 1980.1; 1984.3; 1986.3

219

Subject Index

(Lenin, V.I.)
-on Capri, 1928.8; 1958.16
-correspondence of, 1924,2; 1958.42; 1961.9; 1968.124; 1970.1
-Gorky on, 1934.3; 1958.17; 1967.2
-impact on Gorky, 1947.2; 1970.2
-Iskra, 1968.11, 68
-Leninism-Stalinism, 1947.1
-and socialist realism, 1969.5; 1970.2
-See also "V.I. Lenin"
Leonov, L.M., 1963.8; 1967.9; 1968.78; 1974.7; 1978.10, 15
-Badgers, 1953.3
-Gorky on, 1974.5
-Gorky's impact on, 1953.3; 1961.3; 1968.61
Leopardi, G., 1938.1
Lermontov, M.Iu., 1949.1
Leskov, N.S., 1969.14; 1984.6
-Gorky on, 1962.17; 1968.130
-narrative technique, 1962.17
Leto. See Summer
Letopis', 1916.2; 1956.6; 1963.5; 1966.16
Levin, D., 1965.28
Levin, I.D., 1965.15
"Lev Tolstoy," 1922.3; 1926.5; 1928.1; 1929.4; 1946.6; 1955.6; 1958.5; 1959.3; 1963.10; 1976.4, 34; 1982.3
-structure of, 1926.4; 1968.43
"The Life of a Jew," 1941.6
The Life of a Superfluous Man, 1981.11; addendum 1
The Life of Klim Samgin, 1928.6; 1938.9; 1957.2; 1958.37; 1960.18, 24; 1964.20; 1965.4, 17; 1966.23-24; 1968.10, 26, 43, 122; 1969.36; 1970.19; 1971.15, 17, 20; 1976.32; 1977.20; 1978.18, 22; 1980.12; 1981.5, 11; 1982.10, 24
-as bildungsroman, 1933.1; 1982.6
-characterization in, 1965.29; 1981.15A
-cultural subtext, 1963.16

-early drafts, 1951.5; 1965.1
-as epic, 1951.4; 1956.12; 1962.18; 1964.26; 1965.22; 1967.13; 1978.10; 1982.2
-folklore in, 1978.10; 1979.11
-genre, 1959.15; 1976.33; 1979.15
-Gorky on, 1951.5
-imagery in, 1951.5; 1961.18
-merchant in, 1959.6
-motherhood in, 1976.33
-narrative technique, 1965.6; 1973.7; 1979.11; 1982.2
-peasant in, 1976.33; 1978.10
-socialist realism, 1967.13; 1968.3
-structure, 1958.19, 35; 1962.18; 1966.8
-style, 1954.9; 1968.121; 1979.2
-translations, 1946.1
The Life of Matvei Kozhemiakin, 1958.28; 1972.2; 1981.16
-merchant in, 1959.6
-See also Okurov cycle
Literaturnaia ucheba, 1965.5
"The Little Boy," 1929.2
Liubitel'skii spektakl'. See The Amateur Show
Lomonosov, M.V., 1953.7
London, J., 1926.4; 1957.5; 1970.17; 1976.14
Longfellow, H.W., 1974.1; 1979.9
The Lower Depths, 1907.5; 1908.2; 1920.3; 1924.7; 1938.5; 1940.3; 1942.2; 1948.3; 1951.10-11; 1952.4-5; 1953.4; 1954.2, 9; 1957.3; 1958.39; 1961.19, 27; 1964.2, 17; 1968.50, 60, 96; 1972.12; 1973.3, 3A; 1975.1; 1976.31; 1977.1A, 19; 1979.11; 1982.27
-and egoism, 1967.5
-English productions, 1973.9A
-film of, 1941.2
-German productions, 1964.28; 1968.69
-Luka, 1903.3; 1906.3; 1908.5; 1920.1; 1947.5; 1958.37; 1968.12, 97, 100, 109; 1977.15; 1978.3

Subject Index

(The Lower Depths)
-materials of, 1947.5
-moral view, 1968.23
-naturalism, 1908.5; 1924.5; 1931.1
-production, 1963.1
-Satin, 1904.1; 1947.5; 1966.4; 1975.5
-as social drama, 1968.69
-social view, 1975.17
-structure of, 1906.1; 1977.7
-as tragedy, 1922.4
Lunacharsky, A.V., 1965.13; 1968.78, 118-119; 1975.8; 1976.6, 12; 1977.23; 1978.1; 1979.6, 11; 1980.5, 8; 1981.11; 1982.11, 23
-Religion and Socialism, 1965.16
Lutokhin, D.A., 1976.12
Luxemburg, R., 1970.21

Maiakovsky, V.V., 1927.2; 1947.2; 1953.2, 8; 1956.4; 1964.24; 1968.27, 90A; 1969.14; 1972.14; 1973.11
"Makar Chudra," 1908.1; 1968.32; 1978.10
Maksimov, P., 1968.67
Malinovskaia, E.K., 1976.12
Maltsev, K.A., 1965.5
"Malva," 1902.5; 1977.2
Malyi Theater, 1961.18
Mamin-Sibiriak, D.N., 1962.12
"Man," 1904.4; 1909.2; 1954.9; 1956.11; 1966.20; 1968.33, 58; 1969.2; 1981.6
Mandelshtam, O.E., 1972.11
"A Man Is Born," 1981.7; addendum 2
Mann, H., 1958.7; 1965.7
-Gorky's impact on, 1974.15
Mann, T., 1965.7; 1967.16; 1969.37; 1978.19
-Buddenbrooks, 1969.41
-Doktor Faustus, 1971.17
Marx, K., 1928.15
Marxism, 1907.3; 1945.1; 1973.2; 1975.20; 1978.1
-and art, 1909.2; 1928.15
-and criticism, 1909.2; 1924.4; 1969.38
Mashitsky, A., 1966.1
Mat'. See Mother

Maupassant, G., 1902.6; 1910.2
Mazzini, G., 1981.11
McBride, I., 1968.44
Melnikov-Pechersky, P.I., 1968.32
Merezhkovsky, D.S., 1922.1; 1941.11; 1948.5
Meshchane. See The Petit Bourgeois
Mikhailovsky, B., 1968.77
Mikoyan, A.I., 1968.25
Miller, A., 1968.17
minority literature, 1968.72
Minsky, N., 1957.1
"The Mistake," 1960.17; 1981.6
modernism, 1927.2; 1938.11; 1959.11; 1969.38; 1975.10
-Gorky in, 1906.2; 1924.6; 1968.86; 1977.2
-Gorky on, 1956.4; 1963.14; 1968.13, 62, 120
Moi universitety. See My Universities
Morozov, S.T., 1979.14; 1983.2; 1984.4
Moscow Art Theater, 1920.2; 1938.3A, 6A; 1943.1; 1954.3; 1961.27; 1968.81; 1979.14; 1981.14
Mother, 1921.2; 1940.4; 1941.2, 7; 1951.8; 1952.4; 1953.7; 1956.11; 1958.37; 1959.8; 1960.2, 19; 1964.10; 1966.13; 1967.17; 1968.38; 1969.3, 24, 43; 1975.1, 16; 1977.4, 20; 1979.19; 1980.8; 1981.5; 1982.5; addendum 1
-and Brecht, 1963.7; 1974.6; 1977.7
-characterization in, 1962.6, 12; 1981.15A
-folklore in, 1961.5; 1983.4
-genre, 1958.38; 1962.6, 19
-as God-building, 1982.23
-impact of, 1966.23; 1979.10
-intended reader, 1908.2
-and Lenin, 1985.8
-narrative view, 1981.9A
-Nilovna, 1974.7; 1976.17
-proletariat, 1962.6; 1966.1
-reception, 1941.4; 1947.4; 1958.12; 1969.38; 1979.10

221

(Mother)
-socialist realism, 1951.2; 1952.1; 1968.3, 32; 1971.7
-style, 1961.5; 1962.6, 19; 1970.14; 1974.7
Muratova, K.D., 1961.21; 1968.77
My Apprenticeship, 1938.5B; 1941.6; 1951.4; 1968.32
-folklore, 1956.15
-religion, 1968.51
-style, 1962.8
My Universities, 1927.3; 1929.4; 1958.6; 1963.10; 1964.29; 1976.34; 1979.22; 1981.11

Na dne. See The Lower Depths
Naidenov, S.A., 1959.10; 1964.3
Nansen, F., 1977.8
"Na plotakh." See "On the Rafts"
Napoleon, 1979.13
Nashi dostizheniia, 1965.5
Nekrasov, N., 1966.16
Neruda, P., 1968.14
Nesvoevremennye mysli. See Untimely Thoughts
Nietzsche, F., 1898.3; 1900.1; 1901.7-8, 10; 1902.4, 7; 1903.4; 1905.6; 1907.4; 1908.1; 1946.4; 1958.30; 1961.3; 1964.7; 1965.12; 1966.4; 1968.70, 77; 1970.9; 1976.20, 23; 1978.8; 1979.5, 12; 1980.2; 1981.6; 1983.3; forthcoming 1
-Nietzscheanism, 1915.4
-superman concept, 1902.5
Nikiforova, L.A., 1959.10
Nikitin, N., 1968.32
Nikolaevsky, B.I., 1983.2
"Nilushka," 1980.15; addendum 2
Nixon, R., 1979.3
Novaia zhizn', 1931.2; 1965.21; 1967.2, 18; 1968.27, 48, 119; 1971.1; 1977.14. See also Untimely Thoughts
Novitsky, A.N., 1960.22
Novyi mir, 1965.5

O'Casey, S., 1970.18
"O chizhe, kotoryi lgal . . . ." See "The Siskin and the Woodpecker"

Ogonek, 1965.5
Okurov cycle, 1928.15; 1957.7; 1972.2; 1973.5; 1979.4; 1980.11A; 1981.16; 1982.17
-style in, 1916.2A; 1960.13A
-variants, 1951.8
-See also The Town of Okurov; The Life of Matvei Kozhemiakin
Olbracht, Ivan, 1978.7A
The Old Man, 1948.1
"Old Woman Izergil," 1968.32; 1977.2
Olesha, Iu., Envy, 1968.122
O'Neill, E., 1951.3; 1971.8
-The Iceman Cometh, 1951.11; 1961.19; 1976.31
"On the Rafts," 1981.14-15
"On the Way to the Bottom," 1941.6
"The Orlov Couple," 1908.1
"Oshibka." See "The Mistake"
Ovcharenko, A., 1968.77; 1977.6

Pasternak, B., 1963.8; 1966.17; 1984.1A
"The Peasant," 1901.3
Peshkova, E.P., 1940.5; 1955.5; 1958.42; 1966.6; 1978.5
"Pesnia o burevestnike." See "The Song of the Stormy Petrel"
"Pesnia o sokole." See "The Song of the Falcon"
The Petit Bourgeois, 1907.5; 1931.1; 1951.10; 1952.5; 1956.11; 1957.3; 1959.3, 13; 1968.17; 1972.10; 1975.1
-early reception, 1979.14
-moral view, 1968.23
-Nil, 1958.37; 1968.2; 1976.3
-productions, 1949.3
-variants, 1964.2
Piatnitsky, K.P., 1954.4; 1959.16
Piksanov, N., 1968.77
Pil'niak, B., 1963.8
Pisemsky, A.F., 1968.101
Platonov, A., 1963.8; 1968.32, 89; 1976.9
Plekhanov, G., 1928.15; 1958.28; 1967.17; 1978.1
Poe, E.A., 1948.5; 1979.9

Subject Index

Pokrovsky, M.N., 1976.12
Polonsky, V.P., 1965.5
Popov, A.D., 1949.3
Popov, N.N., 1976.8
popular literature, 1932.4; 1968.46
Po Rusi. See Around Russia
Posse, V.A., 1959.10; 1968.80; 1978.5; 1981.9
Postupaev, F., 1966.1
"Prestupniki." See "Criminals"
Prishvin, M.M., 1957.5
proletarian art, 1927.7; 1928.9; 1934.3; 1951.5; 1963.2; 1964.16; 1966.13; 1973.1; 1975.12
Proletkult, 1927.7; 1963.2
"The Propagandist," 1941.6
Proskuriakov, V.M., 1965.5
Prosveshchenie, 1968.82
"The Public," 1961.18
Pushkin, A.S., 1937.5, 7; 1938.11A; 1951.8; 1962.6, 10; 1976.26
-Gorky on, 1949.1
-"The Shot," 1982.19

Radishchev, A.N., 1962.16
Raskolnikov, F.F., 1965.5
"Rasskaz ob odnom romane." See "The Story of a Certain Romance"
"Rasskaz o geroe." See "The Story of a Hero"
Razin, I.M., 1965.5
"The Reader," 1967.10; 1981.6; 1982.7A
realism, 1958.47; 1962.5; 1969.26
Reed, J., 1968.44
Renoir, J., 1942.2
Repin, I., 1951.8
Reshetnikov, F., 1974.7
Riabushinsky house, 1972.6
Rilke, R.M., 1962.15; 1974.13; 1975.15
Rizov, D., 1968.78
Rodin, A., 1934.4
Rojas, M., 1975.4
Rolland, R., 1958.7, 24, 26, 32; 1961.16; 1962.12; 1965.24; 1966.10; 1967.1; 1968.92; 1979.11

romanticism, 1967.14; 1969.12
-revolutionary, 1968.115; 1978.14
Rousseau, J.-J., 1940.1
Rozanov, V.V., 1923.3; 1957.2
"Rozhdenie cheloveka." See "A Man Is Born"
Russian national character, 1906.2, 8; 1907.1; 1908.3; 1920.1; 1921.2; 1923.2; 1959.19; 1968.8, 132; 1970.12; 1974.13
-Gorky on, 1916.1-2, 5
Russian Tales, 1978.13

Salgaller, E., 1963.4
Saltykov-Shchedrin, M.E., 1949.1; 1957.6
-The Golovlev Family, 1969.41
-Gorky on, 1968.32
Sand, G., 1962.12; 1965.12
Savinkov, B., 1969.14
Schiller, F., 1904.1
-Gorky on, 1968.32, 63
Schopenhauer, A., 1961.3
Second Writers' Congress, 1956.8
Seghers, A., 1965.7; 1974.6
Seifullina, L., 1982.21
Semenov, I.I., 1978.5
Serafimovich, A.S., 1959.10; 1962.12; 1966.23; 1980.8
Serapion Brothers, 1968.105, 107; 1982.26
Sergeev-Tsensky, S.N., 1941.10; 1966.22-23
Severnyi vestnik, 1968.78
Shaginian, M., 1926.4; 1978.15
Shakespeare, W., 1977.1A
-King Lear, 1969.1
Shaliapin, F., 1954.9; 1963.16; 1968.11; 1969.14; 1971.8, 10; 1972.8; 1980.6; 1986.2
Shaw, G.B., 1938.4; 1958.32; 1961.16; 1973.6; 1977.7, 24
-Misalliance, 1977.13
-Gorky's impact on, 1977.13
Shelley, P.B., 1965.12
Shevchenko, T., 1964.21
Shkapa, I.S., 1965.5
Shklovsky, V., 1968.107
Shmarinov, D., 1958.29

Sholokhov, M., 1956.12; 1961.28; 1963.8; 1968.57, 78; 1975.12, 21; 1982.21
-Quiet Flows the Don, 1968.122
Sholom Aleikhem, 1959.10; 1978.7
Shukshin, V., 1982.21
Sinclair, U., 1962.12; 1968.44; 1977.24
Siomu, N., 1968.55
"The Siskin and the Woodpecker," 1960.17, 1964.10
Skazki ob Italii. See Tales of Italy
Sketches and Stories, 1898.2-3; 1901.3
Skitalets [S.G. Petrov], 1959.10; 1960.6; 1966.18, 23
The Smug Citizen. See The Petit Bourgeois
socialist realism, 1939.1; 1946.1; 1951.2; 1952.1; 1957.12; 1958.19, 21, 23, 37; 1959.5; 1960.9; 1964.32; 1965.16; 1966.13; 1968.2, 14, 125; 1969.5, 26; 1971.7, 15; 1972.2; 1975.1, 10, 21; 1976.11; 1977.21; 1978.14; 1979.7, 9-10, 19-20; 1981.5; 1982.23
-Gorky as model, 1941.7; 1954.7; 1956.2, 11; 1960.3; 1968.64
-Gorky on, 1937.4; 1974.14
-and party loyalty, 1947.1; 1958.33, 35; 1963.11; 1967.2; 1968.32, 123; 1970.2; 1975.16
-and positive hero, 1949.1; 1956.11; 1960.14
-and satire, 1960.26
-in theater, 1962.9
society, 1906.4; 1915.4; 1928.4; 1933.2; 1952.2; 1960.20; 1967.6; 1968.40
-bourgeoisie, 1904.2; 1928.15; 1955.7; 1961.17; 1965.29; 1967.16; 1968.103; 1971.17; 1978.19
-capitalist, 1933.1; 1961.14; 1962.18; 1976.22; 1982.5
-intelligentsia, 1908.2; 1928.8, 13; 1929.1; 1936.7; 1951.5; 1954.5

-merchant, 1901.10; 1959.6; 1963.2; 1981.5A
-peasant, 1901.7; 1945.1; 1954.9; 1966.12; 1968.83; 1969.40; 1975.19; 1977.7; 1978.10
-petit bourgeoisie, 1900.1; 1928.4, 9; 1972.10; 1974.15
-proletariat, 1901.9; 1907.6; 1908.2; 1927.4; 1928.4, 15; 1950.5; 1962.6, 12; 1968.26; 1971.17
-revolutionaries, 1981.15A
-Russian, 1906.4; 1915.4; 1922.2; 1953.5
-Soviet, 1936.7; 1946.1
-worker-revolutionaries, 1957.12
"Soldaty." See "Soldiers"
"Soldiers," 1908.2
Sologub, F., 1940.5; 1941.11; 1957.1; 1959.11
Solovev, E.A., 1968.80
Solzhenitsyn, A., 1966.25
Somov and Others, 1941.6; 1955.8; 1964.2; 1969.39
Son, 1940.4
"Song of the Falcon," 1909.1; 1941.1-2; 1979.5
"Song of the Stormy Petrel," 1964.2; 1974.1
Sorin, V.G., 1957.2
Soviet writers, 1964.18; 1978.15. See also Gorky, Maksim: Soviet writers
Sovremennik, 1968.11
Sreda, 1905.8; 1958.39; 1964.23; 1966.23; 1977.11; 1985.4
Sredin, L.V., 1968.11
Stalin, J.V., 1936.5; 1941.5; 1946.1; 1953.6; 1970.22; 1976.21; 1981.5; 1982.1, 4; 1986.3
-and Gorky, 1947.2; 1958.33; 1965.27
-Stalinism, 1965.28
Stanislavsky, K., 1938.3A; 1947.2; 1963.1
Starik. See The Old Man
"Starukha Izergil'." See "Old Woman Izergil"
Stasov, V.V., 1965.31
Stein, P., 1976.35

Subject Index

Stein, V., 1938.1
Stendhal, 1915.2
"Stepan Razin," 1941.6
"Stories of Heroes," 1955.8; 1972.9
"The Story of a Certain Romance," 1977.22
"The Story of a Hero," 1958.8
Stowe, H.B., 1979.9
"Strasti-mordasti," 1958.6
Strindberg, A., 1958.25; 1962.6
Stürmer, Z.F., 1957.2
Summer, 1927.1; 1951.4; 1969.3
Summer Folk, 1904.2; 1938.9; 1959.3; 1964.4, 20; 1965.19; 1968.29, 116; 1976.35; 1977.20; 1982.11, 27
-early reception, 1905.4; 1952.5; 1979.14
-moral view, 1905.6
"Suprugi Orlovy." See "The Orlov Couple"
Swift, J., 1956.1; 1958.30
symbolism, 1910.1; 1954.7; 1978.8; 1979.24
-Gorky on, 1968.62
-in Gorky's work, 1968.131
-symbolists, 1960.29; 1966.13; 1986.3
Sytin, I.D., 1968.46, 78

Tager, E., 1968.77
Tales of Italy, 1951.4, 8; 1975.9; 1978.13; 1982.10
-motherhood in, 1975.9
-style, 1968.61A
Teleshov, N.D., 1928.8; 1959.10
Tesich, S., 1976.35
textology, 1977.7; 1983.7
The Three of Them, 1907.5; 1926.4; 1948.1; 1961.24; 1977.20; 1982.17
-as bourgeois literature, 1961.17
-Ilia Lunev in, 1949.1
Tikhonov, A.N., 1959.3; 1968.78
Timiriazev, K.A., 1961.12; 1964.11; 1966.16
Tolstaia, S.A., 1968.11, 53
Tolstoy, A., 1956.12; 1958.41
Tolstoy, L.N., 1901.4; 1902.3, 6; 1913.2; 1916.3; 1926.3; 1931.1; 1938.11A; 1959.14;
1960.5; 1961.13; 1962.14; 1967.5, 16; 1968.32, 43, 60; 1969.14; 1971.5, 17; 1974.6; 1976.1, 33; 1977.7; 1982.3, 28
-autobiography, 1966.26; 1969.24
-confession, 1979.8
-as critical realist, 1951.2; 1959.5
-and folklore, 1983.4
-on Gorky, 1928.1
-Gorky on, 1922.3; 1926.5; 1929.4; 1946.6; 1951.3; 1955.6; 1958.5; 1959.5; 1964.25; 1968.85, 130; 1971.8
-Gorky's meetings with, 1961.22
-philosophical influence, 1961.22
-Power of Darkness, 1904.1; 1924.7; 1953.4
-Resurrection, 1968.117
-Tolstoyanism, 1915.4; 1968.18
-War and Peace, 1901.2
-See also "Lev Tolstoy"
"Tovarishchi." See "Comrades"
The Town of Okurov, 1972.2; 1981.16. See also Okurov cycle
Troe. See The Three of Them
Trotsky, L., 1931.2
-Trotskyism, 1938.3, 6; 1950.1
Tumanov, G.M., 1968.25
Turgenev, I.S., 1920.2; 1958.2; 1968.111
-Hunter Sketches, 1905.5
Twain, M., 1911.2; 1942.1; 1947.4; 1970.17; 1973.6
"Twenty-six and One," 1901.3; 1972.14A; 1973.1A; 1974.10; 1982.19; 1983.5
Tynianov, Iu., 1963.8

Ulianova, M., 1958.42
Unamuno, 1961.11; 1963.4
Untimely Thoughts, 1963.2; 1968.48; 1971.10; 1972.10A; 1980.1. See also Novaia zhizn'
Upit, A., 1980.8
Uritsky, S.B., 1965.5
Uspensky, G., 1903.5; 1963.12; 1984.6

Vakhtangov, E., 1947.2
"Varenka Olesova," 1901.2; 1972.14A
Varvary. See Barbarians
Vasileva, Z.V., 1978.5
Vassa Zheleznova, 1953.1; 1962.6; 1965.1; 1969.17; 1975.2
Veizenborn, G., 1979.11
Veresaev, V.V., 1959.10; 1968.78, 80
Verlaine, P., 1937.5; 1948.5
Vico, G., 1957.5
"V.I. Lenin," 1940.5; 1953.9; 1958.17; 1979.11
Vinci, L. da, 1970.23
Vinogradov, A.K., 1968.1
V liudiakh. See My Apprenticeship
Voitinskaia, E., 1969.33
Voitinsky, V.S., 1969.33
Voloshin, M., 1976.18
Voltaire, 1956.1
Volynsky, A.L., 1957.1; 1975.8
Voronsky, A.K., 1965.5; 1968.66
Vorovsky, A., 1978.1
Vragi. See Enemies

Weil, I., 1970.13
Wells, H.G., 1926.3; 1941.11; 1958.32; 1964.11; 1971.5; 1977.24; 1982.1A
Whitman, W., 1970.17; 1979.9
"Workman Slovotekov," 1941.6
Wolfe, B.D., 1968.34; 1970.8
Wolfe, T., 1968.17
Wright, C., 1957.2

Yavorskaia, L., 1979.1

Zaitsev, B., 1969.14
Zametki iz dnevnika. See Fragments from My Diary
Zamiatin, E., 1936.9; 1969.14; 1970.22
Za rubezhom, 1965.5
Zazubrin, V.Ia., 1965.5
Zhizn', 1964.23
Zhizn' Klima Samgina. See The Life of Klim Samgin
Zhizn' Matveia Kozhemiakina. See The Life of Matvei Kozhemiakin
Zhizn' nenuzhnogo cheloveka. See The Life of a Superfluous Man
Zhukovsky, V.A., 1937.5
Zinovev, G.E., 1940.5
Znanie, 1926.3; 1954.4; 1956.6; 1958.10-11, 39; 1959.11; 1964.2-3; 1966.2, 9, 13; 1967.8; 1982.14
Zola, E., 1908.5; 1962.12
 -Germinal, 1962.19
Zolotarev, A.A., 1966.2, 23
Zoshchenko, M., 1957.9; 1963.8
Zozulia, E.D., 1965.5
Zweig, S., 1958.32; 1965.7; 1969.14; 1977.24; 1982.3
Zykovs, style, 1916.2A

RAYMOND H. FOGLER LIBRARY
DATE DUE

BOOKS ARE SUBJECT TO
WEEKS